Early Communication Skills for Children with Down Syndrome

Early Communication Skills for Children with Down Syndrome

A Guide for Parents and Professionals

Libby Kumin, Ph.D., CCC-SLP

Woodbine House ◆ 2003

Originally published as *Communication Skills in Children with Down Syndrome*, © 1994, Woodbine House
Second edition 2003

All rights reserved. Published in the United States of America by Woodbine House, 6510 Bells Mill Rd., Bethesda, MD 20817. 800-843-7323.
www.woodbinehouse.com

The illustration of the ear on page 14 is by Jason Chin. Photographs of PECS materials on pages 71 and 197 are courtesy of Andy Bondy and Lori Frost.

Library of Congress Cataloging-in-Publication Data

Kumin, Libby.
  Early communication skills for children with Down syndrome : a guide for parents and professionals / by Libby Kumin.—2nd ed.
    p. cm.
"Originally published as Communication skills in children with Down syndrome, 1994."
Includes bibliographical references and index.
  ISBN 1-890627-27-5
  1. Down syndrome—Patients—Rehabilitation. 2. Down syndrome—Patients—Education. 3. Communicative disorders in children—Treatment. 4. People with mental disabilities—Means of communication. 5. Child rearing. I. Kumin, Libby. Communication skills in children with Down syndrome. II. Title.
  RJ506.D68K86 2003
  618.92'858842—dc21

2003008742

Manufactured in the United States of America

10 9 8 7 6 5 4 3 2 1

Dedicated to

Dr. Herbert and Berniece Kumin, my parents, who have always been committed to me and who nurtured my commitment to others

Dr. Martin Lazar, my husband, whose love and encouragement support my professional and personal growth

Dr. Jonathan Lazar, my son, who infuses every day and every experience with joy and sunshine

Table of Contents

Acknowledgements

For many years, I have worked with infants, toddlers, children, adolescents, and adults with Down syndrome and their families. I have seen many positive changes, and knowing that I have been a part of making those changes happen is deeply satisfying. There is still a great deal to be done to ensure that people with Down syndrome, at all ages, are able to communicate and live a fulfilling life, and I intend to continue to work for that goal.

Many people have helped me in my work. My parents, Herbert and Berniece Kumin, have always been and continue to be a tremendous source of love and support. They were my first role models of people who use their knowledge to make the world a more caring, responsive place for all people. My husband, Martin, has provided a nurturing environment in which I have grown personally and professionally. He believes in my abilities and is always in the background encouraging my efforts. My son, Jonathan, is a source of great joy. His enthusiasm for his work and for living life is wonderful to share.

My professional colleagues, Lisa Schoenbrodt and the faculty of the department of Speech-Language Pathology, and the administrators, faculty, and staff at Loyola College are intelligent, thoughtful colleagues whom I respect and admire. The Down Syndrome Center for Excellence at Loyola College is a joint effort. For over twenty years I have worked side by side with Cheryl Mazaika Councill and Mina Silesky Goodman. Together, we have developed ideas and practical strategies that are now used in clinical settings around the world. I value their knowledge, experience, hard work, and friendship. We are on this journey together and we are making a difference.

This is the third book that I have written for Woodbine House Publishers. I have developed a wonderful working relationship with Susan Stokes, who has edited all of the books. Susan asks the questions that the readers want to know. She ensures that the books are understandable and practical. She brings knowledge and insight to the task. It is a pleasure to work with Susan. Thanks also to Brenda Ruby, Fran Marinaccio, and Beth Binns at Woodbine House for their efforts. Thanks to Joan Medlen for her insights regarding dual diagnosis and augmentative communication. I have enjoyed our discussions relating to this book and her work with *Disability Solutions*.

There are many other colleagues with whom I have had discussions that have shaped my professional views. There are also many parents who have shared their experiences with me. There are too many to name, but I want you to know that I value your knowledge, your insights, and the time we have spent together.

Introduction

Communication is an essential part of our daily life. We need to communicate with our parents, grandparents, siblings, friends, fellow students, teachers, and co-workers. We are always communicating, sometimes intentionally, sometimes unintentionally—through our words, gestures, facial expressions, and dress. We communicate when we say good morning. Our smile and bouncy walk communicate that we are happy. Our red eyes and sad face communicate that we have been crying. Our clothes communicate—the tuxedo or velvet dress say that we are bound for a formal event; the shirt and tie that we are ready for business. An infant communicates when he smiles at seeing a familiar face. A toddler communicates when he cries because he cannot reach the cookies that he wants.

We communicate from the moment we are born, and continue to communicate throughout our lives. We communicate from the moment we wake up to the moment we go to sleep. Whenever we interact with people, we communicate.

For children with Down syndrome, communicating is just as urgent and essential as it is for anyone else. And children with Down syndrome communicate early through their cries, smiles, and gestures. Of course, in infancy they don't yet know that they are sending messages and communicating with us, but our reactions and the reactions of other people in their environment help shape those expressions, gestures, and vocalizations into communication.

Despite their inborn drive to communicate, children with Down syndrome often have physical and cognitive characteristics that can make speech and language difficulties more likely. These characteristics include fluid accumulation in the ear; repeated middle ear infections; hearing loss; low muscle tone in and around the face and mouth; a mouth that is relatively small in relation to tongue size; over- or under-sensitivities to touch in and around the mouth; and mental retardation.

Some communication challenges are common to many individuals with Down syndrome and others are less common, but there really is no such thing as "Down syndrome speech." Many factors that can affect the speech and language skills of children with Down syndrome can also affect the speech and language skills of other children and adults. This means that we know how to help with specific communication problems. Some factors affecting speech can be controlled or treated (e.g., fluid in the ears); others can be greatly helped by appropriate techniques (e.g., low muscle tone in the facial muscles). This book discusses not only how each of these potential difficulties can affect communication skills, but also what you can do to help your child work on these areas of challenge. The emphasis of this book is on the communication skills of children with Down syndrome from infancy through about kindergarten age; a later volume will focus on the communication skills of older children and adolescents.

Your child may face a few, some, or many communication challenges. Children with Down syndrome have a wide range of speech and language abilities, just as other children do. Your child will usually be able to master all of the skills that he needs to understand and use language, but he may master them more slowly. He may babble and make lots of sounds in the first year of life, or he may be a quiet baby. He may begin to speak at about the same age as typical children and may be using short, understandable sentences by kindergarten age. Or he may use very little speech until the age of four or five and need to rely on sign language or a visual system to communicate. Most young children with Down syndrome will probably fall somewhere between these two extremes.

Although there are similarities among children with Down syndrome, the combination of communication strengths and challenges varies. For example, children with complicating factors such as hearing impairments, autism, or serious medical problems usually experience more difficulties in speech and language development than those with Down syndrome alone. Most children with Down syndrome understand more than they can say. Many children have no trouble getting their message across to family members and friends, but experience more difficulty making themselves understood by strangers. Still, they will learn more language from each new experience, from your models, from siblings, grandparents, cousins, and friends, from playing with other children, from listening to stories, from going on trips, and from school.

There are many people who can help children with Down syndrome master communication skills. Chief among these is the speech-language pathologist—the professional trained to understand the process and development of communication skills, as well as to assess and treat communication problems. In addition, early interventionists, feeding specialists, occupational therapists, sensory integration specialists, music therapists, and preschool teachers can help children learn skills that contribute to speech and language development.

There are also many ways that you, the parent, can help your child improve his communication skills. As described above, communication *is* an integral part of life, so it is best learned and practiced as part of real life. Since parents spend the most time with their child doing real-life activities, you are in the ideal position to work on communication skills. Parents and others who are with a child on a daily basis are the primary teachers of infants, toddlers, and school-age children simply because they are the only ones who can carry over learning into daily life. You are the only ones who are there at breakfast, at bedtime, on trips to buy groceries or shoes.

If your child is young, the idea of being one of his primary communication teachers may seem intimidating. In reality, though, teaching communication skills to a child with Down syndrome is not that different from teaching any other child. It is true that you may need to take things more slowly, provide more practice, and put more conscious thought into teaching him. But you can also use many of the same techniques that worked with any older children you may have. For example, songs such as "The Wheels on the Bus" and games such as "Patty-Cake" can be just as effective in helping your child with Down syndrome learn communication skills as they can with any child. Likewise, involving your child in typical life experiences such as shopping for food, preparing for a holiday, or going to the beach can provide the basis for learning vocabulary and other language elements.

The major difference between working with your child on communication skills and working with a typically developing child is that you need not—and should not—do it alone. You need information and guidance to maximize your child's communication potential. There are methods, such as using sign language or picture communication systems, that facilitate the acquisition of speech and language in children with Down syndrome. The speech-language pathologist (SLP) can provide knowledge, information, insight, suggestions, and directions to help you. You, the parent, can also help the speech-language pathologist work more effectively with your child. You can provide him or her with information about your child's daily activities and feedback about how the therapy program is or isn't working. This will help the SLP design a therapy program that will best meet your child's unique needs.

Obviously, helping children with Down syndrome develop optimum communication skills should be a team effort between the family and the SLP. This book therefore has two purposes. First, this book is intended to give you some practical suggestions and guidance in helping your child learn communication skills at home. It provides background information about communication and Down syndrome and specific suggestions for home activities and home- and community-based language experiences, and also includes many suggestions for further reading. Second, it explains how to work effectively with your child's SLP. It explains the process of communication, the professional terminology you may encounter, and the ways the SLP will assess and treat your child's communication difficulties.

In the end, I hope this book not only enables you to enhance your child's communication skills, but also to open the door to greater community participation for him. After all, communication abilities and community inclusion *are* related. I look at the many young children and their families in the speech-language therapy program at Loyola College today and I am amazed at how far we have come in the past thirty-five years. In the past, children with Down syndrome, for the most part, lived in a separate world that did not promote communication. Today, children and their families truly are experiencing life together and communicating with each other. This is clear from the excitement they show when they bring in photographs of their softball games, their experiences as flower girls in weddings, their roles in the school play, their participation in their church's winter concert, or their Brownie and Cub Scout badges, and want to tell us about their experiences.

We have made the difference—parents, professionals, families, friends, and courageous young people who test their skills and try their best every day. Parents and professionals must continue to work together and advocate together because we share the same goal—to maximize the communication potential of children with Down syndrome.

CHAPTER 1

Language, Speech, and Communication

Understanding Basic Terminology

Language, speech, and communication. You have heard the terms, and in general conversation, they are often used interchangeably. But, they really have very distinct meanings. The differences among the three are important to learn about in order to understand the abilities of children with Down syndrome and the ways children with Down syndrome can best learn to communicate with others.

WHAT IS COMMUNICATION?

Communication is the process by which one person formulates and sends a message to another person, who receives and decodes the message. Adults communicate primarily through speech, but they also use many gestures, facial expressions, body postures, and tones of voice to get their messages across. In fact, researchers have found that in most daily interactions, the nonverbal cues (such as a scowl or a smile) and vocal inflections (such as anger in the voice) carry the meaning of the message more than the words themselves. So, if I say, "I'm so glad she came with us" with a scowl on my face and sarcasm in my voice, the listener will assume that I am actually not glad that she came.

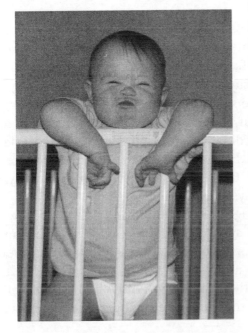

Communication is *holistic*. That is, it is more than the sum of its parts. Rather, its parts get their meaning from their relationship to one another. To understand its meaning, you need to pay attention not only to what is said, but also to how it is said. Communication includes how close I stand to you, whether I shrug my shoulders, whether I look confident or defeated, how my voice sounds, and whether I am smiling, smirking, or scowling.

There are many different forms of communication systems. We can communicate through sign language, facial expressions, gestures such as pointing, and even Morse code and smoke signals. Even very young infants can communicate on a basic level by crying or making faces to let Mom or Dad know that they are hungry or uncomfortable.

When people communicate, they usually use some kind of symbolic code or language. That is, they do not use the actual objects to relay a message; they use symbols to represent those objects. They do not, for instance, hold up a shopping bag to indicate they are going to the mall. *Language* is a structured, arbitrary system of symbols used to communicate about the objects, relations, and events within a culture. It is a shared code that is understood by the members of a language community, and that infants and toddlers learn through social interaction. We must *learn* language, because language is an arbitrary code.

Why do we call a television a television? The word is an arbitrary symbol. There is no intrinsic "television-ness." We call it a television because that is what we have been taught and because everyone in our language community understands what we mean when we say "television." We could call it an "entertainment viewer." But no one would know what we mean. We use the words in our language in order to be understood.

Using language involves both receiving and understanding messages and formulating and sending messages. When we receive a language message and try to understand that message, we are *decoding* language. This is called *receptive language*. When we put messages together and send them, we are *encoding* language. This is called *expressive language*.

One of the ways of encoding and expressing language is through speech. Other ways of expressing language are through sign language, pointing to words or pictures on a communication board, or formulating written messages on a computer. Different ways of receiving and sending messages are sometimes referred to as *channels,* so we may talk about the auditory channel or the visual channel. Children with Down syndrome are usually more advanced in receiving and understanding language messages than they are in encoding and producing language messages.

Speech is verbal language or the process of producing voice and sounds and combining them into words to communicate. Speech makes it possible to be very specific when communicating. It is easier for you to know what your child wants when she uses speech. For instance, if she says, "I want apple juice," you easily understand what she means. It sends a more specific and easily decodable message than pointing to the refrigerator would. But, speech is a more difficult system to learn and use. Speech involves strength, coordination, and timing of precise muscle movements. Speaking also involves the coordination of many brain systems to formulate and then produce the spoken message. It is the most neurologically and physiologically complex of the communication systems.

When we compare speech, language, and communication, speech is by far the most difficult for children with Down syndrome to use. Children with Down syndrome usually understand the concepts of communication and language very well and have the desire to communicate at an early age. Most children with Down syndrome are capable of communicating and using language many months and sometimes even several years before they are able to use speech. Most children

with Down syndrome will, however, progress to using speech as their primary communication system.

In the early years, it is most important for your child to develop adequate communication skills while developing the bases for speech. Since speech builds on the systems used for breathing, swallowing, and eating, we don't have to wait until speech begins before working on the necessary skills. For instance, we can begin working on strengthening and lengthening the exhalation phase of breathing and on strengthening the oral muscle movements for eating. These will help your child develop *oral motor* (mouth movement) skills that will be needed for speaking.

Meanwhile, your infant or toddler needs a way to communicate with those around her. Like most young children with Down syndrome, she will probably figure out for herself how to transmit some messages without speaking. For example, if your child points to the door or walks with you to get a cookie, she is communicating. If she cries or laughs or looks angry or hurt, she is communicat-

Points to Remember

COMMUNICATION

- Communication is holistic.
- Communication can be powerful in affecting the environment.
- Communication may be intentional or unintentional.
- Communication includes verbal and nonverbal messages.

LANGUAGE

- Language is a shared code.
- Language is an arbitrary code that uses symbols to represent real objects and events.
- Language has rules that specify how to use the code.
- Language is used intentionally or purposefully.
- Language is a learned code.
- Language is learned through social interaction.
- Language may include gestures, signs, pictures, and/or speech.

SPEECH

- Speech is verbal language.
- Speech uses the same systems in the body used for breathing, swallowing, and eating.
- Speech involves muscle programming, movement, and coordination.

ing. Most likely, she will need assistance in learning communication skills that will enable her to send more complex messages and to communicate with people who do not know her well. For this reason, the next few chapters focus on ways parents can help their child acquire the building blocks for both receptive and expressive language skills.

In addition, most families find it very helpful to start working with a speech-language pathologist when their child is very young to make sure that:

- their family has the information they need to help their child at home;
- their child has an efficient means of communication at all stages;
- eating and play activities provide the exercise and practice needed to lay the foundation for later speech skills.

Finding a Qualified Speech-Language Pathologist

Dr. Alan Crocker of Children's Hospital of Boston, a leading expert on people with Down syndrome, has stated that appropriate behavior *and* the ability to communicate and be understood are the two most important factors affecting the

quality of life for a person with Down syndrome. And in my opinion, speech-language therapy is essential for most children with Down syndrome to maximize their communication potential.

Speech-language therapy (also known as speech-language pathology services) is the specialized evaluation and treatment of difficulties in communication, language, and speech. Later chapters will provide more specifics about what speech-language therapy for your child might involve. Suffice it to say here that a good speech-language therapy program for an infant or young child with Down syndrome should:

1. be provided by a qualified speech-language pathologist (see the next section);
2. be individually designed to meet all of your child's communication needs;
3. use technology and visual systems such as sign language as needed to help your child communicate before she can use speech;
4. use best practices (methods that have been used successfully with other children);
5. educate and include your family, so that practice is part of daily life and is not limited to therapy sessions.

WHAT MAKES A
SPEECH-LANGUAGE
PATHOLOGIST
QUALIFIED?

Although everyone who provides speech-language therapy may be referred to as a "speech therapist" for short, not all speech therapists are alike. There are many titles that are used, including speech therapist, language specialist, and speech teacher. Your child should receive speech therapy from someone who has earned the credentials of a "speech-language pathologist," although she may refer to herself as a "speech therapist," since that is the term the public is familiar with.

The speech-language pathologist (SLP) should have the professional credentials Certificate of Clinical Competence in Speech-Language Pathology (CCC-SLP), awarded by the American Speech-Language-Hearing Association. To earn those credentials, SLPs must complete an undergraduate and graduate level program that includes intensive supervised clinical practice with children and adults in the areas of speech, language, hearing assessment, and remediation. They must earn a master's degree from an accredited training program. They must pass a national certification examination and complete a clinical fellowship training year (CFY) following graduation. If the professional lists "CCC-SLP" following her name, you know that she has completed a rigorous professional program.

Speech-language pathologists are generally licensed by each state and hold a state license, usually granted by the Department of Health. If you need to check whether a professional holds the CCC-SLP and/or the state license, you can call the professional board in your state or call the American Speech-Language-Hearing Association. You can also check the ASHA website for contact information. (See the Resource Guide at the back of the book.)

Speech-language pathologists who work for a school system are required to hold the appropriate certificate from the State Department of Education, such as a license as a speech and hearing teacher, K-12. In some states, SLPs in the schools are required to hold the CCC-SLP, but in many states, they are not required to have earned the ASHA certification, or are not required to maintain current certification or a current state health department license. Since the dues and fees to maintain these two credentials are high, many professionals in the school choose not to apply for them or not to renew them and keep them current. In the schools, there are also rules that allow systems to hire professionals on a temporary or emergency basis. And, there are speech-language pathology assistants who help in therapy. So, you cannot be certain what level of credentials the person providing speech therapy services has unless you ask.

Of course, none of the credentials lets you know whether that professional has any experience in working with children with Down syndrome. All of the communication problems encountered by children with Down syndrome also occur in other children, but an inexperienced SLP may conclude that the speech problems she is observing are part of "Down syndrome" and may not realize that they are responsive to treatment. Children really benefit from the expertise of a SLP knowledgeable about the unique challenges that Down syndrome often poses.

You may not be able to pick and choose among SLPs if your child is receiving services exclusively through an early intervention program or school and you cannot afford private therapy. But if you are able to choose your child's SLP, the best source of information on qualified professionals who have experience with children with Down syndrome is your local Down syndrome family support group. Parents have a strong resource network that can help you find professionals who have worked with other children with Down syndrome, who work with families, and are well regarded by members of the local parent support group. For information on local support groups, contact the National Down Syndrome Congress, the National Down Syndrome Society, or search through websites such as the Down Syndrome Health Issues website, which has links to many local family support groups. (See the Resource Guide.) Also refer to the section on "Seeking Private Therapy" in Chapter 13, if that is an option for you.

WHAT IS AN INDIVIDUALLY DESIGNED SPEECH-LANGUAGE PROGRAM?

If your child is receiving early intervention or preschool special education services, you are probably already acquainted with the idea of IFSPs or IEPs. For every area of demonstrated need and eligibility, your child is supposed to receive services individually designed to help her with those needs.

Early intervention programs and schools are not supposed to have one program that they routinely offer to children with Down syndrome, another for children with cerebral palsy, etc. Nor should families be told, "We don't provide speech-language therapy for children with Down syndrome until they are two," or, "We don't provide speech-language therapy until your child begins to talk." That kind of statement is against federal law. Speech-language treatment should address your child's individual areas of need through treatment.

There are many areas that can be worked on in therapy with young children with Down syndrome before they begin to talk. At the Down Syndrome Center for Excellence, the speech and language center program that I founded at Loyola College in Columbia, Maryland, we work with families from the very beginning. In our program, children with Down syndrome generally begin receiving formal speech and language therapy at the center at about the age of eight months or once they can sit with support, can focus on objects and people, and can pay attention to a therapist. Before that time, we consult with parents regarding activities they can do at home to promote communication development. In therapy, we work on visual skills such as reciprocal and referential gaze, auditory skills, and receptive vocabulary. We observe how the child is communicating, and, by the child's first birthday, we develop a transitional communication system (such as sign language and/or a picture communication system) to ensure that she will be able to communicate her messages. At the same time, we use oral motor play (such as making kissing sounds and clicking sounds) to strengthen the muscles that will be used for speech. In addition, we help parents learn how to help facilitate their child's language development.

I have developed communication guidelines for parents and SLPs that identify the areas of speech and language that should be assessed to determine which areas should be targeted for treatment. (See pages 314-15 in the Appendix.) I have also developed communication referral guidelines for pediatricians to provide information on speech and language characteristics that they might observe at a visit, or information from case histories or parental report that would indicate that a referral to a speech-language pathologist might be needed. The guidelines for pediatricians are included in the Appendix on pages 316-20.

For more information on legislation and speech-language pathology program planning in the schools, see Chapter 13. Also see the Early Intervention Speech & Language Treatment Program Plan in the Appendix for an idea of areas that should be considered in individualizing a program for young children with Down syndrome.

Getting Started in Early Intervention

If your baby is not yet enrolled in early intervention, you can get the process started at any time by contacting the Child Find or early intervention outreach program from your local school district. (Usually a school district is composed of all the schools in the city or the county, but sometimes several counties combine to form a single school district, or small local jurisdictions may form their own school district, resulting in multiple school districts within the same county.) That contact should, at the very least, provide you with information on the services available in your district.

Since speech is an "output system" that depends on well-functioning "input systems" such as vision, hearing, and touch, early intervention may first work on hearing, stimulating visual skill development, feeding/eating, and sensory integration. These types of intervention will help lay the foundations needed for speech and language development. In other words, your child may not receive speech-language therapy *per se* when she first enters early intervention. Instead, she may receive services from an infant educator, physical therapist, and/or other professionals that are designed to lay the foundation for communication and other skills. Remember, though: Treatment has to be provided or denied based on your child's needs, not the needs of "children with Down syndrome." If your child is beyond the age of one year (but under three years old), she should at least have been evaluated to see whether she qualifies for speech-language therapy through local early intervention programs. See Chapter 12 for information about evaluations.

HOW CAN YOUR FAMILY BE INCLUDED IN THE THERAPY PROGRAM?

The speech-language pathologist has the professional knowledge to guide, inform, and help facilitate and enhance the process of learning communication skills. However, your family (including siblings and extended family), day care workers, classroom teachers, other educational specialists, other therapists (occupational and physical therapists), friends, and community members also can contribute to your child's communication success. Language is part of daily living and needs to be practiced and reinforced as part of daily life. Although a skill may need to be learned in a therapy session, communication practice must go on in the real world. That's what counts!

At the Down Syndrome Center for Excellence, new parents or parents who have received a prenatal diagnosis of Down syndrome are given suggested readings to help them learn how to work with their infants at home. We suggest that they read books such as this one, and attend talks and conferences to learn more about pre-language, pre-speech, and early communication skills. (See Chapters 3 and 4.) They may come to observe in the clinic, so that they can see how young children progress in their speech and language and the kinds of stimulating activities that can help the learning process. In addition, families are given activities to use with their children at home to help teach and reinforce language and speech skills. If the professionals in your child's early intervention or speech-language program do not suggest these kinds of activities to you, let them know that you would like to have this kind of family involvement.

Conclusion

Children with Down syndrome clearly understand the concepts of language and communication very well and *want* to communicate from an early age. However, most children with Down syndrome will need a transitional system, such as sign language, to use before they are able to speak. For this reason, it is essential that communication be worked on early through a partnership between parents and professionals. Communication skills should definitely not be postponed until your child can master the skills necessary for speaking. The next chapter reviews some of the difficulties your child may need to overcome in order to master various communication skills, while Chapters 3 and 4 explain how you can help your child communicate and master pre-language skills before she is ready to speak.

CHAPTER **2**

Speech and Language Characteristics of Children with Down Syndrome

No child, with or without Down syndrome, develops speech and language skills on exactly the same timetable as any other child. That is why charts showing typical ages for developing particular skills usually give a range of ages. For children with Down syndrome, the average age for acquiring communication skills is usually later than it is for typically developing children, but there is still a wide range for acquiring skills. Table 1 on the next page gives an idea of when you might expect your child with Down syndrome to reach certain communication milestones. Based on current research and therapy manuals, it summarizes the information that is currently available.

Why are children with Down syndrome delayed in reaching communication milestones? There are many sensory, perceptual, physical, and cognitive problems that can occur with Down syndrome and affect the development of communication skills. Your child probably won't have all of the problems described in this chapter, but he will have some of them. Identifying which areas are difficult for your child and which affect his speech and language development is very important. Identifying your child's particular challenges is the first step in doing something about them. Speech-language pathology treatment is not a general plan where the same treatment is used for every child with Down syndrome. Treatment is always individualized based on your child's strengths and challenges. Depending on your child's needs, specific techniques and information can be used to help him make maximum progress in communication development.

Sensory and Perceptual Skills

In order to develop speech and language skills, children need certain fundamental sensory and perceptual skills. Sensory skills include the abilities to see, hear, touch, taste, or smell objects and people in the environment. Perceptual skills refer to the

Table 1: Development of Early Communication Skills in Children with Down Syndrome

Skill	Age	Research
Crying	By 12 months	Buckley, S. (2000); Buckley, S. & Bird, G. (2001)
Eye contact/looking	By 12 months	Buckley, S. (2000); Buckley, S. & Bird, G. (2001)
Joint attention	By 12 months 12-24 months	Buckley, S. & Bird, G. (2001) Buckley, S. (2000)
Smiling	By 12 months	Buckley, S. (2000); Buckley, S. & Bird, G. (2001)
Laughing/giggling	By 12 months	Chamberlain, C.E. & Strode, R.M. (2000)
Listening (voices and sounds)	By 12 months	Chamberlain, C.E. & Strode, R.M. (2000); Buckley, S. (2000); Buckley, S. & Bird, G. (2001)
Vocalizing, cooing, vowel-like sounds	By 12 months	Chamberlain, C.E. & Strode, R.M. (2000); Buckley, S. (2000); Buckley, S. & Bird, G. (2001)
Turn taking with actions and vocalizations	By 12 months	Chamberlain, C.E. & Strode, R.M. (2000); Buckley, S. (2000); Buckley, S. & Bird, G. (2001)
Babbling	By 12 months	Chamberlain, C.E. & Strode, R.M. (2000); Buckley, S. & Bird, G. (2001); Buckley, S. (2000)
Uses loudness and pitch variations when vocalizing	By 12 months	Chamberlain, C.E. & Strode, R.M. (2000)
Facial expressions, gestures, or signs	By 12 months 12-24 months	Chamberlain, C.E. & Strode, R.M. (2000); Buckley, S. & Bird, G. (2001) Buckley, S. (2000)
Imitates sounds, actions, syllables, and an occasional word	12-24 months	Chamberlain, C.E. & Strode, R.M. (2000)
Points when requested to 3 body parts (eye, nose, mouth)	13-25 months	Buckley, S. & Sacks, B. (2001)
Jabbers expressively	12-30 months	Buckley, S. & Sacks, B. (2001)
Says or signs first word	12-60 months	See page 66
Uses jargon with some true words mixed in	24-36 months	Chamberlain, C.E. & Strode, R.M. (2000)
Points to pictures when named	24-36 months	Chamberlain, C.E. & Strode, R.M. (2000)
Initiates conversations— pointing, requesting	24-36 months	Chamberlain, C.E. & Strode, R.M. (2000); Buckley, S. & Bird, G. (2001)
Comprehends 50-100 words	24-36 months	Chamberlain, C.E. & Strode, R.M. (2000); Buckley, S. (2000)

ability to give meaning to this sensory input. Thus, your baby's ability to hear your voice is a sensory skill; recognizing that it is Mom's or Dad's voice and interpreting the sounds you make as words are perceptual skills.

Clearly, children need to be able to hear what is being said in order to learn speech and language, but they also need perceptual skills to be able to make sense out of what they hear. They must also be able to see and focus on objects in order to learn the labels of objects. And they must be able to receive and interpret touch sensations in and around the mouth in order to learn how to make speech sounds. The sections below explore how sensory and perceptual characteristics of children with Down syndrome affect speech and language abilities. Chapters 3 and 4 provide suggestions for addressing these areas in therapy and at home.

AUDITORY SKILLS

The typical way to learn language is through hearing the language spoken in your environment. Unfortunately, the majority of children with Down syndrome have some degree of hearing loss, at least some of the time. This has an impact on speech and language development. Consequently, there is a need to use visual cues such as gestures, pictures, and reading to help stimulate language. In addition, children with Down syndrome often have difficulty distinguishing between the figure (speech) and the background noise (ground), especially in the classroom. We need to make the language pop out of the environment, so that children can hear it and learn.

Because good hearing is so essential to speech and language development, your child should be seen regularly by an otolaryngologist (ear, nose and throat specialist), a medical specialist who can treat hearing disorders, and an audiologist who can evaluate hearing and provide therapy or assistive listening devices such as hearing aids. The Healthcare Guidelines for Individuals with Down syndrome of the Down Syndrome Medical Interest Group (DSMIG) recommends that babies with Down syndrome have a hearing test soon after birth, every six months until three years of age, and annually thereafter into adulthood. (See the References and Suggested Reading list for information on the Healthcare Guidelines.)

UNDERSTANDING THE RESULTS OF HEARING TESTS

A variety of methods can be used to test an infant's or young child's hearing, depending on their age and ability to indicate what they hear. For example, otoacoustic emission testing (OAE) and auditory brainstem response testing (ABR) are passive tests that require no voluntary response from the child, and sound field testing requires little response. (See "Understanding the Terminology," below.)

Hearing test results tell you the sound threshold—that is, the softest sound that your child consistently responded to on the test. Children with sound thresholds of 15 decibels (dB) or less have normal hearing. (A decibel is a unit of loudness, so a child with a sound threshold of 15 decibels would only hear sounds that were 15 decibels or louder.)

Children who have sound thresholds from 15-30 dB have a mild hearing loss. They will be able to hear vowel sounds clearly, but may have difficulty hearing some consonant sounds. They may also have difficulty understanding speech when there is background noise.

Children who have sound thresholds from 30 db-50 dB have a moderate hearing loss. They will have difficulty hearing sounds at normal conversational level, and need amplification to help them learn sounds and learn language. Children who have sound thresholds from 50-70 dB have a severe hearing loss and will usually need to wear hearing aids to be able to hear and learn speech.

Children who have sound thresholds greater than 70 dB have difficulty learning to speak, and need ongoing treatment. Children with Down syndrome who have severe or profound hearing loss would have a dual diagnosis of Down syndrome and hearing impairment.

Most children with Down syndrome who have a hearing loss have a mild to moderate conductive hearing loss. Children with Down syndrome who have mild to moderate hearing losses can usually still learn to use speech as their primary communication method. However, they may need to use sign language as a transi-

Understanding the Terminology

Often when your child has fluid in the middle ear or a hearing loss, diagnoses are given rapidly and acronyms are used as a medical shorthand. Following are explanations of the terms typically used to describe the various conditions:

Eustachian tube: A tube that connects the middle ear to the nasopharynx (back of the nose). The Eustachian tube equalizes the pressure between the ear and the outside air. When the air pressure is not equal on both sides of the eardrum, the eardrum can't vibrate and transmit sound well. If the Eustachian tube is swollen due to allergies or colds, the middle ear fluid can't drain and it builds up behind the eardrum.

Middle Ear: The portion of the ear that transmits sound from the outer ear canal to the inner ear. It is behind the tympanic membrane (eardrum). The middle ear includes the eardrum, auditory ossicles (malleus, incus, and stapes, also known by their shape as the hammer, anvil, and stirrup), facial nerve, and Eustachian tube. When physicians examine the ear for fluid, they are looking for fluid through the tympanic membrane.

Otitis Media: Inflammation of the middle ear.

Otitis Media with Effusion (OME): In addition to inflammation of the middle ear. Other terms used to describe this condition are Serous Otitis Media (SOM) and "glue ear" (in the United Kingdom).

Chronic Otitis Media with Effusion (Chronic OME): When fluid is present in the middle ear for longer than three months.

Acute Otitis Media (AOM): Infection of the middle ear, which may be accompanied by pain, earache, and fever. Fluid may or may not be present. There may be a bulging eardrum and there may be drainage from the ear.

Conductive Hearing Loss: Decreased hearing acuity resulting from difficulty in sound transmission in the middle ear (between the eardrum and the oval window).

tional communication system for longer than usual. When children with Down syndrome have a severe or profound hearing loss, there needs to be consultation with the otologist, audiologist, speech-language pathologist and special educator to determine what method of communication will be most effective for the child.

HEARING LOSS AND DOWN SYNDROME

In children with Down syndrome, hearing losses can be conductive, sensorineural, or mixed (a combination of the two).

Conductive Hearing Loss. An estimated 65 to 80 percent of children with Down syndrome have conductive hearing loss. This means that a problem, such as infection or fluid accumulation in the ear, is preventing sound from being transmit-

Decibel: A measurement of sound level—the intensity or loudness of the sound. Abbreviated dB. Conversational speech is usually about 60 dB. Sounds over 130 dB, e.g., subway, jet engine noises, jackhammer, are painful and can damage hearing.

Frequency: A measurement of sound waves; specifically the number of vibrations that occur in one second. Frequencies are measured in Hertz (Hz) and correspond to the pitch of a sound. The speech frequencies are 500-2000 Hz. A high frequency sound may be at 8000 Hz, whereas a low frequency sound may be at 250 Hz.

Pneumatic Otoscope: A medical instrument used to look at the eardrum. It can send a puff of air into the ear canal so the physician or audiologist can observe the movement of the eardrum.

Tympanometry: A test for middle ear fluid and middle ear pressure that examines how well the eardrum is moving to transmit sound. A soft plug is placed in the ear canal and your child hears a low noise. The probe (plug) is connected to the tympanometer, which measures how well the eardrum moves. If there is fluid, the eardrum moves less than when there is no fluid present. A "type B" result is a flat profile, which means that fluid is affecting the movement of the eardrum. Tympanometry and pneumatic otoscopy are often used in combination to obtain an accurate diagnosis.

Otoacoustic Emission Testing (OAE): The cochlea, in the inner ear, contains hair cells that help us hear soft sounds and inhibit loud sounds. Otoacoustic emissions are signals generated by the normal inner ear either spontaneously or in response to sounds. Testing of otoacoustic emissions is painless and can screen for hearing and middle ear problems even in newborns or in individuals with middle ear fluid or infection.

Auditory Brainstem Response Testing (ABR): During ABR testing, a series of clicks are presented to each ear through special earpieces, then brain wave activity in response to the sounds is measured in the auditory centers of the brain. This is an objective, noninvasive way of measuring hearing sensitivity that can be used to screen newborns or to identify infants and young children with a hearing loss.

Sound Field Testing: A method of testing hearing used for infants and children who cannot indicate whether they hear sounds. Speech, pure tones, and noise are piped through speakers and the examiner judges whether the child is hearing the sounds based on behavioral responses such as sound localization (looking toward the sound), eye widening, eye shifts, changes in sucking and breathing patterns, and smiling.

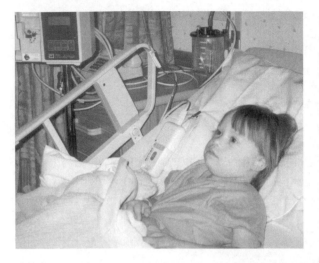

ted effectively and consistently. The most common cause of conductive hearing loss in children with Down syndrome is recurrent otitis media with effusion (fluid in the middle ear), or acute otitis media (more commonly known as ear infections). Many infants, toddlers, and young children have multiple and recurrent ear infections. In addition, many children have an accumulation of fluid behind the eardrum (tympanic membrane) in the ear canal even when they don't have infections. This occurs, in part, because they have small, narrow ear canals from which fluid has difficulty draining. Due to anatomical differences such as Eustachian tube dysfunction or ear canals that are even shorter and narrower than usual, children with Down syndrome are especially prone to fluid that does not drain.

The relationship between fluid in the ear, hearing loss, and speech and language development is an important one. Your child needs to hear adequately to be able to maximize speech and language development. Two researchers reviewed over seventy-five studies on the relationship between otitis media and language and found that children with a history of recurrent OME scored lower on tests of receptive language, expressive language, and speech production (Roberts and Wallace, 1997).

A conductive hearing loss not only affects your child's actual hearing, it also affects auditory awareness and listening skills. If your child doesn't consistently hear the sounds in his environment, he won't learn to pay attention to those sounds. He needs to hear the doorbell ring repeatedly to learn that this is a sound to pay attention to. However, with a conductive hearing loss, hearing levels usually fluctuate—sometimes your child is able to hear softer sounds,

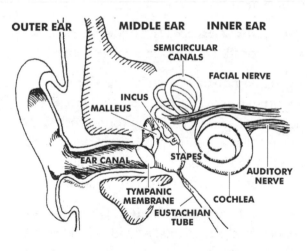

and other times sounds need to be considerably louder for him to hear them. Fluctuating hearing loss also affects phonological development or the development of speech sounds. If your child doesn't hear all of the sounds clearly, he may have difficulty learning the sounds. If he can't hear all of the sounds in a word, he may have difficulty learning to include all of the sounds in the word.

Table 2 gives some examples of how hearing of speech sounds was affected for one child with Down syndrome during a bout of middle ear fluid. This child, who was eight at the time of testing, was able to express when things didn't make sense to her and ask for clarification. Imagine how confusing it must be for a baby or young child to try to understand sounds filtered through middle ear fluid when he doesn't know enough about the language to know what does and does not make sense.

Table 2: Examples of How Middle Ear Fluid Distorts Hearing

What Was Said	What Child Heard
Give her a *treat*	Give her *three*
I need something to *read*	I need something to *eat*
Let's *go get* Kathy	Let's *forget* Kathy
Keep *the ants* out	Keep *your hands* out
She has *measles*	She has *needles*
Pizza with *sausage*	Pizza with *dog spit*
Goody goody	*Kitty kitty*
Daisy	*Baby*

TREATING MIDDLE EAR FLUID AND INFECTION

To minimize the effects on hearing, ear infections should be treated promptly. Antibiotics can sometimes help to clear up ear congestion. Some physicians prescribe antibiotics on a preventative basis if a child is prone to middle ear fluid and infection. In some cases, small tubes may need to be surgically implanted in the eardrum to allow fluid to drain away. In the U.S., these tubes may be referred to as PE tubes (for pressure equalization), tympanostomy tubes, or myringotomy tubes; in other English-speaking countries they may be referred to as grommets. The PE tubes allow air pressure in the middle ear to equalize air pressure outside the ear. The surgery to implant these tubes is called a myringotomy. Ordinarily it is performed under general anesthesia by a pediatric otolaryngologist (ear, nose, and throat doctor) and is a short procedure, usually taking ten or fifteen minutes. Ear tubes are most often intended to be a temporary "fix" for fluid in the ears and come out on their own after several months to a year.

Sometimes children with Down syndrome require only one set of ear tubes. Many, however, have continuing difficulties with middle ear fluid for years and benefit from a series of ear tubes. For example, one child with Down syndrome I know had his first hearing assessment at three months of age, using sound field testing (sound coming through speakers in the room). Tympanometry revealed normal tympanic membrane/middle ear mobility and pressure in the right ear and no observable mobility in the left ear. These results indicated the possibility of a moderate to severe hearing loss. At eight and twelve months, test results were similar. At the age of thirteen months, the ENT performed a myringotomy with the insertion of pressure equalization tubes. At the age of sixteen months, with the tubes in, his audiological reevaluation found significant improvement in his hearing. By his next hearing test at twenty months, however, audiological testing using sound field testing found that he had a slight hearing loss at 2000-4000Hz, and before long he needed to have a new set of ear tubes inserted.

Inserting ear tubes can often make a remarkable difference in a child's hearing abilities. On page 16 are some results of hearing tests completed before and after the same boy, now aged four, had tubes implanted. He was tested using sound field testing rather than earphones, so the results are not shown individually for his right and left ears. The audiologist used visual reinforcement audiometry (providing visual rewards, such as activating an animated stuffed puppy) for looking in the direction of sound to determine whether he could hear particular frequencies at different decibel levels. The testing results on the left show that the boy could not hear any sounds consistently above 30 dB (the moderate hearing loss range) and at some frequencies was hearing in the severe hearing loss range. At the time, he had a cold and fluid in his ears. The results on the right show how his hearing had improved seven months later, following the insertion of ear tubes. The audiologist who performed the test now rated the child's hearing at normal to borderline normal for all frequencies.

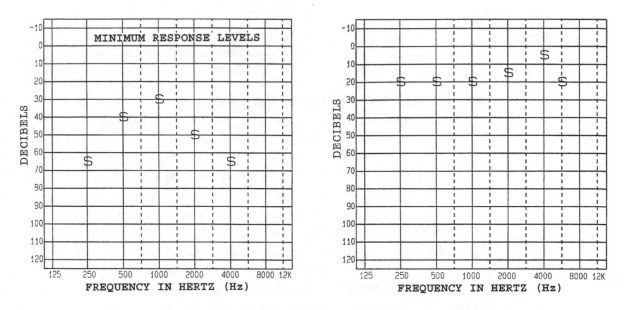

You should know that there are specific guidelines for treatment of middle ear fluid in typical children that were developed by the American Academy of Pediatrics in consortium with the American Academy of Family Physicians and the American Academy of Otolaryngology, among others. These guidelines recommend how to treat middle ear fluid that has lasted for specific lengths of time (e.g., whether to just use "watchful waiting" or to prescribe antibiotics or to insert ear tubes.) These guidelines have been distributed widely to pediatricians and to parents as the updated treatment for serous otitis media. But, the guidelines specifically state: "The guidelines do not apply to children with abnormalities of the nervous system or head and face structures such as cleft palate and Down's syndrome, or who have sensory problems."

Be sure to consult your physician for information on how the treatment recommendations for typical children are or are not applicable to children with Down syndrome. At least one study by ENTs who specialize in treating children with Down syndrome has shown that middle ear fluid in children with Down syndrome should be treated, if anything, more aggressively than in typical children. In a five-year longitudinal study of forty-eight young children with Down syndrome, these doctors were able to preserve normal hearing in all but two of the children by checking the children's ears every three to six months and using ear tubes to treat chronic otitis media (in forty of the children). They concluded that "aggressive, meticulous and compulsive diagnosis and treatment of chronic ear disease in children with Down syndrome, started soon after birth, provides significantly improved hearing levels than reported previously" (Shott, Joseph, and Heithaus, 2001).

Most children with Down syndrome have very small ear canals, making it difficult to examine them properly with the instruments found in the pediatrician's office. Consequently, it may be necessary to refer your child to an ear, nose, and throat physician (or possibly a pediatric ENT who has specialized equipment and specialized training) to visualize the tympanic membranes using the microscope otoscope. Ask your pediatrician for a referral to an ENT physician and an audiologist for ongoing hearing evaluation.

An ENT physician should evaluate all children with an abnormal hearing evaluation and/or tympanogram in order to aggressively manage treatable causes of hearing loss (using antibiotics and/or tympanostomy tubes as indicated). Aggressive medical care can minimize the effect of any hearing loss on language development.

Is There a Connection between Feeding Position and Ear Infections?

Researchers have reported that children who are breastfed have fewer ear infections. This seems to be related to the differences in the feeding positions during breastfeeding and bottle feeding. Infants fed in a supine position (lying on their backs) have an increased risk of ear infections, apparently because this position may result in the milk or formula refluxing up the Eustachian tube into the middle ear (Roberts, Wallace, and Henderson, 1997). Sara Rosenfeld-Johnson (1997) suggests feeding babies by holding them in a position in which their head is more upright—that is, with the mouth lower than the ear—to prevent milk flow into the Eustachian tubes. This is possible with the bottles that have disposable liners; the child draws the milk up the nipple using tongue retraction (backward movement of the tongue in mouth), which is a movement that we want to encourage anyway.

Sensorineural Hearing Loss. Some children with Down syndrome have sensorineural hearing loss. This is a more permanent type of hearing loss caused by damage to the inner ear, the auditory nerve, or both. It may affect the ability to hear at certain frequencies (pitches), and thus may affect the ability to hear certain sounds. Children with this type of hearing loss often need hearing aids to amplify sounds.

Hearing aids are generally small electronic boxes that are worn on the body in a pocket or strapped to the chest area (body aids) or miniaturized electronic aids worn in back of the ear or inside the ear canal. It can be difficult to get a baby or small child to tolerate hearing aids. But it is essential to try to gradually get your child to wear them at all times, or as directed by the audiologist. One way that we have found that helps encourage children to wear their hearing aid(s) is to attach a similar aid to a doll (large doll such as Cabbage Patch Kids) in the same way that your child wears the aid (behind the ear or on the body).

Hearing in a Noisy Classroom Environment

In a typical preschool or kindergarten classroom, the teacher stands about six to ten feet from children in the front row, and farther from children sitting further back. The background noise in a typical classroom is about 60 decibels. Measurements of teacher's voices have found them to be about 62-64 decibels. Because the teacher's voice is only a few decibels louder than the background noise, it is often very difficult for children with a mild to moderate hearing loss to make out what the teacher is saying.

Assistive listening devices and FM systems can help amplify the teacher's voice so that your child can hear better. FM systems transmit sounds from a microphone inches from the teacher's mouth to the listener's ear, so they amplify what the teacher is saying without amplifying the background noise. Sound field or personal FM amplification are generally the systems used for children with mild hearing loss. Binaural FM, behind-the-ear FM, or personal FM systems are used for children with moderate to profound hearing loss. An audiologist can work with you to determine your child's needs and prescribe appropriate systems.

VISUAL SKILLS Children learn language by connecting a label with an object. To learn a word, it helps a great deal if your child can look at you in order to learn how to say the word. It also helps if he can look with you at the object or situation that the word is representing. For example, to learn the word "butterfly," it helps if your child can look at you and look with you at the butterfly perched on a flower. The ability to visually track, or follow a moving object, is also important in learning labels. Thus, to learn the word "dog," it helps if your child can look with you at the dog and follow the dog as it moves.

If your child cannot see clearly or has difficulty focusing on objects, he will naturally have more trouble learning to attach particular words to particular objects. Many children with Down syndrome have visual difficulties. At least 50 percent have strabismus, or muscle imbalance problems that cause one or both eyes to turn outward or inward. Nearsightedness (blurred distant vision) and farsightedness (blurred near vision) are also common problems.

These vision problems are all easily correctable and should not be allowed to interfere with your child's communication development. If you suspect a vision problem, you may want to ask your pediatrician for a referral to a pediatric ophthalmologist—a medical doctor specializing in evaluating and treating vision problems of children. This doctor can test your child's vision even before he is able to talk and let you know how often you should come back for routine checkups.

TACTILE SKILLS

In infancy, most children learn a lot about the world through the sense of touch, the tactile sense. For instance, when a baby is first handed a new object such as a block or a set of plastic keys, he explores it by putting it in his mouth. Touch and sensation around the mouth are particularly related to speech development.

Children with Down syndrome may have difficulty with sensory awareness. For example, if a child with Down syndrome chews a cracker or cookie, he will often not be aware of any food remaining between his lips, cheeks, and teeth. He will generally not use his tongue to clear the area automatically, but he can be taught to do this. He may also have difficulty with tactile feedback; that is, knowing where his tongue is and where it should be placed for a specific sound.

Children with Down syndrome sometimes have trouble processing sensations in their mouth, which can eventually lead to speech difficulties. Some children have reduced sensation to touch in the mouth. Consequently, they may not enjoy exploring objects with the mouth and will get less practice moving the lips and tongue. As a result, they may have more difficulty feeling where their tongue is touching when they try to make speech sounds. Other children with Down syndrome are oversensitive to touch (*tactilely defensive*) and may find any kind of touch around their face or mouth intolerable. If your child is tactilely defensive, you may notice that he doesn't like to be touched when you are giving him a bath, dressing him, washing his face, shampooing his hair, or cleaning his ears. He might not enjoy exploring objects with his mouth, resulting in limited practice exercising the lips and tongue.

If your child is either over- or undersensitive to touch, consult an occupational therapist who is trained in sensory integration therapy (see below). The occupational therapist can use activities and exercises to help your child learn to respond more normally to touch. More information on oral and tactile sensitivity can be found in Chapters 3 and 4, including activities to do at home.

SENSORY INTEGRATION

Much of language learning involves the ability to simultaneously process and organize input from more than one sense. For example, to imitate a word his mother says, a child must be able to hear each sound in the word and then figure out where to touch his lips, tongue, etc. to make those sounds. And to learn which words correspond to which objects in his environment, he must be able to see what adults around him are talking about. This ability to organize input from various senses and apply them to everyday life is known as sensory integration.

A child's sensory integration ability often forms the basis for the way that we view him and his behavior. For example, we generally judge whether a child is listening by whether he looks at us or follows our instructions when we talk to him. That is, we judge him by whether he is able to hear what we say and then translate what he hears into the appropriate movements. If we call him and he does not look up or respond, or if we ask him to come over and he does not move, we assume that he is willfully not following our instructions. Not listening and not looking give a perhaps unfair impression of noncompliance.

Children with Down syndrome may need particular help in learning to pay attention, listen, look, and respond. One reason is that they may have trouble pro-

cessing input from more than one sense at once—for example, if they are asked to look and listen at the same time. They may be overwhelmed by the many sensations around them—the pinch of their new shoes, the feel of a label inside their shirt or a scratchy sweater, the hum of the air conditioner, the smell of baking cookies—and be unable to focus on what is being said. Children with Down syndrome may exhibit behaviors such as hyperactivity and impulsiveness that can be signs of sensory integration difficulties. Sensory integration problems of this nature not only make it difficult to learn communication skills, but many other skills as well.

An occupational therapist may be able to help your child overcome sensory integration problems. An occupational therapist may already be a part of your child's early intervention or education team. If not, the American Occupational Therapy Association or Sensory Integration International can help you locate a therapist trained in sensory integration techniques. See the Resource Guide at the end of this book for contact information. Also check the References and Suggested Reading list at the end of the book for publications that have suggestions about how to work on those difficulties at home.

PHYSICAL CHARACTERISTICS

Children with Down syndrome frequently have differences in the muscles or structure of the facial area that can result in speech difficulties. These differences include:

- Low muscle tone (hypotonia)—muscles that are more relaxed and "floppy" than usual, and therefore more difficult to control. Muscles in your child's lips, tongue, and jaw might be affected
- Difficulty moving the lips, tongue, and jaw independent of each other (SLPs call this "dissociation")
- A mouth that is relatively small in relation to tongue size
- A tendency to breathe through the mouth due to enlarged adenoids or tonsils or to recurrent allergies or colds
- A high narrow palate that might limit tongue movements for speech

See Table 3 on pages 22-23 for a more exhaustive listing of physical differences that can lead to speech and language delays.

The problems above can all affect your child's *speech intelligibility* (how easily his speech is understood) in different ways. Your child may have trouble with:

- **articulation,** or the ability to move and control the lips, tongue, jaws, and palate to form sounds correctly and clearly;

- **fluency,** or the ability to speak smoothly and rhythmically;
- **sequencing,** or the ability to pronounce sounds in the proper order within words (for example, your child may say "efelant" for "elephant");
- **resonance,** or the tone and quality of speech sounds your child produces (for instance, whether sounds are too nasal or "twangy" or not nasal enough and sound as if your child has a stuffed nose).

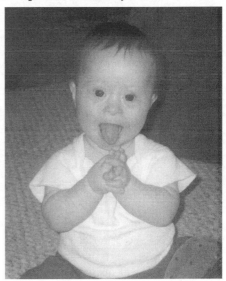

Although the problems above can make speaking more difficult and frustrating for your child, they need not prevent him from communicating effectively. Chapter 5 explains how your child can learn to supplement speech with sign language and other visual communication systems until he is able to speak more intelligibly. Chapter 8 suggests ways you can work with your child on specific factors affecting his intelligibility.

Cognitive Characteristics

Children with Down syndrome often have more difficulty learning because of the mental retardation that is usually present. Mental retardation can have an especially big impact on communication skills, because so much of language learning depends on cognitive or thinking abilities such as reasoning, understanding concepts, and remembering.

These problems will have a significant impact on your child's communication skills, but he can continue to make considerable improvement all his life. As a parent, you can help by providing language experiences as the basis for learning language concepts, by giving your child many opportunities to use old words in new situations, and by giving him plenty of practice in using new language skills. Later chapters explain how, specifically, to do these things.

Some of the specific cognitive abilities that mental retardation can affect are discussed below.

 Generalization is the ability to apply information learned in one situation to a new situation. For example, a younger child may be able to identify the color green

Table 3: Physical Differences That Affect Speech and Language

Physical Characteristic	Effect on Speech/Language
Low tone in mouth, tongue, pharynx muscles (hypotonia)	Articulation and intelligibility problems; imprecise speech; voice and resonance problems
Underdevelopment of midfacial bones, also known as midfacial hypoplasia	Articulation and intelligibility problems
Lax ligaments in TMJ (loose connections in the jaw bone area)	Articulation problems; imprecise speech
Drooling	Difficulty with sensory awareness and feedback for articulation
Open mouth	Articulation problems, especially for /p/, /b/, /m/, /f/, /v/
Mild blockage of nasal airways	Hyponasality (voice quality sounds "stuffy")
Velopharyngeal insufficiency (difficulty using the soft palate and throat wall muscles to seal off the nasal cavity to keep air/sounds out of the nose)	Hypernasality (voice quality sounds too nasal); intelligibility problems
Mouth breathing	Hyponasality; articulation and intelligibility problems
Open bite (upper and lower teeth do not meet)	Articulation problems, especially for /s/, /z/, /sh/, /t/, /d/
Tongue protrusion	Articulation problems, especially for /t/, /d/, /s/, /z/, /sh/, /l/, /n/; intelligibility problems
Angle's Class III maloclusion with prognathism (lower jaw juts out in front of upper jaw)	Articulation and intelligibility problems
Tongue large in relation to mouth	Articulation problems, especially, for /t/, /d/, /s/, /sh/, /z/, /l/, /n/; intelligibility problems
Limited distance and range of motion for tongue movements	Imprecise articulation
Abnormalities of the neuromuscular junctions of the tongue	Articulation problems
Narrow upper jaw	Hypernasality; intelligibility problems
Palate height too low	Intelligibility problems
Palate height too high; v-shaped palate	Hypernasality; intelligibility problems
Irregular dentition (teeth)	Articulation problems
Difficulties with coordination, accuracy, and timing of mouth movements	Articulation and intelligibility problems

Difficulty with graded jaw movements (ability to make small precise movements throughout the range of jaw mobility)	Articulation and intelligibility problems
Sequential processing difficulties	Problems with phonemic processing, auditory memory, morphosyntax
Apraxia or motor planning difficulties	Severe delays in speech; groping and struggling to form sounds; intelligibility problems
Dysarthria or oral motor difficulties	Intelligibility problems
Sensitivities to touch, sound, or movement	Oral motor difficulties
Otitis media with effusion and fluctuating hearing loss	Delayed language development; difficulties with auditory discrimination (telling sounds apart) and auditory localization (telling where sound is coming from)
Impacted cerumen (ear wax)	Delayed language development; difficulties with auditory association and localization
Sensorineural hearing loss	Difficulties with speech perception; phonemic processing
Conductive hearing loss	Difficulties with hearing conversational level speech; difficulties hearing instructions in school without amplification

when he has a group of color blocks, but have difficulty identifying the many shades of green on trees, grass, and signs and advertisements. An older child who has learned to form the plural of the words "dog," "ball," and "cookie" by adding an "s" to the ends of the words might not be able to figure out that he can form the plural of a new word such as "dinosaur" in the same way. He may learn a skill in one situation, and not automatically generalize it to similar situations. With training and practice, however, he can learn to apply a skill to different situations.

MEMORY

Memory can be defined as the ability to store and recall information, actions, and events. Memory can be divided into long-term memory and short-term memory. Long-term memory may involve skills learned over time, such as playing a musical instrument or swimming, or recall of information and events. Short-term memory is the working memory that you use every day as you process information. Short-term memory is important for speaking and for processing language. Generally, children with Down syndrome seem to be better at remembering what they see (visual memory) than at remembering what they hear (auditory memory).

Auditory Memory. Auditory memory is another term for verbal short-term memory—that is, retaining and remembering information that you have heard. Processing and remembering the sounds for speaking are known as the phonological loop. The phonological loop is involved in short-term storage of verbal information.

Ideally, auditory memory allows us to remember words long enough after they have been spoken so we can process and respond to them. Children may have trouble with this, however. For instance, if you ask your child to get his winter jacket and gloves, he may only remember the first thing, the jacket. Since children with Down syndrome respond well to visual cues, your child may be able to follow the instructions more easily if you point to the door or the car and add, "Because we're going outside," or if you are already wearing your coat and gloves.

Visual Memory. Working memory for visual-spatial activities appears to be stronger for children with Down syndrome than working memory for verbal activities. For example, when your child sees you get the cereal from the third shelf, he is more likely to remember where it is than if you tell him verbally, "The cereal is on the third shelf." Put another way: children with Down syndrome learn more easily by watching demonstrations than by listening to verbal instructions. They are also capable of learning signs to represent words and concepts earlier than they are able to learn to say the word, because they usually have stronger visual than auditory skills. This is why reading can be effective in helping children with Down syndrome progress in language. For more information, see Chapter 14.

ABSTRACT THINKING

Abstract thinking refers to the ability to understand relationships, concepts, principles, and other ideas that are intangible. Difficulty with abstract thinking may make it harder for your child to understand language concepts such as:

- that words can identify the extremes of characteristics (hot/ cold, short/long);
- that the same word can be used to label several objects that seem quite different (poodles, German shepherds, and Chihuahuas are all dogs);
- that the meaning of a sentence depends on the order of words ("Joe hit the ball" vs. "The ball hit Joe").

In addition, your child may have trouble understanding and using words for time concepts like "today" and "next year," and will tend to use concrete vocabulary, describing events and objects currently in his environment, rather than those he encountered at a different time or in a different setting. You may need to be sure that you use concrete language when giving instructions. For example, use "sit down" rather than "take a seat."

PROCESSING SKILLS

Our brains are constantly processing information received from our senses. We take in, interpret, and respond to sights, sounds, and other types of stimulation in our environment.

Visual Processing. Just as it is more difficult for children with Down syndrome to remember auditory information than visual information, it is also more difficult for them to process auditory information than visual information. This is because visual information is not as fleeting as auditory information, so children with Down syndrome can take the time to make sense of it before it's gone.

This relative strength in visual processing is one reason that computer-based learning is so successful with children with Down syndrome. It provides visual cues that can be repeated as many times as desired. For similar reasons, perhaps, reading often is a relative strength for children with Down syndrome. It also means that pictures or written words or sign language will help children learn concepts more easily than spoken words.

Auditory processing, or how quickly and efficiently your child takes in, interprets, and responds to spoken words, can be a problem. Children with Down syndrome generally need more time to process and understand what is said to them, and may therefore be slower to answer questions or respond to instructions even when they aren't experiencing auditory memory problems.

Auditory discrimination, or the ability to hear differences between sounds, can also be difficult for children with Down syndrome. This influences whether the child can understand which word is being said—for example, "road" and "rose" or "land" and "sand" may be confused. Not surprisingly, middle ear fluid exacerbates this problem.

Word retrieval, or the ability to select the appropriate word in a given situation, is an issue for many children with Down syndrome. This problem may affect the complexity, accuracy, or length of the phrases and sentences your child uses. Sometimes when children are having difficulty with word retrieval, they may use words that are closely related to the word they are thinking of, such as using "sock" for "shoe." Or they may say "you know" or "whatever." It is often frustrating for children or adults when they cannot retrieve the word they are thinking of.

Asynchrony of Language Skills

Children with Down syndrome do not achieve at the same level in all language areas. This results in what speech-language pathologists refer to as an *asynchrony* of language skills—some skills are more advanced than others. Most notably, children with Down syndrome are usually better at comprehending language (receptive language skills) than at putting thoughts and ideas into words (expressive language skills). As explained below, however, there may also be other patterns of strengths and weaknesses.

RECEPTIVE-EXPRESSIVE GAP

Children with Down syndrome usually can understand language more easily than they can express themselves. Although they may have auditory processing problems, as well as a variety of other difficulties that interfere with language comprehension, they usually have far more difficulty expressing themselves. Thus, they often have difficulty sequencing words to express an idea or asking for clarification when they do not understand something that has been said. This results in the so-called "receptive-expressive gap." For example, a six-year-old who has the receptive language skills of a typical four-year-old may have only the expressive skills of a typical two- to three-year-old.

This gap may be a problem if people who do not know your child well assume that he knows less than he does because he has trouble verbally responding to questions. People tend to underestimate children who cannot speak or speak very little. They wrongfully conclude that the person who has difficulty speaking does not understand what they are saying. At home, too, if your child is slower to formulate a response, you might assume that he does not comprehend what you said. You may need to wait longer for a response to find out whether he actually understood you or not. Your child may need a cue or a prompt or more time to organize his response.

One consequence of your child's expressive language delay is that he will probably have shorter mean length of utterance (MLU) than other children. This means that, on average, his phrases and sentences will contain fewer words. For example, at the age of four years, typically developing children have an MLU of 4.5 words, while children with Down syndrome have an MLU of 1.5 words. By age six and a half, the average MLU for children with Down syndrome is 3.5. Although this may be a problem in school for academic learning, it does not have to be a problem in daily living. Most of the time, it is possible to get our meaning across with short sentences. In addition, environmental stimulation and language intervention do make a difference. Research has shown that parents who are trained to help their children learn language can improve their children's language skills, especially in the areas of mean length of utterance and structural complexity.

MORPHOSYNTAX AND SEMANTICS

Two additional areas of language affected in children with Down syndrome are:

1. **morphosyntax**—the grammar or structure of language (the order of words in a sentence and what function they serve). This area includes word parts (morphemes) such as prefixes and suffixes that signal structural relationships (possession, past tense); and

2. **semantics**—the meaning of words (including usage and understanding of vocabulary).

Research has found that children with Down syndrome have more difficulties with expressive and receptive morphosyntax than do other children of the same mental age. That is, even though an intelligence test might show that your six-year-old is generally performing at the level of a typical four-year-old, his morphosyntax (grammatical) skills would be lower than those of a four-year-old. Up to seventeen months, no difference is found between children with Down syndrome and typically developing children in syntax and vocabulary, but by twenty-six months, children with Down syndrome lag behind. For more information on morphosyntax, including home activities, see Chapter 7.

Although your child's vocabulary may be limited in the early years, vocabulary is an area of relative strength for children with Down syndrome. Studies have shown that children and adults with Down syndrome can continue to develop their vocabularies all their lives. The more experiences your child has, the more new words he will learn. There is no limit or ceiling to vocabulary acquisition, and the acquisition of new vocabulary words and concepts should be a focus from early intervention through adult life. It is true that your child may tend to use concrete words, especially nouns, because of his difficulties with abstract thinking. And he will likely use the same words over and over rather than using a variety of words, but if the words are appropriate to the situation, this may not be a problem in real life. Think of how frequently we say, "Hi, how are you?" or "See you later" without varying the structure. Much of communication is repetitive. Also, there is a wide range of vocabulary level in individuals with Down syndrome. Many adolescents and adults have rich and varied vocabularies; others have more limited vocabularies. See Chapter 7 for a discussion of semantics.

PRAGMATICS

One area of language that is often a relative strength for children with Down syndrome is *pragmatics,* or the social use of language. Pragmatics encompasses such skills as using social greetings appropriately and understanding the unwritten rules of conversation (for example, everybody usually doesn't speak at once, but waits their turn). With practice and experience, children with Down syndrome usually do

well in these areas. Children with Down syndrome also generally learn how to formulate appropriate messages for their listeners. For example, they learn to speak to their teacher using different vocabulary and syntax structure than they would use with their two-year-old cousin.

In addition, most children with Down syndrome are skilled at the nonverbal aspects of pragmatics—for instance, making gestures and facial expressions to help people understand their messages. Other areas of pragmatics such as asking questions, requesting clarification, and staying on topic are more difficult for children with Down syndrome. With help from therapists and parents, however, they can usually make good progress in these areas. Working on social communication skills with your child is essential, as they contribute greatly to inclusion within the community. For a more detailed discussion of pragmatics, see Chapter 10.

Conclusion

Although the long list of communication problems that children with Down syndrome might have may seem daunting, much can be done to help overcome or alleviate the problems. As a parent, you can involve your child in activities and experiences that will help him overcome difficulties in many areas. And speech-language pathologists can use and explain special techniques, materials, and exercises that can help him optimize his communication skills. We are learning more every day about the potential of individuals with Down syndrome. The next few chapters will focus on how to begin the process of communication for infants and young children with Down syndrome. Later chapters will explain specific areas in speech and language and suggest ways you can work on them at home.

Chapter 3

Busy Baby—Busy Parents

Your baby is home. There is much to do physically for her and for yourself. Besides trying to get some rest, you need to adjust to the special needs that your child will have. Remember that your baby needs to be held and cuddled, fed and burped, changed and bathed, talked to and loved just like any other baby. Babies with Down syndrome are far more like other babies than different from other babies. There may, however, be additional medical or feeding concerns for children with Down syndrome. It is not uncommon for children with low muscle tone to have difficulty with sucking and swallowing during feeding. There is information and there are feeding specialists (usually speech-language pathologists or occupational therapists) who can help you give your baby a good start. You can contact other parents who have walked the road before you. Family support groups are available in many parts of the United States, Canada, and other areas of the world. If there is no local parent group, there are Internet support groups that are as close as e-mail.

If you haven't already done so, enroll your child in an early intervention program where she will receive the specialized help she needs to maximize her learning. As part of early intervention, you can request evaluations for feeding difficulties and for early language progress. Early intervention services are federally funded and available in all states in the United States, as well as in Canada and other countries. The special education department at the nearest elementary school or your local ARC can help you locate an early intervention program. Information on how to find services and the laws governing services provided by the school system can be found in Chapter 13.

To learn and grow, every baby needs to have a wide variety of sensory experiences and to experience a stimulating environment. Your baby learns about her world through looking, listening, touching, and sensing position and movement. Interact with your baby from the very beginning. Teach her the skills that are basic to communication development. Talk to her, sing to her, rock her to music. We know that babies recognize familiar voices at a very early age and will respond. Put your face close to your baby when holding her; stare into her face while feeding her. Teaching and practice can be part of your daily activities. When you are bathing or dressing your child, you can teach names of body parts. At mealtimes, you can label the different types of food, and work on "open" and "close" as she opens and closes her lips and mouth for feeding. Communication is part of daily life, and it is natural to talk about certain activities as you go about everyday living.

This chapter focuses on the earliest skills that form the bases of language, and the feeding and pre-speech skills that help develop the skills needed for speech. The activities suggested are generally appropriate for babies with Down syndrome during the first six to eight months of life. The time framework, however, may be different if your child experiences early surgery, or is tube fed rather than bottle- or breastfed. The next chapter focuses on the precursor skills for language and speech. Some can be worked on early, but others may need to wait until after six months of age.

When to start work on specific areas depends on your child's readiness. For example, you can't work on imitation activities until your child is ready to imitate your movements or your sounds. Early intervention specialists can provide information on the steps and stages needed to master sensory, motor, tactile, and speech skills. Remember, speech development is intertwined with development in many other areas. For your child to progress in language and speech use, she needs to learn from her environment through the senses of vision, hearing, and touch. And, you can begin working on sensory input and sensory issues from birth. Think of your child's development as a sequence rather than a time schedule.

Sensory Experiences

Sensory input is all around us. Through our senses, we learn about the world. The more familiar senses are sight (visual), hearing (auditory), touch (tactile), taste (gustatory), and smell (olfactory). But, even the familiar senses are complex. For example, the tactile sense lets us perceive whether an object is smooth or rough, sharp or dull, large or small, hot, cold, or lukewarm.

Lesser-known senses are:

1. **the vestibular sense**—the sense of balance and movement; and
2. **proprioception**—the internal awareness of where our joints and muscles are at any moment.

The vestibular sense is involved in muscle tone, coordinates the two sides of the body, and coordinates the movements of the eyes, head, and body to help us maintain our balance. Proprioception processes feedback from the muscles and joints to keep the body on track. Because of proprioception, we can bring the soup spoon to our mouths without undershooting or overshooting. We automatically and unconsciously bring the spoon accurately to our lips. The vestibular and proprioceptive senses are both involved in articulation and speech intelligibility.

Sensory Integration. Sensory integration (SI) is the term used to describe the ability to receive and absorb accurate sensory information from the environment and to coordinate and integrate the information to function appropriately in your environment. It includes the ability to take in information, as well as the ability to screen out information (such as noise in the environment).

Sensory Integrative Dysfunction. When children have difficulty processing and organizing sensory information, it is known as sensory integrative dysfunction. Sensory integrative dysfunction is more common in children with Down syn-

drome than it is in children with typical development. Clinically, we have observed that many young children with Down syndrome seem to have some difficulties with SI, such as tolerating loud noises, having their teeth brushed, getting haircuts, or handling mixed textures in their food. An excellent source of information on sensory integrative dysfunction is *The Out-of-Sync Child* by Carol Stock Kranowitz. See the box on the next page for information on sensory problems and communication skills.

Your child's early intervention team should be able to assess any sensory difficulties that she is experiencing and provide an appropriate treatment program. You are an important part of the early intervention evaluation team and can provide vital feedback. The early months, at home, are the time to get to know your baby's preferences and learning styles. Does your baby crave more stimulation—such as listening to music or sucking a pacifier? Is she overwhelmed by sensations—perhaps closing her eyes, putting her hands over her ears, or crying because she is overstimulated? The first few months are an excellent opportunity to get to know how your child functions best, what delights her, and what upsets her.

VISUAL EXPERIENCES

Infants learn a great deal by observing their environment, and especially by observing the people in their world. In the early months, babies are attracted by certain kinds of things in the environment. Research has shown that infants prefer bright colors, such as red, as well as black and white contrasts. They can focus best on objects close to them. Research has also shown that infants prefer to look at the human face. Encourage your child to look at you, by holding her so that she can see you. Cradle her in your arms facing you. Hold her in the air with her face near yours. Or, place her in her infant seat on a table at your eye level so that you are looking right at each other. Smile, laugh, and talk and sing to her. Attract her attention to your face.

Once your baby is looking at your face, try to increase the time that she stares at it. Make funny sounds or funny faces to stimulate her and keep her attention. Act as a mirror and imitate any movements that she makes. Use a full-length mirror, lie next to your baby, and look at each other in the mirror. Make it fun for her to look at your face and show delight in looking right at her face. The closeness helps her develop the skill of looking at you.

Be sure that the environment is visually stimulating. Hang colorful mobiles and pictures around the room. Encourage your child to look with you at objects in the room. Pick up a large toy animal or a giant beach ball and hold it close to her. Move it until you can see her looking at the ball and say, "Look at the ball. Isn't it big? It's fun to look at the ball!" Show delight in what you observe together. Have fun explor-

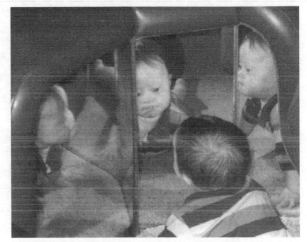

Sensory Difficulties and Communication Skills

In general, there are five types of sensory difficulties that can affect communication. Many children with DS have at least one of these difficulties when they are young; some have all of them. If a child also has autism, she may be more likely to have severe sensory difficulties.

Hypersensitivity—The child is oversensitive to sights, sounds, touch, or movements. She may jump, withdraw, or appear fearful of situations because they are uncomfortable for her. She may eat a limited number of foods, because she does not like crunchy foods or mixed textures (peas or lumps in the mashed potatoes).

Hyposensitivity—The child is undersensitive or less responsive to stimulation, and therefore may appear unaware. As a result, she seeks out intense sensory experiences such as biting and sucking on her fingers, twirling, stuffing her hand in her mouth, or stuffing her mouth with food. Some children have a combination of hyper- and hyposensitivity, and may fluctuate between them.

Unusually high or low activity level—The child is constantly on the move or appears lethargic and tired and is slow to move.

Coordination difficulty—The child may have poor balance. She may have difficulty learning a new task, especially in motor planning. She will appear clumsy and awkward. (Children with Down syndrome usually have coordination difficulties due to low muscle tone, but if these occur along with sensory problems, there may be even greater coordination problems.)

Difficulty with organization of behavior—The child may have difficulty adjusting to new situations or shifting tasks. She may have difficulty falling asleep and waking up. She may appear impulsive or distractible.

If your child is hypo- or hypersensitive to touch throughout the body and does not like to be touched, it is important to consult an occupational therapist (OT). If any of the other symptoms appear to describe your child, request an occupational therapy/sensory integration evaluation. An OT can help your child learn to respond more normally to touch and other sensations. A speech-language pathologist who is trained in sensory integration can help by providing oral sensory experiences that will help your child experience more normal sensation in the lips, tongue, and mouth area and therefore make it easier for her to learn to speak.

ing the visual environment with your baby. Watch as she learns to swat at the mobile. Observe and note when she follows the animals on the mobile as they move around. Watch how alert she is to the music, and when the music stops.

Sometimes babies with Down syndrome have more trouble focusing on faces or objects because of low muscle tone or difficulties in lifting the head. So, be sure to cradle and support your baby's head. Once you have her in a position where she can see your face clearly, she will want to look at your face and will delight in it in the same way as any other baby. Some babies are more responsive, and obviously enjoy looking at faces. Other babies are less responsive. This is sometimes difficult for new parents. We all want feedback. There is nothing that is more reinforcing than a baby who smiles or laughs every time that your face appears. Some babies with Down syndrome take longer to show that response. But, the response will come. Your baby needs to see your face frequently and to be held close to your face and to see that you enjoy looking at her. Eventually, she will learn to look back, to recognize your face, and to think that it is a wonderful face that is special to her. This early visual training is very important. In order to learn to speak in later months, it will help a great deal if your child can look at you, and this is the beginning of that skill.

Most babies respond well to visual stimulation, but they do not all crave the same amount of visual stimulation. Observe your child to see how much stimulation is adequate and how much stimulation distresses her. You want to find that balance. An occupational therapist who is knowledgeable about sensory integration treatment can help you identify the levels of stimulation that are best for your child. You can always increase the stimulation later when your baby seems ready for additional stimulation.

AUDITORY EXPERIENCES

To learn language skills, your child has to be able to listen. Not only must she be physically able to "hear" but she must also be able to focus on sounds. Listening skills are developed through experience. You can help by providing many sounds for your baby to hear. Try one activity at a time, so that she is not overwhelmed by too many competing sounds. Some children have difficulty listening to loud sounds, while others have difficulty focusing on the important sounds in the environment when there is background noise (this is known as figure-ground difficulty).

Play sound games with your baby. For instance, when she makes a screeching sound, imitate that sound. If your baby says "eeee," repeat the sound and then make it into a song. When your baby says "ah," imitate the sound and then repeat it again using a high-pitched voice or a very low voice. Your baby may have a short attention span and lose interest, so keep the practices short. But, it is likely that she will enjoy hearing you make "her" sounds.

Some other ways to train your child to hear sounds, listen, and increase her attention span include:

- *Connect sounds with their sources.* Make animal sounds for your baby's toy animals, and then ask, "What sound does the duck make?" Then say, "Quack, quack." Don't expect your child to join in the sound play for many months, but usually before twelve months of age, she will try to imitate some sounds.
- *Use a variety of rattles, bells, and noisemakers to provide different types of sound stimulation* and to attract your baby's attention. Encourage her to play with the sound toys, too. This gives her practice in hearing sounds and in exploring where those sounds come from.
- *Call your child by name consistently.* If she does not respond, attract her attention by waving a favorite toy and then call her name again.

■ *Use a musical mobile for both visual and auditory stimulation.*

Remember that fluid in the ear and fluctuating hearing loss may sometimes make it more difficult for your child to hear your sounds, so she may sometimes seem not to be paying attention. On those occasions, make sure that she can see your face. Get close to her and say the sounds more loudly so that she can see and hear you. And be sure to seek prompt medical attention for hearing problems, as your child needs to hear as well as possible to learn language. For more information on auditory problems, see Chapter 2.

TACTILE EXPERIENCES

There are many tactile (touch) skills necessary for speaking. To speak, we not only have to be able to move our lips, we also need to be able to sense how our lips are moving: Are the lips tight together? Is the tongue applying pressure on the gum ridge?

There are more sensory nerve fibers present in the mouth than in any other part of the human body. When your baby explores the world by putting objects in her mouth, she is activating this sensitive sensory system. As she gains many experiences in infancy with touch, she also develops "feedback loops"—that is, her brain forms connections between an action and a resulting sensation. When she puts a toy in her mouth or touches something soft and squishy or hard and solid, her body

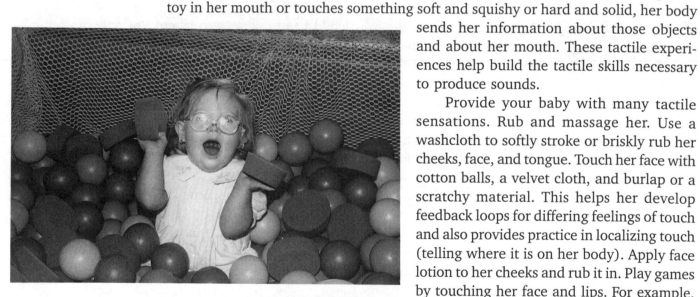

sends her information about those objects and about her mouth. These tactile experiences help build the tactile skills necessary to produce sounds.

Provide your baby with many tactile sensations. Rub and massage her. Use a washcloth to softly stroke or briskly rub her cheeks, face, and tongue. Touch her face with cotton balls, a velvet cloth, and burlap or a scratchy material. This helps her develop feedback loops for differing feelings of touch and also provides practice in localizing touch (telling where it is on her body). Apply face lotion to her cheeks and rub it in. Play games by touching her face and lips. For example, rub her lips, then rub your lips with your finger or a washcloth. Bath time is a natural time to do these activities, and once daily is sufficient. Let this be a special time of closeness that your baby looks forward to.

Encourage exploration with the mouth by providing sponge, rubber, or other soft, safe toys that your baby can easily put into her mouth and stimulate the lips, cheek, and tongue area. Provide a variety of textures in toys so that your child feels different tactile sensations. Soft toy animals with protruding parts such as dinosaurs or a giraffe are especially useful. If your baby does not voluntarily mouth objects herself, an OT can show you how to wipe her gums with a soft washcloth or a NUK toothbrush to help her tolerate touch within her mouth.

Encourage your child to imitate oral movements such as smacking the lips, clicking the tongue, and making funny sounds by holding your face close to her face while you make the sounds.

Communication Experiences

Several very important foundations to communication are laid during infancy. These include learning the concept of turn-taking and that communication allows you to have control over your environment. As a parent, you play a central role in helping your child master these concepts.

<table>
<tr><td>

EARLY TURN-TAKING

</td><td>

All communication depends on turn-taking—on the fact that there is a speaker and a listener and that they can change roles. This is something that you can teach your baby very early through play and sound making. Although your child may need more practice to develop turn-taking skills, she will learn to use this skill correctly.

</td></tr>
</table>

When your baby begins to make sounds, even crying or screeching sounds, imitate her sounds. Then wait, and allow her time to make more sounds. Sometimes children with Down syndrome are slower to take their turn, so be sure to give your child long enough to respond. You might want to position a mirror so your baby can see it, as babies often increase their sound play when looking in a mirror. Keep your face close to your baby's, and play back and forth with sounds. If she bangs her hand on the mattress, wait until she stops and then bang your hand on the mattress. Any movement or sound-making activity can lend itself to turn-taking practice.

React to your baby's sound making as if it has meaning. Listen intently; when she stops making sounds, say, "You don't say" or "Tell me more" or "You want your bottle now, don't you?" Have a conversation with her. When your baby has taken a turn, you respond, then watch her and allow her time to take her turn. When she is able to hold a toy phone, have play phone conversations. This sound play is the beginning of conversational routines. Your baby will love having these conversations with you.

In "conversing" with your baby, use a high-pitched voice, speak in short, simple sentences, talk more slowly, and use a lot of repetition. This is sometimes referred to as "motherese" or "baby talk." Motherese appears to help all infants—including those with Down syndrome—learn language. Once your child has reached the age of two to three years and has begun to use speech, some characteristics of motherese, such as using a high-pitched voice, will begin to feel unnatural or inappropriate. That's the time to fade out those characteristics. But, using shorter sentences and talking more slowly are characteristics of motherese that may be helpful even when your child is older.

For suggestions for teaching turn-taking to children above six months of age, see the next chapter.

<table>
<tr><td>

THE POWER OF COMMUNICATION

</td><td>

To help your baby learn that sound making can influence her environment and get results, respond quickly to her cries and sounds. Help her learn that sounds can bring help. When she cries, pick her up, give her a bottle, or change her diaper, depending on what she wants. Talk about and respond to what your baby is interested in at that very moment. "Did you hear that airplane? It made a loud noise." Or, "You're wet, aren't you? We need to get a diaper very fast and make you dry."

</td></tr>
</table>

Feeding

Feeding is an important activity in your baby's daily life. Not only does it provide her with the nourishment she needs to survive and grow, it also helps exercise the muscles needed for speech. This is because feeding relies on many of the same muscles that are used to produce speech. Through feeding, your baby gains practice in the movements of the lips, tongue, and other parts of the mouth area that are needed for speaking. She also develops sensory awareness, perception, and discrimination within her mouth.

Sometimes children with Down syndrome have medical, sensory, or other problems that make it harder to feed, and therefore, to develop the movements needed for speech. When a child experiences difficulty, it is best to seek a full diagnostic evaluation by a team of specialists. The team should include:

- an occupational therapist who can evaluate sensory issues that may be interfering with feeding,
- a physician who can investigate medical issues such as reflux that may affect feeding,
- a speech-language pathologist who can evaluate oral motor difficulties, and
- a dietitian who can design a dietary plan.

For instance, low muscle tone can make it harder to suck and swallow or to maintain head and trunk control while sucking and swallowing. If your baby has trouble sucking, a speech-language pathologist, occupational therapist, or nurse may be able to suggest changes in the bottle nipple that will help. Some specialists have found that a preemie nipple makes sucking easier. If your baby has trouble closing her lips around the nipple, rub her lips while she is drinking and massage under her chin. Use ice on the lips or lip balm to highlight the sensation of the lips touching at other times, when she is not sucking or feeding. When your baby begins to move on to cereals and spoon feeding, using a small, shallow-bowled spoon and feeding her small spoonfuls at a time can be helpful.

There are also some exercises you can do to help increase the muscle tone of your baby's tongue. First, try tapping the tongue to rhythmical music—bounce or pat the tongue with a clean finger, a pacifier, or a teething biscuit. As the muscle tone increases, there will be an increase in tongue movement. You can then gently stroke your child's tongue to form a central groove or to move it sideways or upward.

As your child progresses to semi-solid foods, it is important to give her foods with a variety of textures so she can continue to develop sensory awareness in her mouth and develop feedback loops for different types of textures. You might begin with foods such as baby cereal, applesauce, oatmeal, cottage cheese, and mashed potatoes. Gradually, you can introduce foods of different textures, including mashed fruit, soups, pureed meats, and yogurt.

Once your child is ready for solid foods, you should be sure to offer her foods that encourage sideways movement of the tongue and biting. Foods such as Junior or chopped baby food, cooked vegetables, flaked tuna with mayonnaise, and spaghetti rings, as well as cookies and crackers such as zwieback, arrowroot, and graham crackers may be introduced during this phase. Other foods that require your child to practice chewing and tongue movements are scrambled eggs, ground beef patties broken up, casseroles, small pieces of cut-up meat, raw fruits and vegetables, and small pieces of dried fruits. If she is hypersensitive to touch (tactile defensiveness), this may show itself as strong food preferences. She often will not want to eat foods of mixed textures such as macaroni and cheese with peas. She will want to keep her foods separate, and may be willing to eat only a limited number of foods. She may have strong temperature preferences, and only eat food that is hot or food that is cold.

Many children with Down syndrome have difficulty shifting from bottle- or breastfeeding to cup feeding. Cup feeding involves different, more complex movements and greater muscle control. It may be easier for your child to begin cup drinking using thicker liquids such as thinned pudding or baby fruit thinned with water or juice. Thicker liquid is easier for infants to swallow. Your child may also have difficulty drinking when the cup is nearly empty. Typically, we bend our head back to drink the liquid from the bottom of the cup. This backward head movement causes some children with Down syndrome to choke. A cut-out cup will often make drinking easier. Cut a semi-circle out of one side of a plastic cup and have your child drink from the uncut side. When she tips the cup back to get the remaining liquid, the cutout provides a place for her nose and she doesn't need to tip her head back to drink. Cut-out cups can also be purchased from several companies listed in the Resource Guide at the end of this book.

Straws can be used to strengthen the lip muscles and the muscles involved in sucking. Straws with a larger opening are generally easier than those with a narrow opening. Likewise, it is usually easier to suck liquids through shorter straws than through longer ones, or through crazy straws with loops. The consistency of the material to be sucked through the straw also has an effect. Thicker liquids such as milkshakes or pudding are more difficult to suck through a straw than thin liquids, and thus provide more of a challenge. See the box on the next page about Sara Rosenfeld-Johnson's oral motor program.

If your child has a great deal of difficulty making the movements necessary for feeding, consult a speech-language pathologist or occupational therapist specializing in feeding therapy. Feeding therapy focuses on developing the muscle movements and the muscular coordination needed for safe and nutritious eating. If, on the other hand, your child is hypersensitive to touch in the mouth (tactilely defensive), you may need to find a therapist (usually an occupational therapist) trained in sensory integration therapy. Otherwise, your child's hypersensitivity may cause her to gag or choke on foods, or to refuse to eat foods with certain textures.

Finally, if your child needs to be tube-fed for any reason, it is important that the speech-language pathologist work with her on an oral motor therapy program. The exercises and activities in an oral motor therapy program will give your child practice in sucking and swallowing, as well as in making other important movements needed for later speech development.

For further information about feeding your baby with Down syndrome, see *The Down Syndrome Nutrition Handbook* by Joan Medlen, listed in the References and Suggested Reading list at the end of the book.

Oral Motor Exercise Programs

Sara Rosenfeld-Johnson, CCC-SLP, has developed several oral motor exercise programs that can be helpful for children with Down syndrome. There are exercises that help children learn to separate tongue and jaw movement, exercises that help children hold their tongue in their mouth, and exercises to improve lip closure and jaw movement.

Rosenfeld-Johnson has also designed tools for oral motor treatment, including bite blocks to work on strengthening the jaw, and a collection of straws and horns (whistles) of increasing difficulty for practice sessions. Some straws have wider openings while others have small, narrow openings. Some horns have flat, broad mouthpieces while others have small, rounded mouthpieces. Rosenfeld-Johnson has set up the tools into a treatment hierarchy based on her clinical experience. Typically, the straws are used with young children and the horns are not introduced until later.

For more information about Rosenfeld's oral motor exercise programs, see her book, *Oral-Motor Exercises for Speech Clarity* or her website for Innovative Therapists International: www.oromotorsp.com.

Your Baby's Learning Styles

The early months are the time to get to know your baby's learning styles. What are her preferences? Which sensory channels does she seem most interested in? Is she more alert in the morning or at night? When does she like to make sounds? Does she enjoy mirror play? Does she like to play in the bath? Does she like to listen to sounds? Does she like to look at an object or would she rather explore it by touch? What textures of food does she like and dislike? What activities are fun for you both?

Once you have determined your baby's preferences, you can teach her by working with her strengths and with what she enjoys. For example, if she likes music, you can sing to help her relax during her "fussy" times. If she seems to enjoy looking around the room but does not look at your face, you can place your face closer to hers, and give her more time to learn to focus on your face. If she seems to enjoy looking at her musical radio or her red stuffed dolphin toy, use those toys frequently. If variety attracts her, vary the toys. Enjoy each moment together as you begin the process of communicating together.

CHAPTER 4

Before the First Word— Precursors to Language

You are undoubtedly anxious to hear your child's first word. But, many small steps need to occur before he says that first word. When you know the many challenges that infants, toddlers, and young children face as they master speech and language, you can see the triumphs as each step is mastered. Instead of waiting for the first word, you can have many celebrations along the way. You will also realize that there are many ways you can help your child with language, communication, and speech before he begins to speak. You don't need to wait passively. You can actively help your child work on the "precursor" or prerequisite skills upon which communication, language, and speech are based. These skills are also known as *pre-language skills* or *linguistic precursors*. They can be organized into communication skills, pre-language skills, and pre-speech skills. Each precursor skill is described in this chapter. Then, activities designed to help develop the precursor are presented.

Once you understand your goal in practicing a particular activity, you can vary the activity with your child. For example, if the goal is for your child to look at you and focus on your face, and your child seems to do that when you sing a specific song or make a funny expression, use those activities with him. Do this practice as part of your daily activities, not as a separate practice time, because children with Down syndrome learn best when practice is a part of daily life. If your child appears to be frustrated or tired, stop the activity and do it some other time. Children with Down syndrome sometimes need shorter, more frequent practices because they often have shorter attention spans.

Especially if your child is not yet receiving speech and language services through his early intervention program, you need information so that you can work with him at home to develop the foundation skills he needs to learn to communicate, to use language, and to speak. Prepare to be patient, but also to enjoy watching your child develop communication, language, and speech. It is a fascinating learning process and you will see many areas of progress. Rejoice in the small gains! Let your child know how happy you are with his progress. Be generous with hugs and smiles. With patience and practice, most children with Down syndrome can succeed in developing all of the communication and language precursors described in this chapter within the first three to four years.

Early Communication Skills

A great deal of learning about communication takes place long before your child uses speech or any formal language system. Early communication skills that are the foundation for later communication include:

- Communicative intent,
- Turn-taking,
- Requesting/reasons for communicating, and
- Social communication.

COMMUNICATIVE INTENT

Communicative intent is the single most important foundation skill because it leads to further communication growth and to an increased desire to communicate. Communicative intent is the knowledge and understanding that you can influence your environment and get results by communicating. For example, if you cry, someone will come to relieve your distress; if you make noises, you will attract others' attention. Research on infants in institutions has demonstrated that if they do not receive any attention when they cry, scream, or make noises, the cries and screams and noises decrease in number. In other words, children who get no response to their communication attempts stop trying to communicate.

The best way to help your child develop communicative intent is to be responsive. You don't even have to wait until he actually communicates. Begin to interpret his sounds and even his movements as communication. If your child kicks his feet, assume that he is asking you to play with his feet. Respond by playing a game with his toes or put a balloon near his feet so that he can kick it. Put bells on his socks so that when he kicks his feet, he will hear them tinkle. Comment on what is happening and the fact that he is making those bells ring: "You're kicking your feet. Kick, kick, kick. You're ringing those bells." If your child points to his stuffed bear, give him the bear and label it as "bear." Interpret looking, kicking, making noises, and pointing as your child's desire to communicate with you. Show him with your actions that you have heard him and that his communication can bring results. That's very powerful motivation to communicate more.

When you observe that your child is pointing and watching for your response, or appears to be expecting your response, you know that he understands communicative intent. When he makes noises and strains to move toward his bottle that has fallen out of the crib, then points and makes noises, he understands communicative intent. He understands that by making sounds, he can have an impact on his environment. He will demonstrate communicative intent through pointing and making noises and sounds way before he begins to use spoken words.

If your child does not try to initiate communicative interactions to affect the environment, you want to look further. He may need specialized training techniques to help him develop the awareness that his communication can help get him the things that he wants. Picture Exchange Communication System (PECS) training can help develop these skills. For more information, see Chapter 10.

TURN-TAKING

When human beings communicate, they take turns. One is the speaker and the other is the listener and they can change their communication roles as speaker and listener. The way to help infants and toddlers develop this skill is to create and model turn-taking opportunities. You can begin with turn-taking for simple things such as tapping on the side of the crib. If your baby happens to tap on his highchair or the side of the crib, you tap on the side of the crib, then wait and give him a turn to tap again.

When your baby makes sounds, imitate his sounds. These may be screeching or cooing sounds or any other sounds, and probably won't be recognizable speech sounds or words until much later. Then wait and allow your child time to take his turn by making more sounds.

HOME ACTIVITIES

- When your child can consistently imitate and perform a movement, such as banging a toy drum, use this drumming play to practice taking turns. Drum for a couple of seconds and then hand him the drum. If necessary, use hand-over-hand assistance to help him tap the drum. When he is finished, take the drum back and take a turn. Mark the turns by saying "Mommy's turn," or "Billy's turn." The goal of this activity is not to have him play the musical instrument accurately, but for him to take turns with you. Keep your turn and his turn short, so that he learns about taking turns. Siblings who have learned to share can be great allies in this activity. You can demonstrate or model the activity using a brother or sister—"Mommy's turn," "Freddy's turn," "Jenny's turn," "Mommy's turn." Many musical toys such as bells, xylophones, piano, and sandpaper blocks lend themselves to turn-taking practice. Depending on your child's interest in the toy, either demonstrate the use of the musical toy first or let him explore sound-making with the toy himself before trying to take turns with him.

- Rolling balls back and forth is another way to practice turn-taking. Beach balls are an excellent choice for teaching turn-taking, since they are colorful, lightweight, and easy to move and roll. Roll the ball to your baby and let him roll it back. Or if he is not yet sitting, hand him the ball and hold it while he pushes the ball against you. As you roll the ball, say "My turn." As your child pushes the ball, say "Baby's turn" or use your child's name.

- Make a tunnel out of a shoebox or other box. Roll a toy car through the tunnel and have your child send the car back to you through the tunnel. Label as "Baby's turn" or "Daddy's turn." There are endless variations on this game.

- Many infant game routines and songs foster turn-taking. These include Peek-a-Boo, Pat-a-Cake, This Little Piggy, etc.

- When your child can imitate a speech sound, wait until he finishes. Then say, "My turn" or "Mommy's turn" and imitate him. When you finish, say "Baby's turn" or use your child's name, and let him take a turn. You can point to the person who has the turn to reinforce the concept of a turn.

REQUESTING/ PROTESTING

Babies have many different reasons for communicating. The most common reason is to request something. Your baby may cry to request his bottle or to refuse it, or he may reach toward you because he wants you to continue making that funny face. He may put his hands high over his head because he wants to be picked up, or he may coo and gurgle because he is satisfied and warm and dry after finishing his bottle and being changed.

Observe how your baby protests. Does he cry or try to push something away? Does he close his eyes to try to block out the thing or event he is protesting? What situations make him protest? Does he prefer soft things and protest about anything that is scratchy or itchy? Does he dislike being wet or cold? Does he protest at bath time? Try to determine whether certain sensory messages are uncomfortable for him. It is possible that he is having difficulty with processing some types of sensation, and that can be worked on through sensory integration therapy. Protesting empowers your child. Responding to his protests helps foster communicative intent.

SOCIAL COMMUNICATION SIGNALS

Social gestures are body movements that are used to communicate. Usually they take the form of greetings such as waving hello or good-bye, shaking your head yes or no, or blowing kisses. Most of a baby's early communication attempts are nonverbal and interactive; they are either facial expressions such as smiling or sounds such as laughing, crying, or grunting. Early social communication attempts usually consist of gestures and body movements that are used to interact with others. Infants and toddlers with Down syndrome usually have the desire to interact with people and are socially responsive. The exciting part for

your child is that these communication attempts are easily understood by most people. So, he gets an enthusiastic response from those around him when he waves bye-bye.

HOME ACTIVITIES

- Practice waving hello. Provide hand-over-hand assistance and help your child move his hand. Don't use imitation because your child will then probably wave backwards toward himself because that is what he is seeing. Wave hello consistently every time you see a new person or wave hello to objects in the environment. Say, "Say, hello to Grandma. Say hello to Uncle Andrew," etc. Now you are teaching your child the meaning of "hello" as well as the gesture.

- Do the same activity as above, waving good-bye. Say, "Say bye-bye to . . . ."

- Read a book with your child that highlights social gestures such as *Good Night Moon*.

- Use a puppet and say, "Wave hello to the puppet" when it appears and, "Wave bye-bye" when it is leaving.

- Line up all of your baby's stuffed animals and dolls or action figures. Walk into the room, and cue your baby, "Wave hello to Bo-bear. Wave hello to Paddington. Wave hello to Betsy. Wave hello to Pooh. Wave hello to Raggedy Ann . . . ."

- Practice waving with a brother or sister, going in and out of the room.

Prerequisite Skills for Language

There is growth and maturation as your child moves from learning early communication skills to being able to learn and use language. The prerequisite skills for language are:

- attention skills,
- visual skills,
- auditory skills,
- tactile skills,
- imitation skills,
- cognitive skills, and
- referential knowledge.

Remember that language is based on the sensory experiences in your child's environment. So, he needs to receive and make sense of the information in his environment to be able to learn labels and names for those experiences. According to research, children learn to handle sensory information in a set order. Children progress from tactile skills to visual skills, then to auditory skills, and only then are they ready to master language and cognitive skills (Ayres, 1980). These tactile, visual, and auditory skills help us move along the pathway to speech and language (Ayres & Mailloux, 1981). They help us learn sounds and words, and enable us to set up feedback loops between the eyes, ears, mouth, lips, tongue and jaw, and the brain.

ATTENTION SKILLS

Attention means being able to focus in on a person, object, or event. We observe this skill in an infant as he focuses in on his parent's face and as he listens attentively to sounds in his environment. We teach attention skills through sensory experiences. For example, your child learns visual attention when you help him to visually explore objects and to focus on objects and faces in his environment. You teach auditory attention by providing experiences such as listening to music and by increasing the amount of time your child focuses on listening. This learning is based on well-functioning senses. It is important to have vision and hearing checked regularly to make sure that it is sufficient to support your child's attempts at learning.

VISUAL SKILLS

VISUAL RECEPTION

Visual reception is the ability to use the sense of vision. It depends on the physical ability to see, as well as the ability to understand what you see. As Chapter 1 explains, vision problems are fairly common in children with Down syndrome. This makes it important for your child to have his vision regularly screened by a pediatrician or ophthalmologist. Current recommendations by the Down Syndrome Medical Interest Group are for your child's vision to be assessed once by the age of six months, and then annually thereafter (more often if a vision problem is diagnosed).

RECIPROCAL GAZE

Reciprocal gaze, conversational gaze, and communicative gaze are all different terms for what is commonly called eye contact. Reciprocal gaze means I look at you and you look at me. In American culture, people interpret looking at them as a sign that you are listening to them, and not looking at them as a sign that you are not listening or are uninterested. Common expressions such as "He looked me straight in the eye" or "He was hiding something, he wouldn't look me in the eye" exemplify the interpretation that American culture gives to reciprocal gaze. In some cultures, such as African cultures, it is a sign of respect to look away, and a sign of aggression to look someone right in their eyes. So, culture has an influence on when it is appropriate or acceptable to use eye contact.

For children to learn speech and to learn facial expressions, they need to tune in to the faces of those around them. Engaging a child's interest and attention and increasing the time that he will look at your face teaches and practices these important skills. Research has shown that the most intriguing sight to the infant is the human face. The animated face costs nothing but your time, and is capable of providing endless entertainment for an infant or toddler.

Because of low muscle tone, infants with Down syndrome may find it more difficult to lift their heads. Visual difficulties may make it harder to focus on the face. So, you may have to provide more support for your child's head and neck, and compensate for visual difficulties as suggested by your pediatrician or ophthalmologist. Reciprocal gaze is an important skill, and children with Down syndrome can practice and master it early in development, usually before one year of age.

HOME ACTIVITIES

- Position your baby so that he is at eye level with your face and no more than eight to twelve inches from your face. You may hold him in the air or on your lap facing you, or sit down next to his infant seat or crib so that you are at eye level with him. To gain his attention, put your face close and talk to him in a high-pitched voice: "I see you now. What a nice baby you are." Make funny faces or smile. Make noises and move your tongue in and out while making funny sounds. You might sing to him, too. Any facial movements and happy sounds are fine as long as they engage your baby's interest. Siblings like to help with this kind of activity, especially when the baby is old enough to react to them by laughing.

- Initiate interactions with your child by physically moving closer to him or by moving toward his face and then away from his face. Zoom in close and then zoom out slowly.

- When you are gazing into your child's eyes, make sounds or smiling or dramatic faces. Sing a short song or call your child's name. Do anything to get his attention. When you are finished, look away or move your child away.

- If your child doesn't look at you or fails to make eye contact, gently direct his face so that he is looking at you. Try to maintain his interest by singing, making funny faces, etc.

- When your child looks at you, assume that this is an initiation of reciprocal gaze. Begin smiling or say, "I see you."

- Make your face even more interesting to look at by introducing surprises. For example, put a sticker on your cheek or forehead. Or, put on funny eyeglasses (such as sunglasses that are heart-shaped, star-shaped, or have bunny ears, frogs, or other animal figures on them). Use these props sparingly and when your child is not expecting them. This will keep him looking. He will never know what he might see!

- When your child is able to use reciprocal gaze, reinforce the learning through play. Games such as Peek-a-Boo are especially good. For older children, Simon Says, Hokey Pokey, and Head, Shoulders, Knees, and Toes promote reciprocal gaze.

VISUAL TRACKING

Visual tracking, or being able to follow the movement of an object as it moves with your eyes, is an important skill in language learning. This skill is sometimes called visual pursuit. It's a skill that helps infants learn about the world around them. Your child will be better able to learn new vocabulary if he can look with you at a moving object such as a squirrel or an airplane as you name it for him. One of the ways to stimulate development of visual tracking is to provide colorful, interesting objects that can be made to move, and to use interesting sounds to help attract your child to the object.

Children with Down syndrome often need more practice and more stimulation to learn visual tracking, but they are usually successful in learning it early in development.

HOME ACTIVITIES

- Move a toy stuffed sheep to the right of your child's visual field and then to the left. You could say "baa-baa" or you could sing "Baa-baa Black Sheep" to attract his attention.

- Blow bubbles through a variety of wands. Watch the bubbles as they move, and get your baby's attention by popping the bubbles as you say, "Pop-pop-pop." The purpose of the activity is to watch the bubble and follow it as it moves slowly through the air. Your baby can begin to imitate you popping the bubbles. Later on, you can use the same activity and he can say, "Pop pop" as he pops the bubbles.

- Use a large attractive toy, such as a clown that has moving parts. Hold it right next to your face. When your baby looks at it, move it very slowly away from your face. Follow the movement with your own gaze. It helps to make noises as the toy moves to further attract your child's attention. You can use squeaking or noisemaking toys or you can make vocal sounds to accompany the movement.

- As you move a toy away from you and your baby, make your voice go up high. As you move the toy back towards you and your baby, make your voice go down low. Any interesting change in your voice will attract your baby's attention.

VISUAL ATTENDING

To learn language concepts, it helps a great deal if your child can visually attend to an object—look at it for a prolonged period of time. So, once your child can look at you, look at an object, and follow a moving object, you want to keep him looking and prolong the time that he looks at an object. How do you help him learn to visually attend? By using your voice, delight, and visual gaze to focus him on the objects. Use sounds to help keep your baby interested in looking and exploring. For example, say, "Look at that" and then look with him at an ant crawling on the ground. Or focus him on an interesting toy such as a music box and help him explore everything that the toy can do. Look at it, shake it, touch it, wind it up, and listen to the music. Young infants will mouth a toy and then throw it away. We want to help prolong the infant's visual interest and visual exploration of the object.

REFERENTIAL GAZE

Referential gaze means focusing in on an object and looking intently at that object. This skill is also known as *joint gaze, shared focus, joint attention,* and *visual regard.* In the beginning, your baby may simply look at an object. Responding to his lead, you can then label the object. In the second phase, shared gaze, your baby watches you, follows your line of visual gaze, and looks at and pays attention to whatever you are looking at. You can promote this skill by cueing your baby verbally: "Look at that bird." Referential gaze is one of the bases for learning the names of objects. In order to learn the name of an object, your child needs to be able to look at the object when you are looking at it and remember what it looks like. When you label the object, your child needs to be able to look at the object in order to connect the label with the object.

HOME ACTIVITIES

- Hold a bright toy such as a ball near your face. When your child looks at you, squeak the toy. Move it a short distance and keep looking at it. With an exaggerated and dramatic voice say, "Ball, look at the ball!"

- When you see a favorite person or a favorite toy, move your head obviously to look at the object, and say, "Look, *Daddy.*" You also can point to the person or object, and use a loud, dramatic voice to focus your child's attention on the object.

- As part of your daily activities, name objects as soon as you see your child looking at them. Focus his attention on the object by using an animated voice or by searching for the object with your child. For example, "Here's your bottle" or "Let's find the rubber ducky. Here it is." Or, "I see a cookie. Here it is."

AUDITORY SKILLS

AUDITORY RECEPTION

Auditory reception refers to the physical ability to hear, as well as to receive messages through hearing. Children with Down syndrome are at increased risk for hearing loss, so it is especially important to have the pediatrician and the audiologist monitor hearing on a regular basis and treat any hearing problems (Cohen et al, 1999, Roizen et al. 1994, Shott, 2000). Hearing testing can begin early, even within the first week of life.

Otitis media with effusion (OME), inflammation of the middle ear with fluid build-up behind the eardrum, is the most common problem related to hearing. The fluid interferes with sound transmission, and the result is a hearing loss that fluctuates. It is difficult for infants and toddlers to learn to listen and to attend to sounds when they sometimes can hear the sounds clearly and other times, cannot. Hearing problems and hearing assessment are discussed further in Chapter 2.

AUDITORY ATTENDING

When you are sure that your child is able to hear environmental and speech sounds, practice in listening or "attending" to sounds can begin. The goal is to lengthen the time that he attends to sounds.

Songs and musical games with hand movements are useful because they engage your child in listening and in movement and hold attention longer. Music and tapes of familiar sounds, See 'n' Say toys (pull the string and you hear the sound associated with the picture the arrow is pointing to), and musical wind-up toys can be used to help children learn to attend to sound. Reading books such as *Look and Listen* by A. Ricketts and *Mr. Brown Can Moo, Can You?* by Dr. Seuss can also reinforce the concepts of listening to sounds. Reading about different sounds is an excellent way to help your child get ready to listen carefully to the sounds of speech.

LOCALIZATION TO SOUND

Localization to sound refers to the ability to turn toward a sound source when you hear the sound. As your infant develops, he should not only turn, but also search for and fixate on the sound source. Listening to a person or several people in a conversation depends on the ability to localize sound and to listen to the source of that sound.

HOME ACTIVITIES

- Use a variety of sound makers: whistles, bells, cellophane crunched in your hand, hand claps. At first, make the sound in front of your child so that he can see what is producing the sound. Then produce the sound distinctly to one side of him. If he does not turn, say "Listen," make the sound again, and say "What was that?" or "Look at that!" Then reveal the source of the sound. Make the sound so that he can see and hear it, then move the sound maker out of sight and try again.

- If your child has difficulty turning to the source of the sound, put him on your lap, facing away from the sound source. Produce the sound. Say, "Did you hear that?" and turn your child toward the sound. Give him a reward such as a hug and a big smile for turning. Some children respond well if this activity is done with you and your child sitting in a swivel chair. Have a friend or sibling ring a bell or start an audiotape out of your child's view, to the side. Say, "Do you hear that bell?" Then, swivel the chair and look directly at the source of the sound. "There's the bell." Then have the person ring the bell again within your child's sight to reinforce the connection between the bell and the sound. Practice sound localization for short periods many times during the day. If you have swivel chairs in the kitchen, dining room, or home office, do this activity whenever you are sitting in the swivel chair. Make it part of your day, not a separate practice time.

ATTENDING TO SOUNDS

When you know that your child is able to hear sounds, you can help him practice listening or paying attention to sounds. Your child needs to learn which sounds are important for him to listen to (people's voices, the telephone ringing) and which are not (the clock ticking, the refrigerator turning on and off). Otherwise, if there are too many competing sounds in the environment, your child might learn to tune out sounds, rather than listening to them. This is referred to as figure-ground discrimination—that is, being able to distinguish between the primary sound and the background sounds or noise. The listening activities below can help with auditory attention, as well as with increasing attending time and sound localization.

HOME ACTIVITIES

- Record and play back familiar sounds, such as the doorbell, a dog barking, or a favorite song. Watch your child's reaction. If he is listening, he will generally stop moving or widen his eyes. When you watch your child, you will be able to determine what he does when he is listening. Comment on what your child hears. Say, for example, "You heard that music. It's pretty music, isn't it?"

- Talk to your child's grandmother on your phone, or talk to your child from work. When your child listens, say, "That's Grandma on the phone. It's fun to listen to Grandma, isn't it?"

- Make your voice the sound source. Call your child by name or make a variety of sounds that will attract his attention. Move around the room. This activity can be used both to help him localize sounds and listen to sounds.

- Gradually strive to lengthen the time that your child pays attention to sounds. Sing a longer song or lengthen the time of a conversation.

AUDITORY ASSOCIATION AND LISTENING

Listening is an important part of learning language. Auditory association is making sense out of what you hear. This goes beyond hearing the sounds. Association implies that the brain is processing the sounds and understanding what they mean.

If your child has fluid in his ears and is having difficulty hearing, don't use the activities below that involve soft sounds because it may be frustrating. Try using louder sounds that you feel he can hear at that moment.

HOME ACTIVITIES

- Put "listening hats" on you and your child. (Mickey Mouse hats or other hats with ears work well.) Talk about listening: "Whenever we are wearing our listening hats, we will listen to all of the sounds around us." Go outside and just listen—to an airplane droning, a bird chirping, the dog barking, the cat meowing, a car going by, sounds of animals at the zoo, sounds of trucks and cranes at a construction site. Point out the source of each sound. Frequently say, "Did you hear that? What was that? An airplane!" For younger children, it is easiest to start with animal sounds, such as oink or meow or bow-wow. Help your child listen to a toy making the sounds or to the real animal sounds on a farm or petting zoo.

- Take photographs, make computer-generated pictures, or cut out illustrations from magazines of the various "sound makers" you listened to on your walk. Then write a book about the sounds you heard. Use a photo album with plastic pages. Put the text on index cards, add the pictures or photos, and insert into the album. You've made a personalized book that will help you and your child review the sounds that you heard.

- Take a tape recorder with you to the farm or zoo and record the sounds. Talk about sounds that animals and things in the environment (such as a dripping faucet) make. Imitate the sounds. Reinforce the concepts by reading books such as *Mr. Brown Can Moo, Can You?* by Dr. Seuss or *One Red Rooster* by Kathleen Carroll. If you cannot listen to sounds live or on an audiotape, watch videotapes that have many sounds, such as tapes of trains or animals. Once your child has the connection between the object and sound, use audiotapes or live listening rather than videotapes, so that the focus can be on the sounds.

- Talk about the sounds that a car horn makes, or a train or bus. Talk about city and country sounds. Talk about the sizzling of fries, the chopping of onions or peppers, the sound of kitchen equipment such as the blender, the sound of outdoor equipment such as lawnmowers or tractors. Daily activities and field trips can provide many opportunities to focus on listening. Go to the fast food restaurant not just to eat, but to listen to the sounds of sizzling fries and whooshing drinks as cups are filled. City transportation noises and country nature and farm equipment noises can provide more listening experiences.

- Audiotape environmental sounds. At the same time, take a photo of what is producing the sound. When you develop the photos, have double prints made. Then make two lotto cards by gluing or taping each set of photos on a piece of construction paper. (Begin with three photos on a card and increase the number as your child's listening and association skills increase.) Now, you can play a Sound Lotto game with one or several children (such as with older children or with siblings helping a preschooler). Listen to the sound, then find the picture of what makes the sound on your lotto card, and cover it with a marker such as a checker.

- Assemble a listening box. Some objects that may be used include a whistle, a horn or recorder, a shoe (a tap shoe could also be used to make a tapping or shoe clopping noise), a maraca, a musical triangle, two blocks of wood with sand paper to rub together, some beans in a see-through plastic jar (securely fastened). First, help your child explore and play with these objects. Then listen to the sounds together, and for older children, you may talk together about the sounds. The goal should be to listen, discriminate among the sounds, and identify the sounds individually by pointing to them. You can even play a game in which you have your child cover his eyes and try to identify the objects by the sounds that they make.

TACTILE SKILLS

Tactile skills involve touch—touching with the hands, as well as touching with the lips, mouth, and tongue. Tactile skills not only help infants establish attachments to people and objects, but also provide a means for exploring their world. Babies have many more nerve endings in the mouth area than in the fingers so it makes sense that they explore objects with their mouth. As your baby explores objects with his mouth, he sets up feedback loops that help him integrate information about the objects that he is touching. These tactile feedback loops will help him later in placing his tongue, and knowing where it is, for the movements of speech.

Many children with Down syndrome are very sensitive to touch. This hypersensitivity to touch is known as tactile defensiveness. Children who are tactilely defensive need more practice with touch, but you may have to move at a slow pace. Because they have difficulty processing touch, it is uncomfortable for them. They don't like you to touch their mouths. They may fight having their hair shampooed, getting a haircut, combing or brushing their hair, or using a washcloth. They don't like labels from their clothing rubbing against their necks.

Seek professional guidance from an occupational therapist and move more slowly if your child appears to be tactilely defensive, but don't avoid touching him or providing the various sensations. Experience indicates that exposure to various sensory experiences often leads to increased tolerance of a variety of sensations. Sensory issues are discussed in greater detail in Chapter 2.

HOME ACTIVITIES
- Some children enjoy learning by touching. Different textures and different feelings are very interesting to them. Follow through on this interest by making a *Touch Book*. Collect items with different textures. You might already have many of these items at home. Start with sandpaper, cotton balls, a piece of velvet fabric, fur or faux fur, aluminum foil, fabric swatches such as satin, vinyl, or wool, a plastic basket from strawberries, thin wood. Many stores will be glad to give you small pieces of fabric or leftover corrugated cardboard, Styrofoam, bubble wrap, carpet, etc. Mount each swatch on a separate page of a sketchbook or scrapbook, or onto large index cards. Double-sided tape, glue, or rubber cement may be used to mount the pieces. You can also place the different textured pieces in a box. Then feel the pieces with your child. Comment on their texture. Give your child plenty of practice in using textures. Save the book. You can use it when your child is older to teach adjectives and descriptions.

- To reinforce the concepts and read about textures, some excellent books are: *Find Out by Touching* by Paul Showers; *Pat the Bunny* by Dorothy Kunhardt; *What Is Your Favorite Thing to Touch?* by Myra Gibson; and *Is It Rough? Is It Smooth? Is It Shiny?* by Tana Hoban.

- In the course of playing with and caring for your baby, provide as many texture sensations as possible. You might have your child play with a bowl of cooked macaroni or even sit in a tub of macaroni. Many children love the squishy feel of gelatin.

- Rub nubby washcloths and smooth washcloths on your child's face and body.

- Massage your child's arms and legs and gradually move towards the face and lips. Use lotion to vary the experience.

- Encourage your child to explore toys with his mouth so that he can develop the feel of the tongue, lips, and jaw moving.

- Brush your child's teeth and gums with a toothette, NUK toothbrush (see photo on page 249, or a soft toothbrush to help him explore different feelings of touch in his mouth. These can be purchased in baby superstores, in many supermarkets, or on websites that sell oral motor practice tools (see the Resource Guide).

Imitation/Modeling

One of the most important ways young children learn is through imitation. Generally, children learn to imitate movements before they learn to imitate speech sounds. Although not directly related to language development, working on motor imitation is helpful because it teaches your child valuable imitation skills. Your child is usually ready for this type of practice when he can move his hand independently of other parts of his body. He may be swatting at his mobile, holding his own bottle, and exploring toys by using his hands to put them in his mouth. Some children are not ready to imitate movements until they are able to sit up. Your physical or occupational therapist can help to determine when your child is ready for this type of practice. In the beginning, you can place your hands over your child's hands and "walk" him through the motions to help him learn the movement. Then try to move to visual imitation. If your child does not seem ready or interested, wait a month and try these activities again.

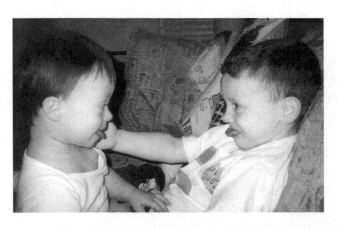

HOME ACTIVITIES

- Follow your child's lead. If he is playing with a toy and bangs it on the table, wait. Then, take the toy, and imitate your child by banging the toy on the table. Next, give the toy back to him. Demonstrate your pleasure in the activity by smiling and laughing. Research has shown that your child is more likely to imitate your movements when you begin by imitating his movements.

- The next time, you become the leader. You can roll a ball, push a truck, tap a xylophone, beat a drum, tap a block on the table, put a block in a box, etc. If your child does not imitate the movement, use hand-over-hand assistance—that is, hold your hand over your child's and demonstrate the movement by tapping the xylophone or pushing the truck.

GESTURAL IMITATION

Once your child understands the concept of motor (movement) imitation, practice imitation using various parts of the body. This is a bit closer to imitation for speech. Some of these movements, such as waving good-bye, will become meaningful movements later, but for now the goal is motor imitation. You may also add sounds to help stimulate your child and keep him interested, but remember that your child is not ready to imitate your sounds yet.

HOME ACTIVITIES

- Wave bye-bye.

- Touch your nose.

- Place your hands on your head.

- Shake your head up and down.

- Shake your head side to side.

- Close your lips tightly.

- Smile.

- Clap your hands.

- Touch your toes.

- Lick your lips.

- Blow out your cheeks.

- Open your mouth.

- Pucker your lips.

- Smack your lips.

- Play "so big." You say, "How big is (your baby's name)?" Then raise your arms high over your head as you say, "So big!" Assist your baby by physically lifting his hands over his head at the beginning. After doing this many times, you may just need to gently touch your child's hands. Later, your child will imitate the movement.

After your child is able to imitate movements involving the body, try getting him to add some sounds to the movements. These activities act as a transition to imitation of sounds for speech, because they provide practice in vocalization for your child as well as an opportunity to hear the sounds of speech in small sound bites. The discrete and precise movements needed for imitating speech sounds accurately are not yet developed at this stage, but will emerge later.

HOME ACTIVITIES
- Blow your cheeks out and make a popping sound.

- Make circles on your tummy, rub, and say "mm-mm."

- Wave your hand and say, "Bye bye."

- Move a toy car and say "vroom."

- Move a toy dog along the table and say "woof-woof."

Cognitive Skills

Cognition is one of those developmental areas you probably didn't think about much before your baby was born with Down syndrome. Now you probably know that cognitive skills are skills that are usually delayed in children with Down syndrome and that your child will need extra assistance to learn. But what exactly *are* cognitive skills? They are not simply what we think of as intelligence, but rather a whole set of skills that enable us to receive, process, analyze, and understand information. They are the skills that allow us to think, to solve problems, and to make sense of our world. Some early cognitive skills that prepare your child to use language and that you can help him master are described below.

When a child masters the concept of object permanence, he understands that an object still exists even though it cannot be seen. For example, he knows that his favorite ball does not cease to exist simply because it is out of sight in the toy chest.

We know that a child understands object permanence when he searches for a hidden toy or a favorite toy he cannot see or when he throws toys over the side of the highchair and then looks for them. So, remember that he is developing the concept and is practicing the skill as you bend to pick up the spoon he has just thrown off the highchair for the tenth time!

Hand-Play Songs

Many hand-play songs are very appropriate for children at this stage. They enable your child to participate in speech or singing without really saying the words. By moving his hands, he is part of the activity. He can imitate the movements to the song, and later may begin to imitate some of the words.

The Patty Cake song is one that helps children learn to imitate clapping. Sit facing your child. Begin singing or chanting the song as you clap along. If your child imitates the clapping, encourage the imitation. If not, teach the clapping movement by hand-over hand-assistance—that is, put your hands over your child's hands, and "walk" him through the clapping movement. Play the game every chance that you get. Babies love repetition and familiar things. Gradually fade out your assistance, so that your child is clapping hands in imitation of your movement.

The References and Suggested Reading list at the back of the book includes some excellent books and tapes to help you learn hand-play songs such as:

- The Bumble Bee Song,
- No More Monkeys,
- The Eensy Weensy Spider,
- If You're Happy and You Know It, Clap Your Hands,
- Where Is Thumbkin,
- Here We Go Round the Mulberry Bush,
- Hokey Pokey,
- London Bridge,
- Ring around the Rosey,
- Ten Little Indians,
- The Wheels on the Bus.

This understanding is an important precursor for labeling through speech or through signing. Until your child learns about object permanence, he is not ready to give objects names. Before this stage, objects seem to appear and disappear from your child's world without rhyme or reason. When your child has mastered object permanence, he is ready to understand that a label not only is the name of an object, but it can also be used to symbolize the object when the object is not present.

Object permanence may be a difficult concept for children with Down syndrome to learn. This is because understanding the concept involves abstract reasoning, which is typically harder for children with mental retardation. Consequently, your child will probably need more practice to learn about object permanence. But unless he has a severe cognitive disability, he will probably be able to master this skill during the same age range that he learns the other skills in this chapter.

How Can You Tell Whether Your Child Understands Object Permanence?

Many young children with Down syndrome do not talk about objects that are not in plain sight. But that does not mean that they do not understand that objects continue to exist when they are out of view. A study using parent surveys demonstrated this disparity (Kumin, Councill, and Goodman, 1998).

In a study of 115 children aged two to five, we found that the following percentages of children could demonstrate an understanding of object permanence:

- *At age 2:* 37% often could, 37% sometimes could, 26% never could;
- *At age 3:* 50% often could, 47% sometimes could, 3% never could;
- *At age 4:* 64% often could, 27% sometimes could, 9% never could;
- *At age 5:* 73% often could, 27% sometimes could.

But although 74% of two-year-olds could sometimes or often *show* that they understood object permanence, only 48% ever *talked* about absent objects. Based on this information, parents should persist in doing the activities below even if your child doesn't let you know that he understands the concept of object permanence.

HOME ACTIVITIES

- Show your child a large toy such as a beach ball. Hide the toy while your child is watching. Say "Where is the _____?" Then find the toy, and say, "Here is the _____." Large toys or toys that make sounds work well. Your child can still see the outlines of a large toy even when it is hidden. In the beginning, you may want to "hide" the toy with a sheer scarf through which your child can still see the toy. Musical toys are wonderful. Even when they are hidden, they can be heard, making them easier for your child to find. Once your child is showing signs of understanding object permanence, take away the visual and sound cues.

- Move your child's hands in front of his face. Say, "Where's baby?" Then move his hands away from his face and say, "There's baby." This is an early variation of Peek-a-Boo.

- Play Peek-a-Boo. "Where's baby?" and "Where's Mommy? . . . Here she is." Children never tire of this.

- Hold a handkerchief so it only partially covers your face, or later on, hide under a blanket so it is obvious that you are there but can't be totally seen. Ask, "Where's Daddy? Here he is."

- Place the series of rings from a plastic stacking toy under a small blanket. Say "Where are the rings?" Let your child find the rings. When he locates the rings each time, say, "Here they are."

- We've all seen the carnival trick where someone hides a pea under walnut shells, and then moves the shells around, while the observer tries to keep track of which shell the pea is under. Here's a variation that babies six months of age or older will enjoy. Brothers and sisters will have fun helping with this activity. Show your baby a lemon. Have him feel and smell the lemon, and give him a chance to explore the lemon with you. Then, take three clear plastic cups. Put the lemon under one cup. Ask your baby, "Where's the lemon?" For a younger baby, show him where the lemon is. For an older baby, use hand-over-hand assistance to teach him how to point to the lemon. Say, "Here's the lemon." When your baby is able to find the lemon using the clear cups regularly, switch to cups you can't see through. If he doesn't find the lemon, pick each cup up slowly, and say, "Is the lemon under here?" And give the answer. When you find the lemon, say "Here's the lemon." Babies will find this a funny game to play.

- Hide a small toy under a plastic bucket such as a sand pail. Look for the toy together by removing the bucket. Progress to having your child find the toy, and to increasing the number of buckets to two or three.

- Hide a small toy in your hand while your child is watching you. Say, "I'm putting the ball in my hand. I'm hiding the ball behind my back." Put your hand behind your back. Let your child see what you are doing, then ask, "Where's the ball?" Then let him find the toy.

- As you walk around the house, make a game out of finding familiar objects in their places. You might say, "Where's the apple juice? I found it. It's in the refrigerator." After you pour the juice and put it back in the refrigerator, close the door. But, then re-open the door, and say, "Look, the apple juice is in the refrigerator." This helps with both object permanence and labeling.

CAUSE AND EFFECT

One of the important concepts that infants and toddlers must learn is cause and effect. That is, if I do something, there is a result. If I push a button on the baby activity box, a Disney or Sesame Street character will pop out. If I push a switch, a toy will begin to move. This type of early learning is also known as *contingent learning*. The infant is learning that his actions can make things happen, and he is gradually mastering the skills that he needs. So, he knows that if he swats at his mobile, the hanging figures will move; if he flips a switch, his toy car will move. Many children's toys, such as a Jack-in-the-Box or a Busy Box, help children learn about cause and effect.

Understanding cause and effect relationships is vital to understanding *communicative intent*—that is, that when you make a sound or a gesture, your communication can get you a desired result. Children demonstrate communicative intent when they point at the cookie jar to indicate that they want a cookie or say "Up" to indicate that they want to be picked up. Again, the concept of cause and effect can be more difficult for children with Down syndrome to understand because predicting the consequence of an action involves abstract reasoning. But with practice and repetition, you can help your child master this important concept.

HOME ACTIVITIES

- Use toys that have a beginning and end sequence and a definite cause and effect, such as a Jack-in-the-Box. Turn the handle and the Jack-in-the-Box will pop out. Say, "Turn-turn-turn-turn . . . pop!"

- Securely sew bells to elastic that can go around your child's wrist or foot. Or, sew bells securely onto socks and decorate the socks with a face or animal picture using fabric paints, appliqués, or thread. When your child moves his hands or feet, he will hear the bells. You will notice that he will stop moving, and listen to the sound. If he likes the sound, he will increase the number of times he shakes or moves his feet. The ability to ring the bells is under his direct control. You can use the little bells that are widely available around the winter holidays. Just be sure that there is no way your child could swallow the bells and monitor him when he's using them.

- A variation of the previous activity is to sew bells onto a fabric picture panel, then stretch it across the width of the crib, just below your child's feet. Make it taut. When your child kicks the panel, the bells will ring. Again, your child will learn to master this activity, and learn about cause and effect.

- Use toy tops, especially visually interesting tops that have trains or cars circling inside. Say, "Go, go, go, go . . . stop." You control the movement so that the top stops when you say "stop" and goes when you say "go."

- Use Busy Box or pop-up toys. When your child pushes a button or pulls a lever, a figure will pop up.

- Children often like to turn a light switch on and off and see the results. This is a good example of cause and effect play. If you don't want your child playing with the room lights, make a play board with a switch and a small colored light or adapt a battery-operated toy so that when your child pushes a paddle, moves a joystick, or pushes a button, the toy will begin to move. An information packet on adapting toys is available from the National Lekotek Center in the Resource Guide, under "Toys/Play," and adapted toys and switches can be ordered from the companies listed under the same section.

MEANS-END

Means-end is the concept that you can plan a course of action to solve a problem or reach a desired object. For example, if a bolster has fallen from the sofa and is in front of the television, it needs to be pushed away so you can see the screen. This cognitive ability, which develops over time, is one of the bases for the skill of creating sentences or planning a language message. The earliest means-end activities usually involve crawling to reach a toy that is out of reach. More advanced problem solving would be demonstrated when your child moves a chair to the counter in order to reach the cookie jar. There are three types of means-end planning:

1. *Displacement of barriers*—for example, if a sand pail is in front of the toy radio, your child pushes the pail out of the way in order to reach the radio.
2. *Movement as the means*—for example, your child crawls to a desired toy or walks to the VCR and starts the video he wants to watch.
3. *Use of tools*—for example, your child uses a string to pull a toy or a stick to retrieve a ball that has rolled under the sofa.

Infants and toddlers need lots of experience with this skill in play.

HOME ACTIVITIES

• Provide toys that promote means-end learning, such as pull toys that move along as you pull the string.

• Set up play situations that encourage your child to figure out how to get what he wants. For example, place a ball out of reach and encourage your child to crawl toward it. "Come on over, come get the ball, come right over here," etc.

• Put a small barrier between your crawling infant and what he wants. Make the barrier lightweight and easy to move. A small inflatable beach ball or a transparent, blow-up cylinder are good choices.

• Show your child how to use tools. Use a shovel and pail in the sandbox, and fill the pail with sand. Demonstrate or help your child with the action.

• Use communication temptations in which your child has to create a plan to solve a problem. For example, place a toy just out of reach or put a desired food in a plastic container with a secure top that your child cannot easily open. This is also good for practice in making requests and asking for help.

• Clear off the top of a table so there are no other objects to distract your child. Set up blocks so they are in a line, like cars lined up. Move one block so that it pushes the next block. Keep pushing with the block until the end block falls off the table. You might use the word "push" as you are moving the block, and "block fall down" as the block falls off the edge of the table. At another time, use a line-up of toy cars, toy trains, or wooden or plastic people toys or figurines.

• Once your child can produce sounds, you can play a game involving siblings, friends, or grandparents. You need a few people to make it work well. One of the siblings can serve as a model. Have the sibling make a loud sound. Choose a sound that your infant or toddler can make, such as "bababa," or a laughing or screaming sound. Whenever the model makes that sound, another person will do something funny and repetitive. For instance, Grandpa will put on a hat and begin marching around while Grandma sings. Or, brother will squirt the mirror with a water pistol. Or, Mom and Dad will start dancing. Any movement activity can be used, as long as it is something your child will like to watch and will want to make happen. After a few models, your child will probably either try to make a sound, or may just inadvertently make a sound. Be sure that the sound immediately sets off the activity. Once your child understands the game, watch how he begins to make sounds to set off the activities. He is learning to plan to make something happen.

REFERENTIAL KNOWLEDGE

Referential knowledge is the ability to make the connection between the object and the linguistic label—for example, between the actual ball and the word "ball." Visual skills such as referential gaze and cognitive skills such as object permanence are the basis for this ability. The best way to provide practice is to label items that your child looks at or shows interest in. Professor Sue Buckley, a psychologist in the United Kingdom, has done a great deal of research about how children with Down syndrome learn best. She suggests that toddlers with Down syndrome can often learn the relationship between a word and a concept by using sight reading. You may want to try labeling items in your house with a written word in addition to using verbal stimulation to assist your child with understanding the connection between words and the objects they stand for.

Pre-Speech Skills

As discussed before, speech uses the same structures and movements used for breathing and eating. There is no bodily structure used exclusively for speech. Thus, through feeding, breathing, and oral motor exercises using horns, straws, and bubble blowing, we can practice many of the movements that will be needed for speech. It also means that you can work on movements that will be needed for speaking before your child is speaking.

Some pre-speech skills have been discussed earlier in this chapter. For example, tactile skills and motor imitation skills both help lay the groundwork for communication skills. Other functions essential to speech include respiratory (breathing) skills, oral motor skills, sound production, and vocal and speech imitation skills.

RESPIRATORY SKILLS

When we breathe, we inhale and exhale about the same amount of time, but speech is spoken on exhalation only. When we are speaking, we need to use about 90 percent exhalation and only 10 percent inhalation.

Through practice and vocal play, you can help your infant or toddler learn to lengthen the exhalation phase of breathing. Crying builds up exhalation, as does early sound making. Provide early models by holding your baby so he can see your face and making sounds such as "ah" or sighing. In the beginning, your baby may laugh or smile and think that the sounds and the faces are funny.

When your baby begins to make cooing noises, imitate them and then vary the sound. For example, when he says "ah," you make a string of five "ah" sounds, or make a high-pitched and a low-pitched "ah," sing "ah" going up and down the scale, or prolong the "ah" sound.

This practice serves several purposes. First, it helps your baby learn to attend to sounds. Second, it helps him prolong his attention because you are making interesting sounds that he likes to listen to. Third, when your baby is ready, he will begin to practice making sounds and playing with sounds. You can provide reinforcement and stimulation that will encourage him to practice and subsequently to learn how to expand exhalation to meet the needs of speech, and to make sounds on exhalation.

When your baby makes sounds, imitate those sounds. Repeat them, so that you are serving as an echo of his sounds. When he is playing with you by imitating your sounds and there is a nice back-and-forth flow (this activity is also good for turn-taking practice), repeat the sound but make it longer.

Over a period of weeks or even months, try to extend the amount of time your child can prolong and produce a sound. These sounds may be coos, screeches, screams, or any other sounds. The sounds may be said or sung. Singing and making sounds to music are good practice activities for infants and toddlers. They may be vowel-like sounds, but they need not be recognizable speech sounds. The idea is to help your child expand and extend his capacity to prolong the exhalation. This capability will be needed later when your child begins to speak.

FEEDING SKILLS

Feeding uses many of the same structures and movements that are used for speaking, although the neurological control and monitoring for feeding and speech are different. Feeding gives your child practice in muscle movement and coordination. Children with Down syndrome may have difficulty with feeding because of low muscle tone, inability to form a seal with the lips, difficulties with jaw or tongue control, and increased tactile sensitivity or tactile defensiveness (Kumin & Bahr, 1999, Medlen, 2002). Speech-language pathologists or occupational therapists can work on feeding as part of your child's early intervention program. You may also need to consult a registered dietitian if your child is having trouble taking in enough nourishment.

ORAL MOTOR SKILLS

It is very common for infants and young children with Down syndrome to have low muscle tone and weak muscles in the lip, tongue, and palate. In fact, many of the speech intelligibility problems in children with Down syndrome are due to this low muscle tone. Many speech-language pathologists think that helping the child improve muscle strength and muscle control in these areas can help with later articulation and speech intelligibility.

The term oral motor therapy describes activities used to help improve muscle strength, range of motion, movements, and coordination in the mouth. This can be done with stimulation and with imitation. Theoretically, you could use your fingers, but young children often chomp down and bite your fingers. So, tools such as the NUK exerciser have been developed. This is a rubber implement about the size of a toothbrush that has bumps at one end, rather than bristles, and can be used to rub the gums, cheeks, tongue, and lips to accustom children to touch around the mouth area.

Using a mirror to provide visual feedback is also very effective. Infants and toddlers often like to explore the use of the various parts of their bodies while looking in a mirror. They are intrigued as they move their hands and see what those hands can do. It's harder for babies to explore the movement of various parts of the face and mouth in play, but mirrors allow them to watch themselves, to see their mouths and faces as they make sounds. Research has found that mirror play increases a child's sound-making. Watch your child in the bathroom, where there are large mirrors. Notice how interested he is in looking at himself in the mirror.

Play with your child, while looking in the mirror together. Comment on what you see. "See the pretty baby. Look at your mouth. I'll throw you a kiss. Where is your tongue? See it in the mirror." This activity will hold your child's attention. Babble strings of sounds with your child in the mirror, using a consonant sound plus a vowel sound: "puhpuhpuh" or "beebeebee," for instance. The most effective are the sounds made with the lips (*m, p, b, w*) or the sounds made with the lips, tongue, or teeth where the placement is easy to see (*f, v, th* as in *thin, th* as in *the*).

SOUND PRODUCTION SKILLS

The first sound that most infants make is a crying sound. As the child develops, he will begin to make a wider array of sounds. Laughing, grunting, cooing sounds, popping, screeching, and raspberry sounds are early sound productions. When your child begins to produce strings of sounds—"babababa," "mamamama"—this is known as *babbling*. In early babbling, the child appears to like the feel of the sounds, whereas in later babbling, the child begins to narrow his sound production to the sounds of his native language. You can help encourage babbling, by showing delight and by playing with your child's sound making (see Vocal Imitation section below).

As your child progresses, he will begin to have what sound like mini-conversations using *jargon*. This demonstrates understanding of the rhythm and inflection of the language. He knows the song of the language, but still has to learn the words. He will also begin to imitate and echo words. This is the final pre-speech stage. It means that your child is almost ready to begin to use spoken words.

VOCAL IMITATION

Within the first six months of life, your child will probably begin to make sounds and noises other than crying. For instance, when he has finished nursing or taking a bottle, he will begin to gurgle or make cooing or happy sounds. You can reinforce these sounds if you simply imitate or repeat them. The combination of your delight in your child's sounds and your reinforcement of the sounds is very powerful.

Over a period of time, try to establish a little conversational routine with your child making sounds and then you making sounds. By six to nine months of age, your child will usually begin to babble—making strings of sounds, such as "dadada" or "bababa." Repeat the strings of sounds your child makes. You can then vary your imitations. For example, when your child says "bababa" in one tone, you can say the sounds in a very high or very low voice. Have fun making sounds with your child and help him practice making sounds. This sound making is the beginning of speech.

By the time your child is one to two years old, he will probably be ready to begin imitating sounds. Imitation of environmental and vocal sounds can give your child practice in making oral movements and in coordinating breathing and muscle movements needed later for speech.

If your child does not respond to speech imitation activities at first, go back to working on motor imitation with toys and sounds, as described earlier in the chapter. Wait awhile and then try again with sound imitation. Your child will let you know when he is ready for sound imitation by responding and by being interested.

HOME ACTIVITIES

- Smack your lips and make kissing sounds.

- Make crying sounds.

- Make nasal sounds, letting air come through your nose like a foghorn.

- Make sneezing sounds.

- Make coughing sounds.

- Make yawning sounds.

- Make happy sounds—cooing and "ahhh."

- Make environmental sounds: car motor sounds, beeping horn sounds, vacuum cleaner whooshing noises, etc.

- If your child has difficulty imitating or initiating sound making, try using a sound light. This is a light that is activated by sound—many electronics stores sell such lights or the materials to make them. The light will turn on whenever your child makes a sound and stay on only while he continues to vocalize. For added motivation, you can use voice-activated toys that will move as soon as your child makes a sound. Voice-activated toys are available from several companies listed in the Resource Guide section or can be adapted from any battery-operated toy.

IMITATION OF SPEECH SOUNDS

Once your child has begun to get the knack of verbal imitation, you can move on to imitation of speech sounds. You should begin by practicing individual sounds used in speech and gradually progress to real words. Chapter 5 provides many more activities designed to help your child master single words.

HOME ACTIVITIES

- Make any of the speech sounds individually and repeat them—for example, /bababa/, /lalala/, /tatata/.[1] Try to vary the sounds that you use, but if your child is especially intrigued with the /p/ sound or the /v/ sound, stay with that sound. The easiest sounds to begin with are /p/, /b/, and /m/, because your child can see how your lips move to make those sounds.

- Take one vowel sound and vary the intonation pattern—that is, the sequence of pitches or the sing-song melody. For example, say "aaaah" with upward inflection and then with downward inflection, or sing "ahahahaha" with varying patterns. Take turns with you and your child being the initiator.

- Say a familiar word such as "mama," "dada," or a sibling's name. If your child imitates the word, give a big reaction. Remember that the imitation will probably be approximate, so "grandma" may be "gaga." Always provide the correct model after your child's imitation, but don't correct his pronunciation at this stage. Say, "Grandma, you said grandma; what a big boy!"

What if Your Child Struggles with Speech Sounds?

When your child practices oral movements, he sets up feedback loops for how movements feel. He also develops "templates" in his brain which help the movements become almost automatic. This practice is helpful for all children with Down syndrome. If your child seems to have quite a bit of trouble in developing sound patterns, it may be because he has difficulty planning the movements needed for speech. This problem is known as childhood verbal apraxia, and it will not generally be evident until later in development. Apraxia is covered in more detail in Chapter 8.

Conclusion

The period before the first word is a very active period in language development. Your child will develop skills in the areas of communication, pre-language, and pre-speech that will help him progress toward using speech and language to communicate. There are many home activities that can stimulate your child during this period. It is a wonderful period in which you can take the time to explore the world together with your child and enjoy the many learning opportunities around you.

---

[1] Slashes are used to set off sounds or strings of sounds that go together. Speech-language pathologists often use slashes and brackets for this purpose.

CHAPTER 5

The One-Word Stage

When will my child begin to talk? This is a question that parents often ask. As we have previously discussed, the road to speech is a process with many skills to be learned as your child progresses. Most children with Down syndrome are able to understand the relationship between a word (symbol) and a person, place, thing, or event well before they are able to speak. So, they make the connection and are ready to learn to use words months or even several years before they may be able to use speech.

For typically developing children, the one-word stage begins when they use true speech—when they consistently use sounds or word-like consonant-vowel combinations to represent objects and people. For children with Down syndrome, the one-word stage begins when they are either ready to use speech or an alternative language system such as sign to represent an object or person. In other words, this is the period when your child makes the connection that symbols represent ideas, people, and objects. It is when she first says or signs "mama" and "dada" and means *you*.

The use of a word or symbol to represent the real object is the basis of language. When your child says "da" for daddy, "ma" for mommy, and "ba" for teddy bear, she is demonstrating that she has learned the code and understands the concept of true speech. That is, she understands that a word has meaning and that others will understand what she means when she uses that word. When we, as adults, use a word such as "table," the word has meaning because it is part of our language. There is no innate meaning in "table," no "tableness." "Table" is understood because we learned the code of our community as a child and everyone in the community uses the same code.

During the one-word period, most children's first words may not sound exactly like the word intended. For instance, an infant may say "ad," and use that sound combination consistently whenever she wants a drink. Eventually, her parents will figure out that she is using "ad" to mean apple juice. "Apple juice? You want apple juice?" they might say, assigning meaning to their child's early speech attempts.

Also during this stage, children often use one word or sound to mean more than one thing. For example, a child may sometimes say "ba" and mean "I want a bottle." Other times, she may say "ba" and mean "Take away this bottle" or "I dropped the bottle and I can't find it." It is up to the parents to deduce the meaning of the word based on context.

By interpreting their child's consistent sound patterns, parents teach their child that the world around her responds to her sound productions. Once a child understands that she is able to influence the world through her actions and especially through her sound-making, she will probably continue to try to get others' attention in this way. This is known as *communicative intent*—the knowledge that what you say will influence your environment and get results. Helping a child develop communicative intent is very important because it forms the basis for your child's motivation to communicate. Chapter 4 provides suggested activities to teach and reinforce communicative intent.

When Do Children with Down Syndrome Enter the One-Word Stage?

Many children with Down syndrome begin using signs to communicate around their first birthday and then say their first true words between ages two and three. Others may begin using speech between ages four and five. Some may use sign and then make a transition to using speech. Still others may progress through a period in which they sometimes use both speech and sign language (or another alternative communication system) simultaneously and sometimes use one system and other times use another. This makes it very difficult to accurately predict an average age when your child will use speech or speak her first word. Table 1 gives an idea of the range of possible ages that your child might say her first word.

Children with Down syndrome are more likely than other children to have difficulty making speech sounds during this stage. As other chapters explain, this is because they often have low muscle tone in and around the face, hearing impairments, and other difficulties that make it harder to process and produce speech sounds. But even children with significant speech production problems can make important strides during the one-word stage. Their first "words" may be gestures rather than spoken words, but they can still improve their abilities in both receptive and expressive language. Often they learn to communicate through one of the transitional communication systems described below.

Table 1: Age When Children with Down Syndrome Produce Their First Word	
Age	**Research**
12-24 months	Buckley, S. (2000); Buckley, S. & Bird, G. (2001); Chamberlain, C.E. & Strode, R.M. (2000)
18 months	Buckley, S. & Sacks, B. (2001)
2-5 years	Chamberlain, C.E. & Strode, R.M. (1999)

Transitional Communication Systems

Children with Down syndrome are usually ready to communicate well before they are able to speak. Some children have mastered all of the pragmatic and language prerequisites and are ready to use language to communicate two to three years before they are ready and able to use speech. Speech is the most complex communication system because it relies on:

- respiratory support to supply the air stream for speech,
- vibration of the vocal bands for voice,
- resonation of the sound within the mouth or nose, and
- adequate muscle strength and coordination and accurate movement of the *articulators*—the teeth, lips, tongue, and hard and soft palate.

Transitional communication systems enable children to communicate before they are able to use speech. They cut down on frustration and allow the child to continue to make progress in vocabulary development and other areas of language when she is not yet physiologically and developmentally ready to use speech.

Many children will begin using natural gestures to make their needs known. They will point to a favorite toy so that you will bring it to them. Or, they will try to pantomime a situation such as holding a bottle to send the message that they are thirsty. But these natural gestures are usually not sufficient for a child to continue to develop her language skills and make her needs known. It is difficult to pantomime some concepts, and not everyone will understand the child's gestures. So, it is almost always a good idea to introduce a formal transitional language system so that your child can continue to communicate well and to develop language while she is developing the skills she will need to speak.

Your child will be ready to use a communication system when:

1. she understands representation (that a symbol "means" a concept or object); and
2. she is able to remember the meaning of a gesture or picture.

A variety of transitional communication systems may be used with children with Down syndrome. The purpose of the transitional system is to enable your child to communicate her needs effectively until she is able to use speech to get her needs met. So, a transitional system needs to meet her communication needs, but also needs to facilitate her mastery of speech. That means that your child should hear speech, in order to learn to speak, even though she cannot yet use speech. Types of transitional communication systems include:

- Total Communication/sign language,
- communication boards,
- portable books,
- notebooks or photo albums,
- Picture Exchange Communication System (PECS).

These methods are discussed briefly below and explored in more detail in Chapter 11.

TOTAL COMMUNICATION

Although most young children with Down syndrome are delayed in speech development, they usually have relative strengths in motor development and visual learning. As a result, it is often easier for them to recognize and make gestures with their hands or to use pictures to communicate than it is for them to make speech sounds. Total Communication enables your child to progress in language, even though she is not yet ready to use speech, and overcome her frustration at not being able to be understood. Total Communication is the combined use of signs or gestures with

speech to facilitate communication development. It has been demonstrated through research and clinical experience to assist in acquiring speech. It is the most commonly used transitional language system for children with Down syndrome.

Some speech-language pathologists may tell you that sign language may prevent your child from speaking—that your child will take the easy way out and sign instead of speaking. Over the past ten years, however, we have learned more about the effectiveness of using signs with children with Down syndrome. Research and clinical findings point so strongly toward the need to use Total Communication with children with Down syndrome that it would be wise to seek out a speech-language pathologist who can implement a Total Communication program for your child. The same system should be used at home, in school, in therapy, in day care—in short, in all of your child's settings throughout the day.

Parents are sometimes concerned that signing will prevent or delay the acquisition of speech, but the opposite is actually true. Without signing, children with Down syndrome—who can usually understand much more than they can express verbally—sometimes become very frustrated and resort to screaming or give up trying to be understood. By enabling your child to communicate, signing reinforces basic language concepts while empowering her to influence her world. Studies with children with Down syndrome have demonstrated increasing language usage with sign language, as well as decreased frustration. And studies of typically developing children have demonstrated that children who use sign language before they speak have a 30 percent larger vocabulary than those who do not use sign language (Acredolo & Goodwyn, 1996). In our experience, children as young as eight to twelve months can effectively learn signs and use sign language. But, it is important to always use Total Communication (signs plus speech) to provide the verbal model for your child. Signing may be the expressive language system that you child is using to communicate, but she needs to hear speech.

An excellent videotape that presents the use of Total Communication from the parent's point of view is *The Early Use of Total Communication,* which is cited in the References and Suggested Reading section.

SIGN LANGUAGE SYSTEMS

The sign language system that seems to be most often used for Total Communication is the *Signed Exact English System (SEE)*. Another language system, called *American Sign Language (ASL),* has also been used with children with Down syndrome. Both systems use two hands for signing. ASL is a complete language with its own structure that is different from spoken English. For example, spoken English typically uses noun-verb combinations ("The boy runs") while ASL typically uses verb-noun combinations. In addition, ASL has no tense indicators. SEE, on the other hand, is spoken English in a visual mode. It merely translates spoken English into signs. SEE has a sign for most English words. At Loyola College, we use SEE with children with Down syndrome because it uses regular English structures and grammar.

Another system that may be used is *Amerind,* which is derived from American Indian signs. It has easily decodable signs that can be understood by 85 percent of people even if they don't know sign language. *Simplified Signs* is a signed vocabulary system that was developed by a college student for use by adults who could not speak following accidents or neurological difficulties. The system is available on the Internet (see References and Suggested Reading) and has a wide variety of easily recognizable signs. However, it does not have signs for "more" or "all done" or other signs that help a child make the environment more responsive to her desires and needs.

The main considerations when choosing a sign language system are:

- your child's manual dexterity,
- her readiness to use a sign system, and
- whether the people in her daily life will be able to understand and use the sign system (or the signs).

If your child is in an early intervention program, you want her to be able to "talk" with the teachers and other children and get her needs met. You also want her to be able to be understood by siblings, daycare workers, grandparents, and significant others in her environment, and for them to be able to communicate with her. She needs communication partners who understand what she is trying to "say." After all, the purpose of using Total Communication is to provide a language system for your child so that she can communicate with others and learn that she can get her needs met through communication.

CHOOSING SIGNS

Whatever sign system is chosen, the first signs taught are usually "more" and "finished" or "no." These are powerful signs for your child to use. They help her communicate her needs, and enable her to control the continuation or termination of an event. Later, a sign vocabulary should be individually chosen to meet the needs of your child and your family. Favorite snacks, favorite toys, favorite destinations, favorite activities, and photographs or names of important people in your child's environment can be other early language choices. For example, if you live in a warm climate, "pool" or "swim" might be an early sign. Likewise, the sign for "sister" or "grandma" might be needed by a specific family, or a sign for "out" for a child who particularly loves the outdoors.

The speech-language pathologist (SLP) will depend on you to let her know which signs you feel are important for your child to communicate. You might keep a list and discuss the needs with the SLP at the therapy sessions. You can rely on the SLP to teach you the signs and provide information on the use of Total Communication.

In general, the signs you choose for your child should:

- empower her and lead to improved communication;
- be functional so that they can be used often in her daily activities;
- be easy for her to make; and
- be easily understood by the significant people in her life.

Children with Down syndrome typically begin using Total Communication at about one year. When your child is able, she will generally begin verbally imitating your words while she is using the signs. Once your child is able to say the words, the signs will drop out of her repertoire. This usually occurs by age five. Talk with parents of older children with Down syndrome. They will reassure you that your child will stop signing once she can say words. Your child wants to speak, and signs will lead to speech.

Making Total Communication a Family Affair

1. Remember that when you use Total Communication, you should sign and speak simultaneously. Don't concentrate so hard on the sign that you forget to use the word.
2. Be sure that your child is looking at you when you present a sign or verbal model. Look at her when she is communicating.
3. Provide hand-over-hand assistance when teaching a sign. Place your hands on your child's and move her hands through the making of the sign. Accept approximations of signs or your child's versions of them, as long as the sign can be understood.
4. Make sure that the signs you teach are meaningful and useful for your child in her environment and will be practiced as part of her activities every day.
5. Encourage your child to make sounds while signing, by repeating the word after your child signs it, but respond to the sign as you would to speech until your child is ready to speak.
6. Make sure that family members, day care providers, and significant others can understand and respond to the signs your child uses.
7. Keep one step ahead of your child when learning signs. Ask your SLP to teach you signs you anticipate your child needing, or see the References and Suggested Reading section for books and materials on Total Communication.

OTHER TRANSITIONAL SYSTEMS

Communication Boards. Communication Boards are individually designed communication systems that may involve the use of pictures, photographs, rebus or pictographs, alphabet letters, or words. These pictures may be kept in small notebooks or displayed on "boards" made of wood, plastic, or tagboard. To communicate, the child typically points to or otherwise indicates the picture for the word she wants to say.

Communication boards that use pictures, words, or symbols can be designed on the computer using programs such as *Boardmaker*™ (Mayer-Johnson Company) or *Picture This*™ (Silver Lining Multimedia). Multiple boards for home, school, friends, morning, afternoon, and evening can be easily designed. Your child might have different "topic boards" to use at different centers in kindergarten, or to use at lunch or snack time.

Notebooks or Photo Albums. These are communication books that include pages of signs, often organized by category or some other system that makes sense to the child (such as putting pictures of foods on one page and pictures of activities on another). These are often used in school or in specific situations. Since they are larger, they are a bit less portable, but they can hold more pictures, photos, symbols, or words than a board.

Picture Exchange Communication System. The Picture Exchange Communication System (PECS) is a communication system originally developed by Andy Bondy and Lori Frost to help individuals with autism communicate. Using the system, communication partners physically give each other communication symbols

such as photographs or line drawings to communicate. PECS is especially helpful for the child who is having difficulty initiating communication. The child learns to give the picture to the "listener" to get her needs met. It enables her to communicate a message that is important to her (such as getting a favorite snack food) almost immediately. This can be a good system for children with Down syndrome who need help learning the skills for communication such as turn-taking or requesting or who don't have the fine motor skills to make signs. It teaches a child how to communicate, while providing a system that will enable the child's desires to be understood.

The PECS system is designed to be taught in six phases:

1. The child is taught to initiate communication by giving a picture of a desired item such as a pretzel to a communication partner. She is then given that item in exchange for the picture. Physical prompting (using hand-over-hand assistance to help the child understand what she needs to do) may be used at first.
2. Picture use is expanded to include more people, places, and rewards that the child might want to request.
3. The child is taught to make specific choices between pictures. (Pictures of disliked items can be used in addition to pictures of what the child wants.)
4. The child is taught to construct simple sentences with pictures, such as "I want pudding." Attributes such as colors, size, shape, position, and temperature are also taught.
5. The child is taught to use the pictures to respond to "What do you want?" (Child uses the "I want" picture card plus the pictured item that she desires.)
6. The child is taught to comment on various items and activities for social reasons, not only to get a tangible reward. For example, she might use the pictures to say, "I see black dog" to make conversation, rather than to indicate that she wants the dog.

Electronic Devices. Electronic devices are technologically based communication systems that enable the child or adult to communicate through speech or writing. Many devices use speech synthesizers that can "speak" for the child or adult. They are not used as frequently as transitional communication systems as are sign language or communication boards, because they are more expensive, funding is difficult, and they are usually used for a short period of time. They also involve a highly specialized evaluation to determine which system best matches the child's communication needs and abilities. However, an electronic device may be appropriate for a child who has a great deal to communicate but is having difficulty learning sign.

Transitional Communication Systems

Total Communication
- American Sign Language
- Signed Exact English

Communication Boards / Communication Books
- Pictures
- Symbols
- Writing

Picture Exchange Communication System (PECS)

Computer-Based Communication
- Synthesized Speech
- Direct/Scanned Access System

These transitional communication systems are not mutually exclusive. Your child might be using signs for "juice" but then you might have magnets on the refrigerator with pictures of apple juice and grape juice so she can clearly communicate her specific desires. Your child may point to tell you that she wants to go outside, but then use signs or a picture communication board to indicate that she wants to go get ice cream at the store.

Whatever transitional systems you use, your child needs to be taught language concepts that are meaningful for her. They should enable her to communicate what she really wants to communicate so that she can get her needs met and make her wants known. This will greatly diminish her frustration at not being able to communicate with her environment.

On the next page is a form that you and your child's SLP can use to figure out the most useful transitional communication system for your child.

Environmental Stimulation

Although your child may only know ten to thirty signs or words at this stage, that does not mean that these are the only words you should use with her. On the contrary, your child needs to be exposed to a rich variety of language all her life so that she can reach her potential in communication skills. Only by hearing many

DEVELOPING A TRANSITIONAL COMMUNICATION SYSTEM

1. **Type of System(s):** What type of communication system(s) will your child use? Check all that apply.

   Unaided: Sign Language   *Aided:* Communication board ❑
               SEE ❑   Communication notebook ❑
               ASL ❑   Picture Exchange System (PECS) ❑
             Other ❑   Electronic high tech system (specify) ❑ _____
                                  Other ❑ _____

2. **Symbol System:** What kinds of symbols will be used in the communication system?
   Objects ❑   Photographs ❑   Pictures ❑   Words ❑
   Other ❑ _____

3. **Number of Symbols Used:** How many different words is she able to use? How many words can she handle on one board? Is there a need for different communication boards/overlays for different settings?

4. **Content of System:** What does she want to communicate?
   Requests: More; All done/finished; Ask for help ❑
   Family members ❑   Favorite activities ❑   Favorite foods ❑
   Other ❑ _____

5. **Settings:** Where will your child need to use a communication system?
   Home ❑   Day care ❑   Community ❑   School ❑
   Other ❑ _____

6. **Purposes:** For what purposes will your child need to communicate?
   Requests ❑   To get help ❑   Social communication ❑   Learning ❑
   Other ❑ _____

7. **Organization of Information:** How will the information be organized in the communication system? Can your child use 8 pictures on a page? Or only 2 choices on a page? Would it make sense to put all the choices that related to home on one page and all the choices related to the playground (toys, playground equipment, and friends she sees at the playground) on another?

8. **How will your child access the information?**
   (pointing; switches)

9. **Training Needed:** Who will need help learning the communication system?
   Child ❑   Parent ❑   Siblings ❑   Grandparents ❑   Day care ❑
   Other communication partners ❑ _____

10. **Maintenance of System:** Who will take care of the system? What happens if the system breaks down or requires maintenance?

10. **Funding of System:** How will the system be financed?

different words used many different ways by many different people can she learn how to communicate in the real world. This was proven in decades past when children with Down syndrome were all too often shut away in institutions, where they learned little, if any, useful language. All of the tremendous strides—the discoveries about the true capabilities of people with Down syndrome—have occurred because parents now provide their children with stimulation, improved health care, and opportunities for inclusion and experiences.

Constantly stimulating your child's language can seem like a daunting prospect. But it is really not. Much of the language stimulation you provide your child can—and should—be worked into naturally occurring activities and routines. And you need not do all the stimulating on your own. Siblings, babysitters, grandparents, and friends will all be willing to help if you show them what to do. As an example of how learning can be incorporated into your daily life, here are some ways you might help your child learn the word "red":

HOME ACTIVITIES

- Gather many red things from around the house—red towels, a red skirt, a red tie, baby's red stuffed fish, a red bell. Put them all in a "treasure" bag or a red laundry basket. Have your child pull them out one by one. Parent, sibling, babysitter say (and sign) "red" for each object as it is pulled out. You can make this an after-dinner game.

- Sort the colored laundry together and put all of the red items together in a red basket.

- Go shopping and look for red things. Wear a red scarf or hat, or carry a square of red fabric so your child can match the color and "learn" the concept of redness.

- Consider having a "red day." Wear a red shirt. Serve spaghetti, red fruit juice, strawberries, and red apples. Go to the firehouse, where many objects, including the fire truck, are red. Read a book about red.

- Once your child has learned the word "red," put all of the objects back in place, go back to a variety of foods and regular daily activities. But every time a red item is encountered in the normal flow of daily routine, label it as "red."

- When your child is able to say or sign the word, ask the question and provide immediate feedback: "What color is it?" (Wait for your child's response.) "Red. That's right. It's red."

Teaching Words and Concepts

At the one-word stage, your emphasis should be on teaching vocabulary and concepts, both receptively and expressively. Later on, you can work on pronunciation, grammar, and pragmatics. For now, just focus on helping your child master important single words and their meanings. Below are some principles to keep in mind when working with your child on words and concepts.

Remember that language is more than spoken words. When you are teaching a word or concept, focus on the meaning and on conveying that meaning to your child through play or through multisensory experiences with the word. Don't focus on the accuracy of the pronunciation. If you want your child to learn the concept of a car, ride in a car, talk about how a car looks and sounds, and play with toy cars. If it helps, use Total Communication and help teach the concept with a sign.

Provide many models. Children with Down syndrome need many repetitions and experiences to learn a word. When you are teaching the concept "in," for example, provide as many experiences as you can with the concept, and label the action each time. Put the block in the box and say "in." Put the apples in the bag and say "in." Put the bag in the shopping cart and say "in." Pour the orange juice in the glass and say "in." Put the envelope in the mailbox and say "in." Put the toy coin in the toy cash register and say "in." Put the toys back in the toy box and say "in."

Use real objects and real situations. Use daily activities and real situations as much as possible when teaching a concept. If you are teaching "drink," do it at snack time. If you are teaching body parts, do it at bath time. If you are teaching clothing names, teach while dressing your child or while shopping in a store. If you are talking about fruits and vegetables, teach while shopping in the produce section. Using real objects and experiences helps children with Down syndrome learn because they tend to have trouble with abstract thought. They may have difficulty understanding that a plastic apple or a picture in a book represents a real piece of fruit, but if they can hold, sniff, and taste a real apple, they can more easily see the relationship between the word and the object.

Teach, don't test. When you are teaching a concept, you want to provide models. You *don't* want to ask questions and demand answers. For example, don't go through stacks of picture cards representing the concept "in" and ask your child each time, "Where is the block?" Instead, provide experiences, as described above. Language stimulation should not be "work." In fact, it is detrimental to set aside a half-hour for practice each day with a young child. After a while, the child shuts down and refuses to practice. Practice should be part of life and should use real objects and situations.

Reinforce the concepts with toy objects during play. Once your child knows a sign or word, reinforce the learning during play. If she knows "up" and "down," use a toy garage, and have the cars go up and down on the elevator, while you and your child say "up" and "down." If she is learning the names of foods, reinforce the learning through pretend shopping trips with toy food, a toy shopping cart, and a toy cash register.

Generalize the concepts. Children with Down syndrome frequently have difficulty generalizing—applying the skills they have learned to use in one situa-

Slipping Concepts into Your Daily Routine

Here are some suggestions and examples for teaching concepts as part of your daily routines:

Dressing Time:

This is a natural time for teaching about:

- Body parts: arms, legs, head, neck, finger, toes, foot, eyes, shoulder, knees
- Clothing: sock, shirt, underpants, pants, dress, shorts, shoes
- Colors: red, blue, yellow, black, white, pink, green, orange
- Number concepts: one and two
- Prepositions: in, on, off, open, close
- Relational terms: back, front, first, next, last
- Verbs: button, zip, pull, sit, stand, snap, button, bend

Meal and Snack Times:

- Food terms: names of food items, types of drinks, snack foods, meats, dairy products, vegetables, fruits
- Meals: breakfast, lunch, dinner, snack
- Utensils: cup, plate, bowl, fork, spoon, dish
- Verbs: eat, drink, chew, cut, wipe, open, close
- Adjectives: hot, cold, empty, full, all gone, more
- Prepositions: in, out
- Expressive terms: m-m-m

Driving or Walking Outdoors:

- Vehicle terms: wheel, car, horn, stroller, truck, airplane
- Weather terms: cold, hot, wet, rain, snow, wind
- Outdoor objects: trees, leaves, acorn, sun, flowers, dog, cow, light, store, door
- Clothing: jacket, coat, gloves, hood, hat

tion to another similar situation. For example, your child may be able to identify the roses in your garden as "flowers," but have trouble understanding that the neighbor's daffodils are also flowers.

Provide many experiences with a word or concept once your child has learned the basic concept. Help your child learn, for example, that many different-looking animals can all be called "dog" and that many different things she eats can all be called "food." Label "car" so that your child learns that a red car, a blue car, a convertible, and an SUV are all "cars." If you are teaching the body part "nose" and its function of "smell," say, "My nose can smell popcorn. What can your nose smell?" Keep the game up until you have named a dozen items that you and your child can smell. Comment on a smell when it occurs. For instance, in the bakery, say "My

- Verbs: stop, go, open, close, push, pull
- Prepositions: in, out, up, down
- Sounds: beep, honk, vroom
- Greetings: hello, bye, see you later

Play Time:
- Nouns: playground, ball, top, books, blocks, names of toys, sand, flowers, trees
- Verbs: kick, roll, push, pull, throw, drop, catch, stack, swing, slide, jump, run, stop, go
- Colors and shapes
- Prepositions: in, under, on, through, up, down, over
- Weather terms: sunny, cloudy, cold, warm, hot, sun, wind, snow, rain
- Other terms: all done, uh oh, fall down, I see

Shopping Time:
- Grocery shopping: meat, vegetables, fruits, bread, cereal, box, can, jar, big, little, take out, put away
- Clothing shopping: hat, gloves, jacket, coat, shoes, socks, pants, skirt, blouse, shirt, sweater, belt
- Hardware/houseware shopping: trash can, lamp, paint, clock, hammer

Bath Time:
- Nouns: body parts, water, duck, boat, bathtub, soap, shampoo, towel, bubbles
- Verbs: pour, splash, squirt, turn on, turn off, blow, pop, rub, wash, smile, kiss, shake, show, point
- Adjectives: wet, dry, hot, cold, big, little

Bed Time:
- Nouns: bed, blanket, pillow, quilt, light, bear, doll, door, window, moon, star
- Verbs: read, kiss, hug, close, sleep, cover
- Greetings: good night

nose can smell bread." Use the game repeatedly over time, and your child will learn the concepts of "nose" and "smell" and be able to apply the concepts to many different situations. Do the same for many other concepts, including "bell," "music," "horn," and "dance," "jump," "hop," "run."

Repeat what your child says. When your child attempts a word, repeat that word. Always provide a correct model when you repeat the word, but do not correct her attempts or make her repeat the word correctly at this stage. For example, if your child says "kee" for cheese, you could reply, "You want cheese. Here is your cheese!" Let your child know by your repetitions that you are listening to her and responding to her communication attempts. Repetition and responsiveness are very important.

Follow your child's lead. If your child shows interest in an object, person, or event, tell her the word for that concept. If you are using Total Communication, ask the SLP at the next session to show you how to sign the concept, as well. Focus on your child's current interest and use that interest to teach your child new vocabulary or new sounds. For example, your child might show an interest in a toy ambulance at the toy store. Talk about the toy's color and size, what's in the ambulance, and that the ambulance has a siren that makes a loud noise. When you see an ambulance go by, point out the ambulance, or drive by the hospital to increase your chances of seeing an ambulance. Go to the library and take out a book about ambulances.

When spring comes and the trees and flowers begin to sprout and grow, go for a walk with your child. If your child shows interest, go to the nursery and buy seeds or plants. Plant some flowers. Visit an arboretum. Plant some vegetables. Read books about spring and plants, flowers and vegetables. When the vegetables have grown, make vegetable soup. Use your child's interests to teach new concepts.

Practice active listening. Show your child through your repetitions, shared focus, and attention that you are listening to what she is trying to say. If you aren't sure what she is trying to say, guess. "You want a hamburger? You want a hug?" You will probably guess the meaning fairly quickly because you know your child's routines and needs best. But even if you guess wrong, you will still show your child that speech can get attention; she can influence her environment through speech. You will also show her that you value her communication and communication attempts.

Provide cues to help your child learn. Once your child understands a concept and is beginning to use the word or sign, provide cues or prompts when she forgets to use the word or sign or appears to have difficulty getting started. These might include:

- *Physical cues*—Make a gesture or provide hand-over-hand assistance (actually hold your child's hand and put it through the motions) to help her point to a picture or make a sign.
- *Imitation*—Say the word for your child so that she can imitate your production.
- *Initial phonemic cues*—If your child is having trouble giving you the word or getting started, you can provide the initial sound, such as /b/ for ball, to help her. If you are using Total Communication, you might show your child the first hand configuration for the sign.
- *Fill-in sentence*—Provide a framework for the word by providing the beginning of the sentence or phrase. If you want your child to say "cookie," you might say, "You want milk and ____." This would be spoken with upward inflection, so that your child will fill in the space. If you want your child to say "shoes," say "socks and ___."

Use paralinguistic cues. These are the rhythm, stress, inflection, and emotion in the voice, and singing-like production which can all help in teaching a concept. If you are teaching "big" and "little," use a deep, booming voice for "big" and a quiet, high-pitched voice for "little." Let your voice go up while saying "up" and down while saying "down." Commercials, advertising jingles, and *Sesame Street* all make powerful use of paralinguistic cues.

Reading with Your Child

All children need to get to know about books. Children need to see books, magazines, and other reading matter at home and in early school settings. They need to be read to, and to have time to explore books. Children may turn the pages and look through the pictures in a book well before they are actually able to read the book. When adults and children read a book together, children learn many pre-literacy skills, such as how to hold a book, reading from top to bottom and left to right, recognizing that printed words have a regularity and differ from marks or scribbles on a page, and progressing from page to page. In fact, the factor that has been found to relate most highly to learning to read is reading to the child.

Reading also helps teach and reinforce language concepts. When you read to your child, you help her develop receptive language skills, help increase her understanding, help her hear differences between sounds, and in general, provide language stimulation. For example, if you go on a picnic and then read a book about a picnic, or perhaps make a personal book using your own photos, you reinforce the vocabulary and concepts that go with "picnics."

CHOOSING BOOKS

Here are some tips to keep in mind when choosing books for your child during the one-word stage:

- Choose books based on your child's interests and experiences.
- Choose books with brightly colored illustrations.
- Limit the number of pictures on a page to match your child's visual skills and attention level.
- Limit the text so that the story is the appropriate length to hold your child's interest. Shorten the text as you read if your child squirms when you linger on one page too long.
- Make reading a loving, shared experience.
- Provide opportunities for your child to participate in reading.
- Gradually increase your child's participation level, as discussed directly below.

HELPING YOUR CHILD PARTICIPATE IN READING

There are many ways to help your child participate, including:

- Point out the characters in the book, then have your child point to the characters as you talk about them. Talk about what is happening (the plot), and describe the action.
- If your child enjoys books that have individual pictures of objects (e.g., Brimax books), you can use them to teach language labels such as cup and table. Let your child point to the cup or make the sign for the word. Or say, "Oh, look, a teddy bear! Where's your teddy bear?"

- When you read books with a great deal of action (such as Richard Scarry books), encourage your child to pantomime or imitate the actions. Or let her use a stuffed animal or puppet to make the actions.
- Let your child star in her own personalized books to increase her motivation to "read." Children love to read books about themselves and their own experiences. Use photos of your child and her activities to make books that relate directly to her daily experiences.

See Chapter 14 for more suggestions about how to help your child actively take part in reading, such as adapting books so she can turn the pages more easily and reading predictable stories with her. Also see the References and Suggested Reading section at the back of the book for titles of books that can be used for one-word stimulation. Talk to the children's librarian in your local library for other suggestions.

Conclusion

Children with Down syndrome can learn many different concepts and can continue to expand their vocabularies all through their lives. But it is during the one-word stage that your child first begins to lay the real groundwork for later language learning. As a parent, you can provide her with experiences that will expand her vocabulary while teaching her about the many people, objects, and events in her world. Reading can help develop word concepts and can also reinforce language experiences. Remember, though: don't get so caught up in teaching your child that language learning becomes drudgery for her. If you can show your child that communicating is rewarding and enjoyable and that you value her communication, she will be far more motivated to learn.

CHAPTER 6

The Two- and Three-Word Stages

The one-word stage can be very empowering and exciting for children with Down syndrome and their families. Your child will learn many new words and concepts during this stage. And, whether he uses speech, signs, or another communication system to communicate, he will learn to pack a lot of meaning into single words. At this stage, however, much of the meaning is subject to interpretation by others. For instance, when a child says "Ball!" in a certain way, is he saying, "That's my ball"? Or, "Let's play ball"?

In the next stage, your child learns how to communicate his meaning more precisely. He will combine the words that he has already learned to make into two-word ("Throw ball") and then three-word combinations ("Daddy throw ball"). During this period, there will be horizontal growth as your child continues to learn new vocabulary words. There will also be vertical growth as he combines the words that he knows into multiword utterances. During this expansion period, your child begins to learn about semantic relationships between words and how to express them. For example, if he wants you to take him outside, he may say, "Mommy out," and if he doesn't want to eat cereal, he may say, "No O's." He is learning how to convey more complex meanings through language.

When Do Children Put Two Words Together?

Researchers have studied how and when children shift from using single words to using multiword combinations. This is a process that occurs over time. Typically developing children combine words into two-word phrases when they have a fifty-word vocabulary at an average age of nineteen months to two years of age (Nelson, 1973). When do children with Down syndrome begin to combine words into multiword phrases?

The short answer is that the average age that children with Down syndrome start using some two-word phrases seems to be around age three. See the chart below for a summary of what several studies have found.

Table 1: Emergence of Two-Word Phrases in Children with Down Syndrome	
Mean Age for 2-Word Phrases	**Study**
24-36 months	Chamberlain, C.E. & Strode, R.M. (2000)
30 months	Buckley, S. & Sacks, B. (2001)
Before age 36 months	Mervis (1997)
36.9 months overall (34.6 months for females; 42.5 for males)	Oliver and Buckley (1994)
36-48 months	Chamberlain, C.E. & Strode, R.M. (1999)
Not usually until 48-60 months	Rondal (1988)
36 months (62%); 60 months (100%)	Kumin, Councill, and Goodman (1998)

Even though the mean age for using some two-word phrases appears to be around age three, in my own center's study, we found there was a wide range for children with Down syndrome to acquire this skill (Kumin, Councill, and Goodman, 1998). For instance, in a study of 168 children, we found that a few children with Down syndrome were using multiword phrases (in sign or speech) at age one and that 33.3 percent (one-third) were sometimes using multiword phrases by age two. By age three, the number of children combining two or more words had climbed to about 62 percent, but only 32 percent were *often* using multiword utterances. By age four, nearly 80 percent used multiword utterances at least some of the time, and by age five, 100 percent of the 168 children in our study were sometimes or often producing multiword phrases.

Besides needing more time than typical children do to begin using multiword phrases, there is some evidence that children with Down syndrome also may need to have more words in their vocabularies before they start putting them together. For example, Sue Buckley initially found that most children with Down syndrome had a vocabulary of about 100 words before they began to combine words (Buckley, 1993). In a later study, she and a colleague reported that the mean vocabulary size when children began to combine words into multiword utterances was 54.4 words, but there was a wide range, from 21-109 words (Buckley & Oliver, 1994). In the 1998 study cited above, we found that the children who began using multiword utterances at age two (about one-third of the children) had an average of 54.9 words in their vocabularies, with a vocabulary range from 8-226 expressive vocabulary words.

The Two-Word Stage

During the two-word stage, your child will be able to transmit a great deal of information. For example, he can make simple requests ("More juice"), describe his own and others' actions ("Daddy go"), and indicate possession ("Mommy coat"). Also during this stage, your child begins to learn the semantic (meaningful) and syntactic (structural) relationships between words. He learns that the order in which words are placed affects meaning. For example, the sentences, "The girl chases the dog" and "The dog chases the girl" may contain the same words, but they have two different meanings.

Table 2 shows some of the many types of relationships between people and objects that can be expressed using two-word phrases. Note that—just as in the one-word stage—the same words may be used to mean more than one thing. For example, the words "no milk" may represent three different meanings:

1. *Rejection:* I don't want any milk.
2. *Nonexistence:* There's no milk here.
3. *Denial:* This isn't milk; it's juice.

Table 2: Types of Two-Word Phrases	
Agent – Action (subject – verb)	"Mommy come," "Daddy throw"
Action - Object	"Drink juice," "Roll ball," "Push car"
Agent - Object	"Mommy shoe," "Daddy toy," meaning "Mommy, put on your shoe," or "Daddy, get the toy"
Possessive	"Bobby bike," "Daddy car," "Dolly sock"
Descriptive	"Blue ball," "Big truck"
Locative (location, positions)	"On table," "In box"
Temporal (time)	"Go now," "Eat later"
Quantitative	"One ball," "Two socks"
Conjunctive (goes together; and)	"Cereal milk," "Shoe sock"
Existence	"This doll," "That cookie"
Recurrence	"More cookie," "More music"
Nonexistence	"No juice," meaning "No juice is here"
Rejection	"No juice," meaning "I don't want any juice"
Denial	"No juice," meaning "It's not juice"

These early word combinations consist of high information words. These are known as *contentives* or *content words*. Later, children learn words such as "the," "is," and "or"; these are known as *functors* or *function words*, or grammatical words.

WHEN IS A TWO-WORD PHRASE NOT A TWO-WORD PHRASE?

A two-word phrase occurs when your child combines two words he already knows in order to make a new statement. The important part is that he is creating (encoding) a new thought. When children use two words that always go together, it is not really a multiword phrase. For instance, "Teddy Graham," "Grandma Jane," "Barney Show," or "Blue's Clues" are not considered two-word phrases. Likewise, if your child is saying "Go bye-bye" to mean "Let's go out" or "Go round and round" to describe the top spinning, those are not considered to be true multiword phrases. They are like one long word because they are learned and used as a unit.

IMITATION WITH EXPANSION

One of the best ways to help your child make the transition from the one-word to the two-word stage is to use *imitation with expansion*. Using this technique, you first repeat a word your child has said, then expand what he said by one word. For example, your child might say "car" while pushing a toy car on a play road. You would imitate "car" and then expand it by one word—for instance, "Car, car go." Or your child might say "ball" while looking around for the ball, and you could respond by pointing to the ball in the toy box and saying, "ball, see ball."

Imitation with expansion helps children learn how to combine words, and it provides the stimulation right at the level where they can learn. It is a technique that takes them from where they are into the next stage.

Three points are important to remember about imitation with expansion:

1. Repeat what your child says.
2. Validate that what he says is correct—demonstrate that you understand him and that he used a correct word.
3. Expand what your child says by one word.

You may present the imitation with expansion many times before your child begins to use two words; just keep at it. Repetition is essential, so provide many opportunities to practice. This type of activity lends itself well to play and to activities of daily living. Once you get used to using repetition and imitation with expansion, it becomes an easy technique to incorporate into almost any activity, including eating, dressing, taking a walk, etc. For suggestions, see the section on activities during daily living in Chapter 5. You can also teach grandparents, siblings, babysitters, and others to use repetition and imitation with expansion with your child.

Imitation with expansion is just as helpful with children who use Total Communication as it is with children who use speech alone. To use the technique with Total Communication, you would imitate the single sign your child makes and then add another sign while accompanying the sign with speech. For example, if your child points to his glass and signs "more," you would sign and say, "More, more milk."

Sometimes parents encounter difficulties in using imitation with expansion because their child may not initiate the first word. For example, your child may not talk as he plays, even though you know that he can speak or sign the words for the toys and for what he is doing with the toys. If your child does not initiate the first word, you can begin the conversation by talking about the activity. Your child may then repeat one of your words, such as bear, and you can then expand what he said by one word. Remember, too, that your child may initiate conversations without using speech. For instance, he may gaze or point at an object. Whenever possible, follow your child's lead. You can respond to his initiations by labeling the object, and then expanding—for example, "Ball, want ball." "Want" and "more" are always good words to introduce in two-word phrases because they teach your child to use communication to get *his* needs met.

PACING BOARDS

Another technique that you can use to help your child progress from the one-word to the two-word stage is the use of a *pacing board*. A pacing board provides a visual and tactile reminder of the number of words your child is able to use in combination. It is a cueing system. The pacing board may consist of two colored dots on a piece of cardboard, two teddy bear blocks put next to each other, a square of velvet and a square of sandpaper mounted on a board, two colorful dinosaur stickers mounted on a piece of cardboard—or anything else that your child likes. When you use imitation with expansion, point to the spots on the pacing board as you say each word. For example, in modeling the phrase "Car go," point to the first spot as you say "car" and to the second spot as you say "go."

Use hand-over-hand assistance to help your child get accustomed to using the pacing board for practice. Hold your hand on top of his hand and take him through the pointing motion. Using the pacing board provides multisensory cues—visual and tactile reminders for your child to use two separate words. Pacing boards are especially helpful for children with Down syndrome because they make use of their visual strengths to remind them to include two words.

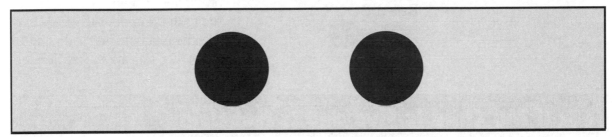

Pacing board with dots

Pacing board with pictures

PRACTICING TWO-WORD COMBINATIONS

At this point in his development, your child will probably not use appropriate word endings. For instance, he will probably say "mommy shoe" or "daddy car" meaning possessive. When you provide the model, use the correct possessive forms, "mommy's shoe" and "daddy's car," but don't expect your child to use the correct endings. You might try to exaggerate the word ending by making it louder or more clearly articulated to draw your child's attention to the ending, for example, by saying "mommy'sss shoe." Children with Down syndrome often leave off the final sounds in words. Research has shown that children understand the concept of possession long before they begin to use an apostrophe "s" to denote possession.

Once your child is able to use two-word combinations, encourage him to do so consistently. Ask day-care workers, grandparents, adult friends, family, and even siblings to encourage your child to use two words. Give your child a big positive reaction whenever he uses two words: "You're so grown-up; you sound like a big boy now." This usually motivates children with Down syndrome to continue to use two words. If your child is tired, don't push him to produce the two words, but use imitation with expansion and provide the two-word model for him.

Read BOOK

The section on "Learning and Play" offers suggestions for incorporating the learning of both two-word and three-word phrases into play. Also see the References and Suggested Reading list for books that discuss ways to combine language learning with play. There are some books that have only two words on a page and can help provide practice in combining words and expanding phrases. You can adapt these books so that they are similar to pacing boards by placing stick-on circles (usually used for color coding file folders) under the words in the book. See the example, left, adapted from *Find Cat, Wear Hat*, by Karen Gundersheimer.

What If My Child Is Five and Is Not Using Two-word Phrases?

Although all of the five-year-olds in the Loyola study cited above were using two-word phrases by age five, some children with Down syndrome do not accomplish this milestone by age five. Some of these children may be combining words using a language system such as sign language, but not with spoken words. In any case, you need to schedule a speech and language evaluation if your child is five or over and is not speaking in two-word phrases. The focus of the evaluation should be to determine whether any of the following are interfering with speech and language progress:

- oral motor skills
- childhood verbal apraxia
- hearing
- cognitive impairment
- another diagnosis such as autism co-occurring with Down syndrome

During that evaluation, the SLP should also assess your child's need for an Alternative or Augmentative Communication (AAC) system. See Chapter 11 for information on AAC and Chapter 12 for an explanation of the evaluation process.

The Three-Word Stage

When your child is consistently using two-word phrases, you can begin to encourage him to use three-word phrases. This will enable him to express an even wider range of meanings, as shown in the table on the next page.

Table 3: Types of Three-Word Phrases

Agent-Action-Object	"Sister kiss doll"; "Brother throw ball"
Agent-Action-Locative	"Mom go store"; "Baby fall down"
Action-Object-Locative	"Drink juice kitchen"; "Throw ball outside"
Phrases with Prepositions	"Toy in car"; "Hide under table"; "Put in box"
Modifying Phrases	"Want more cheese"; "See my cat"
Carrier Phrases	"I want cookie"; "I love mommy"

As before, he will be using the words that he knows and combining them into phrases. As before, you can use repetition with expansion to help your child progress from the two-word to the three-word stage. For example, your child might say, "Car go." You then repeat, "Car go." You have imitated, but have also validated the accuracy of his statement. Then you might say, "Car go fast" and make motor "vroom" noises, or you might say, "Big car go." As with the transition from the one- to two-word stage, a great deal of repetition and practice is needed, but the practice can be incorporated into play and daily life. In time, your child will use the words that he already knows from the one- and two-word phases and begin to combine them into three-word phrases.

If your child is able to use three-word phrases but doesn't seem to want to, try putting the three words to a musical tune. Say them very dramatically like an opera singer. Make it fun to sing the three words. Or make it sound like a TV jingle. This works on expanding phrases and also works on the rhythm (prosody) of speech, at the same time.

Two types of three-word phrases should be taught in different ways and therefore deserve special mention: carrier phrases and prepositional phrases.

CARRIER PHRASES

Carrier phrases consist of words such as "I want____ please" that often occur together in a particular order. They can be taught as a unit because your child will use them as a unit in daily conversation. When your child uses the phrase, he only needs to vary one or two key words. For instance: "I want *candy* please"; "I want *play* please"; "I want *more cookie* please." Or: "I like *Chris;*" "I like *Grandma;*" "I like *big drink.*" Carrier phrases are very useful because they transmit a great deal of information. They are also easier for your child to learn because they don't have to be formulated word by word each time he wants to use the phrase. He only needs to add the important word and his message will be understood.

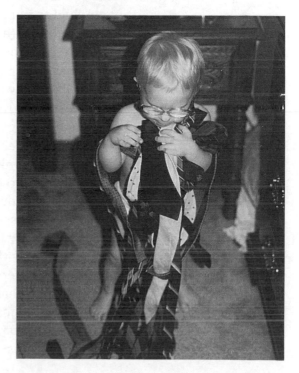

There are many ways to practice carrier phrases as part of play. For example, you can use puppets, dolls, or stuffed animals to practice. "What do you like to eat for dinner? I like pizza. What do *you* like to eat? I like hot dogs." You could model the phrase using puppets, and try to get your child to imitate and then use the phrase. A toy grocery game or a toy fast food counter can be used for role playing to practice carrier phrases. For example, "What do you want to buy? I want soda. I want ice cream. I want peanut butter." At home, you can look at the pictures in the newspaper supermarket ads, and you can ask your child to tell you three things he wants to buy. Paste the pictures on a paper, and bring the picture grocery list to the store. In the supermarket, using the list as a cueing system, your child can use his carrier phrase to tell you, "I want____."

Encourage your child to use the entire carrier phrase. If he uses only part of the phrase, provide the correct model, and try to have him repeat the model. You can set the phrase to a melody like a jingle, if your child enjoys music. You can use a pacing board with the appropriate number of dots. You also can write the carrier phrase right above the dots, and point to the dots as you say the carrier phrase.

PREPOSITIONAL PHRASES

The other special type of phrase your child will learn during the three-word period is the prepositional phrase. Prepositional phrases begin with prepositions (relationship words such as about, around, above, across, in, under, through) and often provide the answer to a "where is" question. Examples of prepositional phrases are "in the box," "under the table," and "on the porch."

Your child will best learn specific prepositions if he can directly experience the direction and location they express through play. You might want to start off on the playground where you can experience *in, on,* and *under* with the equipment. Then, you can use a big box to practice the various preposition "locations." Put your child *in* the box, *on* the box, and *under* the box. Then, use a smaller box and put a doll or stuffed animal *in, on,* or *under* the box while you label "in box." Work up to asking your child to put the doll *in* or *under* the box. While you are playing, be sure to use different boxes (a shoebox, a gift box, a plastic box). You want to make sure that your child will be able to generalize what he is learning to different situations. If you always teach prepositions by putting the same block on, under, or in the same box, your child will tend to identify prepositions only with that situation.

Most playgrounds are ideally suited to teaching prepositional phrases. Not only can you begin your preposition exercises on the playground, but you can use playground experiences to practice and reinforce the concepts. Your child can go *through* the monkey bars, *down* the slide, *under* the swing, and *up* the ladder. Again, be sure to provide many experiences, and to vary the equipment and situations to help your child generalize the concepts. When your child is able to use prepositions in speech, ask, "Where do you want to go?" and then respond to his answer, whether it be "in the sandbox" or "on the see-saw." What if he answers your question with "sandbox" or "see-saw," even though you know he knows the prepositions? Repeat the question, and then give the answer emphasizing the preposition by making it louder or more dramatic: "Where do you want to go? *On* the seesaw." Signs can be used to cue the preposition. An additional benefit is that the signs for prepositions, such as "through" or "between," look very much like the concepts they represent.

Language and Play

Play will be an important learning tool for your child during this stage—and indeed, all through childhood. As he begins to understand concepts, he will often play with toys as if they were the real objects. For example, he may pretend to drink from a toy cup (functional play), or pretend to feed a doll. Later, your child might build a bridge from blocks and have his toy car travel over the bridge (representational play). Play can be used as a window to observe your child's level of cognitive development. Excellent discussions of play are provided in *The New Language of Toys,* which is listed in the "Communication Skills" section of the References and Suggested Reading list at the end of the book.

There are many ways you can use play activities to stimulate language development during the two- and three-word stages. Some tips to keep in mind are:

- Use your child's favorite toys.
- Follow your child's lead. Talk about and play with the toy that your child has chosen at that moment.
- Use imitation with expansion, validation, and repetition as you play with your child.

HOME ACTIVITIES

Here are some ways you might incorporate language learning into play activities at this stage:

- Put a toy car in the elevator of a toy garage. Have the car go up and say, "Car up" or "Car go up." As the car goes down the ramp, say, "Car down" or "Car go down." Use a high-pitched voice as the car goes up and a low-pitched voice as the car goes down to further enhance learning.

- Use real or pretend cooking activities. Make chocolate milk or spread cheese on celery. Use vocabulary at the two-word or three-word level; whichever is appropriate for your child at the time. Some examples are "in milk; stir milk" or "syrup in milk; stir with spoon."

- Use a toy shopping cart and pretend food. Put the food in the cart: "Soup in; cereal in; juice in." Then take them out at the toy checkout. This is a wonderful activity because it is so true to life.

- Use a large doll such as a Raggedy Ann doll or Dressable Madeline doll. Dress the doll: "Socks on," "shirt on," "shoes on," etc. Children seem to relate well to a large doll and you can use real clothes and many of your child's own clothes to dress the doll.

- Use the *Motor Mat*, *Thomas the Tank Engine Village*, or some other town-like plastic mat. You can also make your own mat of felt or quilted fabric and customize it to represent your street or the land-marks of your town. Plastic mats are available at dollar stores, and fabric stores often have fabric by the yard imprinted with a town setting and a shopping mall. Use toy cars and travel around the village, talking about what you pass and what you see—the library, post office, supermarket, and park.

Teaching Questions and Responses

Play activities and reading activities are excellent ways to teach your child about questions and responses, as well as how to use prepositional phrases. In school, your child will particularly need to understand "Wh-" questions—the where, why, when, and who. As you play and as you read, ask your child "Wh-" questions. Remember to provide many examples of the answer. Model the answer—teach, don't test your child. Say, "Where are your shoes? On your feet. Where are your gloves? On your hands." When reading a book, ask "Where is the car? In the garage." "Where is the car now? On the bridge." "Where is Waldo? Behind the tree. . . ." There are many books that focus on wh- questions. See the References and Suggested Reading List for some suggestions. The possibilities are vast, and play and reading are pleasurable activities for you and your child to share.

Language and Reading

Reading with your child is an excellent time to work on receptive language. Reading again takes advantage of the visual strengths of children with Down syndrome, and many children greatly enjoy being read to. Sometimes, though, children with Down syndrome have short attention spans and may find reading too slow-paced. To help maintain your child's interest in reading, here are some suggestions:

- Choose books that have large print and colorful, interesting illustrations.
- Follow your child's lead and interests. Let him choose books.
- Make visits to the library a regular part of your weekly routine.
- When your child has a favorite library book, purchase the book for your own home library.

- Choose books with thick pages that your child can turn himself. (Or see Chapter 14 for tips on making pages easier for your child to turn.)
- Make reading a special time. Try not to have interruptions. Make reading a loving time of closeness. Sit in a favorite chair, snuggle together, and read.
- Children love repetition. If your child asks you to read the same book again and again, read that favorite book.
- Read dramatically with expression, and show that you are enjoying reading with your child.
- If your child points to a picture or a word, follow his lead and talk about it.
- Point to the name of the object in the book, then point to the picture that represents the object.

Many children with Down syndrome enjoy books about activities they can do themselves. You might read a book about autumn leaves, for example; then, follow up the reading activity with a real experience. Collect leaves, do an art project with leaves, or make cookies shaped like leaves. Then re-read the book and talk about your autumn leaves. Or, write your own story, and help your child illustrate it, or take photographs to illustrate the story.

With a little creativity, you can probably think of ways to directly involve your child in reading other types of books. For example, you might choose books with an animal or a famous character (Curious George, Big Bird) in it. Use a stuffed toy of that animal or character and act out parts of the book. Or you could select a book that focuses on sounds, such as *Mr. Brown Can Moo, Can You?* and together make the sounds that are described in the book. Or you can make character puppets by coloring in pictures of the characters from the book, and mounting them on Popsicle sticks or tongue depressors. Then use the paper puppets to retell the story. Or have your child act out what is happening as you read the story together.

After you finish reading a paragraph or a page, ask questions. Ask your child to show you who is jumping or where Grover is going. Have him point to the pictures in the book that answer the question. If you have a doll or stuffed animal that could represent a character from the book, you might ask your child to follow directions using the doll or show you the answer to the question using the doll.

If your child cannot answer your question, give him the answer. Remember, you are reading with him and teaching him, not testing him. If he cannot yet give the answer, try to have him imitate the answer. Emphasize the important word in your question—"WHERE was Grover hiding?" Once you have given the answer on several different occasions, try providing cues instead of giving the answer. You might give the initial sound of the answer, or give a phrase that will help your child say the answer. For example, say, "J" or "He ate bread and ___" to stimulate the word "jam," or use a signed cue to stimulate the word. Try to vary the way in which you ask the questions once your child is familiar with the content of the book. This helps in teaching and generalizing the concepts learned.

Conclusion

When your child is in the two- and three-word stages, he uses many modifiers. He not only says the one-word name of an object, but also talks about sizes, shapes, and colors. He uses adjectives and prepositions, and begins to talk about daily routines. And he learns to answer "Wh-" questions. The References and Suggested Reading list includes some readily available children's books that may be used to help teach these concepts in expressive and receptive language. In addition, Chapters 5 and 14 include information about how learning to read may help your child learn and strengthen many speech and language skills.

CHAPTER 7

The Nuts and Bolts of Language Comprehension

Your child with Down syndrome will probably continue to have communication challenges throughout her childhood. After mastering three-word phrases and short sentences, children with Down syndrome usually need continued help to improve upon the communication skills they have already acquired. We can discuss the development of the next set of skills best by focusing on the language areas one at a time. This will help you understand the language skills children need to learn and how you can help your child at home in each of these areas.

The next few chapters discuss the communication problems and challenges of children with Down syndrome who already have basic speech and language skills by focusing on semantics, morphosyntax, speech intelligibility, articulation and phonology, and pragmatics. If your child is over the age of three or four and is not able to use speech to communicate her needs (whether or not she has been using a transitional communication system), you may want to turn to Chapter 11 instead and learn how augmentative and alternative communication strategies can help her develop communication skills.

As discussed in Chapter 2, communication ability is made up of many skills. This chapter covers basic difficulties with language vocabulary and structure (morphosyntax). Chapter 8 covers problems with speech intelligibility and provides home and community activities to improve speech. Chapter 9 goes into more detail about articulation problems and phonology, which are usually involved when a child has difficulties speaking intelligibly. Chapter 10 addresses pragmatics, or how a child uses the language skills she has in real-life situations.

The Components of Language

Language is a very complex area because it includes many specific skills. For example, to effectively express and understand messages, we need to know a certain number of words and understand what they mean; understand how to make plural and possessive nouns and how to put verbs into the past and future tense;

know how to order words in a sentence; know which words are appropriate to use in different situations; and on and on. It takes a lot of time for *all* children, and especially children with Down syndrome, to learn how to use language effectively.

Children with Down syndrome may have trouble with all areas of language development or they may have trouble with only a few. Most, however, need help in almost all areas of language. The sections below look at the specific language areas of *semantics, morphology,* and *syntax (*sometimes combined as *morphosyntax)* and offer suggested activities to help in improving language skills.

Semantics

Semantics is the study of meaning in language. It is sometimes referred to as the *content* of language. Each language has its unique set of words for every object and concept. In American English, there are words for objects ("ball"), actions ("throw"), and descriptions ("good"). Children learn about meaning by pairing the concept or object with the appropriate word. But for all children, including children with Down syndrome, we know that learning is not that simple. There are many subtleties to master, such as the idea that specific words are used in specific situations—for example, you can "break" a plate but you don't break paper, you "tear" or "rip" it.

The major skills in semantics that children from birth to six years of age are developing are vocabulary skills.

Vocabulary. This includes the words and concepts a child understands (receptive vocabulary), as well as words she can use in speech (expressive vocabulary). We know that children with Down syndrome can usually understand many more words than they can produce—that is, their receptive vocabulary is larger than their expressive vocabulary.

Vocabulary skills in general appear to be one of the strongest areas of language for children with Down syndrome. Research has documented that children with Down syndrome begin to acquire receptive and expressive vocabulary at an early age and that vocabulary can continue to grow during childhood, adolescence, and adulthood. There is no plateau and no ceiling on vocabulary. Vocabulary is an area in which teaching by the family, as well as practice and experience, play a key role.

Sub-areas of vocabulary that you may hear discussed include:

- *Concrete words and labels/basic words:* Concrete or basic words and labels such as "ball" and "milk" are learned early, but we continue to learn concrete words through adulthood. Any new technological advances, concepts, or products will probably lead to a new word or label for that concept or product, such as "microwave" or "software."
- *Relational words such as time and space terms:* These are words that derive their meaning only in relation to other words. For instance, you don't know what someone means by

"early" in the morning unless you know what they think is "later." These words are learned through experience. What will we do now and what will we do later? What is early and late, before and after?

- *Classification:* Classification and categorization skills include the ability to sort things into categories (such as types of clothing or types of food), as well as the ability to name six animals or foods, or things that are orange.
- *Synonyms and antonyms:* Synonyms are words that have similar meanings, such as "small," "little," and "tiny," whereas antonyms are words with opposite meanings, such as "fast/ slow," "hot/cold," "loud/quiet." Synonyms and antonyms are often tested in language tests. Home and school experiences, including reading, can help children learn about similarities and differences.
- *Associated meanings:* These are words that are related to each other by meaning. They are not synonyms but are in the same meaning category. That is, they "go together"—e.g., "socks" and "shoes," "milk" and "cookies."
- *Subordinate/Superordinate:* When we group words together, we often group words because they are examples of a larger or smaller unit. Subordinates are words that are specific examples of a larger category—e.g., "goldfish" or "salmon" are in the category "fish." Superordinates are larger categories such as "food." For instance, one superordinate of "fruit" would be "food," while a superordinate of "orange" or "apple" would be "fruit."

HOW DO CHILDREN DEVELOP SEMANTIC SKILLS?

As infants grow, they share many experiences with their parents, siblings, and caretakers. During these joint experiences, objects, actions, people, and events are labeled with words by the adults for the infant.

Infants also learn about objects, people, and events in their environment through their sensory exploration. When infants and toddlers explore objects by putting the objects in their mouths or by looking at them intently, they are learning about the attributes of objects. Is the object soft or hard, big or little? Can it bounce or roll? Can you eat it? When children begin to use symbols to describe these objects, people, and events, they can connect the word with the object that they know about through shared experiences and through their exploration.

Young children also need to learn the actual word to use to describe objects and experiences. They learn these labels through using *referential gaze*—that is, by looking at objects with an adult, who then labels the object for them. Referential gaze is also known as shared gaze or joint attention. Labels are known as *referential meaning* or *referential vocabulary*, and the child's ability to use labels is known as *referential production*.

Developing referential meaning appears to be one of two separate skills involved in learning vocabulary. The other important skill is developing *grammatical classification*, or understanding what part of speech a word is. Researchers have

found that children with cognitive disabilities acquire object names (content words) in the same manner as children without cognitive disabilities, but they experience difficulty in acquiring function words, such as prepositions and connectives (conjunctions). This suggests that they develop adequate referential meaning (they know what the word is referring to and understand what the word represents) but have difficulty learning the grammatical category of words (whether a word is a noun, verb, or preposition) and how you use it in a multiword phrase or sentence.

During the one-word stage, young children learn the names of people and objects in their environment. They learn the names or nicknames for family members, and they learn the labels for things that they want in their environment—juice, ball, doll, car, outside. Their language focuses on the here and now. Research tells us that the best way to teach vocabulary to young children with Down syndrome is to follow their referential gaze, what they are looking at. That means that you follow your child's lead and teach her words for what she is most interested in. For typically developing children and children with Down syndrome, the early words are similar. The first ten words learned are usually names for important people in their environment ("mama," "dada," "nana," labels for objects or toys ("ball") or pets ("dog"), and greetings or words that refer to daily routines ("bye-bye").

Children use single words as *holophrases*. They put more complex meanings behind their use of single words, and the same word can have a different meaning depending on the context. For example, "milk" may mean "want more milk," or "no milk," or "milk spilled," depending on the situation. As children develop semantic concepts, their word choices may be accurate or may be mismatched with the adult model. As they learn, they often use underextension and overextension.

Underextension occurs when the child uses a word such as "jacket" only to describe the specific jacket in her experience. So, if there is a picture of a blue jacket, and her jacket is red, she will not use the word " jacket" to describe the blue jacket. Her word use is specific to her experience. As children develop and have more experience with various types of jackets and learn the *semantic features* of jacket (a short coat with buttons or zipper), they learn to generalize the usage of the word "jacket."

Often, when children are learning new words and concepts, they use *overextension* or *overgeneralization*. In this case, they learn one characteristic of a vocabulary word and then they use that word for any object that shares that characteristic. For instance, a child may learn that a dog has four legs and then use the word "dog" for any animal with four legs. Or, she may learn that Daddy is a man, so any man that she sees becomes "daddy." With language experience, children learn the appropriate word for the object, person, or event, and modify their vocabulary to match the adult model.

When children begin to combine words into two-word and three-word phrases, there are various semantic relationships that they learn to understand and produce. For example, during the two-word phase, children learn to combine words to demonstrate possession ("Dolly sock") or action – object ("Eat cracker"). During the three-word stage, children expand on the semantic relationships by using their vocabulary words to form relationships such as phrases with prepositions ("Hat on head"). See Chapter 6 for more detailed lists of semantic relationships explored at these stages.

<table>
<tr><td>

RESEARCH ON SEMANTICS IN CHILDREN WITH DOWN SYNDROME

</td><td>

When a young child uses her first spoken or signed word, she shows that she can connect a symbol with an object, person, or event. That is, she understands what that symbol *means*. When does this typically occur in children with Down syndrome?

</td></tr>
</table>

The average age that children with Down syndrome produce their first spoken word is eighteen months (Gillham, 1979), but some children are able to sign words that show expressive vocabulary knowledge before twelve months of age (Kumin, Goodman, Councill, 1991). (Also see the table on page 66 of Chapter 5.) Researchers have documented that vocabulary development and the words included in the early vocabularies of children with Down syndrome are similar to those of typically developing children (Gillham, 1979, Mervis, 1997). Researchers do not always agree, however, about other aspects of vocabulary development in children with Down syndrome. Below are some of the results researchers have reported.

DO CHILDREN WITH DOWN SYNDROME HAVE SMALLER VOCABULARIES?

It is clear that when children with Down syndrome are compared with typically developing children of the same chronological age, the children with Down syndrome have smaller vocabularies. However, in studies comparing children with Down syndrome with typically developing (TD) children using other criteria, researchers do not always agree whether children with Down syndrome have smaller vocabularies.

One researcher found that children with Down syndrome produced *more* different vocabulary words than TD children when they were matched by linguistic stage rather than chronological age (Rondal, 1978). His conclusion was that since the children with Down syndrome were chronologically older at each linguistic stage, the results reflected the influence of life experience. (See page 105 for an explanation of linguistic stages.) Jon Miller, a speech-language pathologist at the University of Wisconsin who has done a great deal of research into communication skills in Down syndrome, had similar results. In one study, Miller matched children with Down syndrome and typically developing children by their mean length of utterance (MLU). He found that children with Down syndrome produced significantly more different words than typically developing children matched for MLU (Miller et al, 1987).

Several researchers have matched children with Down syndrome and typically developing children by mental age—that is, matched by scores on cognitive tests rather than chronological age. In one study, when children with Down syndrome were matched with typically developing children by mental age, the two groups produced similar levels of different vocabulary words in a language sample (Cardoso-Martins et al. 1985). Another researcher originally found that when children with Down syndrome were matched with typically developing children by mental age, children with Down syndrome produced fewer different words than typically developing children (Miller et al. 1987). However, when the same researcher conducted another study matching children for mental age and also for socioeconomic status, he found no significant differences in the number of different words used by the two groups of children (Miller, 1992). In yet another study, this same researcher found that most children with Down syndrome have smaller vocabularies compared to typically developing children matched for mental age, but that 35 percent of the children he studied with Down syndrome had rates of vocabulary growth consistent with mental age (Miller, 1995).

In plain language, this research means that your child will probably not have as large a vocabulary as a typically developing child of the same age. But it is possible that her vocabulary will be average for her mental age. In addition, the size of your child's vocabulary is very likely to be appropriate for someone who is at that general linguistic stage.

DO CHILDREN WITH DOWN SYNDROME LEARN NEW WORDS AT A STEADY RATE?

Typically developing children experience a steady growth in vocabulary with rapid acceleration at around seventeen months of age. Jon Miller found that children with Down syndrome progress in vocabulary development at a steady rate up to twenty-three months of age (1992). At that time, there is often a rapid acceleration in their vocabulary acquisition. Two British researchers confirmed that this "vocabulary explosion" occurs in many, but not all children with Down syndrome, and that

the mean age for this rapid vocabulary progress was 30 months when the child had reached a mean vocabulary of 24.4 words (Oliver and Buckley, 1994). Yet another researcher found a period of rapid vocabulary growth at about three years of age (Mervis, 1997).

For parents, this means that you might expect to see a surge in acquisition of new vocabulary words when your child with Down syndrome is between the ages of two and three.

After this surge, at least one study suggests that there may be a brief slow-down in vocabulary acquisition around the ages of three and four. At my center, we conducted a survey of parents of 115 children with Down syndrome between the ages of two and five (Kumin, Councill, and Goodman, 1998). Using the MacArthur Communicative Development Inventories, we collected information about how many spoken and/or signed words were in the children's vocabularies. There was a great deal of variability among children, but we found that most five-year-olds could express significantly more words than two-, three-, and four-year-olds. However, there was not a significant difference in vocabularies between three- and four-year-olds. (See Table 1 in the next section to get an idea of the numbers of words used at different ages.) One possible explanation for this slow-down is that many children with Down syndrome may be shifting from signing to speaking when they are between the ages of three and four. So, perhaps children with Down syndrome are concentrating on the oral-motor tasks needed for speech during that year.

WHAT ABOUT THE RECEPTIVE-EXPRESSIVE VOCABULARY GAP?

Previous chapters have pointed out that children with Down syndrome frequently understand much more language than they are able to express. That is, their receptive language skills are usually better than their expressive language

Table 1: Expressive Vocabularies of Young Children with Down Syndrome

Age	Mean Number of Words (spoken and signed)	Study
15-23 months	11-14	Buckley, S. (2000)
24-35 months	28 55 (range of 8-226)	Buckley (2000) Kumin, Councill & Goodman (1998)
36-47 months	117 168 (range of 5-675)	Buckley (2000) Kumin et al. (1998)
48-59 months	218 251 (range of 22-645)	Buckley (2000) Kumin et al. (1998)
60-71 months	272 391 (range of 62-611)	Buckley (2000) Kumin et al. (1998)

Table 2: Receptive Vocabularies of Young Children with Down Syndrome

Age	Mean Number of Words Understood	Study
15-23 months	125	Buckley, S. (2000)
24-35 months	167	Buckley, S. (2000)
36-47 months	233	Buckley, S. (2000)
48-59 months	300	Buckley, S. (2000)
60-71 months	334	Buckley, S. (2000)

skills. Over the years, many researchers have actually counted the number of words that young children with Down syndrome can comprehend or produce at different ages. Although different researchers came up with different totals of words for children at different ages, the gap is clear if you compare the results in the two tables. Some studies have found that children with Down syndrome have even larger receptive vocabularies than shown above. For example, Sue Buckley and Gillian Bird estimated that children with Down syndrome could comprehend over 2000 words by age 7 (Buckley & Bird, 2001).

IS VOCABULARY DEVELOPMENT LINKED TO COGNITIVE ABILITIES?

It is generally accepted that people with Down syndrome have lower communication skills overall than would be expected based on their cognitive skills. That is, there is a perception that many people with Down syndrome know more than they are able to communicate. There is no general agreement, however, whether there is a similar discrepancy between cognitive skills and vocabulary skills.

In one study of 35 children with Down syndrome from ages 5.5 to 20.5 years, researchers concluded that vocabulary comprehension was *higher* than cognition levels. In another study of children from ages 17 months to 39 months, researchers concluded that vocabulary levels were *lower* than cognitive developmental levels (Cardoso-Martins, Mervis and Mervis, 1985). The question that needs to be asked is how the cognitive developmental levels were measured. Were language-based tests used to determine cognitive levels? If so, it should be expected that developmental levels for language and cognition would be similar. This is because most cognitive tests are heavily language based, so if a child has lower language skills it will affect her ability to understand and answer the questions. Research has shown that language scores are often below cognitive scores, so when a language-based IQ test is used, it may actually "lower" the cognitive score.

Sue Buckley has cast some light on how using a non-language-based test of intelligence can clarify the differences between cognitive abilities and language skills. In a study of 12 teenagers with Down syndrome with a mean chronological age of 14 years 11 months, she found a mean score of 7 years on the Raven's Coloured Matrices, a test of nonverbal reasoning ability, as compared to an average score of 5 years 6 months on a picture vocabulary comprehension test and 5 years on a grammar comprehension test (Buckley, 1993, 1994). In other words, the teenagers' vocabulary comprehension skills were a year and a half behind their nonverbal reasoning skills (and their skills in understanding grammar were about two years behind).

What is clear is that people with Down syndrome—no matter what their cognitive abilities—can continue to acquire new vocabulary throughout their lives. Even though learning new vocabulary words may take longer, children with Down syndrome can develop rich and varied vocabularies.

READING AND SEMANTICS

British researcher Sue Buckley believes that the brain can go straight from print to meaning, without translating the visual image to speech and then determining the meaning (Buckley, 1996, 1997). She thinks that this can make reading a fruitful avenue to explore for teaching vocabulary words to children with Down syndrome. Indeed, several studies have found that children with Down syndrome sometimes make errors in reading such as saying "closed" instead of "shut" (Buckley, 1993, 1996). The words do not look the same visually; the similarities are in meaning. So, Buckley feels that the children decode the word for meaning directly from print and then retrieve a word associated in meaning.

One implication is that if a child is having a lot of difficulty with learning new words that are spoken, she could use reading as an alternative way to learn new words. For more information on using reading and visual cues as assists in language learning, see Chapter 14.

HOME ACTIVITIES

Chapter 13 explains how semantic difficulties are addressed in speech therapy. Here are some activities to try at home.

- Label objects that seem to interest your child. Follow her gaze, and see what she is looking at. Then give her the name for that object or person. If she is looking at the balloon, say "balloon." Then point out other balloons when you see them. Give her many opportunities to hear the word when it is paired with the item in real life. Seize the opportunities!

- Use pointing to help your child learn new words. Point to the object, be sure that she is looking at it, and provide the label several times. For example, look at the beach ball that is being tossed around on the beach, make sure that your child is looking at it, and then label it "ball, ball, ball."

- Teach vocabulary concepts during real-life activities. For example, when you are at the supermarket, name all of the foods that you see. Talk about what is in the produce section, what's a fruit and what's a vegetable, and name specific items.

- If your child can ask "wh-" questions, have your child ask store employees at grocery or variety stores where items are located, "Where is the cereal? Where is the corn?" This is a good way to practice vocabulary words and "wh-" questions at the same time.

- Reinforce concepts learned in real-life experiences by role playing real life experiences. After the trip to the supermarket, play Supermarket. Use a toy shopping cart, a toy cash register, and play food or boxes and cans of real food. If you regularly go to the same supermarket, they may be willing to give you some props such as a supermarket cap or an apron to use in your play.

- Read a book about subjects that relate to your child's experiences to reinforce the vocabulary she learned. For example, if you vacationed at the beach, read a book about the beach. Ask her to show you, or to identify sand, shells, waves, etc. Or, when it is snowing, read a book about snowy days and activities such as sledding and making snowmen.

- Use a photograph album and "memory" photos to reinforce vocabulary concepts. During the summer, go to your neighborhood pool or park or to the beach and label what you see. Take photos of your friends and family at play. Then use the photos as cues to talk about the pool, park, or beach, and your experiences. In the winter, use the photo album to help remind you about summer experiences and the vocabulary that goes with summer. Rich and varied experiences help in vocabulary development. Many parents have noted increases in vocabulary after family trips or vacations or have commented on spurts in vocabulary growth with school inclusion in preschool and kindergarten.

- Use your photographs from a family outing to create your own book. Mount the photos or draw your own pictures and create a custom-designed book for your child. Then, using the photos as guidelines, write a story together about your experiences on the outing.

- Categories are an important part of vocabulary. To teach and reinforce category concepts, take two carts when you go to the discount variety store. Bring two small signs (index cards or post-it notes), one saying "clothing" and the other labeled "appliances" (or "hardware" or any other category that you need to buy that day). As you shop, put all clothing into one cart and all hardware into the other. Some stores have kiddie carts that your child can push. Or go to the store as a family, involve siblings, and make this a family game.

- Teach children about categories by labeling and sorting objects at home. You can do this in the context of cleaning a room—putting books on the bookshelf, toys in the toy box. Or sort laundry or put clothes in the appropriate dresser drawers. Be sure to verbally label each item. This is a good way to teach superordinate-subordinate relationships. Call the shirt a "shirt" and then discuss how it is clothing. Name the specific book titles, and then put them into the larger category of books as you place them onto the bookshelf.

- Use word games to teach both superordinate categories (generic categories such as "fruit" or "animals") and subordinate categories (specific examples within categories such as "orange," "apple," and "banana"). After a trip to the zoo, ask, "How many animals can you think of?" or "A bear is an *animal*. What's a banana? Is it an animal? No, it's food."

- Help children learn about associated meanings by using games such as lotto or match-ups. Choose or design lotto cards based on a specific topic. For instance, make a dog lotto card, which includes pictures of dog food, a bone, a leash, etc. Discuss what goes with dogs.

- Reading to young children helps them develop vocabulary skills. In fact, research has demonstrated that the best predictor of vocabulary size in typically developing children is how much they are read to. Refer to Chapters 6 and 14 for guidance on reading to your child.

- Help your child learn verbs by identifying motor activities. Go to the playground and play on the equipment together. If your child can use verbs, model the sentence, "I am jumping." Ask, "What are you doing?" She can either jump and say, "I am jumping" or change activities and say, "I am running." If she cannot yet say the words, you can describe what you are doing and then describe what she is doing.

- Have your child demonstrate that she understands verbs by asking her to make a doll or stuffed animal do certain actions. For example, "Make Pooh Bear jump" or "Make Pooh Bear dance."

- Play Simon Says. Ask your child to do actions with her own body such as "Put your hands on your head." Or vary the game by using toy props or pictures: "Simon Says, Put Batman in the car." Or "Simon Says, put the fork on the table." This activity helps children with following directions as well as vocabulary.

Morphosyntax

Until recently, morphology (the study of word parts such as verb tense endings, plurals, and possessives) and syntax (the study of grammar) were considered two separate areas of language. In recognition of how closely the two areas interact in understanding and formulating messages, the areas are now often combined and labeled as morphosyntax.

Morphology

Morphology is the term used to describe how people use the individual elements of language—root words, prefixes, or suffixes—to form words. These individual elements are called *morphemes*. Morphemes are typically used to express concepts such as plurals and present and past tense. Words may contain one or more morphemes that are built on the root word. For example, the word, "phone" has one morpheme; the word "telephone" has two morphemes (tele + phone); and the word "telephones" has three morphemes (tele + phone + s). For another example, the root word "walk" and the suffix "ed" are both morphemes, and may be combined to form the past tense "walked."

Children learn the morphological rules of their language by listening to people around them. We know that children have learned a morphological rule by the structures they use in their own speech. When they use correct structures, such as "He walked," we know that they have learned how to convey past tense. But even when they use incorrect structures, such as "He runned," we can tell that they have learned the morphological rule for past tense and are applying the rule; they just have not learned the exceptions to the rule. That comes with time and practice.

Children with Down syndrome often have difficulty with morphology. In conversation, many word endings are said softly or unclearly, and children who have a hearing loss may have difficulty hearing them. Also, morphological concepts may be abstract, such as using "un—" to mean negation or "—ed" to mean past tense, and consequently are more difficult for children with cognitive delays to learn. Another complicating factor is that children with Down syndrome often leave off final sounds when speaking, and many morphemes occur as the final sounds in words. For example, it is often much easier for children with Down syndrome to pronounce the word "bike" than it is to say the word "bikes." As a result, they may not get the amount of practice they need to consistently know when to add the "s" to the end of some words.

If your child is working on morphemes in school or in speech-language therapy, ask which morphemes she is working on, so you can think of activities to do with her at home to practice those morphemes. For examples, see the Home Activities on the next page.

HOME ACTIVITIES

• Plurals can be worked on as soon as your child understands the concept of one and more than one. Work on plurals during daily activities that involve more than one. For example, have your child count the number of Cheerios she eats using the plural form Cheerios. Give her five M&M's. If she counts them using the plural form, she can eat them. Make cupcakes and then decorate them. Your child can ask for the decorations using plurals: "I want two hearts." "Can I have more chocolate chips?"

• You can also use laundry to practice the possessive "'s" morpheme. As your child helps you sort the laundry, say "Mommy's shirt," "Haley's shirt," "Daddy's shirt," being sure to emphasize the ending /s/. Or sort toys, books, children's artwork, etc. this way. Be aware, however, that your child will probably understand the concept of possession long before she uses the proper possessive form in speech. That is, many three-year-olds with Down syndrome can point to Mommy's shoe, even when Mommy is not there, and say "Mommy." But it may take several years for them to learn to say, "Mommy's shoe." In one study, only 20 percent of three-year-olds ever used the possessive /s/, about 42 percent of the four-year-olds did, and about 78 percent of the five-year-olds did (Kumin, Councill, and Goodman, 1998).

• Teach morphemes that involve verb tenses through real-life activities. For example, when you are cooking, say "I *will mix* the cake," "I *am mixing* the cake," "I *mixed* the cake." Be sure to emphasize the last morpheme of the word, the ending.

Syntax

Syntax is the term used for grammar, or the rules governing the form of the language. Syntax includes word order, sentence construction, and how to ask questions. Syntax is not really a consideration until children are beyond the one- and two-word stages. (Very few grammatical sentences can be constructed with just two words, other than very simple noun-verb sentences such as "You go" or "I eat.")

One researcher documented that children with Down syndrome who are learning Swedish develop skills in morphosyntax in the same *order* as typically developing children do (Berglund, 2001). The *rate* at which they develop these skills is slower than in typical children, however, and they also acquire these skills more slowly than they acquire skills in semantics. Perhaps this relative slowness in developing grammar is linked to slower growth in vocabulary growth. At any rate, one study found that children with Down syndrome need to have a minimum vocabulary of 250 vocabulary words before they begin to use early grammatical markers for possessives, plurals, and verb tenses (Buckley, S. & Pennanen, T., in press).

What Are the Linguistic Stages?

If you ever read accounts of research studies into children's language skills, you may come across references to the children being at, for example, "Brown Stage I" or "Brown Stage IV." What the researchers are referring to is the length of the children's typical utterance, as well as how far they have progressed in mastering the first fourteen morphemes typically learned in the English language and basic semantic skills. A description of the order in which young children typically learn to use morphemes was originally published by Roger Brown in his book *A First Language*—hence the references to "Brown stages."

These are the five stages and how they affect a child's morphosyntax:

Stage I: *MLU of 1.75 words; typically reached at 22 months.*
Children form sentences without using morphological word endings. For example, they say "Mommy shoe" to mean "Mommy's shoe" or "Baby cry" to mean "Baby is crying."

Stage II: *MLU of 2.25 words; typically reached at 28 months.*
Children use the following morphemes:
   1. Present-progressive verb ending ("-ing"): For example, "Julie eating"
   2. Preposition "in": "Billy in car"
   3. Preposition "on": "bowl on table"
   4. Regular plural ("-s"): "toys," "cars," "fingers"

Stage III: *MLU of 2.75 words; typically reached at 32 months.*
Children add the use of the following morphemes:
   5. Past irregular verbs: "toy broke," "you fell down," "Susie came home"
   6. Possessives: "Mommy's cars," "Joey's shoes"
   7. Uncontractible copula (using "to be" words without contractions): "What is that?" "Where are they?"

Stage IV: *MLU of 3.50 words; typically reached at 41 months.*
Children add the use of the following morphemes:
   8. Articles (the, an, a): "the ball," "a hat"
   9. Past-regular tense endings ("-ed"): "Kelly walked yesterday."
   10. Third-person-regular tense endings ("-s"): "Josh carries teddy," "Susie sees cookies"

Stage V: *MLU of 4.00 words; typically reached at 45 months.*
Children add the use of the following morphemes:
   11. Third-person-irregular tense endings: "Mom does."
   12. Uncontractible auxiliary (full form of "to be" used as a "helping verb": "The dog is barking."
   13. Contractible copula (contracted form of "to be" used as only verb in sentence: "Brian's silly," "Where's mommy?"
   14. Contractible auxiliary (contracted form of "to be" used as a "helping verb": "The dog's barking."

Usually, it takes children with Down syndrome much longer to acquire a 250-word vocabulary than it does typically developing children.

As discussed in Chapter 2, syntax is a difficult area for children with Down syndrome because it is abstract and complex. At least one study has shown that children with Down syndrome reach a period during adolescence where there is a slowdown in morphosyntactic development and that there is little spontaneous progress beyond that period (Rondal and Edwards, 1997). There has not been any research to investigate whether morphosyntax can continue to improve with treatment—that is, whether specific interventions can result in progress when children do not spontaneously improve their skills.

In my experience, the areas of syntax that are especially difficult for children with Down syndrome are:

1. the use of past tense;
2. agreement of pronoun and verb (for example, "He walks," "We walk");
3. the use of personal pronouns ("he," "she," "himself," "herself," "his," "hers," "theirs");
4. active versus passive construction ("the dog chased the cat" vs. "the cat was chased by the dog");
5. correct use of negatives ("I'm not ready") and interrogatives ("Are you going to go with me?"); and
6. difficulty with the use of articles such as "the" and "a" (using telegraphic speech).

Again, we don't know how great an impact oral motor ability and speech ability contribute to some of the difficulties with syntax children with Down syndrome have. For example, do they have trouble forming past tense because of difficulties pronouncing the "–ed" on the ends of verbs? difficulties hearing the "–ed" on the ends of verbs? Or is it difficulty in understanding and using when and why to use the past tense?

In general, children with Down syndrome have more trouble with syntax (grammar) than with semantics (vocabulary). The difference between vocabulary and grammatical development gets larger as children get older. Still, children with Down syndrome learn grammatical structures in the same order as typically developing children—just at a slower pace.

RESEARCH ON SYNTAX IN CHILDREN WITH DOWN SYNDROME

A number of researchers have documented that syntactic (grammar) skills are especially difficult for children with Down syndrome, and that semantic (vocabulary) skills are relatively easier for them. Some of their findings and theories about these areas include:

- Children with Down syndrome may have difficulties with syntax due to underlying sequencing difficulties (knowing what order to put words in) and this is their major language learning problem. Vocabulary learning may be easier for them because learning new words is not dependent on sequencing skills (Fowler, 1995).
- The reason children with Down syndrome are delayed in vocabulary compared to typically developing children may be that children with Down syndrome have trouble learning

Table 3: Morphosyntax Development in Children with Down Syndrome

Skills	Age	Study
Understand grammatical concepts such as possession and past tense, but not usually able to use the grammatical markers that represent these concepts	3 years	Kumin, L., Councill, C., & Goodman, M. (1999)
Present progressive tense of verbs (-ing) denoting an activity in progress ("He's drawing")	30-52 months 3-5 years or older	Rutter & Buckley (1994) Kumin, L., Councill, C., & Goodman, M. (1999)
Preposition "on" ("Put it on the table")	28-49 months	Rutter & Buckley (1994)
Preposition "in" ("It's in the cupboard")	30-54 months	Rutter & Buckley (1994)
Plural /s/ ("Dogs")	28-50 months 2-8 years (most often between 4-5 years)	Rutter & Buckley (1994) Kumin, L., Councill, C., & Goodman, M. (1999)
Irregular past tense of verbs ("It broke"; "He ran")	28-51 months	Rutter & Buckley (1994)
Possessive /s/ ("Tom's book")	31-52 months	Rutter & Buckley (1994)
Articles "a" and "the"	31-56 months	Rutter & Buckley (1994)
Regular past tense forms (-ed) ("Sally picked the flower")	40-54 months usually after 4-5 years	Rutter & Buckley (1994) Kumin, L., Councill, C., & Goodman, M. (1999)
Irregular third person singular /s/ for present tense ("He has"; "She does")	44 months	Rutter & Buckley (1994)
Contractible copula form (contracted form of "to be" used as only verb in sentence: "They're inside"; "The boy's dirty")	42-79 months	Rutter & Buckley (1994)
Contractible auxiliary form (contracted form of "to be" used as a "helping verb": "He's laughing")	44-45 months	Rutter & Buckley (1994)
Mean length of utterance 1.5 words	4 years	Chamberlain, C.E. & Strode, R.M. (1999)
Mean length of utterance 3.5 words	6 years	Chamberlain, C.E. & Strode, R.M. (1999)
Mean length of utterance 5+ words	15 years	Chamberlain, C.E. & Strode, R.M. (1999)

words with grammatical meanings (for example, "but," "if," "then") (Barrett and Diniz, 1988).

■ Young children with Down syndrome use many more referential vocabulary words (words for objects or things that can be experienced) than grammatical classification words (words that are only used to hold sentences together, such as "however" or "or") (Kumin, Councill, and Goodman, 1998). Typically, they do not use any grammatical vocabulary words until at least age five, and begin to increase their use of words with grammatical meanings around age six.

When Do Children with Down Syndrome Begin Using the Plural /s/ ?

According to one study (Kumin, Councill, and Goodman, 1998), children with Down syndrome most often begin using the plural /s/ between the ages of four and five. There was, however, a great deal of variability. (A child was considered to be forming plurals correctly when she included a final /s/ sound (as in "tops"), final /z/ sound (as in "cars"), /es/ (as in "bases"), or /ez/ (as in "houses"). The following percentages of children used the plural /s/ correctly:

- At age 2: 85% never did,   15% sometimes did,   0% often did;
- At age 3: 56.6% never did,   26.6% sometimes did,   16.6 often did;
- At age 4: 57.5% never did,   33.3% sometimes did,   09% often did;
- At age 5: 27.7% never did,   55% sometimes did,   27.7% often did;
- At age 6: 20% never did,   46.7% sometimes did,   30.8% often did;
- At age 7: 7.7% never did,   30.8% sometimes did,   61.5% often did;
- At age 8: 0% never did,   30% sometimes did,   70% often did.

This delay in mastering the usage of plurals may be related to delays in phonology and articulation. In other words, some of the delay in using the final /s/ may be due to difficulty hearing the endings of words. And some of it may be due to difficulty in pronouncing all the sounds in a word. Delays may also occur due to difficulty in understanding why or when to make words plural.

HOME ACTIVITIES

As mentioned above, learning about syntax becomes more important as children use longer multiword utterances and begin formulating sentences. Therefore, it is probably best to use home activities in the area of syntax to supplement classroom or therapy activities in order to focus on and reinforce specific skills suggested by the classroom teacher or SLP. (See Chapter 13 for information about how the SLP works on problems with syntax.) Most of the work on syntax is beyond the age range of this book, and occurs during the elementary and middle school years.

- Make verb books (picture cues of verbs your child knows) to help her remember to use these words in her speech. She might respond best to photos of herself or siblings, cousins, or friends making movements depicting various verbs.

- Use gross motor activities to teach verb usage. For instance, when you are learning the verbs "jump," "bend," and "stretch," actually make those movements. This is similar to the way that *Sesame Street* presents new concepts, but they use animation. Later on, use stuffed animals, puppets, or family members to illustrate how the verbs change depending on tense. For instance, make Teddy Bear jump off the bed while you say "Teddy is jumping," then comment, "Teddy jumped."

- Use manipulative materials to emphasize verbs, prepositions, etc. For example, use a rubber stamp or stickers to learn and practice concepts such as "press," "lift," "stick," "on top," and "under."

- Use a pacing board to teach verb forms such as "-ing."

He is go ing

He is sing ing

Pacing board with print cues

- The basic technique that you used in imitation with expansion when your child was ready to use two- and three-word phrases can apply here. Expand on your child's phrases so that they become short grammatical sentences. Provide the correct model for her. So when she says, "Where Dad?" you say, "Where is Dad?" Provide the model and then answer the question: "He went to the hardware store."

- To help teach negatives, line up your child's toy animals or small action figures. Designate one toy as the one you are looking for. "Where's Mickey Mouse?" For each toy, point and ask your child, "Is this Mickey Mouse?" Your child has to say, "No, this is NOT Mickey Mouse." Model it so she can imitate you at first, and make the word "not" much louder to emphasize it. Then, try to help her say it spontaneously. You may need to provide a cue, such as moving your lips for the first letter or saying some of the words in unison with her. When you get to Mickey Mouse, have her say, "Yes, it is Mickey Mouse," and remove Mickey from the group. Then designate another character as the one you are looking for.

- A variation on the previous activity: ask your child which color of clay or Play Doh she wants. Then point to all of the other colors first. For example, "Is this red? No, it's yellow." You may need to give her models or use the carrier phrase, "No, it's ____" and let her fill in the color. You can do this with ice cream flavors or when choosing a t-shirt when shopping. When she expresses a preference, ask her whether that is what she wants as you point to the others. Make it a game so that she will not get upset or frustrated.

- Mark the activities you do with your child on a calendar. Look back at the calendar at the end of the week and discuss what you have done. This gives you an opportunity to teach the past tense, referring to events that are still recent so that your child is likely to remember those events. "What did we do on Monday?" "We met Grandma. We went out to lunch." "Tuesday, we went to the playground."

- To work on word order, cut out photos from magazines, use family photos, or use a software program such as *Picture This!* to make a large collection of pictures depicting people, things, places, and verbs. Using the picture cards, make picture sentences, and then model sentences for your child: "Dad throws the ball to Bill." "Dad throws the ball to me." "Dad drives the car." "Mom drives the car." "I feed Rover."

- Teach your child to use more carrier phrases, as described in Chapter 6.

- Use toy cars, trucks, animals, and other props to work on word order. Move the objects, make the sentence, and then discuss the difference between the sentences. For instance, act out "The car hits the truck" vs. "The truck hits the car," or "Mickey is driving the car" and "Minnie is sitting in the car."

- To help your child learn to answer "wh-" questions, try some of the activities in the box on "Mining Ads and Catalogs for Language Activities."

Mining Ads and Catalogs for Language Activities

A great way to practice both language and early reading skills is to use the colorful advertisement pullouts from stores (usually the sales sections in the Sunday paper, but sometimes separate mailers). This is a free, colorful, interesting resource. It is also a resource in which the items change from week to week, but the basic format usually remains the same. One use of the ads is to practice asking and answering "wh-" questions. Pull out the supermarket section and ask, "What do you want to buy?" If your child does not give an answer, provide some cues in the form of questions. "Do you want to buy juice? Do you want to buy cereal?" or "Which cereal should we buy?" Try to buy at least *some* of her choices the next time you visit the store.

Then, try a clothing store advertisement. Ask, "What should we buy?" If there is an ad for men's, women's, and children's shorts, ask, "Who needs these shorts?" or if your child is working on colors, "What color are these shorts?"

When it's close to your child's birthday or Christmas or Hanukah, let her page through a flyer or catalog from a toy store. Ask her, "What do you want?" then let her circle or put her initials or a sticker next to the items she is interested in receiving.

Once you have looked at two or three different ads from different stores, ask questions such as, "Where can we buy shorts?" "Where can we buy M & M's?" "Where can we buy a new Wiggles video?" "Where can we buy a new dress for your Barbie doll?"

When Do Children with Down Syndrome Learn to Use Verb Endings?

As with many language concepts, children with Down syndrome appear to understand the concepts underlying verb tenses (the difference between past and future) before they are able to express that understanding as a typically developing child would.

In a 1998 study, Cheryl Councill, Mina Goodman, and I tried to determine when children with Down syndrome begin talking about past and future events, and when they begin using the appropriate verb endings. What we found was that many children with Down syndrome can remember and talk about past or future events around the age of three or four. For example, your child may have seen a parade on Saturday, and on Wednesday she says "band" or "clown." Or she may mention her upcoming birthday party or a family vacation you are planning to take to Disney World. However, most five-year-olds with Down syndrome are still not using the past tense of verbs when discussing past events *or* the –ing verb ending when talking about an ongoing action.

Some statistics for when the children with Down syndrome in our study formed past tense with –ed (such as adding –ed to "kiss" to form "kissed"):

- At age 2: 100% never
- At age 3: 93% never, 07% sometimes
- At age 4: 78% never, 19% sometimes, 3% often
- At age 5: 77% never, 18% sometimes, 5% often

Some statistics for when the children used the –ing ending:

- At age 2: 96.3% never, 3.7% sometimes
- At age 3: 73% never, 13% sometimes, 13% often
- At age 4: 61% never, 27% sometimes, 12% often
- At age 5: 52% never, 26% sometimes, 22% often

Conclusion

Studies and experience show that children and adults with Down syndrome can continue to expand their vocabularies throughout life. Vocabulary gets your message across; with an extensive vocabulary and intelligible speech, you can communicate your message even if you use short sentences or incorrect morphological endings. Speech and language treatment and inclusion in community expe-

riences, family outings, vacations, and religious activities can all contribute to vocabulary growth.

Your child's morphosyntax may not develop adequately without assistance through treatment (see Chapter 13). Children with Down syndrome need lots of models and practice opportunities to learn the grammatical structures, word order, and word endings. They are not likely to just learn by listening to speech in the environment. Morphosyntax needs to be taught, or at least the learning needs to be facilitated. A treatment program with home practice will help your children learn how to formulate grammatical sentences and also help her learn in school.

CHAPTER 8

Speech and Intelligibility Problems

Children with Down syndrome have a lot to tell us. But, many times, we cannot understand what they are saying due to difficulties with speech *intelligibility*. Intelligibility is the "understandability" of speech—that is, how easy or difficult it is for the listener to understand what the speaker is saying.

Being able to convey a message clearly so that the listener can understand it is important. It is frustrating to constantly have people ask, "Can you say that again? I didn't understand you." Parents share the frustration their child feels when they cannot understand what their child is trying to say. It is also difficult and worrisome when parents can understand their child but the school bus driver, teacher, or childcare person cannot. Parents feel helpless standing by watching their child's attempts and often step in to translate after a few tries. Parents also feel helpless when their child gives up. It is sad to watch your child give up when he had so much to say just a few minutes ago.

With increasing inclusion in school and in community life, as well as expanding opportunities for community interaction, intelligibility of speech becomes an extremely important issue. As your child's circle of friends, acquaintances, and co-workers becomes larger, he interacts with many more people who may have difficulty in understanding his speech. Intelligibility is important not only because it aids or hinders understanding of the person's message, but also because it plays a major role in our judgment of the speech, and sometimes in our judgment of the person's abilities. When a child with Down syndrome has trouble speaking understandably, listeners may underestimate his capabilities. Many people with Down syndrome have speech that makes them appear

less capable than they are. Many clinicians and researchers feel that some behavior problems in children with Down syndrome stem from the inability to be understood, resulting in frustration and acting-out behavior (Reichle & Wacker, 1993).

Some children with Down syndrome have intelligibility problems from an early age. Other children may not be difficult to understand when they are speaking in one- and two-word phrases. Later on, however, when they are having long conversations or trying to tell about something that happened at school, it may be more difficult to understand what they are saying. This chapter describes the speech problems that can affect children with Down syndrome of all ages, but only provides home activities for problem areas typically confronted by children ages six and younger. Intelligibility problems in older children will be addressed in a later volume.

How Is Intelligibility Judged?

Intelligibility is influenced by many different factors. A person's intelligibility is never consistent; it varies greatly from one situation to another and between listeners. It is not a static condition. Many children with Down syndrome are difficult to understand sometimes, especially when they are trying to tell you about something upsetting that happened to them. But, at other times and in other situations, such as when greeting their friends, their speech may be very understandable. So, your child's "intelligibility" is a subjective judgment or rating made professionally by a trained listener, usually a speech-language pathologist (SLP), but it is also a judgment that is made by all listeners, on a daily basis.

The factors that affect whether or not speech is understandable vary from child to child. Difficulty with speech intelligibility is a global diagnosis. If a child has a "speech intelligibility" problem, we do not know, just from that diagnosis how to help that child. Here are four children who are receiving speech and language services for "speech intelligibility":

- **Rebecca:** Rebecca speaks very quickly. She leaves off the sounds at the end of words, so you can't tell whether she is trying to say "two," "toot," or "tooth."
- **Joshua:** Joshua speaks very softly; you have to strain to hear him. He always sounds as if he has a cold or as if he is "stuffed up." It is difficult to understand what he is saying.
- **Ben:** Ben speaks slowly, stutters, and makes many errors on speech sounds. Sometimes, he repeats a word many times.
- **Karen:** Karen produces sounds inconsistently. Sometimes she can say /b/ and /f/ and other times she cannot. Karen also leaves out syllables, reverses sounds, and leaves off most final sounds in words.

Rebecca, Joshua, Ben, and Karen are each rated as having fair intelligibility, yet their speech is not at all similar. This global rating does not provide enough information to be helpful. Looking for and documenting the reason a child has trouble being understood provides a basis for successful treatment.

Speech Intelligibility Problems of Children with Down Syndrome

A variety of speech problems make it more difficult for children with Down syndrome to be understood. But if the specific speech problems affecting intelligibility can be identified, a great deal of information is available that can be applied to help improve intelligibility. For example, if your child is known to have weak tongue muscles, he can do exercises to strengthen those muscles. Much has been learned about the potential of people with Down syndrome to speak intelligibly and about the therapy and educational techniques to fully tap that potential.

You may encounter professionals and nonprofessionals who act as if your child's intelligibility problems are "part of Down syndrome." They may say, "Of course he has difficulty in being understood; he has Down syndrome." In fact, until the mid 1990s, speech intelligibility difficulties in people with Down syndrome were rarely discussed in the research literature and were rarely addressed in therapy, although parents saw evidence of the difficulties every day. In 1994, using a survey of families, I was able to document that speech intelligibility was a major problem for individuals with Down syndrome. Over 95 percent of the almost 1000 families responding reported that their children sometimes or frequently had difficulty being understood by people outside of their immediate circle.

Despite the prevalence of intelligibility problems among people with Down syndrome, none of them are exclusive to people with Down syndrome. All of the factors that might affect your child's intelligibility can also be found in children and adults without Down syndrome, and there is no one specific speech pattern that is characteristic of all children with Down syndrome.

Speech Problems Affecting Intelligibility

When we think of intelligibility, we usually think about the way children make the sounds. Many parents say, "If my child could only produce the sounds more clearly, people would understand him." *Articulation,* or the ability to produce the sounds of language, is an important factor in intelligibility, but there are many other factors that also need to be considered. Intelligibility is often thought of globally—as just a part of Down syndrome. Thinking about intelligibility in general terms is not helpful, however. It is important to address the *specific* speech, language, and conversational characteristics that influence whether your child can be understood. The box on the next page summarizes these areas, which are discussed in detail in the sections below. Bear in mind that different children have different combinations of these factors. It is highly unlikely that your child is struggling with all of these areas. It is likely that he experiences a combination of them.

Typically developing children are generally expected to have developed speech that is intelligible 100 percent of the time by four years of age (Weiss et al, 1981). It is rare for speech to be 100 percent intelligible for individuals with Down syndrome at any age, so the problem is *not* simply a delay in development.

Factors Affecting Intelligibility

- Anatomical factors
- Physiological factors
- Neurological functional patterns
- Perceptual speech symptoms
- Language factors
- Nonverbal factors
- External and situational factors

Anatomical and Physiological Factors

Clinicians and researchers have identified anatomical and physiological differences in individuals with Down syndrome that make speech difficult. That is, there can be differences in the *anatomy* or structure of the body (a small upper jaw, for example). And there can also be differences in the *physiology* or function of body parts (weak muscles in the palate, for example).

Anatomical differences may include:

- A high narrow palatal arch: that is, the roof of the mouth, or hard palate, is sometimes narrower and higher than usual, which can make speech sound more nasal.
- Irregular dentition: that is, the teeth often come in more slowly, perhaps in an unusual order, some teeth may be missing, and other teeth may be crowded. When there are spaces between teeth or teeth are crowded, it will make it more difficult to articulate sounds.
- An open bite: this occurs when the upper and lower teeth do not meet in the front. In this case, the child's tongue is likely to protrude through his teeth when he tries to make the /s/ sound, so when he tries to say "sun," it will sound like "thun."
- A small and narrow upper jaw: this may restrict movement of the tongue, making articulation more difficult.
- A relatively large tongue: that is, the tongue is usually a normal size, but because the mouth may be smaller than usual, the child's tongue may be somewhat crowded inside his mouth and have limited space to move. This will affect many speech sounds, including /t/, /d/, /s/, /n/, and /l/.

Physiological differences may include:

- Low tone (hypotonia) in the oral facial muscles. Hypotonia contributes to difficulty in articulation.
- Lax ligaments in the temporomandibular joint: that is, the tough bands of tissue holding the joint together are looser

than usual. (The temporomandibular joint (TMJ) is the area where the lower jaw meets the temporal bone in the skull, right in front of the ear.)

■ A tendency to develop otitis media with effusion (fluid in the ear) with subsequent fluctuating hearing loss. When a child's hearing is sometimes clear and sometimes muffled, he does not receive consistent information about how speech should sound, which will affect language learning. (See the next section for more information.)

Combined anatomical and physiological differences may include:

■ Enlarged tonsils and adenoids, with mild blockage of the nasal airways, in combination with low muscle tone of the muscles in the palate and the pharynx (back of the throat). This can result in *hyponasality*—sounding as if you are "stuffed up" when you speak.

■ Low muscle tone, mouth breathing (due to allergies, enlarged tonsils or adenoids, or other reasons), a relatively large tongue, and a relatively small jaw. Children with this combination of factors may habitually hold their mouth open and develop tongue thrusting (protruding the tongue when swallowing instead of moving it upward and backward). This can affect eating because food may be propelled out of the mouth and it can affect articulation, including the ability to produce the /s/ and /z/ sounds correctly. (See below.)

HEARING IMPAIRMENTS

Most of us learn the sounds of our language by hearing those sounds. The typically developing child will probably hear a word 2000 times or more before he uses that word in speech. Children with Down syndrome often need to hear a word even more times before they can say it. This can be difficult when a child has recurrent middle ear infections with fluctuating hearing loss—as many children with Down syndrome do. Ear infections complicate learning the sounds of the language, because your child may accurately hear the sounds at one time but not at another. He needs to hear the sounds frequently and consistently in order to learn them accurately.

As a parent, the best way you can minimize the effects of hearing problems on speech production is to seek prompt medical attention for ear infections, and to follow through on the physician's treatment plan. Sometimes when your child constantly has ear infections, it can get to the point where you feel that the ear infection is a very minor medical situation. You may feel that "it's just another ear infection." But "just another ear infection" can have a major impact on hearing and can further delay speech development. For example, children who have fluctuating hearing loss may not hear the final sounds in words such as "coat*s*," "walk*ed*," and "fel*t*" because they are typically said more softly. Consult Chapters 2 and 3 for information that you can use to help your child develop the auditory bases of language. Research has shown that hearing loss has a negative effect on speech and language development.

I think that some of the speech and language difficulties that people ascribe to Down syndrome are actually related to the fluctuating hearing loss that children experience. If your pediatrician does not seem to recognize the importance of doing anything about continued ear infections or doesn't seem concerned if he can't see the eardrum and determine whether or not there is fluid, ask for a referral to a pediatric otolaryngologist (ENT) or get a second opinion. ENTs have specialized equipment so that they can better view the ear through tiny or narrow ear canals. Remember, fluid in the ear can damage the middle ear bones over time or result in your child missing a critical language learning period if he is not hearing well.

TONGUE THRUST

Many children with Down syndrome have difficulty with tongue thrust—that is, with the tongue protruding and thrusting out of the mouth during eating, speaking, and other times. You may have been told that your child has a deviate swallow, a reverse swallow, myofunctional problems, or difficulties in orofacial myology. These terms all describe the same pattern of tongue thrust.

A speech symptom that often accompanies tongue thrust is the substitution of /th/ for /s/—for example, saying /thun/ for /sun/. This is sometimes referred to as an *interdental lisp*.

A tongue thrusting pattern can be diagnosed by the speech-language pathologist. It is then usually treated together by an orthodontist and speech-language pathologist working together. This is usually worked on later than the birth- to six-year-old period covered by this book.

Some parents have tried facial reconstructive surgery, specifically tongue reduction surgery, to improve their child's speech. In Israel, tongue reduction surgery is routinely performed for children with Down syndrome before the age of two years. Some research has found that this can help a child keep his tongue inside his mouth. Based on current research findings, however, it does not appear that tongue reduction surgery improves speech or articulation. Although tongue reduction surgery reduces the size of the tongue (the anatomy), it does not affect its function (the physiology). In my experience, the strength and mobility of the tongue muscles have the biggest impact on a child's speech, not the size of the tongue.

Any activity in the following sections that strengthens the tongue muscles and the lip muscles will help your child keep his tongue in his mouth and keep his lips closed. These exercises can include tongue touching and lip pursing. There are specific exercise programs that accompany myofunctional therapy, but those must be prescribed by a professional depending on your child's specific myofunctional pattern. Myofunctional therapy (also known as orofacial mycology) requires daily practice and relies on the child's conscious effort to change the tongue movement patterns. Therefore, therapy is often delayed until the child is committed to the program, often after ten to twelve years of age.

Neurological Functioning

For muscles to function smoothly, accurately, and in a coordinated manner, the various parts of the nervous system (brain, spinal cord, nerves) must communicate with one another well. The nervous system is also involved in processing and making sense of sensations such as pain, touch, position, and muscle tension experienced by the body. Any problems with neurological functioning (or how the nervous system works) can clearly affect speech.

Two better-known neurologically based problems that directly affect speech intelligibility in some individuals with Down syndrome include:

1. oral motor difficulty (*dysarthria*): a condition that affects the strength and precision of muscle movement, resulting in speech that sounds "thickened" or imprecise, and

2. motor planning difficulty (*childhood verbal apraxia* or *developmental apraxia of speech*): a condition that affects the ability to plan and sequence sounds for speaking.

In addition, hypotonia, especially in the oral area, is a proven contributing factor to difficulties in speech intelligibility. Difficulties in auditory perception and processing, as well as oral-sensory function (perceiving sensations in the mouth), also contribute to speech intelligibility problems.

LOW MUSCLE TONE

As earlier chapters discuss, children with Down syndrome frequently have hypotonicity or low muscle tone. Muscles in the facial area, as well as in the arms, legs, and neck may be floppier or more relaxed. When muscles in the lips, tongue, and cheeks have low tone, speech may sound imprecise, thickened, or slurred. Children might talk in shorter utterances because they are unable to sustain a breath long enough to say a whole sentence.

If your child has low muscle tone in the lips, tongue, and cheeks, his speech-language pathologist will work with him in therapy to improve his muscle tone and coordination. There are also some exercises that you can use with your child in the Home Activities section on pages 125-26.

AUDITORY PERCEPTION

Research has shown that children with Down syndrome have more difficulty with auditory perception or auditory processing than with visual perception or visual processing (Pueschel et al. 1987). That is, they can understand and make sense out of things they see better than things they hear. Moreover, they have specific difficulty on tasks in which they must discriminate and reproduce speech sounds. That makes it difficult for children to learn the sounds of the language solely through their sense of hearing. This is sometimes known as difficulty with the phonological loop. This difficulty is in addition to the impact that hearing loss may have on learning sounds.

Because of these difficulties, children with Down syndrome usually do not learn how to make sounds just from listening to the sounds adults make. It is often easier for children with Down syndrome to learn sounds through using visual models—that is, if adults make the sounds visible to them and help them to "pull" the sounds out of the environment. Using a mirror, using signs or gestural cues, and using written alphabet letter cues can help children learn how to make sounds. For example, you might point to your lips when you are showing your child how to make the /b/ sound. Or, you could use a mirror so that he can see that you make the /b/ sound by closing your lips.

ORAL MOTOR SKILLS/ DYSARTHRIA

The ability to produce speech sounds is also affected by the development and maturation of the nerves and muscles. Some children with Down syndrome have gaps in neurological development that make it harder to control and coordinate the complex movements needed for speech. For example, the words "*splash*" and "*sprinkle*" require complex movements. The difficulty may occur because certain infant reflexes that usually disappear in early childhood persist. It is believed that these "primitive" reflexes, such as the rooting reflex that makes a child open his mouth when an object such as a nipple comes near, interfere with higher levels of neurological development. Likewise, the inability to move one part of the mouth—such as the tongue or lips—without moving the whole body can also hinder development.

When a child has difficulty with oral motor skills, also known as dysarthria, he usually has difficulties with chewing and swallowing in addition to trouble articulating speech sounds. He may also have difficulty with other aspects of speech discussed later in this chapter, including voice, resonance, and fluency.

Children who have dysarthria are very consistent in the types of speech problems they have. For example, they may always mispronounce their name in the same way, or always run out of breath after saying three words. Generally, if the muscles can perform a task, they will work in approximately the same way each time, but if the muscles have difficulty performing a task, they will have consistent difficulty. Usually the difficulty is not linked to specific sounds. That is, it is not simply that a child has trouble with the /t/ sound, but that he has overall difficulties producing speech sounds. Dysarthria can improve with therapy and practice.

CHILDHOOD VERBAL APRAXIA

In contrast to dysarthria, childhood verbal apraxia is a motor programming problem, not a muscular problem. Children with apraxia, often called developmental verbal apraxia, developmental apraxia of speech (DAS), or pediatric verbal apraxia, have the physical ability to make the movements needed for speech, but have difficulty putting them into proper order. The muscles themselves are not affected, and there may be no difficulty in using the muscles for eating or swallowing.

Children who have childhood verbal apraxia are very inconsistent. One time, a child may be able to produce his cousin's name clearly; another time, he may have great difficulty. Typically, children with apraxia also make many sound reversals in their words. They might say "aminal" or "hopsital" or "efelant." They may be physically capable of producing all the speech sounds, but have trouble putting them in the proper sequence. When the speech-language pathologist tests for this problem, she usually asks the child to say multisyllabic words such as "hamburger," "elephant," or "hospital," or complex words such as "aluminum," "linoleum," or "statistics." As words get longer, children with motor programming problems such as apraxia start to have difficulty. So, a child might be able to say "light," but "lightning bug" may be difficult. Or "eel" might be fine, but "electricity" will be difficult.

Many children with Down syndrome appear to have difficulties with motor planning for speech. In a survey of over 1000 families that I conducted in 1994, 48 to 72 percent of parents reported that their children had signs of motor planning problems, including difficulty in sequencing sounds and making sound reversals and sound errors. The parents of younger children reported fewer problems; the parents of older children reported more problems, which is why there was such a range. This is probably because younger children are using shorter, less complex words, while older children are using longer phrases, sentences, and conversation.

Strangely enough, children with Down syndrome have historically not been identified as having childhood verbal apraxia. This is because early studies that identified and described the disorder included only individuals who demonstrated "normal intelligence," hearing within normal limits, and absence of muscle weakness or paralysis. The diagnosis of childhood verbal apraxia was not generalized beyond the original subject groups. Another problem is that children with Down syndrome often have oral motor difficulties such as feeding problems and low muscle tone, in addition to motor planning difficulties. Sometimes problems that are really due to apraxia are attributed to the oral motor difficulties alone. The bottom line is that assessment and treatment for childhood verbal apraxia has usually not been provided for children with Down syndrome.

In a recent survey of over 1500 families (Kumin, 2003), to determine whether apraxia is a widespread problem for individuals with Down syndrome, results confirm that children with Down syndrome are not being diagnosed with childhood verbal apraxia. Whereas 61 percent of the families had been told that their child had oral motor problems (such as low muscle tone in the facial muscles), only 16 percent of the parents had been told that their child had apraxia. (And those who were told that their child had apraxia were always given that diagnosis in conjunction with a diagnosis of oral motor problems. That is, no child with Down syndrome was diagnosed solely with childhood verbal apraxia.) And yet, even when parents had not been given a diagnosis of apraxia, survey responses often documented that the children were exhibiting many symptoms characteristic of childhood verbal apraxia. The survey also documented that children with Down syndrome who have apraxia tend to begin speaking at a later age (average five years) and have more difficulties with speech intelligibility than other children with Down syndrome.

Some current definitions of motor planning difficulties are beginning to include children with Down syndrome (Hall et al, 1993). Whether the motor planning difficulty in children with Down syndrome should or should not be labeled as childhood verbal apraxia, developmental apraxia of speech, etc. can be debated by others. My concern is that we learn more about the difficulties so that children with Down syndrome get the help they need.

CHARACTERISTICS OF APRAXIA

Childhood verbal apraxia is defined by a cluster of characteristics of speech. No one symptom must be present for a diagnosis, but having certain symptoms in combination leads to the diagnosis. The most frequently reported symptoms that differentiate this disorder from other speech disorders include:

- Struggling or groping when speaking or trying to speak. Your child seems to be working hard to talk, but the correct sounds are not coming out. Sometimes, you may even see him move his lips or tongue, but he is not saying the correct sounds.

- Inconsistency in sound and speech production. One time, he can say a sound or a word clearly, but at other times, he has great difficulty with the same sound or word.
- Less sound play (babbling and cooing) as infants. A tendency to use a small number of sounds. More vowels are used, without consonants attached, which makes the speech hard to understand.
- A difference in intelligibility between automatic, frequently used phrases and more spontaneous speech. He may say "I don't care" or "I don't know" very clearly but have great difficulty in spontaneous conversation or when asked for a specific answer to a question.
- Difficulty combining and sequencing phonemes. Your child may be able to imitate or produce individual sounds, but when he tries to combine them into words, he has difficulty, especially as the word gets longer or more complex. So, he can say "ham," but when he says "hamburger," it may come out as "hangurber." "Banana" may be "nabana." Sounds and syllables are frequently reversed. This reversal is known as *metathesis*.
- Decrease in intelligibility as utterance length increases. He has more difficulty with longer words and phrases. So, he may say "key" easily, but have difficulty with "mon*key*" or "mon*key* bars."
- Prosodic or rhythm difficulties. Your child may talk slowly or rapidly or have an uneven pace.
- Children with apraxia appear to understand (receptive language) more than they can produce (expressive language), but this is characteristic of most children with Down syndrome.

Although all children with apraxia show some difficulty in planning and sequencing motor speech behaviors, they have a wide variety of error patterns and a wide range of severity. Some children have a great deal of difficulty developing speech and are very delayed. Other children may not display any signs of difficulty until after they have developed speech, and only have difficulty when the task becomes more complex. Perhaps this is a reason why some children with apraxia are not diagnosed right away. The signs may be subtle.

HOME ACTIVITIES
Regular practice is critical for children with apraxia, and the SLP should provide a home practice program for you and your child to work on together. Here are examples of activities and strategies the SLP might suggest for you to use at home:

- Use singing and melody, especially songs with hand movements or songs with repeated choruses. The repetition will make it easier for your child.

- When you read with your child, use repetitive books or books with predictable phrases. *Chicken Soup with Rice; Four Furry Feet;* and *Are You My Mother?* are examples of this type of book. Children know what the repeated phrase is and can practice it in advance and say it in a singsong manner. If they cannot say the phrase, they can say some of the words. This will give them successful experiences saying words.

- During daily routines, use scripts and phrases that are repeated. For example: "Hi, how're you doing?" Or, "See you later." This will also provide successful experiences, and opportunities to practice familiar phrases.

- If your child is having difficulty speaking, never insist that he say a word in order to receive a reward or receive a desired item. Don't say, "I won't give you this ice cream until you ask for it."

- To promote communication when your child cannot speak, Total Communication using signs or picture communication systems can be used. You use speech and the sign or picture, but your child can respond using only the sign or picture, if necessary, to request things that he wants or to communicate with you in other ways. For children who are having difficulty speaking, this can cut down on frustration.

- Many of the therapy methods suggest helping children practice with slowed-down speech. You can slow down songs and sing them together with your child like a choir in slow motion. Or play *Time to Sing!*—a new CD that contains slowed-down versions of twenty-six popular children's songs that has been helpful for children with apraxia who want to sing along but can't sing the words at fast speeds. (See the Resource Guide.)

MOTOR SPEECH PROBLEMS AND CHILDREN WITH DOWN SYNDROME

In my experience, many children with Down syndrome exhibit symptoms of oral motor problems (dysarthria), some exhibit symptoms of apraxia, and some exhibit symptoms of both. Despite the lack of formal research into the incidence of dysarthria or developmental apraxia of speech in children with Down syndrome, there is no doubt that, when present, they affect speech intelligibility.

The movement components of speech production skills are developed through experience and practice. Early movements such as those involved in crying, sucking, and feeding are precursors to movements and skills needed in early speech production. For example, the sucking pattern that infants use provides practice for the movements that will be used later for

lip rounding and tongue retraction skills needed for certain speech sounds. If a child is not able to integrate all of the incoming sensory information, it will be difficult to organize and sequence the movements necessary for precise, articulate speech. It is necessary to process all incoming sensory input in order to develop the motor plans in the brain that are needed to make speech sounds, and those plans develop through experience.

In evaluating your child's speech, the speech-language pathologist should always consider whether intelligibility problems are complicated by dysarthria or verbal apraxia. Determining which of these problems is present is important because remediation techniques for the problems are very different. For some types of dysarthria, such as hypotonicity, it is important to use muscle strengthening exercises for the lips and the tongue, cheek, and jaw muscles. For apraxia or motor programming problems, it is important to use drill and repetition, with many visual-tactile cues. For example, the SLP might place her fingers on her lips when your child is learning the /p/, /b/, or /m/ sounds, or have your child touch the throat area when learning the /k/ and /g/ sounds. The bottom line is that therapy needs to be different for the two problems if the therapy is to be effective.

ORAL SENSORY FUNCTION

Children with Down syndrome may have many problems with oral sensory function (that is, with how the mouth perceives sensations). These problems can make it

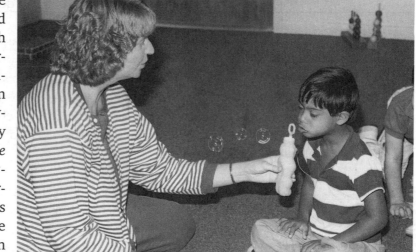

harder to gain the experience needed to learn speech movements. In particular, many children with Down syndrome have hypersensitive (overly sensitive or *tactile defensive*) or hyposensitive (undersensitive) reactions to touch around the mouth. Children who are hypersensitive do not like to be touched in or around the mouth. They don't like it when you brush their teeth or wash their face. Children who are hyposensitive get insufficient tactile feedback from their bodies, so they suck their fingers or jam their fingers back into their mouths. They like pacifiers and chewy toys and foods.

If your child is reluctant to explore things with his mouth or has reduced sensation in his mouth, he may have trouble feeling where his tongue is or whether his lips are open or closed. He may also not practice speech sounds enough to develop the feedback loops in his brain that will let him know if sounds "feel" right when he makes them. If your infant or toddler has difficulty with oral sensory skills, early speech intervention and home activities for practice can help him progress in oral sensory development.

HOME ACTIVITIES
For Promoting Oral Motor Strength and Coordination:

1. Look in a mirror together with your child and have fun moving your lips and tongue.
   - round your lips
   - blow kisses
   - smack your lips
   - smile and then pucker
   - say /oo/ as in "soup" and then /ee/ as in "meet"
   - frown
   - open your mouth wide
   - close your mouth tightly
   - reach for the sky with your tongue (move your tongue up as if to touch your nose)
   - lick your lips (try smearing peanut butter, jelly, or ice cream on your child's lips to encourage him to lick)
   - say "mmmm"
   - yawn
   - sigh

2. Do the same activities without the mirror. Look at each other when you make the sounds and then imitate each other.

3. Blow bubbles. For a long time, your child will not actually blow bubbles. It's the lip rounding that you're practicing first. The bubble blowing will start as your child gains additional breath control. Older children with Down syndrome can blow bubbles to delight younger siblings.

4. Whistles provide excellent practice for the lip rounding and lip compression needed for making sounds such as /p/, /b/, /m/, and /w/. When you begin practice, you will need a whistle with a large, round mouthpiece. If your child cannot seal his lips around the whistle, increase the circumference of the mouthpiece. This can be done in two ways: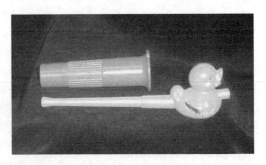
   - Take the rod out of a foam hair curler. Stretch the foam curler over the mouthpiece of the whistle.
   - Wrap a piece of sponge around the mouthpiece. Secure it around the mouthpiece.

To make practice more interesting, get a variety of intriguing types of whistles or horns. Some that we use in our center have miniature trains circling and a whistle with a slide. We use the Sara Rosenfeld-Johnson horn hierarchy; MORE whistle sets available from PDP Products; or whistles from Therapro. All are cited in the Resource Guide section. Play rhythms with the whistles, take turns blowing, or simply blow long and loud. The lip compression and lip rounding practice helps strengthen the lip muscles.

5. Use real or toy musical instruments such as harmonicas or kazoos for work on lip movements, as well as breath control. Try blowing the toy instrument yourself to be sure that it is not too difficult or frustrating to blow. Consult your SLP or a music teacher to determine which instruments might be beneficial and which instruments your child might be ready for. The recorder is an instrument that many children with Down syndrome play and enjoy.

6. For the older child, design a lip and tongue Olympics. Have events such as the activities used for mirror practice above. Add higher level activities. For example:
   - Hold your tongue up right behind your teeth for a count of ten.
   - See how high the coach (you) can count while your child holds his tongue up.
   - Round /oo/ and retract (smile) the lips alternately ten times.
   - Open your mouth a little, then a little wider, and then close.
   - Open and then close the mouth, increasing the number of times and increasing the speed.
   - Move the tongue from one corner of the mouth to the other.
   - Lick the entire perimeter of the lips (slowly and carefully).
   - Touch the outside of your child's cheek; have him move his tongue to that spot on the inside of his cheek.

   Award prizes for each event mastered, or use a checklist and check off each skill mastered. When your child has completed four events, award a ribbon or a special prize such as lunch or a movie together.

7. For children preschool age and older, design a "Make That Face" game board to help practice the movements. Opened manila folders make wonderful game boards and are easy to store. Use a spinner and game pieces. On selected spaces, draw in cartoons or pictures and instructions such as "Make a kissing sound with your lips." Another variation is to put the instructions on cards and have the game board spaces say, "Pick a red card" or "Pick a yellow card."

8. Use a hopscotch grid on the ground. In each square, place a card listing an activity involving the tongue or lips. Wherever the stone is thrown, everyone has to do what it says.

Perceptual Symptoms

When we listen to someone's speech, what do we hear? Is his speech very loud? Does he stutter? Does he substitute an /f/ sound for a /t/ or /th/? Does he leave off the final sounds in words (cat becomes /ca/)? These are called perceptual symptoms. This is a description of what the listener sees and hears when he listens to someone speak. With a young child who has limited speech, we may not hear all of these symptoms, but with an older child, rate and fluency difficulties will become more obvious. Perceptual symptoms may include:

- Articulation;
- Phonological Processes;
- Voice;
- Resonance;
- Rate of Speaking;
- Fluency; and
- Prosody.

ARTICULATION SKILLS

Articulation refers to the movements of the *articulators* to produce the sounds for speech. The articulators are the lips, tongue, upper and lower jaw, hard and soft palate, alveolar ridge (the gum ridge behind the teeth), and the teeth. When children have articulation difficulty, they have problems producing specific sounds.

The specific articulation errors that your child makes can affect intelligibility. For example, the more frequently the sounds he has trouble with occur in the language, the more his intelligibility will be affected. Think about game shows such as *Wheel of Fortune*. Why will contestants choose the "t" or "s" early in the round rather than the "m" or "z"? Because they want to choose a letter that occurs frequently in words to maximize the chance that it will be in the word or phrase they are trying to decode. Similarly, in speech, if you have difficulty making the /s/ sound, it will seem as if you have more of an articulation problem than if you have difficulty with the /y/ sound, because the /s/ sound occurs with higher frequency than /y/ in English. If a sound is mildly distorted (such as not producing /r/ or /l/ exactly correctly), the word will probably be easier to understand than if the sound is omitted.

Since articulation poses major problems for many children with Down syndrome, a large portion of the next chapter discusses specific articulation problems and what you can do about them. Articulation evaluation and treatment is discussed in greater detail in Chapters 12 and 13.

HOME ACTIVITIES

These are very basic activities to help your child develop foundation skills for articulation. See Chapter 9 for more suggestions.

- Give each sound a name. For example, /z/ is the "buzzing sound" or /p/ is the "motorboat sound." Play with a toy that makes that sound.

- For sound awareness, have a "sound" day. If it's /p/ day, have pizza for lunch, and pork, potato, pasta, and peas for dinner. Make popcorn, or have peanuts or potato chips as a snack. Go to the park or the party store and have a treasure hunt to name as many things as you can starting with the sound. Play Nerf ping pong as a family activity, and read a *Peanuts* book together. (This activity can be adapted for older children by varying the activities. For example, go to the video store or a game arcade and play games that have "p" in their titles.)

- Sometimes, older children can articulate a word accurately when it is said alone. For example, some children with Down syndrome can say the word "cake" alone, but have difficulty when that word is in a sentence such as "I want more cake." One way to practice making longer and more clearly articulated sentences is through using carrier phrases such as "I want more..." and the pacing board as described in earlier chapters. Use a pacing board with four circles, or have your child tap out a rhythm as he says the words. Point to each circle as you say, "I want more cake."

- If your child is having difficulty with multisyllabic words such as "railroad train" or "birthday cake," try having him practice words of similar length he *can* say while he pounds lightly on a drum. For example, "pancake house," "rock and roll," and "hamburger."

- Play a mirror imitation game. You say a word with the sound to be practiced while looking in the mirror. Your child keeps looking in the mirror and tries to say the word exactly the way you did. To keep the practice fun, make some words loud, others whispered, still others dramatic.

PHONOLOGICAL PROCESSES

As young children first develop speech, most use what are called "phonological processes." These are sound simplifications or substitution patterns children discover, usually on their own, that make their speech production easier. It enables them to make a variety of different sounds, even when they can't make all of the sounds. It is a step in learning sounds and the sound patterns (where do sounds go, what sounds can be combined, etc.) of their language. For example, a child may say /tootie/ instead of /cookie/ because he still can't make back sounds. Or he may leave off all of the final consonant sounds in words, saying /ca/ for both /cat/ and /cap/. At the same time, he may say /po/ for /pot/ and /to/ for /top/, proving that he is capable of saying the final consonants of cat and cap. So sometimes the problem is that he doesn't know when to use these sounds, not that he can't say them.

Usually, typically developing children do not use phonological processes beyond the age of five. Children with Down syndrome, however, often continue to use these simplifications much longer. Since this can have a major impact on intelligibility, a large portion of the next chapter is devoted to describing typical problems with phonological processes and to suggesting ways you can help.

VOICE Your child's voice quality, and the volume and pitch he uses when speaking can also affect intelligibility.

Voice Quality. Voice quality is how others perceive the sound of our voice. Your child's voice quality can affect the intelligibility of his speech. If people must focus on his voice when listening to your child speak, it will be more difficult for them to focus on his message. In children with Down syndrome, voice quality is often described as hoarse, rough, or breathy.

For voice difficulties, an examination by an otolaryngologist (ENT) is needed before any speech treatment begins. There may be medical reasons for the problem—such as allergies or anatomical differences in the larynx (voice box)—which would require medical treatment. Voice quality can also be related to low muscle tone, such as in the larynx or throat muscles. These muscles adjust the tension on the vocal bands as they vibrate.

Pitch. There have been conflicting findings about vocal pitch (how high or low the voice sounds) in the speech of individuals with Down syndrome. Generally, because listeners hear hoarseness in the voice of people with Down syndrome, they perceive that the pitch of the voice is low. However, studies of both children and adults with Down syndrome have found that they actually have higher fundamental frequencies (pitch) when they are speaking, not lower. Generally speaking, the range of pitches children and adults with Down syndrome are able to use is similar to the range used by people without Down syndrome.

Volume. To be intelligible, your child needs to speak at the appropriate volume level. The volume or loudness of your child's voice may be too loud, too soft, inconsistent and uncontrolled, or inappropriate to the occasion (for example, screaming in school). Often this is not due to respiratory or voice production difficulties, but related to the child's lack of awareness of volume.

Some children with Down syndrome speak very loudly or even scream. It is very important to teach children not to shout or scream constantly because this can result in damage to the vocal mechanism. This problem is not unique to children with Down syndrome; many typically developing children shout to the point of needing voice therapy.

Usually when children with Down syndrome have difficulty with volume, it is because they are speaking too softly, rather than too loudly. Sometimes problems with volume can be traced to a physical condition. For example, a child who has fluctuating hearing loss because of recurrent ear infections may have trouble monitoring his own volume. Or a child with low muscle tone may not have the breath support to speak loudly. If your child has difficulties with volume, the first step is therefore to consult an otolaryngologist (ENT)—a physician who specializes in the diagnosis and treatment of conditions in the ear, nose, and throat. If there is a problem such as lack of sufficient breath to produce adequate loudness, that must be addressed by your child's doctor and speech-language pathologist.

Usually there is no underlying physical cause for chronic low speech volume. Low volume may be related to lack of confidence, lack of experience, or overcompensating when trying not to shout. In addition, your child's volume may be inconsistent, or he may not modulate his volume appropriately to the environment. Volume needs to be adjusted for the size of the room, the setting (outdoors or indoors), and the number of communication partners and their ages and abilities. For example, it is appropriate to speak loudly or shout when playing dodge ball on the playground with other children, but not at the movies. So, what your child may really need to learn is *when* to be loud and when to use a quiet voice. This is best taught at home and in the community in real-life situations. At home, you can let your child know that you are having difficulty hearing him and that he needs to speak more loudly. You can let him know when you are on the phone and he needs to use a soft voice. You can also discuss and practice different situations. Practice may be all that is needed to increase or decrease his volume.

Failing to use appropriate volume is a problem many "typically developing" children experience. If you have found a method for helping your other children learn when to be loud and when to be soft, it will likely work for your child with Down syndrome.

HOME ACTIVITIES

- Talk about loud and soft voices. Label voices as your "inside" and "outside" voices. Practice using a loud voice (in a tunnel so you can hear the echo) and a soft voice (from a whisper to a quiet voice).

- Comment on loud and soft noises in the environment. For example, when you hear the lion at the zoo, comment on the loud roar. Listen to quiet sounds in the environment, such as water dripping and birds chirping, and comment on them.

- Talk about places where you need to use a soft voice, such as at school or church, and places where you can use a loud voice, such as at baseball or hockey games or on a roller coaster. This is most helpful if you can talk about loudness/softness immediately before your child will encounter the situation.

- Read books about whispering and loud and soft sounds. Some favorite books for talking about volume include:
  - *Mr. Brown Can Moo, Can You?* by Dr. Seuss,
  - *Noisy Nora* by Rosemary Wells,
  - *SHHH!* by Suzy Kline,
  - *Noisemakers* by Judith Caseley,
  - *Helen and the Great Quiet* by Rick Fitzgerald,
  - *The Quiet Noisy Book* by Margaret Brown, and
  - *The Very Quiet Cricket* by Eric Carle

- Other books that focus on voice that can help you in discussing voice with children are :
  - *The Three Billy Goats Gruff,*
  - *Hester* by Bryon Barton,
  - *Mice Squeak, We Speak* by Tomie DePaolo,
  - *I Am Phoenix: Poems for Two Voices* by Paul Fleischman,

- ○ *Joyful Noise: Poems for Two People* by Paul Fleischman
- ○ *Hattie and the Fox* by Mem Fox
- ○ *I Unpacked My Grandmother's Trunk* by Susan Hoguet
- ○ *Hiccup* by Mercer Mayer

● Play games where your child has to use a loud or soft voice or a whisper. "Telephone" is a good game to use, but remember to keep the messages short. Several children stand in a line. The first child whispers a message in the ear of the next child in line, and so on down the line. The last child has to repeat the message he heard and compare it to the message the first child sent.

● When your child has learned how to control volume, but doesn't remember to do so, use a sign at home as a reminder, such as a cartoon that shows Barney holding his hand behind his ear and saying "Speak Up" or Barney holding his finger on his lips as in "Sh-h-h." Or when away from home, agree on a signal, such as a thumbs up for "speak up" and closing and opening your hand for "speak more softly."

RESONANCE (ORAL/NASAL BALANCE)

Resonance refers to how full and vibrant a voice sounds, the tone of the voice. When someone sounds as if they are all stuffed up or "twangy," you are noticing the quality of vocal resonance. When you hear an announcer and his voice sounds rich and full, you are hearing resonance and voice quality at work. In the English language, all sounds except /m/, /n/, and /-ng/ (as in "ring") are resonated in the oral cavity (mouth), not the nasal cavity (nose). For a child to have normal resonance, he needs a clear nasal pathway for the nasal sounds (/m/, /n/, and /-ng/) and adequate muscle function to close off the nasal passage when the air should be resonating in the mouth for sounds like /b/ and /d/.

Many children with Down syndrome have resonance problems. The most common are *hyponasality,* or decreased nasal resonance, and *hypernasality*, or increased nasal resonance.

HYPONASALITY

If your child has allergies or enlarged tonsils and adenoids, he may breathe through his mouth. As a result, sounds may never be resonated through his nasal cavity. He will sound stuffed up, as if he has a perpetual "cold." This is known as hyponasal resonance or hyponasality. When the conditions causing the hyponasality are treated, the hyponasality should improve as well. An otolaryngologist (ENT) can diagnose and treat the medical conditions that may underlie resonance problems, such as swollen adenoids.

HYPERNASALITY

Your child may resonate too many sounds through the nasal cavity if he has a short velum (soft palate area), a high palatal vault, or *velopharyngeal insufficiency* (difficulty using the soft palate and throat wall muscles to seal off the nasal cavity to keep air/sounds out of the nose, and to send air through the mouth). This is known as hypernasality. With hypernasality, your child's speech would sound "twangy."

The speech-language pathologist can give your child muscle strengthening exercises to help him improve velopharyngeal closure. If the hypernasality is severe and affects intelligibility, it may be necessary to seek treatment from a maxillofacial or cleft palate team. These teams are usually made up of dental, medical, and speech specialists. They might prescribe a speech appliance, similar to a dental bridge, that would make velopharyngeal closure easier. Or they might recommend pharyngeal flap surgery, which also aids in the closure. Maxillofacial and cleft palate teams are usually located in university hospitals, children's hospitals, and dental schools. Your pediatrician should be able to refer you to one in your area.

Sometimes, you can hear both hypo- and hypernasality in a child's speech. It is always important to have a full medical ENT (ear, nose, and throat) evaluation to examine causes for some of these conditions before a treatment plan is developed.

THE EFFECTS OF SURGERY ON RESONANCE

Any surgical procedure such as a tonsillectomy or adenoidectomy that removes tissue in the mouth, nose, or throat area can affect the resonance of speech. Consequently, any time otolaryngological surgery is being considered for your child, the possible impact on resonance should be considered carefully.

If your child has normal resonance before surgery, it is possible that he will sound hypernasal following surgery and may require a period of speech therapy to train the muscles for velopharyngeal closure. If your child has hyponasality before surgery, the resonance will probably sound normal after surgery because air is now able to resonate through his nasal cavity for the /m/, /n/, and /ng/ sounds. But, if your child has hypernasality before surgery, it is possible that this hypernasality will increase following surgery. This is because the swollen tonsils and adenoids provided a bulky, large surface for closure. The muscles didn't need to move far, because they could easily close off the nose. That's why your child sounded "stuffed" or hyponasal. Following surgery, the muscles move in the way that they are accustomed, but the swollen tissue is not there to help your child achieve closure. So, the muscles need to learn to move farther and stretch more. They may do that on their own, or your child may need an exercise program to help.

If your physician recommends tonsillectomy or adenoidectomy for your child, request that a speech-language pathologist be included on the team to determine whether follow-up therapy or other intervention will be needed. Although the need for surgery is a medical decision, the possible effects on speech should not be ignored. And, the pre-operative speech should be documented, in the event that therapy is needed after surgery.

RATE

The rate of speech, or how fast we talk, is an important factor in whether we can be easily understood. Children with Down syndrome may have a rapid rate, slow rate, or uneven and changing rate of speech. Rate patterns have not been documented in the literature. In my experience as a speech-language pathologist, I have found that children with Down syndrome often speak rapidly or in spurts.

They may start out at a comfortable rate for the listener, but often speed up as the conversation progresses. Fast or spurted rate may result in slurred or difficult-to-understand speech because there are no pauses between words, and words tend to run into each other. If your child has trouble speaking at an appropriate rate, there are a variety of activities you can try at home.

HOME ACTIVITIES

- A pacing board may be used to help your child develop a more regular rhythmic pattern. Chapter 6 describes pacing boards in detail. Using a pacing board frequently helps slow down speech. If your child is typically using five words, the pacing board would have five circles or five stickers. Your child would put his finger on the first circle as he said the first word, the second circle as he said the second word, and so on. This acts as a visual reminder to speak more rhythmically.

- Lightly beat a drum as your child speaks and have him try to match his speech rate to the drum. For example, have your child practice saying a phrase such as "Hi! How are you? I'm fine. Bye now!" to the accompaniment of a drumbeat. You can also use a metronome for this type of practice.

- Have conversations with your child in which each of you sings your words to a musical rhythm. You can use a song that your child already knows or make up a different tune. You can use slow and fast songs. For example, you and your child would sing, "Good morning. I'm glad to see you. Have a good day." When your child can do this slowly and rhythmically, the "singing" can gradually be phased out. You can also sing to a specific rate and rhythm using a metronome and a specific tune. These types of activities are used with a melodic intonation therapy approach.

- Talk about slow and fast speech and demonstrate slow and fast speech. Play a game in which you say sentences or read a story while your child moves a car along a toy road. When you speak slowly, he moves the car slowly. When you speed up, he should make the car speed up. When this activity becomes familiar, have your child repeat phrases after you, and move the car along at the speed of speech. This activity can be varied with a toy horse on a trail or a toy boat on a river.

- Read the story of *The Tortoise and the Hare*, and talk about slow and fast. You can say a rhyme or sing a song very fast and very slow. You can set up a racetrack with a NASCAR toy car and a very slow moving car and talk at that rate as you play with the cars and race them.

The Motor Boat Activity

Here's a home activity that can be used to introduce language concepts of movement and speed and can easily be adapted as your child grows. Recite the following poem with accompanying body movements geared to your child's age.

Motor boat, motor boat, go so slow.
Motor boat, motor boat, go so fast.
Motor boat, motor boat, step on the gas.

When your child is a baby, hold him securely in your arms. When the motor boat goes slowly, walk slowly or move slowly in a circle. When the motor boat goes fast, circle or walk more quickly. When the jingle says to step on the gas, speed up quickly. This activity can be adapted as your child gains more motor, play, and receptive language skills. When your child begins to walk, you can hold his hands and circle together at a slow or quick speed as indicated in the jingle (similar to "Ring Around the Rosy"). You and your child can also pretend to be motor boats in the pool, or move toy boats around to the rhyme during bath time.

FLUENCY

Fluency refers to the smoothness of speech—how easily one sound flows into the next sound, one syllable flows into the next syllable, and one word flows into the next word. Problems with fluency are sometimes referred to as stuttering. Children who stutter may have repetitions (*clonic blocks*) or periods of silence in which they seem to be struggling to emit a sound (*tonic blocks*).

Stuttering or dysfluency is more prevalent in people with Down syndrome. At present, the best estimates are that approximately 45 to 53 percent of people with Down syndrome stutter (Devenny and Silverman, 1990; Preuss, 1990). Sometimes there are fluency difficulties as the child is developing language. But, more frequently, dysfluency does not become evident until the child is using longer phrases and sentences and more complex language. So, we may not see evidence of fluency difficulty in children from birth to six years.

There is no conclusive data to determine whether fluency problems in children with Down syndrome are related to a neurological or cognitive problem or to a respiratory, motor, or airflow problem. Fluency problems often occur together with rate problems; children who speak rapidly may also demonstrate difficulties in fluency.

If your child has fluency problems, it is important not to draw attention to them. This will only increase tension in the muscles used for speaking and breathing and make fluent speech more difficult. Drawing attention to fluency problems may also make your child avoid speaking. In general, you should maintain eye contact, be very patient, and listen to what your child is saying. Don't fill in the words that are giving him difficulty and don't tell him to slow down. Let him know that you will continue to listen to him until he is finished.

Fluency problems are complex and need to be treated by a speech-language pathologist. He or she will suggest home activities appropriate to the specific type of fluency problems your child has. Evaluation and treatment of fluency problems are discussed in later chapters.

PROSODY Prosody is the general term for the rhythm of speech. Prosody includes how pitch and inflection are used to convey meaning. For instance, in English the voice generally goes up at the end of the sentence for a question and down for a statement. Sometimes, you may hear your child having a play conversation with his toy phone or his teddy bears. He sounds as if he is having a real conversation even though there are no real words. That is because your child understands and is using the prosody of the language correctly. Sid Caesar, the comedian, is a master at using the prosody of foreign languages so well that it sounds as if he is speaking the language, even though he is not.

Prosody in children with Down syndrome is another one of those areas that has been neglected by researchers. However, I have observed that prosody is often difficult for children with Down syndrome, especially as they become capable of longer sentences. They may emphasize the wrong word in a sentence or speak in something of a monotone. Also, as is true for the rest of us, some children with Down syndrome may have more difficulties speaking with expression in some situations (such as when they are nervous) than in other situations (at home with family).

HOME ACTIVITIES
- Help your child learn more about the musicality of language by singing words as a game, as if you were in an opera. So, sing "Good morning. How are you?" That emphasizes the inflection and rhythm.

- Play a game where you pretend to be a robot or alien that speaks in a monotone on one pitch (or use a puppet). Your child's job is to teach you to speak more like a human. For example, you say, "May I have the ball?" robotically. Your child models, "May I have the ball?" with the pitch going up at the end. He doesn't give you the ball until you imitate his model correctly.

- Use the same words with varying inflections, such as for a question and an answer. For example, you ask, "Ice cream?" Your child needs to respond, "Ice cream" with the inflection of a statement if he wants some. If he says it as a question modeling you, you say, "Well, do you want ice cream?" Or, you ask, "tickle?" and your child needs to respond with the affirmative statement "tickle" if he wants to be tickled. Then change roles. Your child asks, "Bubbles?" and you say, "Bubbles" and begin blowing the bubbles.

Language Factors

Up to this point, we have been discussing factors related to the mechanics of speech that can affect your child's intelligibility. That is, we have been focusing on *how* your child speaks and the ways that can affect understandability. But your child's intelligibility can also be affected by *what* he says—by the content of his speech. For example, if your child is sending a social message or a greeting that is expected, it will probably be easier to understand than if he is trying to explain something that happened at preschool that you didn't witness. The higher the unfamiliarity of the message and the more complex the message, the more difficult it will probably be to understand.

Pragmatic language (language in use) factors will affect intelligibility, because they affect whether the message can be understood on a language meaning level. Pragmatics is discussed in detail in Chapter 10, but includes such areas as conversational skills, greetings, and other interactional language. One of the pragmatic areas that directly affects intelligibility is *topicalization*, which includes the ability to stay on a topic and to switch topics appropriately. Many children with Down syndrome wander from the main topic of a discussion or conversation. This makes it more difficult for the listener to follow the conversation and to understand what the speaker is saying, if he has speech intelligibility problems.

Two other language factors that can affect intelligibility are conversational skills and narrative discourse—the ability to retell a story or describe an event. Since conversational and narrative discourse skills involve longer, more complex language output, it may be more difficult to understand what the child with Down syndrome is trying to say. Most children with Down syndrome in the target age of this book (ages six and younger) will probably not have intelligibility problems of this nature since their conversational and narrative discourse skills will be more basic at this age. These issues will be discussed in another volume for children with more advanced communication skills.

Nonverbal Factors

Even if a child has problems with speech intelligibility, there are a variety of nonverbal strategies he can use to help get his message across. Nonverbal factors that match the message that is being communicated increase intelligibility, while those that are at odds with the message decrease intelligibility. For example, if I say, "I'm really happy" and I am smiling, my message is easier to understand than if I say, "I'm really happy," but I am frowning and look sad. Usually, individuals with Down syndrome use appropriate facial expressions and gestures. Nonverbal factors that enhance intelligibility include:

- looking at your communication partner;
- using gestures to help make your message clear;
- using facial expressions consistent with your message (smiling when you are happy, frowning when you are upset);
- keeping the distance between conversational partners appropriate to their age and level of familiarity (for example, not standing too close to someone who is unfamiliar).

Eye contact is sometimes a problem for children with Down syndrome. Many children look down or look away from the person with whom they are conversing. When you look at someone, they know that you are speaking to them and they become more attentive and listen to what you are saying. When you are not look-

ing at them, intelligibility is affected because they may not pay attention to, or listen to, you. Eye contact can be worked on in therapy and in a home program.

Proxemics refers to the use of distance and space in conversations. What is appropriate varies from country to country and from culture to culture. If distance is inappropriate, it will distract the listener, perhaps decreasing intelligibility. Children with Down syndrome often stand too close to others. Proxemics can be worked on in therapy through role playing and the use of floor markers for appropriate distances. It can also be addressed through a home-based treatment program.

A detailed discussion of nonverbal communication is included in Chapter 10

External and Situational Factors Affecting Intelligibility

Intelligibility can change from one situation to another. Some factors that may affect intelligibility at any moment include:

- how well the listener knows the speaker;
- whether the listener is familiar with the topic;
- whether the speaker is calm or upset;
- whether the topic is in context and whether there are environmental cues;
- whether the environment is quiet or noisy; and
- whether there are visual distractions in the environment.

Intelligibility is affected by the speaker, the listener, the message, and the situation. Generally, if the topic is familiar and the context is a discussion in a quiet environment with lots of environmental cues, the speaker will be more intelligible than if the same speaker is talking softly on an unfamiliar topic to a large group of people with background noise and poor visibility. For example, if your child is talking about making a snowman and having hot chocolate and marshmallows while you are building the snowman or immediately afterwards, the environment has lots of cues that support the message and help you understand what he is saying. If he starts talking about snowmen when you are in the car driving to the beach for summer vacation, the cues are not there. When he talks to you at home about events that occurred at home during the weekend, there are more cues than when he talks about something that happened at school that you have no knowledge of. It is the same situation when he tries to tell his teacher about something that happened at home.

The speaker's emotional state can also affect intelligibility. When you are excited, frightened, angry, or anxious, clear intelligible speech may be more difficult to produce. Perhaps you have had the experience of trying to understand your child when he is trying to tell you about an upsetting event that happened at school. He was upset, and there were no environmental cues. Even though you know your child well, you did not know what happened and so you didn't know what questions to ask or if the answers were correct. Communication is more difficult at those times.

When situational factors prevent you from understanding your child, the most important thing to do at that moment is to reassure him that you *want* to understand him. You might suggest that he show you what he's trying to say by having him use gestures, show you an object, or draw a picture. If your child often wants to say things that you can't understand, make sure you read about AAC in Chapter 11.

The More Familiar, the More Intelligible

The listener's familiarity with a speaker's speech pattern is one influence that always affects speech-language pathologists as well as parents. Once we get to know a child and become familiar with his speech patterns, it becomes very difficult to judge the intelligibility of his speech. The speech appears more intelligible to us, because it is more intelligible "to us." We are no longer unfamiliar listeners, but familiar listeners who can understand the speech. This is true for speech that is mildly to moderately difficult to understand. When speech is extremely difficult to understand, even the familiar listener, or the most familiar listener, the parents, may have difficulty.

Clearly, how familiar the listener is with the speech patterns of the speaker will influence intelligibility judgments. This is one reason that intelligibility evaluations are not reliable. Intelligibility is relative. If someone who is completely unfamiliar with your child rates his intelligibility, he will probably understand less than most people in your child's environment. But if someone who knows your child well assesses his intelligibility, he will understand more than someone who is meeting your child for the first time. See Chapter 12 for an in-depth discussion of other issues in intelligibility evaluations.

Increasing Speech Intelligibility

When your child is beginning to speak, it is important to encourage all of his attempts. The chapters on the one- to three-word language stages, therefore, suggest that you respond to the *meaning* of what your child is saying without correcting his speech. You should, however, always provide a correct model for your child. Generally, the right time to begin correcting speech errors is when you know that your child can successfully correct the sound. If he knows how to say the sound correctly, it is fine to comment and correct him. If he would be unable to self-correct, it is not a good idea to correct him.

During any speech-motor practice activities, the movement *and* the sound can be corrected. For example, if you are looking in a mirror with your child and rounding your lips to say "oo," you can comment on your child's movement. ("Let's make our lips into a big round circle.") Another appropriate time to correct your child's speech production is when he can sometimes make a sound correctly, but at other times has difficulty. For instance, he can say "run" correctly but says "wabbit" for "rabbit." Make up a game in which you combine the words "run rabbit" and practice with him. You can also correct your child if he sometimes leaves out a sound in a word but at other times says it correctly. For example, he might say "po" sometimes and "pop" at other times. You can then remind your child to say the end sound in the word.

People with Down syndrome can continue to improve their intelligibility all their lives. And they (and their parents) are usually motivated to keep working on speech so that they can be understood by their friends and later by coworkers. You can help your child develop clearer speech by not getting too accustomed to speech errors that you—but only you—can understand. That is, even if *you* understand him when he leaves out syllables, leaves off sounds, slurs sounds together, or talks too fast, it is still important to have him work on those words/sentences so he doesn't get into careless habits. Other family members should also be instructed not to settle for less than your child's best speech production. It is a good idea to check periodically with teachers, acquaintances, and other people who don't know your child that well to see what they are able to understand and what aspects of his speech are difficult for them to understand.

While trying to improve your child's intelligibility, it is also important not to frustrate or humiliate him with corrections. Be discreet about correcting him in public. For example, don't make him keep repeating his order over and over for the waitress if you can understand him but she can't. In addition, bear in mind that speech will often deteriorate when you are tired or sick, and everyone has times when they don't feel their best. As much as possible, work on speech in quiet, fun, and loving ways, so that your child will want to be understood and will work hard to always use his best speech.

As long as your child receives speech and language therapy, the speech-language pathologist can continue to work with him on intelligibility, as well as to suggest home activities and recommendations about how and when to correct your child at home. Chapter 13 provides information about various therapeutic approaches the speech-language pathologist may use to improve intelligibility.

CHAPTER 9

Articulation and Phonology: Learning the Sounds of the Language

The previous chapter gave an overview of all the factors that can affect speech intelligibility in children with Down syndrome. This chapter takes a more in-depth look at the two factors that often have the biggest impact on intelligibility and sound making: articulation and phonology.

As you may recall, articulation refers to the physical process of producing speech sounds—for example, how the tongue elevates and touches the alveolar ridge on the roof of the mouth to make the /t/ sound. Therapy for articulation is concerned with teaching your child to physically form the sounds correctly. In contrast, phonology refers to the way sounds are organized in a language to form words and how children learn about those sounds. Phonology looks at patterns of sound errors, such as whether your child can pronounce the /t/ sound, but habitually leaves it off the ends of words. Therapy for phonology is concerned with teaching your child to perceive and improve problems with her own sound patterns.

In my experience, young children with Down syndrome usually have difficulties with phonology and articulation. They are likely to progress in the area of phonology, especially as they become aware of correct and incorrect sound patterns through treatment and practice. Articulation is more difficult because it is related to anatomical and physiological factors (such as underbites or problems coordinating muscles), and is complicated by oral motor and motor planning difficulties. It's important for parents and SLPs to understand and identify the differences between articulation and phonology for the child, so they can target their activities appropriately to help with both areas.

Articulation in Children with DS

Articulation is a significant concern for most individuals with Down syndrome, and these articulation difficulties definitely affect whether speech can be understood. Surprisingly, there has been little research on the underlying causes of those problems and how best to help child with Down syndrome in the area of articulation. What *is* known is that:

- ■ *There is a high incidence of articulation problems.* One researcher found that approximately 95 percent of children with Down syndrome have articulation problems (Dodd, 1970).
- ■ *More errors are made on consonants than vowels.* In one study, adolescents with Down syndrome made significantly more errors in articulating consonants in words than did adolescents with mental retardation due to other causes (Rosin et al. 1988). In another study of four children with Down syndrome, over 90 percent of the sound errors were on consonant sounds (Stoel-Gammon, 1980). In this study, children with Down syndrome did not have difficulty with vowel sounds.
- ■ *More errors are made on sounds that typically develop later (e.g., /s/ or /r/)* (Van Borsel, 1996). See the section on developmental norms below for information on the ages that sounds typically develop.
- ■ *Often, speech errors are inconsistent.* That is, sometimes a particular child can produce the sound correctly in one word, but not in another word.
- ■ *More articulation errors are made as words get longer.*
- ■ *More articulation errors are evident in conversations than in single words* (Kumin, 2002; Kumin & Adams, 2000; Stoel-Gammon, 1980).

Some of these patterns of articulation difficulties may be due to underlying problems in sequencing the movements needed for speech. If so, a diagnosis of childhood verbal apraxia may be appropriate (see Chapter 8). Other times, articulation difficulties are the result of one or more of the causes discussed in the next section. Whatever the cause, however, articulation errors affect whether or not your child's speech is understandable to listeners and are therefore important to identify and treat.

Causes of Articulation Difficulties

In children with Down syndrome, articulation disorders can occur due to faulty placement, timing, direction, pressure, speed, or coordination of the movement of the lips, tongue, velum (soft palate), jaw, or pharynx. These difficulties may arise as the result of several factors, including many of the same factors that affect intelligibility in general and are described in Chapter 8:

- ■ hearing loss and middle ear fluid accumulation,
- ■ auditory perception difficulties,
- ■ anatomical and physiological differences,

- oral sensory function,
- oral motor function,
- motor planning skills.

In addition, differences in early sound play may contribute to articulation difficulties in particular.

EARLY SOUND PLAY

All children need time to practice making speech sounds. They do this, as they develop, by playing with sounds, cooing, and babbling strings of sounds. Sound play is reflexive in the beginning, but comes to depend more and more on the sounds that children hear around them. Later, they begin to repeat and imitate sounds. This sound play occurs during the first six months to one year in typically developing children. Practicing sounds and movements sets up touch and movement feedback loops so that a sound "feels" right. This sound practice helps "pro-

gram" the muscles and articulators (lips, tongue, teeth, hard palate, soft palate, upper and lower jaw). It appears to establish patterns of movement so that articulation becomes almost automatic. We can then just make the sounds; we don't have to think about making each sound.

Children with Down syndrome may need more practice and more time to practice sound making. What often happens during this early period in the child's life is that medical issues take precedence, with cardiac and other surgeries needed. So, the child is in a situation where she may not be able to practice making sounds. She may not even be able to practice the feeding movements that help develop speech movements if she needs to be tube-fed. In addition, hearing loss and fluid in the ear, as well as any hyper- or hyposensitivities to touch in the mouth, can also make it less likely that a child will get enough sound-making practice. Usually, when a baby repeats sounds in babbling, it is pleasurable for her. But, if she doesn't hear the sounds consistently, she is less likely to continue to repeat those sounds.

Studies have found that babbling and reduplicated canonical babbling ("bababa") are similar in young children with Down syndrome and typically developing children, in terms of age of onset, vowels, and place of articulation for consonants. In addition, at least one study on early sound development and production has found similar patterns of development for vowels and consonants during the first fifteen months of age (Smith & Oller, 1981). However, in a study that I conducted with colleagues at Loyola College, we found a wide age span in sound development in children with Down syndrome.

In our study, we found that the emergence of phonemes (speech sounds) in children with Down syndrome followed the same general order as speech sound development in typically developing children. But some children were using many consonants in their sound play at age one and other children were just beginning to produce individual sounds at age eight (Kumin, Councill, & Goodman, 1995). In a recent survey study, I was able to discover some factors that were related to early or later sound development. Children who show patterns of childhood verbal apraxia, or a combination of oral motor difficulties and childhood verbal apraxia, were more likely to have difficulty developing speech. They showed a pattern of delays in speech and later development of speech sounds. Children who had low muscle tone alone (oral motor difficulties), however, were not significantly delayed in speech onset (Kumin, 2002).

Understanding Sounds and Sound Errors

To truly understand the nature of any articulation problems your child may have, it helps to understand how speech sounds are described and analyzed.

Each individual sound in a language is known as a *phoneme*. Different languages have different phonemes and may include sounds produced in different ways. For instance, speakers of some languages trill the /r/ sound or make clicking noises that aren't present in English. In English, sounds are made with the lips, teeth, tongue, palate (hard and soft, known as the velum) and upper and lower jaw moving toward or away from each other to produce each sound. These structures are known as the *articulators*. Articulation is the process of moving the articulators to produce the sounds of speech.

When phonemes are written, the phonetic alphabet is used and the phonemes are written between slashes. For example, /p/, /b/, /k/, /l/ are phonemes. Some phonetic symbols are the same as the alphabet letters, but others use phonetic symbols that are not letters, e.g., /ʃ/ is *sh* as in *sh*oe and /ð/ is *th* as in *th*is. If phonetic symbols are used when you get a report of articulation test results, ask the SLP to give you a sample word for the sound, e.g., /tʃ/ is *ch* as in *ch*op.

There are several different systems for describing and analyzing sounds in English. Rather than individually describe how each sound is produced, speech-language pathologists have created systems for grouping sounds, so that we are able to see the factors sounds have in common, and systems for analyzing the sound patterns produced by a child or adult.

The most common systems for describing sounds and analyzing sound patterns for articulation are:

- sound by sound analysis,
- distinctive features analysis (including place/manner/ voicing analysis),
- developmental norms.

SOUND BY SOUND ANALYSIS

When the speech-language pathologist listens to your child's articulation and analyzes the errors, she will often use a sound by sound analysis. She will evaluate how your child articulates each speech sound at the beginning, in the middle, and at the end of words. (These are referred to as *initial, medial,* and *final* positions.) For each sound that is incorrectly articulated, she will determine whether your child is:

- omitting the sound *(omission)* – for instance, saying /do/ for dog;
- replacing the sound with another sound of English *(substitution)* – for instance, saying /tootie/ for cookie or /fum/ for thumb;
- replacing the sound with a variation of the sound or a distortion that is not another English sound *(distortion)* – for instance, producing a lateral lisp when attempting to make the

/s/ sound (sending the air over the sides of the tongue rather than down the center of the tongue);

- adding a sound—for instance, saying /glass/ for gas.

Identifying the articulation errors in this way will enable the SLP to choose sounds to work on in treatment. See Chapter 13 for information on the different types of articulation therapy.

DISTINCTIVE FEATURES ANALYSIS

The individual sounds of any language are composed of distinctive features which make each sound different from other sounds. For example, the /f/ and /v/ sounds in English share four distinctive features. They are both consonants. They are both produced in the front (they are *anterior* sounds). They are both continuant sounds (air is emitted continuously) and they are both strident sounds. But, they differ by one feature. The /f/ sound is voiceless or unvoiced, whereas the /v/ sound is voiced.

Speech-language pathologists use distinctive features to analyze the commonalities of sound production errors. Once the patterns are identified, therapy can focus on remediating features and patterns, rather than remediating individual sounds. Eleven distinctive features can be used to analyze articulation error patterns in research. However, in practice, SLPs generally only analyze three distinctive features—place, manner, and voicing—as discussed in the next section.

PLACE/MANNER/ VOICING ANALYSIS

Rather than individually describe how each sound is produced, as in the sound by sound approach, speech-language pathologists sometimes look for patterns in articulation problems. That is, what do the child's problem sounds have in common? Sounds are usually grouped according to the *place of production*, the *manner of production,* and *voicing* characteristics. SLPs typically use all three to analyze a child's speech. It would be similar to describing your coat as a long black leather coat—you would need the length, color, and material to completely describe the coat.

Place of Production Analysis. Sounds are described according to their place or location of articulation by using the Latin names for the structures that come together to produce the sound:

- bilabial sounds—produced with the upper and lower lip;
- labiodental sounds—produced with the lower lip and upper teeth;
- linguadental or interdental—produced with the tongue between the teeth;
- lingua-alveolar—produced with the tongue tip or blade on the alveolar ridge (the upper gum ridge right behind the front teeth);
- linguapalatal—produced with the tongue and palate;
- velar—produced at the soft palate area;
- glottal sounds—produced at the area of the vocal bands (vocal cords).

It is important to describe the place of production because this enables the SLP to look for commonalities in the sounds that are difficult for your child. This information is helpful in treatment.

Table 1: Place and Sounds

Upper and Lower Lip (*bilabial*):	p, b, w, m, wh
Lower Lip and Upper Teeth (*labiodental*):	f, v
Tongue Between Teeth (*linguadental* or *interdental*):	the "th" sounds in (*This*) and (*Thin*)
Tongue Tip Behind Upper Teeth (*lingua-alveolar*):	t, d, l, n
Tongue Blade and Alveolar Ridge (*lingua-alveolar*):	s, z
Tongue and Palate (*linguapalatal*):	sh, zh, ch, j
Front Palate (*linguapalatal*):	y
Central Palate (*linguapalatal*):	r
Velum (soft palate)(*velar*):	k, g, ng
Glottis (voice box)(*glottal*):	h

Manner of Production Analysis. Manner refers to the way in which the air stream is modified as the sound is being produced. Sounds in English can be described as stops or plosives, fricatives, affricates, nasals, glides, laterals, and rhotic.

- *Stop* sounds (also known as *plosive* sounds) are made by stopping the air completely and then releasing it with a small puff or explosion of air. The *stop* or *plosive* sounds are p, b, t, d, k, g.
- *Fricative* sounds are made by sending air through partially closed articulators (the word "fricative" comes from "friction"). *Fricative* sounds are s, z, f, v, sh, zh, th (*thin*), th (*this*).
- *Affricate* sounds are combinations of a *stop* and a *fricative* sound. Ch as in chime and j as in judge are *affricate* sounds.
- *Nasal* sounds are sounds where the breath stream is sent through the nose. Nasal sounds are m, n, and ng as in ring.
- *Glides* are sounds in which the articulation changes as the sound is being made. Glides are always followed by vowels. W and y are glides.
- The *lateral* sound is made by sending the air stream through the sides of the mouth. L is the lateral sound.
- The *rhotic* sound is complex and involves air being directed in more than one direction. R is the rhotic sound.

Grouping sounds by manner helps SLPs learn more about the types of sound production that are difficult for a child. Is she having difficulty with sounds that are produced by holding and exploding the air stream (stop/plosive sounds), or sounds produced by sending the air stream through partially closed articulators (fricative sounds), or sounds produced by directing the air stream through the nose (nasal sounds)? Then, when one sound is worked on in treatment and the child masters that sound, other sounds with similar manner of production should improve.

Table 2: Manner of Production

stop (plosive)	p, b, t, d, k, g
fricative	s, z, f, v, sh ,zh ,th (thin),th (this)
affricate	ch (chime), j (judge)
nasal	m, n, ng
glide	w, y
lateral	l
rhotic	r

Voicing Analysis. Voiced sounds involve vibration of the vocal bands. When a sound is voiced, you can feel the vibration if you place your fingers on the Adam's apple area. When a sound is voiceless, you will not feel that vibration.

All vowel sounds are voiced. Consonant sounds may be voiced or voiceless (also known as unvoiced). Voiceless sounds are p, t, k, f, s, th (*thin*), sh, ch. Voiced sounds are: b, d, g, z, th (*this*), zh (*measure*), j, m, n, ng. Once your child masters how to voice one sound, she should be able to produce voicing for other sounds.

Sounds that are produced at the same *place of production* and in the same *manner of production*, but differ in *voicing* (one is voiced, the other is voiceless) are known as *cognates*. For example, /p/ and /b/ are cognates and so are /f/ and /v/. When one cognate is incorrectly substituted for the other, it is known as *cognate confusion*.

Table 3: Voicing

Voiced Sounds	**Voiceless (Unvoiced) Sounds**
all vowel sounds	p, t, k, f, s, th (thin), sh, ch
b, d, g, z, th (this), zh, j, m ,n, ng	

Putting It All Together. When the SLP describes your child's articulation, she will often use this place-manner-voicing terminology. She will report that your child has difficulty with *lingua-alveolar* sounds, or *fricative* sounds, or *voiced* sounds. Write down the terms, and then look them up on these charts when you get home. For example, if your child has difficulty with /t/, /d/, /n/, and /l/, she is having trouble making sounds that involve tongue tip elevation. All of these sounds require raising the tongue tip and placing it directly behind the upper teeth, holding the tongue there, and then releasing it. Similarly, the patterns observed may indicate that your child has difficulty with sounds in which she needs to hold her tongue in her mouth or sounds that involve building up air pressure and then releasing the puff of air (plosive sounds). This makes it possible to work on the underlying cause of the articulation difficulty (such as difficulty in tongue tip elevation), rather than work on each individual sound.

One final way of analyzing your child's articulation is in comparison to *norms*. That is, the SLP will look at the sounds your child cannot produce correctly and compare them to a list of sounds that most (usually meaning 75 or 90 percent) typically developing children can produce by a given age. Some norms look at mastery of each sound in certain positions in words, such as at the beginning of words (initial) or at the end of words (final). The norms help us learn which sounds are early developing sounds (such as /d/) and which sounds develop later (such as /r/).

Sometimes norms from tests of articulation are used. Often, norms from research studies that sample large groups of children are used. The most recent articulation norms were collected by Ann Smit and colleagues (Smit, A., Hand, L., Freilinger, J., Bernthal, J., Bird, A., 1990). These norms are given in the two tables below. The first shows the ages that 90 percent of typically developing children mastered single sounds, while the second shows when consonant clusters were mastered. (Consonant clusters are often difficult for children with Down syndrome to produce.)

The problem in using articulation norms with children with Down syndrome is that they were compiled from a sample of typically developing children. The children probably did not have fluctuating hearing loss due to middle ear infections and fluid build-up. They did not have low muscle tone in the oral facial muscles. So, they may not provide accurate information on sound development in children with Down syndrome. Furthermore, the norms are often used as the basis for denying articulation treatment to children with Down syndrome. That is why you, as parents, need to know about them. Norms are often referred to within the IEP process for evaluating and treating articulation difficulties. See Chapter 12 for more reasons that using norms for children with Down syndrome may not be helpful, and for information that will be helpful in understanding articulation evaluation and treatment.

Although children with Down syndrome may not start to use these sounds at typical ages, they do begin to use the sounds in the same order as typically developing children. Knowing about norms provides information on which sounds are produced earlier and which are later.

Table 4: Ages Single Sounds Are Typically Mastered

Age	Sounds Mastered by Girls	Sounds Mastered by Boys
3 years	/m/, /p/, /b/, /h/, /w/, /d/	/m/, /n/, /p/, /b/, /h/, /w/
3 years, 6 months	/n/, /k/, /f/, /g/	/d/, /k/, /f/, /t/
4 years	/t/, /y/ ("yes")	/g/
4 years, 6 months	th as in "the"	
5 years	/l/	/y/ ("yes")
5 years, 6 months	/v/, /f/, final position	/v/, /f/, final position
6 years	th, as in "thin," sh, ch, /j/, /l/, final position	/l/
7 years		th as in "the," sh, ch, /j/, /l/, final position
between 7 and 9 years	/s/, /z/, /-ng/	/s/, /z/, /-ng/
8 years	/r/	/r/, th as in "thin"

Age	Sounds Mastered by Girls	Sounds Mastered by Boys
4 years	/tw/, /kw/, as in twin and queen	
5 years, 6 months	/pl/, /bl/, /kl/, /gl/, /fl/, as in play, blue, clay, glass, and fly	/tw/, /kw/
6 years		/pl/, /bl/, /kl/, /gl/, /fl/
between 7 and 9 years	/spl/, /spr/, as in split and sprinkle, and all other initial consonant clusters	/spl/, /spr/, and all other initial clusters
8 years	/pr/, /br/, /tr/, /dr/, /kr/, /gr/, /fr/, as in pray, brown, fry, drink, cry, green, and fry	/pr/, /br/, /tr/, /dr/, /kr/, /gr/, /fr/
9 years	/thr/, as in three	/thr/

Table 5: Ages Consonant Clusters Are Typically Mastered

Articulation Treatment

When parents first hear the words "speech therapy," they often envision what goes on in articulation treatment. That is, they think about exercises and activities designed to help a child learn to better produce specific sounds. In reality, articulation therapy is only one small component of speech-language therapy, as discussed in Chapter 12. And there are many different approaches to providing articulation therapy, some of them more effective with children with Down syndrome than others. Chapter 13 discusses the approaches to providing articulation therapy, together with the pros and cons of using each.

HOME ACTIVITIES FOR ARTICULATION

What can you do at home? Early on, you can focus in on sound play, using a mirror and heightening the awareness of sounds. Make sounds into games. For example, pretend you are a snake, slithering on the floor and make the /s/ snake sound as you are moving along. You can also help foster awareness of the articulators. When you are bathing or changing your baby or toddler, name the lips, teeth, tongue. Look in a mirror with your child and say, "Let me see your lips," or "Tell me when you see my tongue." Play games with noises, smacking your lips, throwing kisses, and clicking your tongue. Use lip balm or ice to help your child feel her lips smacking. In addition to seeing how sounds are made, children need practice in hearing the sounds. Children with Down syndrome need many repetitions to learn. They need to watch and listen to models of correct sounds. See below for examples of specific activities to try at home.

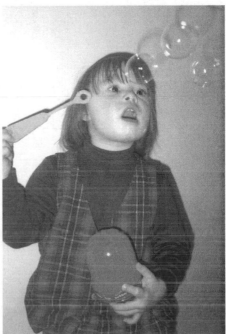

RECORD FORM FOR ARTICULATION

Use this form to keep a record of when your child produces specific sounds. Note when your child can make the sound when she is babbling or playing with individual sounds, and when she begins to make the sounds in words.

Sound	Date Used in Babbling/Sound Play	Date Sound Used in Speech
/m/		
/n/		
/-ng/		
/p/		
/b/		
/y/		
/t/		
/d/		
/h/		
/w/		
/k/		
/g/		
/f/		
/v/		
th as in "thin"		
th as in "the"		
/s/		
/z/		
sh		
ch		
/j/		
/l/		
/r/		

The ideal situation would be for you and your child to be working with a SLP who would provide home activities to practice the sounds that are the focus of therapy at that time. But, that level of service is often not available. Many times, therapy is not provided for articulation until after your child demonstrates a delay based on the developmental norms. So, therapy for articulation may not begin until after age six.

How does that happen? It depends on the eligibility requirements for speech treatment in your school system. Often, the SLP tells parents something like this: "Your child does not say the /s/ sound correctly in any position. But, you don't need to worry. She's only five. According to the norms, the /s/ sound isn't mastered until ages seven to nine, so your child isn't delayed. We don't need to work on the /s/ sound yet." But, in reality, if you wait until age eight, your child still may not say the /s/ sound correctly and will have been practicing saying it incorrectly for an additional three years. So, I believe strongly in teaching the sounds, not in waiting until the norms show that your child is delayed. It is good to be proactive and teach the sounds. See Chapter 12 for more information about how and why speech-language therapy may be denied for children who actually need it.

Whether or not your child's speech therapy program focuses on articulation, there are many areas that you can work on at home. You can:

- heighten visual and tactile awareness of the articulators and articulation movements,
- heighten auditory awareness of different sounds,
- practice sound production through songs and games, and
- practice sound production through reading.

HEIGHTEN AWARENESS OF THE ARTICULATORS AND ARTICULATION MOVEMENTS

When we work in therapy on articulation, we often focus on lip movements. These home activities help your child heighten awareness of lip sensa-

tion and movement. Be sure to use only the activities that are safe for your child. For example, do not blow bubbles with bubble gum if your child will swallow the gum. These activities will be fun for siblings, grandparents, and other family members to use with your child.

- Gently stroke the lips with an ice cube, then smack the lips together. Model this with your own lips.
- Suck hard on a Popsicle. Feel the ice on your lips. Look in the mirror, and see the color on your lips.
- Put lip balm on your lips. Smack the lips together and feel how they almost stick together.

- Hold the lips tightly together and move them as a unit from side to side. This may also be done after rubbing with ice or using lip balm.
- Put lipstick on your lips. Then blot with a tissue held between the lips.
- Put lipstick on your lips. Make kissing marks on a piece of paper.
- Tighten your lips around food such as carrots or pretzels. Suck to a count of five, then release.
- Blow on whistles that have different-sized mouthpieces.
- Play a harmonica.
- Blow on a recorder.
- Play a kazoo.
- Make popping sounds with lips.
- Blow bubbles through a bubble wand.
- Make kissing movements and sounds. Pretend to blow them through the air.
- Blow bubbles using bubble gum.
- Smack your lips at each other, making kissing sounds. Start five feet apart. Move closer and closer until you are kissing each other. Then move farther and farther away until you can no longer hear the lip-smacking sound.
- Hold your lips open. Pull them together quickly. They will make a sound. Then open them quickly. They will make a pop. It will almost sound like "oom-pah."

HEIGHTEN AWARENESS OF DIFFERENT SOUNDS

When your child is an infant, you can begin to introduce her to the sounds of her world—sounds of airplanes, trains, construction equipment, lawn mowers, birds. As part of that practice, you are also trying to heighten her awareness of speech sounds. Suggestions for home activities with younger children are presented in Chapter 4.

When your child is beginning to imitate sounds and is poised at the brink of beginning to use speech, you again want to heighten auditory awareness of speech sounds. One way to develop sound awareness is to focus on a specific sound each week, providing practice for hearing the sound as it occurs in daily life.

For example, you can focus on the /k/ sound. In English, the /k/ sound may be represented by the letter K or C. Rent *The Lion King* and listen for the /k/ sound. Plan your shopping trip to include Kmart and Burger King. Eat Corn Flakes or Captain Crunch for breakfast with milk. Take a walk around the house or the neighborhood and point out everything that has the /k/ sound: car, keys, coins, curtains, cups, calendar, and computer. Have a snack of Coca Cola and popcorn, or cookies or crackers and cream cheese. Have corn on the cob and carrots or corned beef and cabbage for dinner. Or have turkey with cranberry sauce. Have a cupcake or an ice cream cone for dessert.

On the first two days, you can point out whenever there is a /k/ sound. After that, make a sign with a K on it that your child can hold up or create a secret gesture, such as making the "OK" sign every time that she hears a /k/.

You can also read books that have many examples of a specific sound. For example, *The Tale of Benjamin Bunny* has many instances of the /b/ sound, *Night Noises* has many instances of the /n/ sound, and *Hop on Pop* has many instances of the /p/ sound. The first few times that you read the story, your child will be listening to see what happens. Once your child is familiar with the story, then begin to focus on the sound. To heighten awareness, when you read the stories, make the /b/ or /n/ sound louder. Then, clap or hold up a card that has the letter on it every time you read a /b/ sound. When your child is able to hear and identify the sound, have her clap or hold up a card each time that she hears a /b/ sound. Or, you might buy or bake alphabet cookies. Then, she can hold up a /b/ cookie each time she hears the sound. Her reward can be to eat the /b/ cookie when she identifies the sound.

Reading books that have many examples of a specific sound helps your child learn to identify the sound and discriminate the sound from other sounds. Later, when your child can make the sound, books can provide opportunities to practice the sound production. Many of these books are available in bookstores, but some are classics so might not be. All of them should be available at the library. Here is a list of books organized by sounds to get you started:

Books for Phonological Awareness and Sound Practice for Children

The /p/ Sound
Bang, Molly. *The Paper Crane.*
Carle, Eric. *Pancakes, Pancakes.*
De Paola, Tomie. *Pancakes for Breakfast.*
McPhail, David. *Pigs Aplenty, Pigs Galore.*
Oxenbury, Helen. *Tom & Pippo* (series)
Pizer, Abigail. *It's a Perfect Day.*
Prelutsky, Jack. *Ride a Purple Pelican.*
Seuss, Dr. *Hop on Pop.*

The /b/ Sound
Bob the Builder (series).
Barton, Byron. *Boats.*
Berenstain, Stan & Jan. *The Berenstain Bears* (series).
Brown, Margaret. *Big Red Barn.*
Carle, Eric. *The Very Busy Spider.*
Carter, David. *More Bugs in Boxes.*
Gretz, Susanna. *Teddy Bears ABC.*
Isadora, Rachel. *Ben's Trumpet.*
Martin, Bill, Jr. *Brown Bear, Brown Bear, What Do You See?*
Potter, Beatrix. *The Tale of Benjamin Bunny.*

The /t/ Sound
Baker, Alan. *Two Tiny Mice.*
Brett, Jan. *The Mitten: A Ukranian Folktale.*
Crowe, Robert. *Tyler Toad and the Thunder.*

Isadora, Rachel. *Ben's Trumpet.*
Lester, Helen. *Tacky the Penguin.*
McClosky, Robert. *Time of Wonder.*
Mosel, A. *Tikki Tikki Tembo.*
Wiesner, Shirley & Tuesday, David. *Time to Get Out of the Bath.*

The /d/ Sound
Alborough, Jez. *Cuddly Dudley.*
Aliki. *Digging Up Dinosaurs.*
Bridwell, Norman. *Clifford, the Big Red Dog* (series).
Hines, Anna. *Daddy Makes the Best Spaghetti.*
Kirk, Daniel. *Breakfast at the Liberty Diner.*
McClosky, Robert. *Make Way for Ducklings.*
Shannon, D. *Duck on a Bike.*

The /k/ Sound
Burton, Virginia. *Katy and the Big Snow.*
Day, Alexandra. *Good Dog Carl.*
De Paola, Tomie. *Kit and Kat.*
Freeman, Don. *Corduroy* (series).
Hutchins, Pat. *Rosie's Walk.*
Krauss, Ruth. *The Carrot Seed.*
McCully, Emily. *Picnic.*
Rey, H.A. *Curious George* series.
Seuss, Dr. *The Cat in the Hat.*
Seuss, Dr. *The Cat in the Hat Comes Back.*
Slobodkina, Esphyr. *Caps for Sale.*

The /g/ Sound
Brown, Margaret. *Goodnight Moon.*
Carle, Eric. *The Grouchy Ladybug.*
Edwards, Pamela. *Some Smug Slug.*
Ehlert, Lois. *Growing Vegetable Soup.*
Hughes, Shirley. *Giving.*
Rathmann, Peggy. *Good Night, Gorilla.*

The /m/ Sound
Brett, Jan. *The Mitten: A Ukranian Folktale.*
Brown, Margaret. *Goodnight Moon.*
Day, Alexandra. *Carl's Masquerade.*
Dunrea, Olivier. *Mogwogs on the March.*
Gag, Wanda. *Millions of Cats.*
Guarino, Deborah. *Is Your Mama a Llama?*
Kellogg, S. *The Missing Mitten Mystery.*
McCloskey, Robert. *Make Way for Ducklings.*
McCloskey, Robert. *One Morning in Maine.*
Shulevitz, Uri. *One Monday Morning.*

The /n/ Sound

Allard, Harry. *Miss Nelson Has a Field Day.*
Brett, Jan. *Annie and the Wild Animals.*
Brown, Margaret. *Goodnight Moon.*
Ehlert, Lois. *Nuts to You.*
Fox, Mem. *Night Noises.*
Frasier, Debra. *Out of the Ocean.*
Lyon, George. *The Outside Inn.*
Wood, Audrey. *The Napping House.*

The /h/ Sound

Carle, Eric. *The Very Hungry Caterpillar.*
Cauley, Lorinda. *Clap Your Hands.*
Davis, K. *Who Hops? Who Hoots?*
Fox, Mem. *Hattie and the Fox.*
Mayer, Mercer. *Hiccup.*
Seuss, Dr. *Horray for Diffendoofer Day.*
Seuss, Dr. *Horton Hears a Who.*
Seuss, Dr. *Horton Hatches the Egg.*
Zion, Gene. *Harry the Dirty Dog.*

The /f/ Sound

Carle, Eric. *The Grouchy Ladybug.*
Charlip, Remy. *Fortunately.*
Hutchins, Pat. *Don't Forget the Bacon.*
McKissack, Patricia. *Flossie and the Fox.*
McPhail, David. *Fix-It.*
Pfister, Marcus. *The Rainbow Fish.*
Seuss, Dr. *Fox in Socks.*
Waddell, Martin. *Farmer Duck.*

The /v/ Sound

Bianco, Margery. *The Velveteen Rabbit.*
Carle, Eric. *The Very Busy Spider.*
Carle, Eric. *The Very Hungry Caterpillar.*
Carle, Eric. *The Very Noisy Cricket.*
Hoban, Tana. *Over, Under and Through and Other
        Spatial Concepts.*
Hutchins, Pat. *The Very Worse Monster.*
Kvasnosky, Laura. *Zelda and Ivy.*

The /l/ Sound

Brown, Marc. *Pickle Things.*
Guarino, Deborah. *Good-Night Owl!*
Kraus, Robert. *Leo the Late Bloomer.*
Lionni, Leo. *Little Blue and Little Yellow.*
Martin, Bill & Archambault, John. *Listen to the Rain.*

Mayer, Mercer. *Liza Lou and the Yeller Belly Swamp.*
Waber, Bernard. *Lyle, Lyle Crocodile* (series).

The /r/ Sound

Brown, Marc T. *Arthur* (series).
Burningham, John. *Would You Rather?*
Gantos, Jack. *Rotten Ralph* (series).
Marshall, Edward. *Three Up a Tree.*
Marshall, James. *George and Martha* (series)
Rey, H.A. *Curious George* (series)
Sendak, Maurice. *Chicken Soup with Rice.*
Viorst, Judith. *Alexander and the Terrible, Horrible, No Good, Very Bad Day.*
Zion, Gene. *No Roses for Harry.*

The /s/ Sound

Allard, H. & Marshall, J. *Miss Nelson* (series).
Banchek, Linda. *Snake In, Snake Out.*
Keats, Ezra Jack. *The Snowy Day.*
Martin, Bill. *Brown Bear, Brown Bear, What Do You See?*
Morrison, Bill. *Squeeze a Sneeze.*
Pelutsky, Jack. *The Snoop on the Sidewalk and Other Poems.*
Silverstein, Shel. *Where the Sidewalk Ends.*
Viorst, Judith. *Alexander Who Used to be Rich Last Sunday.*

The /sh/ Sound

Cowley, Joy. *Mrs. Wishy Washy.*
Dahl, Roald. *Charlie and the Chocolate Factory.*
Keats, Ezra. *Peter's Chair.*
Henkes, K. *Sheila Rae's Peppermint Stick.*
Henkes, Kevin. *Shhhhh.*
Quackenbush, R. *She'll Be Comin' Round the Mountain.*
Shaw, Nancy. *Sheep in a Jeep.*
Shaw, Nancy. *Sheep in a Shop.*
Weeks, Sarah. *Splish, Splash!*

The /ch/ Sound

Dahl, Roald. *Charlie and the Chocolate Factory.*
Keats, Ezra. *Peter's Chair.*
Martin, Bill Jr. & John Archambault. *Chicka Chicka Boom Boom.*
Mayer, Mercer. *Ah-Choo.*
Rockwell, Anne. *At the Beach.*
Sendak, Maurice. *Chicken Soup with Rice.*
Wells, Rosemary. *Max's Chocolate Chicken.*
Williams, Vera. *A Chair for My Mother.*

The /j/ Sound (as in judge)

Aliki. *Jack and Jake.*
Anno, Mitsumasa. *Anno's Journey.*
Arnold, Ted. *No Jumping on the Bed.*
Dahl, Roald. *James and the Giant Peach.*
Rey, H.A. *Curious George* (series).
Walsh, Helen. *Hop Jump.*

The /z/ Sound

Brett, Jan. *Berlioz, the Bear.*
Kvasnosky, Laura. *Zelda and Ivy.*
Lobel, Arnold. *A Zoo for Mister Muster.*
McDermott, Gerald. *Zomo the Rabbit.*
Peet, Bill. *Zella, Zack and Zodiac.*

The /th/ (voiced and voiceless) Sound

Burningham, John. *Time to Get Out of the Bath, Shirley.*
Crowe, Robert. *Tyler Toad and the Thunder.*
Scieszka, Jon. *The True Story of the Three Little Pigs.*
Sendak, Maurice. *Where the Wild Things Are.*

The /w/ Sound

Cole, Henry. *I Took a Walk.*
Galdone, Paul. *The Teeny-Tiny Woman.*
Hutchins, Pat. *The Wind Blew.*
Kantrowitz, Mildred. *Willy Bear.*
Keats, Ezra Jack. *Whistle for Willie.*
LeSieg, Theo. *Wacky Wednesday.*
Milne, A.A. *Winnie the Pooh* (series).
Rylant, Cynthis. *Henry and Mudge and the Wild Wind.*
Sendak, Maurice. *Where the Wild Things Are.*

The /y/ Sound

Carlstrom, Nancy. *Jesse Bear, What Will You Wear?*
Gey, Judith. *Yummy, Yummy.*
Lionni, Leo. *Little Blue and Little Yellow.*
Reynolds, F. *I am Yellow Bear! Shake Me, Rattle Me!*
Seuss, Dr. *Yertle the Turtle* (and other stories).

Books that Sample Many Sounds

Base, Graeme. *Animalia.*
Cole, J. & Calmenson, S. *Six Stick Sheep: One Hundred One Tongue Twisters.*
Prelutsky, Jack. *For Laughing Out Loud.*

Books for Rhythm and Rhyme

Brown, Marc. *Pickle Things.*

Brown, R. *What Rhymes with Snake?*
Carratello, P. *Skate, Kate, Skate!*
Cox, P.R. & Cartwright, S. *Cat on a Mat Board Book*
Cox, P.R. & Cartwright, S. *Sam Sheep Can't Sleep Board Book*
Cox, P.R. & Cartwright, S. *Ted In A Red Bed Board Book*
Cox, P.R. & Catwright, S. *Toad Makes a Road Board Book*
Degen, Bruce. *Jamberry.*
DeRegiers, Beatrice Schenk. *It Does Not Say Meow, and Other Animal Riddle Rhymes.*
Eichenberg, Fritz. *Ape in a Cape: An Alphabet of Odd Animals.*
Emberley, Barbara. *Drummer Hoff.*
Fleming, Denise. *In the Tall Grass.*
Gregorich, B. *Gum on the Drum.*
Hawkins, Colin & Jacqui. *Jen the Hen.*
Hawkins, Colin & Jacqui. *Mig the Pig.*
Hawkins, Colin & Jacqui. *Pat the Cat.*
Hawkins, Colin & Jacqui. *Tog the Dog.*
Hennessey, B. *Jake Baked a Cake.*
Kalish, M. & Kalish, L. *Bears on the Stairs.*
Morrison, Bill. *Squeeze a Sneeze.*
Ochs, C.P. *Moose on the Loose.*
Roxbee-Cox, P. & Cartwright, S. *Find the Duck* (series)
Seuss, Dr. *The Cat in the Hat.*
Shaw, N. *Sheep on a Jeep.*
Stadler, John. *Cat is Back at Bat.*
Witty, B. *The Raccoon on the Moon.*

Books for Sound Identification

Fox, Mem. *Night Noises.*
Hawkins, C. & Hawkins, J. *Jen the Hen.*
Hawkins, C. & Hawkins, J. *Mig the Pig.*
Hawkins, C. & Hawkins, J. *Pat the Cat.*
Hawkins, C. & Hawkins, J. *Tog the Dog.*
Otto, C. *Dinosaur Chase.*
Parry, C. *Zoomerang-a-Boomerang: Poems to Make Your Belly Laugh.*
Patz, N. *Moses Supposes His Toeses Are Roses.*
Seuss, Dr. *There's a Wocket in My Pocket.*

Voice

Asbojornsen, Peter. *The Three Billy Goats Gruff.*
Barton, Bryon. *Hester.*
Brown, Margaret. *The Quiet Noisy Book.*
Carle, Eric. *The Very Quiet Cricket.*
DePaolo, Tomie. *Mice Squeak, We Speak.*
Fleischman, Paul. *I Am Phoenix: Poems for Two Voices.*
Fleischman, Paul. *Joyful Noise: Poems for Two People.*

Fox, Mem. *Hattie and the Fox.*
Hawkins, Colin & Hawkins, Jacqui. *Old MacDonald Had a Farm.*
Hoguet, Susan. *I Unpacked My Grandmother's Trunk.*
Mayer, Mercer. *Hiccup.*
Wells, Rosemary. *Noisy Nora.*

PRACTICE SOUND PRODUCTION THROUGH SONGS AND GAMES

Some children will need specific, focused help to learn how to make each individual sound. Other children will be able to imitate a new sound by watching you when you provide a model or by looking in the mirror with you as you make the sound. Professional help from a SLP may be needed for your child to make a specific sound. If that is the case, you can stimulate production and heighten awareness, but you don't want to put pressure on your child to produce the sound until she is able to do that.

When she is able to make the sound, songs, games, and finger plays can be great ways to provide practice in making the sound. That practice will help the sound production become more automatic and less effortful. For example, if you are focusing on the /b/ sound, try singing "I'm Bringing Home a Baby Bumblebee" or "The Buzz Song" with your child. If you are focusing on /p/, try playing "Pat a Cake" or "This Little Piggy." More ideas are listed in the table on the next page.

PRACTICE SOUND PRODUCTION THROUGH READING

Once your child is able to produce sounds (even if incorrectly), you can use books to stimulate your child to practice sounds. As described above, you can highlight the words beginning or ending with the sound targeted in treatment by drawing out the sound or saying it louder. Then ask your child to imitate the word from

your model. Try not to correct your child's production of the sound until she is able to make the sound correctly. You don't want to put pressure on her until she is ready to make a sound. For example, if your child has difficulty with the /r/ sound, try reading any of the books about Harry the Dirty Dog, or the Arthur series, Rotten Ralph series, or Curious George series. Or read *Alexander and The Terrible, Horrible, No Good, Very Bad Day* or *Would You Rather....* Or choose a book with a repeated phrase such as *Chicken Soup with Rice*. Your child can chime in with "rice" or with the entire phrase "chicken soup with rice."

The speech-language pathologist will work with you to determine when it is appropriate to correct production. Once your child can make the sound correctly, then reading aloud can provide practice in producing the sound. You can also ask your child questions about the book to provide practice in making the sound while speaking.

To determine whether a book is appropriate to use for stimulation on a specific sound, simply preview the book yourself. What you are looking for is what sounds words begin and end with in the book. Is there a preponderance of one or two sounds used? For example, the children's book, *The Snowy Day*, has many /s/

Table 6: Suggestions for Stimulating Speech Sounds

/p/	blow bubbles and say "pop"; use boat and make putt-putt sound; play "Pat a Cake"; read *Peter, Peter, Pumpkin Eater, Tom, Tom the Piper's Son,* and *Georgie Porgie*
/b/	play with Barney or Blue's Clues toy; wave bye-bye; blow a tissue; hit a balloon; dress Barbie
/t/	point out toes on dolls, stuffed toys; toy clock ticking; crafts with colored tape
/d/	daddy sound: use photos of Dad or activities with Dad; toy duck, doll, dinosaur
/k/	cat - real, toy, photos; toy keys; variety of cups; bake cookies or a cake; read *Caps for Sale*
/g/	toy garage—put cars in; gallop or giddyap
/s/	make hissing snake sound; Santa Claus; plant seeds; take socks on and off doll
/z/	zip and unzip a zipper; buzz like a bee
/f/	make a fan and fan yourself; play Go Fish; toy fish with magnets; play with a football or watch football
/v/	play with a toy van—put things in it and make it go vroom; make a vase and collect flowers to put in the vase
/sh/	make the shhhh sound with finger on lips; shoe on and off doll
/ch/	choo choo train; Thomas the Tank Engine; read *The Little Engine That Could*
/j/	jump; make toy jump; put jelly beans in a jar; put jacket on and off doll
/m/	eat favorite food and say m-m-m; play with a mirror; play with magnets and pick up objects; sing *The Muffin Man.*
/n/	the no sound; feel your nose; identify toys' & dolls' noses; make a necklace with pasta or beads; say night-night and put doll to sleep
/l/	sing lala to a song; lick a lollipop; make a craft project with leaves; recite *Little Miss Muffet, London Bridge, Little Boy Blue,* and *To Market, To Market.*
/r/	play with a toy rabbit or rocket; make a race car move; put rings on a stand; put raisins in a jar; growl like a tiger
/w/	play with a wagon; put water in a bucket; watch the Wiggles
/h/	play with a toy horse; put funny hats on; make paper hearts or cards for Valentine's Day; pant like a puppy dog ("huh-huh-huh")
/y/	yawn and say "ya"; play with a yoyo; make a yarn picture or twist yarn around a bow

sounds. *The Three Little Pigs* has many final /f/ sounds (the wolf appears many times in the story) and can engage your child in practicing the /f/ with the repetitive phrase "I'll huff and I'll puff and I'll blow your house in."

Remember that you are looking and listening for sounds, not alphabet letters, so the /th/ as in *the* is a /th/ sound, not a /t/ sound as in *toe*. Some books have many examples of one sound. Other books can be used to target multiple sounds. For example, in the book, *Hop on Pop*, the following sounds are included:

- *initial p:* past, Pat, pop, pup
- *final p:* hop, pop, cup, jump, pup, up, top
- *b:* back, ball, bat, bad, be, bed, bee, big, bit, bump, but
- *m:* me, mother, mouse, Mr., Mrs., must, my, am, bump, him, jump, tomorrow
- *f:* fall, fast, fish, fight, father
- *k:* call, came, can, cat, cup

- *s:* say , see, sent, sing, sister, song, sat, sad, snack
- *final l:* all, tall, small, ball, will, hill

Listed on pages 153-58 are some widely available children's books that contain many examples of specific sounds. When you go to the library or bookstore with your child, talk with the librarian and ask for suggestions of books that focus in on your target sound. Or, look through the books yourself; just use a different "set of glasses." You are looking for many examples of a specific sound. When you look at books in that way, you can find many wonderful books on topics and at a level appropriate for your child.

You may also want to try making your own books to target particular sounds. For instance, if your child is working on the /p/ sound, you could make popcorn with your child, listen to it pop, and pour it into the bowl. Take photos. Then make your own book about Popping Popcorn. Make a J book and fill it with photos or pictures from magazines of things that begin with J such as jar, jam and jelly, jelly beans. Another idea is to buy or collect old calendars. Many calendars have twelve pictures on a similar topic, such as dogs. You can make a book with the pictures and put in your own titles—big dog, little dog, dog with a hat, dog and cat—then laminate and bind.

ADVICE FOR FAMILIES

When is it appropriate to work on the activities described in this chapter? Or to read books that focus on specific sounds? Or to correct your child when she makes a sound incorrectly?

Children with Down syndrome learn sounds at different ages. Some are just beginning to babble at age three, while others are speaking in phrases at that age. So, look at the activities as possibilities. Try lip smacking or throwing kisses. If your child has difficulty, ask the SLP what activity might be a bit easier for your child. Or what exercises might help your child get ready for lip smacking. Try the activity again every few months to determine whether your child is ready at that time.

Sometimes two activities may seem the same but one will be easier for your child than the other. For example, your child might try blowing two horns. One will be easy for her because it has a wide mouthpiece and does not require too much breath pressure. Another horn will be difficult because it has a very small mouthpiece so your child has to compress her lips hard around the mouthpiece and use a lot of breath pressure. Both activities are horn blowing. Watch your child for signs that an activity is too easy or difficult for her.

When do you start correcting your child if she is saying a sound incorrectly? For example, her name is Sandy and she says /thandy/? First, you want to separate practice from daily speaking. When she says her name for daily speaking, her focus is on meaning—on getting her message across. When she is practicing, she is learning to make the sounds. Practice may involve separate pieces, such as learning to hold her tongue inside her mouth and learning to lift her tongue. In daily living, you want to focus on her message.

Only when your child is able to say the sound in words in practice the majority of the time should you try correcting her in daily speaking. And, even then, it should be with respect—when you are alone or within the family in situations that will not embarrass her. Remember the distinctions that we made in the beginning of the book among speech, language, and communication. If you correct speech in situations that are difficult for your child, you run the risk of her deciding not to communicate, deciding that speech is just too hard, and giving up. Focus on one or two sounds. Focus on sounds that she is successful with in speech sessions or in practice sessions. And be sure to correct her only in comfortable situations, when she feels free to try again.

Phonology

Now we come to the second major topic of this chapter: phonology. As mentioned at the beginning of the chapter, phonology and articulation are closely related. It is important to understand the differences, though, so that a problem with phonology is not mistaken for a problem with articulation or vice versa, and therefore treated in an ineffective way. The distinction between phonology and articulation can be hard to grasp, so I will give some brief definitions and comparisons to start, so you can refer back to them if you get confused.

- *Articulation:* When we focus on articulation, we are concerned with determining whether a child is moving her articulators to form sounds correctly. That is, we are concerned with whether a child has the ability to pronounce particular speech sounds, such as the /s/ sound, correctly. Articulation is a production task.
- *Phonology:* When we focus on phonology, we are concerned with understanding what sounds typically appear in a language (such as English or Spanish), and in what patterns they appear. For instance, English contains the /s/ sound, and it can appear in many positions in a word, in many different consonant combinations (e.g., /sc/, /sh/, /sl/, /sm/, etc., but *not* /sd/).
- *Phonological Processes:* In this area of phonology, we focus on how children change the rules of phonology and make their own (incorrect, but simpler) patterns of sounds. For example, a child may be able to articulate the /s/ sound, but habitually leave it (and perhaps other sounds) off the ends of words.

THE NUTS AND BOLTS OF PHONOLOGY AND PHONOLOGICAL PROCESSING

Phonology studies the sounds of a language. Every language has specific sounds that are used in that language, and the sounds of one language may be very different from the sounds of another language. In some languages, tongue clicks are part of the sound system. In other languages, some sounds are made on inhaled air. In English, tongue clicks are not considered speech sounds and all speech sounds are made on exhaled air.

Sounds are arranged in a very organized, rule-governed way in every language in the world. For example, in English, only the /s/ sound can begin a three-consonant blend. So, "splash" and "sprinkle" are acceptable English words, but "flrash" or "grpinkle" are not acceptable sound sequences for words in English.

(Note: articulation and phonology both deal with sounds, not alphabet letters, so even though some words like "chlorine" and "chloride" have three letters at the beginning of the word, they only produce two sounds, /kl/. Similarly, there are two alphabet letters at the end of the word "ring," but only one sound, /ng/.) And in English, certain sounds, such as /q/, are rarely used at the ends of words. Native speakers do not usually think about these sound combinations. They automatically know what is acceptable and what is not because they have grown up hearing English and learning to speak English as young children. So, native speakers do not need to think about each sound combination and whether it is acceptable in the language.

The way that children develop the speech sound system is very organized and logical. When researchers and clinicians analyze how children learn the sounds of the language, they find that even the errors that children make are very systematic. When children try to produce sounds that are too difficult for them to make, they simplify the standard adult productions of the sounds. That is why many children make the same sound errors when they are learning the sounds of English—for example, saying /thun/ for "sun" or /fum/ for "thumb" or /wawa/ for "water." Researchers have also found that the various sounds in a word or phrase affect each other. That is, your child may be able to say "yes," but she says "lellow" for yellow. The /l/ in the word affects the first /y/ sound and she uses the /l/ sound twice.

These types of simplifications of sounds, sound substitutions, and patterns of sound errors are known as *phonological processes*.

Phonological Process Analysis

Phonological process *analysis* is a method for analyzing your child's phonological processes. That is, it is an approach to analyzing your child's speech that looks at the pattern of sound errors and sound substitutions that she uses when speaking. A phonological process analysis might look at, for example, whether your child makes all sounds in the front of the mouth, or whether she leaves off all of the final sounds in words.

Phonological process analyses are used when your child is able to produce sounds correctly in some contexts but not in others or when your child uses simplifications in her speech that follow definite patterns. For example, your child says the /y/ in yes, but says /lellow/ for yellow. Phonological process theory explains this by saying that it's not that your child cannot produce /y/ or needs to be taught to produce the /y/. It's that the /l/ in yellow is influencing the way that your child produces the first sound in the word (this is known as an *assimilation process*). Or, your child may say /pa/ for pat, but be able to say the /t/ in top. It's not that she can't say the /t/, it's that she is leaving out the last sound in the word; this is called *deletion of final consonants*. Or, that she says /tootie/ for cooky, because she makes all back sounds in the front of the mouth instead; this is called *fronting*.

Phonological process analysis may seem like the sound by sound approach to analyzing sound errors described earlier, but it is not. In a sound by sound analysis, the SLP is looking at the sounds your child *can't* make. In a phonological process analysis, the SLP is looking at the patterns of sounds your child *can* make in different situations. Using the sound by sound approach with the example above of the child saying "yes" and "lellow," it would appear that the child has difficulty producing the /y/ sound consistently, but that is really not the case.

When we analyze the phonological processes that children use, we can figure out the rules that they are using. Phonological processes are based on rules and patterns, not on the articulation and oral motor abilities of the child. How do we know that? Consider the example of the child who says /fum/ for thumb. If the error were based on articulation or oral motor ability, we would assume that the child has difficulty saying the /th/ sound. But, this child also says /thun/ for sun, so she can make the /th/ sound. She just does not make it in the right word at the right time. This tells us that she has a different logical rule system in her mind. She has developed it although no one has taught the rule to her. As for /wawa/, she probably has not heard an adult use that word, but she develops it by reduplicating or repeating the first syllable, /wa/. These are very common substitutions that we hear frequently in young children who are learning English.

Phonological Processes and Children with Down Syndrome

All children use certain sound simplification rules as they develop speech, but children with Down syndrome use these simplifications longer. In one study, researchers found that children with Down syndrome and typically developing children used the same numbers and types of phonological processes at eighteen months to two years of age. At age four, however, the children with Down syndrome were using more phonological processes than the other children. In fact, they continued to use phonological processes at about the level of a typically developing two- or two-and-a-half-year-old (Smith & Stoel-Gammon, 1983).

Other researchers have found that children with Down syndrome use more phonological processes as the length and complexity of their speech increases. That is, they use more phonological processes in connected language samples than when they are naming pictures spontaneously or imitating the names spoken by others (Sommers, Patterson, & Wildgen, 1988).

TYPES OF PHONOLOGICAL PROCESSES

The most frequent phonological processes (simplification rules) used by children with Down syndrome are:

- final consonant deletion (saying "boo" for "boot");
- consonant cluster reduction (saying "gas" for "glass");
- stopping (saying "toup" for "soup");

- fronting, or making all the sounds in the front of the mouth ("tootie" for "cookie");
- backing, or making all sounds in the back of the mouth ("gagi" for "daddy");
- weak syllable deletion ("hamger" for "hamburger.")

FINAL CONSONANT DELETION

Final consonant deletion means that the child leaves out the last sound in the word. So, she might say /boo/ for *boot* or /fi/ for *fish.* (Remember, it's the last sound, not the last letter that is deleted.) This is the most common phonological process used by children with Down syndrome. Final consonant deletion may be related to hearing loss and fluid in the ear affecting hearing. In English, we tend to say the final sounds of words more quietly. So, we say "<u>B</u>ook," not "boo<u>K</u>." It is harder to hear that final sound, and maybe that is why final consonant deletion is so common among children with Down syndrome.

Leaving out final sounds presents a problem in school when children are expected to learn grammar. In English, many verb tenses are marked by final sounds. So are plurals and possessives. So, if the teacher is asking a child with Down syndrome to respond to: "This bike belongs to Fred. It is _____ bike." The child may answer, "It is Fred bi" or "It is Fred bike." The child with Down syndrome may fully understand the concept of possession and the markers that are used for the possessive, but still say "Fred bike." She may also delete the final consonant in both words and say "Fred bi." On the other hand, the child may not know how to use the /s/ to mark possession. How does the teacher know what the problem is? Perhaps the child can write the answer correctly, but leaves out the final consonant sound when speaking. In this case, it is likely that she knows how to use the possessive /s/. Or, if she leaves out the final sound in both "Fred" and "bike," we can see a pattern emerging more clearly. Still, deletion of final consonants makes it more difficult to determine whether and when a child with Down syndrome understands and can use verb tenses, plural, and possessive markers.

CONSONANT CLUSTER REDUCTION

A consonant cluster is a group of two or more consonant sounds occurring in sequence (e.g., /sp/ or /br/). Consonant cluster reduction (sometimes called consonant cluster simplification) means that either one of the sounds of the cluster is omitted (/cown/ for "clown") or that another sound is substituted for one of the sounds in the consonant cluster (/bwown/ for "brown").

Younger children with Down syndrome (ages three to four and a half) are especially likely to use cluster reduction at the start of words, according to one study (Bleile & Schwartz,1984).

STOPPING

As explained earlier, the "stop" sounds (also known as *plosive* sounds) are made by stopping the air completely and then releasing it with a small puff or explosion of air. When a child uses stopping, she replaces a fricative or affricate sound (such as /s/, /f/, or /j/) with a stop sound (such as /b/, /d/, or /t/). For example, your child might say /toup/ for "soup" or /dat/ for "that." This is another phonological process that is common in younger children with Down syndrome (Bleile & Schwartz, 1984).

FRONTING

Fronting means that sounds that should be articulated in the middle or back of the mouth are instead made in the front of the mouth. For example, your child might say /tootie/ instead of "cookie," /ti/ instead of "key," and /do/ instead of "go."

BACKING

Backing means that sounds that should be articulated in the front or middle of the mouth are made posterior to or in the back of the mouth. For example, "do" would be pronounced as /goo/ and "toe" would be /ko/.

WEAK SYLLABLE DELETION

Weak syllable deletion or unstressed syllable deletion means that an unstressed syllable is omitted in a multi-syllabic word. The child is simplifying the word by leaving out a syllable, thus shortening the word. For example, "hamburger" would be /hamger/, "potato" would be /tato/, "telephone" would be /tefon/, and "pajamas" would be /jamiz/.

Treatment for Phonological Processes

If your child is receiving speech-language treatment for phonological processes, the SLP will focus on correcting your child's patterns, rather than the individual sounds. For example, treatment for final consonant deletion will focus on making your child aware that final consonants affect meaning and that she is leaving off those final consonants. This therapy approach will use minimal pairs—words that differ by only one sound in the final position in words, such as "bowl," "boat," and "bone." The next section provides an example of a game using minimal pairs. See Chapter 13 for more information about speech-language treatment.

HOME ACTIVITIES FOR PHONOLOGICAL PROCESSES

For Final Consonant Deletion:

- Play a game called "End That Word." Show pictures of words with three sounds, but only give the first two sounds. For example, /ba/ for "bat" or /ta/ for "tack." Your child has to say the word with the final sound emphasized, such as "battt," and "takkk." Take turns.
- Play a game called "Put the Tail on the Dog." Use cards with pictures of objects; say the word with the final sound emphasized. Discuss that the final sound on a word is like the tail on the dog; it needs to be right at the end. Say the word with the final sound attached and you get to pin the tail on the dog. (You can draw a picture of a dog and let your child draw the tail on, or use a picture of a dog from a magazine and let your child tape the tail on.)
- Play "Let's Match Up" as described in the box on the next page.

Let's Match Up

This awareness activity adapted from the "Go Fish" card game is an example of a home activity to help children learn to include final sounds when speaking.

- Make two copies of pictures of objects that only differ in the final sound, such as boat, bowl, bone, and bow. There are lists of such words in speech therapy books on "minimal contrasts" or you can make up your own.
- Mount the pictures on unlined index cards or cardstock, creating a deck of playing cards. For example, there would be two boat cards with pictures of boats, two bow cards, two bowl cards, and two bone cards.
- Give each player a number of cards (you can use three, five, or seven cards).
- Taking turns, players request specific cards so that they can make pairs. The player with the most pairs wins. For example, your child might ask, "Do you have any boat cards?" Now, if she does not pronounce the final sound correctly or omits the final sound, her card playing partner may hand her the wrong card. This creates awareness that the final sound affects the meaning of the word. Both listening and production practice can be included in the game.

For Fronting and Backing:

- Talk about the fact that some sounds like /p/ and /l/ are made right in the front of the mouth and other sounds like /k/ and /g/ are made at the back of the mouth. Use a toy house with a front door and a back door. Practice making a front sound whenever you open the front door and a back sound whenever you open the back door. Use a mirror to see the front sounds and touch your throat area to feel the back sounds.

For Weak Syllable Deletion:

- Use a drum or pacing board to pound out, count out, or touch the number of syllables. For example, ham-bur-ger, base-ball-bat. Another possibility is to "sing" the word in a three-part rhythm, ham-bur-ger. You might want to emphasize the syllable that is usually omitted or say it louder.

For Consonant Cluster Reduction:

- When your child omits one consonant in the cluster, such as "cown" for "clown," add an "a" sound after the first consonant sound and emphasize the two sounds in practice. For example, for "clown," say, "ca-lown"; for "glass," say "ga-lass." Sometimes children enjoy doing a dance while practicing these clusters.

PHONOLOGICAL AWARENESS In addition to phonological processes, there are other areas of phonology that are difficult for children with Down syndrome to master. In particular, phonological awareness (also known as *metaphonology*) often is challenging for children with Down syndrome.

Phonological awareness is the ability to identify and manipulate the sounds of the language. Another way of looking at it is: the ability to consciously think about and perform actions on speech sounds. It usually includes skills such as:

- breaking down words into their constituent sounds ("map" into m-a-p);
- combining sounds into words (s-n-o-w into "snow");
- identifying words that begin with a certain sound ("bat" begins with /b/);
- rhyming words (hat, cat, rat, sat, mat).

Phonological awareness is related to reading development. Many of the reading and language arts skills that are tested and taught in the early elementary school years are phonological awareness skills. There are many tests and treatment materials available to address phonological awareness skills. It can be worked on by the SLP, at home, and in preschool or kindergarten. Many early learning workbooks, activity books, and software programs address this area. Most of this material is not worked on until kindergarten and first grade, because segmenting words or combining sounds into words are more advanced phonological skills.

To work on phonological awareness at home, you can use some of the same activities described on pages 152-58 in the section called "Heighten Awareness of Different Sounds," above. Choose one or two sounds for your child to work on identifying to begin with. Read books that contain the target sound to her and stop and clap (or hold up a card with the letter) every time you hear the target sound. Then let her try clapping or holding up the card. A book such as *The Cat in the Hat* is appropriate for practicing phonological awareness skills. Children can sound out the words and the book has many rhyming words.

You can also work on rhyming skills at home. Rhyming skills are based on the sounds of the language, and are important skills that help children learn about the sounds of words and word parts. When children can rhyme words, we know that they can hear similarities in sound patterns. Some ideas for working on rhymes include:

- Read books with rhymed texts, such as *Sheep, Sheep, Sheep, Help Me Fall Asleep; Pickle Things; In the Tall, Tall Grass; Sheep in a Jeep; Is Your Mama a Llama?* and *Pigs Aplenty, Pigs Galore.* Using rhyming books helps children learn that language is playful and fun. (See the list of books earlier in the chapter for more examples.)
- When you're reading a book with a strong rhyme, pause at the ends of sentences and see if your child can guess the rhyming word that comes next.
- Play a rhyming variation of "I Spy" when you are waiting with your child in a doctor's office or restaurant. For instance, say, "I see something that rhymes with moon…. Need a hint? You use it to eat with" (spoon).
- Make up riddles for your child that use rhyme. For example: "I am thinking of something that is good for sleeping on. It rhymes with head."

Conclusion

Both articulation and phonology can be quite challenging for children with Down syndrome. They are important to work on, however, since they play a major role in speech intelligibility. In addition, an understanding of phonology is essential to receptive language skill and reading skill mastery. Most children with Down syndrome benefit from speech-language therapy in these areas, but there are also many activities you can do at home to improve your child's abilities to produce sounds and understand the sound patterns that are used in English. With support from you and the speech-language pathologist, your child can continue to make progress in these areas throughout childhood and even into adulthood.

CHAPTER 10

Pragmatics: Communication in Action

If you are familiar with the word *pragmatic,* you probably have a good hunch what *pragmatics* means. It's all about the practical uses of language in real-life communication situations—the social and interactional use of language. Most children, including those with Down syndrome, develop many skills in pragmatics before they speak their first word. That is because some pragmatics skills are as basic as making eye contact and smiling or frowning to make your feelings known. Other pragmatics skills, such as being able to stay on topic during a conversation, do not develop until children have already mastered many other speech and language skills.

There are many different types of pragmatics skills. Some skills, such as facial expressions and taking turns, develop early, while others, such as stylistic variation and presuppositions, are advanced skills that develop much later. Your child may have a good knowledge of vocabulary, but pragmatics involves being able to use that vocabulary to interact with another person and achieve your communication goals. Pragmatics includes:

- *Kinesics:* the use of gestures;
- *Proxemics:* use of distance and space when interacting with others;
- *Intent:* the goal of the communication;
- *Eye contact:* looking directly at the communication partner (also known as reciprocal gaze);
- *Facial expression:* the emotional meaning of the movements of the face such as smiling or frowning;
- *Requests:* asking for something through the communication;
- *Conversational skills:* the social interaction of communication partners, including turn taking;
- *Stylistic variation:* ability to adapt your speech and language to different conversational partners and audiences;
- *Presuppositions:* assumptions a person makes that may influence a conversation;

- *Topicalization:* this includes introducing topics, staying on topic, shifting topics, and ending topics;
- *Clarification and repairs:* asking your conversation partner for information that you don't understand, and providing information that the listener needs.

Once you understand which skills are included in pragmatics, you will be more aware of which skills your child is using and which skills may need to be worked on, in early intervention, in speech therapy, or at home.

Pragmatics and Children with Down Syndrome

There has been very little research on pragmatics skills in young children with Down syndrome. Some of the research has involved comparison of children with Down syndrome and children with autism on social interactive communication skills. Results have shown that children with Down syndrome do better in social interactive language situations than children with autism. What we really need to know from researchers, however, is how we can improve the pragmatics skills of children with Down syndrome, how and when skills develop, and what are the best timetables and the best techniques to treat difficulties in pragmatics.

In my experience, most children with Down syndrome interact very well socially. They can and will communicate with others even before they use speech, through the appropriate use of pointing, facial expressions, gestures, and sign language. In fact, nonverbal social interactional skills are usually a strength for young children with Down syndrome.

Even though most children with Down syndrome find pragmatics easier to learn than many other communication skills, they still often need to work on pragmatics in therapy sessions. This is in contrast to typically developing children who learn the social use of language by observing adults and older children and by practice and trial and error. Of course, many children with Down syndrome also learn skills through observation, but they often need to have the skills brought into their awareness.

Although we may need to teach children with Down syndrome *how* to use language in certain situations, the good news is that they usually *want* to interact and to communicate with others, and are capable of socially interacting. The communication may be through gestures, sign language, a communication board, or speech.

Kinesics

Kinesics is the use of gestures in communication. Pointing to a cookie in the bakery or circling your fingers for the "OK" sign are examples of kinesics. Gestures can support and reinforce communication. For example, people shake their fingers to indicate that they are angry and shrug their shoulders to show that there is nothing they can do. Gestures can also replace communication. For example, your child might wave at you from across the playground or nod his head when his mouth is full and someone asks if he wants more pasta. Gestures are learned primarily through imitation. Different cultures have different gestures, and your child learns his set of gestures from the people around him.

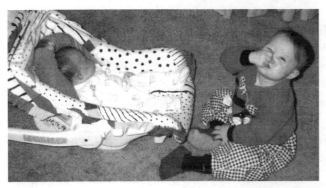

In my work with children with Down syndrome, I have observed that they do not have difficulty with gestures, and usually use them appropriately when they have plenty of practice at home and in the community. In addition, at least one researcher has found that children with Down syndrome generally use gestures very well, including "instrumental gestures" such as "come here" (Attwood, 1988).

If your child is not using pointing and other gestures by the age of three, you might want to seek further diagnosis. Children with the dual diagnosis of Down syndrome and autism often do not point and use gestures to communicate. Or, they may use gestures early in development, and then stop using them, especially the pointing gesture, at older ages. See the box on page 174.

HOME ACTIVITIES

- Play "Show Me." Ask your child a series of questions and allow him to answer with gestures only. For example, "Where is your riding truck?" "Do you want to go to the store now?" Then change places if your child is old enough and can formulate questions. Have your child ask you questions that you answer only with gestures.

- Play the "Yes, No, I Don't Know Game." Ask a series of questions that can be answered only by yes or no. Your child has to answer by moving his head only. If he doesn't know the answer, he has to shrug his shoulders and make the facial expression for "I don't know." Involve siblings and friends in this game and make some of the questions funny, to make this practice a game rather than work. For example, "Is your name Suzy?" "Are you a banana?" "Are you a girl?" "Are you smaller than an ant?" "Are you bigger than an elephant?"

- Pointing is a very specific gesture that language experts call *deixis*. Play the game "Where is It?" Using household objects, ask "Where is the telephone?" Your child needs to answer by pointing. For older children, use cards depicting various rooms, and have your child point to the appropriate picture to answer the question. For example, "Where is the blue quilt? Where is the dishwasher?" In the beginning, it doesn't matter if your child uses his whole hand, his thumb, or his middle finger to point instead of his pointer finger. You are working on a communication skill in this activity, not a fine motor skill. You may, however, need the guidance of an occupational therapist to help your child learn to isolate his index finger to point. (See *Fine Motor Skills in Children with Down Syndrome* by Maryanne Bruni for more information.)

- Make a game board showing rooms of your house, or with spaces on which you have written the names of rooms. Take photos of many objects in your house and place them in the center of the game board. Your child rolls dice, moves his game piece the correct number of spaces, and lands on a room name or picture. He then has to *point* to the picture in the center of the board that goes in that room and put it on that room. This is also good practice for associations and categories for receptive language. Vary the game board and the pictures to include outside activities your child enjoys such as baseball, soccer, or camping.

- Play Simon Says with gestures. You say, "Simon Says do this," but what you are asking your child to do is to copy a gesture.

- Play the Hokey Pokey, which involves modeling and copying gestures.

When Dual Diagnosis Complicates Down Syndrome

Although most children with Down syndrome are delayed in speech skills, they usually find other ways to communicate their wants and needs and seek out others to listen to their message. A toddler may bang on the bathroom door and make noises to tell Mom to get out of the bathroom or hold his arms up to tell Dad he wants to be swung around. It is typical for a young child with Down syndrome to use gestures and pantomime to help get his message across. These attempts at communicating are usually directly related to what is going on in the child's environment at that moment.

If a child with Down syndrome who does not have sufficient language and speech skills does *not* find alternative ways to interact and communicate with people, then we need to consider whether some other complicating condition is preventing him from communicating. Also, if the child has been socializing and then begins to withdraw and not notice others, or seems to lose his ability to use signs or verbal language, we need to consider other diagnoses. Regression is *not* typical for young children with Down syndrome.

An evaluation by a physician and/or psychologist should consider the possibilities of seizure disorders, reactive attachment disorder (especially if your child was adopted), and autism spectrum disorders (including autism and pervasive developmental disability). It has been estimated that 5 to 8 percent of children with Down syndrome have a dual diagnosis of Down syndrome and autism spectrum disorder. The major signs are: 1) absence of or severe delay in using spoken language, 2) lack of communication interaction using speech or gestures, 3) a failure to initiate communication with others, 4) poor social relatedness, 5) a limited repertoire of activities and interests, and 6) poor receptive language skills, which may give the appearance that the child does not hear (Capone, 1999).

A child with autism does not seek communication and does not use speech meaningfully to communicate. He may repeat what you say; this is known as echolalia. For example, you say, "What is your name?" and the child says "name." He may not use gestures or pointing to get his needs met. He may appear as if he does not hear or understand you, but may be uncomfortable when sounds in his environment are loud. Shopping trips to stores where there are lots of people, fluorescent lights, and a

Proxemics

The term proxemics refers to how a person uses space and distance in interpersonal situations. It includes posture, how close we stand to another person, and touch and physical contact. Proxemics vary greatly from culture to culture and even from one geographic region to another. In some cultures, men kiss or hug and women hold hands or walk arm in arm; in others this would be considered inappropriate. Extended families may have varying practices that are confusing to children. For example, the mother's side of the family may hug and kiss in greeting, while the father's side may say, "Good to see you" and wave from a distance.

There is no right and wrong in proxemics; there is only appropriate and inappropriate behavior in a given situation. Typically developing children often learn what is appropriate proxemics by watching, but for many children with Down syndrome, this needs to be taught. Proxemics is best taught at home and in the community, in real-life situations.

variety of noises may be very difficult for him to tolerate. He may rock back and forth or twirl around repeatedly. He may have strong food preferences and go through periods where he will only eat one or two different foods. He may not like the feel of certain textures in clothing, blankets, or toys. When he has a strong response, it may be difficult to figure out what he is responding to. Is it the activity? The lights? A specific person? In short, he finds it difficult to respond to the sensory stimulation he is receiving from his environment.

Important: Just because your child may be very delayed in speech or language skills does not necessarily mean he has autism. Such delays in expressive language are common in children with Down syndrome. Your child most likely does not have autism if he interacts with others in many nonverbal ways, such as by maintaining eye contact, taking turns, and seeking engagement and social interaction with his environment.

Seek out an evaluation if you suspect a dual diagnosis. Ask your pediatrician for a referral to a developmental pediatrician who specializes in this area. The combination of Down syndrome and autism is not frequently seen and is difficult to diagnose. The focus of treatment and specific methodologies used are different, so it is important to determine whether autism is present (Patterson, 1999). Two developmental pediatricians who are active in this specialty area are George Capone, M.D., of the Kennedy-Krieger Institute, Johns Hopkins Hospital in Baltimore, Maryland, and Bonnie Patterson, M.D., of the Cincinnati Center on Developmental Disabilities.

If your child does have one of the autism spectrum disorders (ASD), his treatment program will need to be individually designed, and will probably include an augmentative and alternative communication system. Children with ASD may have difficulty initiating communication, and need to be taught how to communicate, not only how to use language or speak. The Picture Exchange Communication System (PECS) is one useful method for teaching children to initiate communication. For more information on AAC and PECS, see Chapter 11 as well as the materials listed under Autism in the References and Suggested Reading list.

The more practice your child gets in physically approaching people, the better. Proxemics needs to be brought into awareness. Talk about who you shake hands with and who you hug. Talk about how you will greet someone right before you actually greet them. For example, explain, "Ginny is a good friend. We can say hi and hug Ginny." Or, "When we go to the office, let's shake hands with John and say, 'Good to meet you.'"

The most common problem children with Down syndrome have with proxemics is maintaining appropriate physical distance from strangers or acquaintances. Children with Down syndrome may get physically close, hug, and show affection to others, regardless of how well they know them. In my heart, I view this as a strength, as a reflection of the warmth and love that children with Down syndrome feel. But,

as children become adolescents, inappropriate hugging or closeness can get them into trouble. If your child uses hugging or other touch inappropriately, or has other problems with proxemics, a positive behavioral support plan can be written into your child's IFSP or IEP to help him learn appropriate proxemics skills. See Chapter 15 for information on positive behavioral support plans.

Parents of children with Down syndrome need to start working on proxemics early and always keep in mind what is appropriate adult behavior within their culture. For example, strangers may find it cute if a four-year-old with Down syndrome comes up and hugs them, but intimidating if a teenager with Down syndrome does the same. It helps if you help your child understand who is a stranger, who is a friend, and who is a close friend, and what is appropriate behavior. Practice at home and practice in the community to help your child learn what is appropriate. Experience in school inclusion also helps children learn what is appropriate and acceptable and what is not.

HOME ACTIVITIES

- Role playing and acting out real-life situations are terrific ways to teach and practice proxemics at home. Set up a scenario such as going to a fast food restaurant. Use props such as fast food restaurant hats and menus to set the stage. Role play what you would do in the situation. For example, act out waiting in line and talking to employees and customers. Talk about what is appropriate physical distance and behavior. Or role play greeting someone your child will be encountering soon (you can use photos mounted on Popsicle sticks as "people" puppets). Practice giving a handshake or hug, as appropriate.

- To teach appropriate distances, use chalk to draw concentric circles outdoors or in the gym to represent appropriate distances between people for specific situations. For example, draw a small circle to show

how close your child can stand to his brother if each person stands at the outer edge of a circle. Draw a larger circle to show how far apart to stand from the principal when talking with him. For kindergarten and early elementary school age children, these circles can be used with a dress-up activity. A dress-up box containing office clothes, dressy formal clothes, a fireman's hat, a fast food cap, a gas station attendant's hat, a supermarket cashier's apron, and a waitress's apron can be provided. When two or three people are dressed in different outfits, talk about distances and where on the circle they should stand. You can suggest roles and then talk about the circle distances that would be appropriate.

Intent

Intent is the term used to describe the purpose of the conversation, as viewed by the speaker. It is the message that the speaker intends to send. If your child's intent and the message received by the listener are the same, the intent has been successfully communicated. For example, your child says, "no more Lion." You might say, "Are you finished watching *The Lion King*? Would you like to go rent another video?" If your child's intent was to go rent a different video, he has communicated his intent to you successfully. If he was trying to tell you that the Lion wasn't on the screen anymore, he has not communicated what he wanted to. He wanted you to put the video on again, and you did not get that intended message. Intent doesn't even have to involve speech. For instance, your child could show his communicative purpose by getting his coat to show you that he wants to go out.

People have many different types of intentions when they communicate, including:

- requesting,
- greeting,
- socializing/being friendly,
- protesting,
- regulating the environment, and
- asking for information.

Intents are *almost always* part of purposeful communication attempts. That is, we usually have an underlying reason for trying to communicate. You want to encourage communicative intent—using communication to get your needs met. With infants, communicative intent means the realization that you can get needs met through communication. With older children, intent includes "how to" get your message across.

HOME ACTIVITIES
- If your child is speaking, comment on his verbal and nonverbal intent. For example, "I can see that you're watching for the ice cream truck. Do you want to ask me something?" If you get no response, ask, "Do you want an ice cream cone?" Or, "You really like to listen to that song. Do you want to ask me anything?" If you get no response, ask, "Do you

want to listen to it again?" Before your child is speaking, you can comment on his intent without suggesting he follow up with speech. For example, "I can see you're watching for the ice cream truck. I bet you want some ice cream—yum yum."

- If you have a pet, try commenting on its communicative intent sometimes. For instance, if your cat meows a certain way, say, "What is the kitty trying to tell us? Does he want to go out?"

- If you can tell that your child wants something but he is not gesturing or speaking to show what he wants, help him express his intent. For example, your child can't get to his favorite bear because it is on the shelf. You see that he is looking at the bear, but he is not pointing to it. Depending on his skill level, you might take his finger and point to the bear, and say "You're showing me that you want the bear." Or you might say, "Tell me bear" or "Show me what you want."

Eye Contact

Eye contact plays a critical role in social communication. In some cultures, direct eye contact is considered very important. People will say, "Can't you look at me when I talk to you?" or make comments such as "He looked me right in the eye; I could tell he was an honest person." When you are listening and when you are talking, it is considered appropriate to look at the other person. If you are in a group, you are expected to look at the person who is speaking. In other cultures, however, it is considered a sign of respect to look away and is considered aggressive to look directly at another person. So, what is considered appropriate eye contact varies among cultures.

To be accepted, it is important to use the eye contact patterns considered appropriate in your culture. Until children with Down syndrome learn that direct eye contact is expected in school, they may be incorrectly labeled as inattentive or unmotivated. Children with Down syndrome often look down or do not look people in the eye. This is a skill that can be practiced at home.

HOME ACTIVITIES
- Play a "Look Me in the Eye" Game. Every time your child looks you in the eye, make a secret signal such as a wink.

- Place a sticker on your forehead. Your child has to look you in the eye and name the sticker. Do this at odd moments when your child is not expecting to see anything unusual. Make it a game to find the sticker and name it.

- Create a special pair of handmade or purchased eyeglasses that you call the "Look at My Eyes" glasses. These may be funny and wildly decorated. When wearing the glasses, your child must look everyone in the eye. Use additional pairs for siblings and friends who can also participate in this game. Have your child wear the glasses for five minutes each day, and increase the time gradually.

- Purchase a variety of funny eyeglasses. In my collection, I have bunny glasses, frog glasses, Groucho Marx glasses, glasses with rhinestones, star glasses, and heart glasses. Put them on when your child is not expecting it, and time how long it takes him to notice. Once he gets accustomed to looking at you, the time will shorten and looking at you will become a positive habit.

Facial Expressions

According to communications researchers, about 38 percent of the meaning of your message is communicated through facial expressions. So, they are a very important part of communication. Research has also shown that there are universal facial expressions such as happiness, grief, and anger. But, what triggers these emotions varies from culture to culture. What is important is that the facial expressions match the message being sent. For example, if I say, "I love camp" and I am smiling and look happy, it reinforces my verbal message. But, what happens if I look sad and my voice sounds sad or angry even though I am saying "I love camp?" Research has shown that the listener will believe the nonverbal message if the verbal and nonverbal messages being sent don't agree.

Children with Down syndrome are often very adept at reading people's emotions. They might know immediately that you're feeling sad. However, children with Down syndrome some-times have difficulty reading facial expressions. For example, when your child is joking around with his brother and you intervene because it is time to get ready for bed, your child with Down syndrome may keep joking around and miss your subtle facial expressions that show you are becoming increasingly annoyed. You can help your child by providing a verbal cue, such as "I'm getting annoyed. It's not time to joke anymore; it's time to go to sleep. Can you see my face?" Practice can help your child learn to tune in to facial expressions and interpret them.

It is very important for your child with Down syndrome to be able to understand or decode facial expressions and emotions and to be able to use appropriate facial expressions that will reinforce his verbal message. Facial expressions are really best learned at home through real-life experiences, within the family setting.

HOME ACTIVITIES

- At home and in the community, you can talk about how we look when we are happy or sad. You can comment, "You look happy today because you're getting a new bike," or "Bobby looks sad today because his dog is sick."

- Use cartoon-like smiley and sad faces to stimulate discussion about when we feel happy, sad, and angry, and about how we look. These often come in packs of stickers, or you can use photographs or draw cartoons. Talk about when you would make that kind of face; what situations would evoke that kind of feeling.

- You can practice making different kinds of faces in the mirror and comment on them. Again, talk about the situations that would make you look like that face.

- Use photos in which family members or friends look happy or sad, and talk about what they were doing at that time. For example: "Bobby looks scared in that picture. That roller coaster he is on looks very big. Wow, he must feel scared."

- Read a book with your child that explores feelings such as *Alexander and the Terrible, Horrible, No Good, Very Bad Day* by Judith Viorst. Make faces that describe how Alexander is feeling as you read about each situation.

- Play with a puzzle such as the "Moody Bear" puzzle, which comes with different outfits and different expressions (happy, sad, surprised, scared) that you can mix and match.

Requests

The ability to make and respond to requests appropriately is an important skill that helps ensure that our environment will meet our needs. Children begin to use gesture, sound making, and eye gaze to show what they want early in development. They may make a request by pointing to or looking at an object and making some sounds or grunts. Research has shown that young children with Down syndrome are less likely to make nonverbal requests than typically developing children, and that their delays in nonverbal requests are related to later expressive language skills.

Making requests is generally learned as part of daily life, but you can help enhance and reinforce it. Comment on your child's requests when he uses them. For example, "You want more cheese. Sure, I can give you some more." Or, "You asked to watch the cartoons very nicely. I'll turn the TV on for you."

There are different types of requests that children with Down syndrome need to learn. Often, the earliest requests are general ones such as "Help!" *Imperative ellipsis requests,* or requests that name what is wanted without using a verb, are usually mastered earliest, and may be produced using Total Communication, as well as speech. For example, "More juice" is an imperative ellipsis that is learned very early in language development, often first by signing. *Imperatives,* such as "Give me the ball," are usually mastered by children with Down syndrome quite early. Modeling and imitation with expansion (discussed in Chapter 6) can be used to teach the different request forms.

HOME ACTIVITIES

- Explicit needs and wants requests, such as "I want a drink" or "I need my coat," can be taught through pattern practice as follows:

     Parent first models, "I want more cheese" or "I want my coat."
     Child imitates.
     Parent: "What do you want?"
     Child: "More cheese."
     Parent: "*I want* (emphasize) more cheese. What do you want?"
     Child: "I want more cheese."

     Requests can also be taught when your child is signing or using PECS or a communication board.

- Requests can be taught as a part of routines or scripts. Then it will seem natural and familiar to your child to use the request when the situation occurs. For example, you would teach your child the pattern "May I have _____ please?" Or "I want more ____ please." Then, you would provide support and practice through role playing a real-life situation. So, you might play that you are going to the bakery. Prompt your child by saying, "You see the cookies, and you really want one. What can you say?" You may even write out a cue card if your child can read, "May I have a cookie (picture or word), please?" Or you may say the word "may" or put your lips together to make the "m" sound as a visual cue.

- Practicing requests can also be a very good way to encourage your child to speak in complete sentences or phrases. Children with Down syndrome tend to leave out needed elements of sentences, reducing a request such as, "May I have more juice, please" to "Juice." As much as humanly possible, try to insist on complete sentences or phrases when your child makes requests. One method is simply not to respond until your child makes a request with a full sentence. Another is to cue your child with a sign or picture. For example, use the sign for cookie or a picture of a cookie, or a sign for your pet when your child doesn't see him and wants to know where he is. You can use a pacing board and write the words on top of the dots. But, be sure to demand only what your child is able to say so as not to frustrate him. If he can say two words, don't withhold what he wants because he is not telling you in

four words. If your child has apraxia, he may not be able to say sounds
or words consistently. This is not willful. Your child may need to use a
combination of speech and sign language or a communication board
with signs until he is able to use speech alone.

- Put a toy in a plastic canister or jar with a lid secured on it. Give your
child the jar, but do not remove the lid. You are providing a situation
where he needs to request help. If necessary, model how to ask for
assistance or prompt him to do so. He can use a sign, picture, or words
depending on what he is able to use.

More Advanced Skills

The pragmatics skills discussed above are basic to conversation and to functioning well at home, in school, and in the community, and can be learned by most
children with Down syndrome. Other pragmatics skills are more advanced, and
will probably only be mastered by older children and adults who function independently and at more sophisticated cognitive levels. For example, explaining to the
teacher or your boss why you will be late or responding to someone's request for
instructions or information are advanced skills.

Remember, pragmatics skills are learned through interaction and experience.
Every new experience will enhance your child's pragmatics skills and his skills can
continue to grow throughout adulthood. The following skills may be more difficult
for children with Down syndrome, but are worthwhile to work on. For each area,
the basic levels of the skill are discussed.

Conversational Skills

Conversational skills are skills that enable us to participate in conversations both
as a speaker and listener. Some basic conversational skills, such as turn-taking,
are learned even before children begin to speak. Other, more advanced conversational skills, are generally learned over time, through experience. These include:
initiating the conversation; responding; keeping a conversation going and termi-
nating a conversation; and knowing when to pause, how to interrupt, and how to
provide feedback to the speaker. They are all explained below.

One of the basic conversational skills, called simply "conversational manners,"
is knowing when you can interrupt, when not to interrupt, and how to interrupt
either when it is not your turn in the conversation or when you are not part of the
conversation. Role playing, and commenting during real situations (be sure it is
not a situation that will embarrass your child), are the best ways to teach your
child conversational manners. As more children with Down syndrome are included
in their schools and communities, it appears that, although they may interrupt the
teacher, take inappropriate turns, or ask inappropriate questions at the beginning
of the school year, they usually eliminate these conversational behaviors after a

few months. The natural consequences of teachers and other students saying, "Don't interrupt; it's not your turn now" or "Knock it off" modifies the behavior. Experience and practice are the best teachers for conversational manners.

STYLISTIC VARIATIONS

Stylistic variations is the term used to describe a person's skill in adapting his communication to his audience and the situation. It is a common, yet hardly noticed, skill people use in daily interactions. Using this skill means that we modify how we talk to people, not necessarily what we actually say. As children grow, they learn a variety of different rules or formats to use when talking with people in different social roles. This might include knowing how to use polite, formal, and colloquial language. It might involve knowing how to talk to a two-year-old cousin, a peer, a teacher, or the minister in different ways, and understanding what is appropriate for each situation. This is difficult to learn because there are so many possible permutations and different situations. Children with Down syndrome benefit from extra help and practice in this area.

Parents are usually the best teachers of this skill. Usually, it is best to talk to your child about adjusting the way he interacts with someone prior to encountering them or as the situation presents itself. One of the most effective ways to teach stylistic variation is through role playing.

HOME ACTIVITIES

- Practice in the most "natural" setting possible. Set up the situation clearly, and use props and costumes to make the role playing as realistic as possible. For example, if you want your child to practice going to a friend's house for a pajama party, have him pack his pajamas, bring his radio, and take clothes for the next morning. Then set up a part of the room that is "your friend's house" and play out various scenarios to practice what is appropriate communication and what is not appropriate. For example, how do you ask your friend's mother for a soda, or what would be appropriate to say if your friend's younger brother is annoying you?

- Use verbal coaching or provide specific instructions to help your child give appropriate responses during the play or role playing. You might whisper in his ear to provide suggestions, such as "talk softly" or "call him Reverend Brown." Don't assume that your child is going to figure out the rules; teach him the rules of conversation. Role play how to act at the family wedding or the dance recital, and coach your child to help him learn the communication skills needed for the situation. Then praise his successes. "You spoke so nicely to the minister" or "You used your quiet voice and were so polite when you told Aunt Kathy how pretty she looked in her new dress." If you can find a book about a similar situation, read the book together and talk about it. Practice is needed, and experience is very important in teaching this skill.

- Change voices, loudness etc. as you role-play super heroes, Barbie, and popular personalities with dolls or action figures.

- Make stick puppets by drawing, tracing, or copying pictures of favorite characters from a children's story book. Color in the pictures. Then mount the cut-outs on cardboard or tag board to make then stiffer, and attach to Popsicle sticks. Read the storybook to your child, or choose a favorite story that your child already "knows." Retell the story using the puppets, and change the voices and the manner of speaking for each puppet, so that each puppet has a distinctive way of speaking. The superhero may have a deep loud voice, while the kitty cat meows in a high quiet voice.

PRESUPPOSITIONS

Presuppositions are the background information you assume your listener already knows without your telling him or her. Presuppositions require being able to place yourself in your listener's position. What does your listener know? What do you need to tell him? What will be familiar or unfamiliar to him? For example, if a friend asks you the best place to buy a new video, will he know where the store is located if you only name the store? Do you need to give directions?

Young children have difficulty with presuppositions because they are egocentric and because they do not have a great deal of language to explain things to the listener. A child will talk about his friend, Jeffrey, assuming that you know him. He will not stop to explain that Jeffrey is a friend from school. Parents can stop their child and ask, "Who is Jeffrey? I don't know him." This helps teach the child to explain what the listener needs to know. Children with Down syndrome have difficulty with presuppositions, and need more practice, coaching, and reminders to learn about what the listener needs to know. This important skill continues to develop throughout childhood and can continue to develop into adulthood.

TURN-TAKING

Early development in turn-taking is discussed in the beginning chapters. But turn-taking is also one of the important skills required in conversations for older children. Children with Down syndrome often have very short conversations. They will respond to your questions, but won't ask you any questions to keep the conversation going. They won't continue to take turns to keep the conversation active.

James MacDonald, a speech-language pathologist who has worked with many families and children with Down syndrome, feels that learning to take enough turns in conversation is one of the areas that is most important for communication success. The major area that he addresses in treatment is increasing the number of conversational turns, and focusing on engaging the child in conversations frequently and on a regular basis. If the child is not able to take turns in conversation, Dr. MacDonald will take turns by playing games with the child, such as by saying "I'm going to get you," or trying to step on the child's foot.

Conversational length may also be related to difficulties in topicalization (discussed below) and to vocabulary (semantic), grammatical (syntax), and verbal skills, but turn-taking skills play a role in the tendency toward short conversations. You can help your child build up to longer conversations at home, and can also help practice and reinforce those longer conversations. Often, turn-taking and topicalization must be practiced together because they are so intertwined. When you take your turn, you need to know how to continue with the topic and to stay on topic in order to keep the conversation going.

HOME ACTIVITIES

- Play movie director and have your children "act" out roles with dialogue that requires taking turns (write out the dialogue at first or use photos; later try to progress to improvised dialogue). Get a blackboard or a movie board, and a baseball cap or beret for the "director" as props to make this activity more fun and realistic. Cue cards may also be used to provide suggestions for your child on what to say and to emphasize that each "actor" must wait for his turn to speak. Or have a sibling play movie director and point to the person who needs to talk. This can be done even when your child is using two- to three-word phrases or is using signs to communicate. He just needs to have something to "say" and be able to take a conversational turn.

- Pick a topic that you know your child will be interested in, such as an upcoming trip to the baseball game. Use a visual cue, such as a baseball or balloon, to show whose turn it is and to help keep the conversation going. The person who starts the conversation holds the balloon. When he finishes, he passes the balloon to the next speaker. This activity can involve two people or even a small group. Don't make the group too large, however, or your child may get bored or distracted waiting for his turn. The balloon is passed back and forth and the last speaker gets to keep the balloon. This game may motivate your child and provide practice in longer conversations. This is an exercise in turn-taking and topicalization.

TOPICALIZATION

Topics are the material on which conversations are based; they are the subject of conversations. It is important to learn how to choose a topic for a conversation, how to introduce a topic, how to maintain a topic, how to stay on a topic, and how to change a topic. Some of these skills are beyond the birth to six-year-old stage covered in this book, but the basic idea of choosing a topic and staying on topic can be addressed early.

Research has shown that young children with Down syndrome have difficulty introducing new topics and are less likely to introduce new topics in conversations when compared with typically developing children matched by cognitive and linguistic level. Maintaining a topic and staying on topic are also often difficult for children with Down syndrome. These difficulties may result from mental retardation as well as a lack of conversational experience.

When you have difficulty maintaining a topic, conversations are short because you don't know what else to say about the topic. And, when you have difficulty staying on topic, your conversation may seem rambling and listeners may lose interest. Much progress, however, has been made in improving topicalization skills in children with Down syndrome. Increased vocabulary and conversational skills that result from enriched experiences are probably some of the main reasons that current generations of children with Down syndrome are so much more advanced in their use of language and in their conversational ability. Former generations of

children with Down syndrome often didn't have these types of language or life experiences. Parents, grandparents, siblings, and the stimulation of family and community life have made a tremendous difference in the conversational abilities of children and adults with Down syndrome.

Work with your child on topicalization in private, but be discreet when correcting him in public. Practice the skill, but also maintain your sense of humor. Don't expect perfection; sometimes, every child's comments are off the topic, but may be delightful comments on life.

HOME ACTIVITIES

- When you work with young children on categories, you are actually working on "topic" categories. Practice with older children can center on what goes with different topics. For example, if you want to talk about your trip to the aquarium, what could you tell Dad? What did you see? How did you get there? Children with Down syndrome learn well through the visual channel, so you might take photos at the aquarium. Then, give your child those photos plus photos of a trip to a bakery. Sort the photos into two shoeboxes or bins, labeled as "aquarium" and "not aquarium." That sorting activity is really a "staying on topic" activity.

- You can also work on categorization in the course of daily routines. So, if you are making a fruit salad, you can comment that you wouldn't talk about milk or cheese when you are talking about what you will put into the fruit salad.

- Make a game board with different topics on the board, such as "I got a new dress" or "We went to the beach." Use a spinner and a game pieces. Whatever space you land on, you have to say two things about that topic. When your child can say two things, up the ante to three. Use cues, such as "What else could you tell Aunt Sue about your new dress?" or "What did you make in the sand?"

- Words that you associate together are part of the same topic, so association games help children learn more about topics. For young children, picture games such as Baby Animal Lotto can be used. Lotto games that are personalized to your child's toys, rooms, people in his life can be made by scanning in pictures and making two copies, one for the board and one for matching cards.

- Games such as "I Spy" can be played in the car, on vacation, or while waiting for a doctor's appointment. In the beginning when your child has little language, you may need to provide all of the clues, but your child can look around and guess the object from your clues.

- Talk about topics that interest your child. For example, "If we want to talk about the baseball game, what are all the things we can talk about? We can talk about the stadium, the players, what we ate at the game, and what happened in each inning." Photos help with this practice. Reading children's books on specific topics helps too. Talk about what the book included; that's what is on the topic.

- To help your child learn about topics, create "topic totes." Fill a decorated box, basket, or plastic tote with objects and books that relate to a single topic area. For example, make a beach tote by filling a plastic pail with books about the beach and swimming, sunglasses, flip flops, a bathing suit, beach towel, a doll dressed for the beach, shovel, and shells. There are many possible topic totes, depending on your child's age and interests: a fall tote, Halloween tote, winter tote, holiday tote, jewelry tote with beads, macaroni, and string, or a cat or dog tote.

- Language experience activities are excellent for working on the skills needed for maintaining topics. In a language experience activity, the language is combined directly with the activity. For example, going to the supermarket is actually a rich language experience. Here is what you do: In advance, you talk about going to the supermarket, what you *will* do, who you *will* see. Then as you are going through the supermarket, talk about what you *are* doing. Take photographs. Later, using the photographs to guide the conversation, talk about what you *did*, who you *saw*, what you *bought*, or how you carried the groceries home. You might write a story about the trip to the supermarket, using the photographs to illustrate. Ask questions about the book that can't be answered with just "yes," "no," or one word, such as, "What did we do at the supermarket?" This provides a detailed exploration of a specific topic, and can be duplicated for other activities such as baking cookies, preparing for a birthday party, or going to the circus or the ice show.

- Ask questions about experiences your child has had. "What did you do at Jennifer's birthday party?" Ask for details, such as, "What did you eat? Who did you see? What games did you play? What gifts did Jennifer get?" Coach your child to help him stay on topic.

- Practice routines with your child through role playing. For example, discuss going to McDonald's, and point out what is and is not on the topic. Use props to make the situation more realistic, such as a McDonald's Happy Meal box or placemat. You can use a picture menu from McDonald's to visually prompt what is on the topic. For instance, can we buy popcorn at McDonald's? You are pointing out what "goes with" McDonald's and what does not.

- Give your child visual reminders, such as photographs of a trip, to give him practice in lengthening the conversation. For example, talk about Disney World using photographs. Or use sequential photographs or slides of an everyday activity such as food shopping. Each person uses one photo in the sequence to talk about what is happening in the picture. Then it is the next person's turn. Take detailed photos: for example, stopping at a red light, getting the shopping cart, buying milk and eggs, and checking out. Compare the conversation you would have with your child without the photographs, and then with them. The second conversation should be longer. Talk about how each of these pictures is "on topic."

CLARIFICATION AND REPAIRS

Clarification and repairs are two skills that go together. Clarification is asking for more information—clearing up a misunderstanding. The listener may ask for clarification ("What did you say?"), for specification ("Can you tell me what you mean?"), or for confirmation ("Is this what you are saying?"). Repairs involves recognizing when a communication breakdown has occurred, understanding what caused the breakdown, and providing the information needed to "repair" the misunderstanding.

Researchers have looked at how preschool children with Down syndrome respond to signals from adults who are having trouble understanding them. They concluded that the young children with Down syndrome consistently tried to respond to these signals, but they were not always sure how to clear up the confusion. That is, they were aware that the listener did not understand them, but unsure of how to improve the situation.

Although learning to make clarification and repairs is usually too advanced for children in the birth to six-year-old period, you can help your child develop awareness by asking for clarification from him. For example, if he is talking about Beth, ask "Who is Beth? Was she the girl you were playing with at the pool today?" See if you can get a head nod or yes for confirmation and clarification.

If your child uses an AAC system, it is important to make sure that he has ways to request clarification. For instance, he should have a way to express, "I don't understand" and "Could you repeat?" See Chapter 11 for more information about AAC systems.

HOME ACTIVITIES
- To help your child learn to ask for clarification, try giving him instructions that are vague. For example, say, "Bring me that thing." When he looks confused, ask him, "What do you need to know? Say, 'What do you want?'" Provide models and examples, and teach him what kinds of information he needs to ask. For example, "Do I want the telephone?" Name objects that are visible that you might be asking for.

- If your child cannot use speech to ask for clarification, show him how to look quizzical by holding his arms out as if to say "Which thing are you talking about?" Or use a picture cue your child can give to you that asks "which thing do you want?"

- Sometimes deliberately misunderstand your child if you know he can make repairs. For instance, if he asks simply for "more, please" and you are pretty sure that he wants more gravy, give him more of something else instead, like peas, and see if he will make the repair and ask for more gravy.

Conclusion

Your child needs to learn many pragmatics skills to be successful in conversation. Fortunately, there are abundant opportunities to work on pragmatics in real life. With inclusion in schools and in the community, children with Down syndrome have plenty of appropriate peer and adult models, more learning opportunities, and more practice with social interactive communication. Although your child may need more direct teaching to learn some aspects of pragmatics, with steady practice and support he can continue to develop these skills throughout childhood and into adulthood.

CHAPTER 11

Communicating without Speech

Learning and using spoken language can be very difficult for toddlers and young children with Down syndrome. As Chapter 8 explains, many anatomical and physiological factors associated with the syndrome, including low muscle tone, childhood verbal apraxia, and dysarthria, can affect speech development and speech production. In addition, any hearing loss, whether fluctuating or permanent, can affect speech and language development. Speech is rapid and fleeting, so it is difficult to learn language solely through the sense of hearing when you do not hear sounds clearly. Cognitive factors, such as difficulties with memory and attention, can also delay the acquisition of speech skills.

Some children with Down syndrome begin to use spoken words at age two, and a few children use speech before age two, but most children do not use speech until ages three to five years. We have seen children at our center who did not begin to speak until seven or eight years of age. In addition, a small percentage of children with Down syndrome are never able to use speech as their major communication system. Yet, a large number of children with Down syndrome are ready to communicate with a language system such as sign language by ten to twelve months of age. They just are not ready to use speech, which requires more advanced neuromuscular skills.

Whatever a child's age, it is important to ensure that she has an effective method for communicating. When a child can't get her message across, she usually becomes frustrated. She may stop trying to communicate or may find alternative ways of getting her message across. Sometimes, she will use pantomime or drag you over to show you what she wants. But, sometimes her message is more complex and can't be easily pantomimed or shown. She may vent her frustration through behavior, kicking, biting, or screaming to get the attention that she cannot get through communication. In these situations, it is important to provide an *additional method of communicating* or *alternate method of communicating*. This gives your child a way to share her message, promotes communication, and often reduces problem behavior resulting from communication frustration. Some children who are not communicating do not get to that level of communication frustration for a long time—they are passively letting the world go by and do not engage because they do not understand how they can engage.

Since it is critical to enable children to communicate when they are ready, many, if not most, children with Down syndrome, should be considered as candidates for *augmentative and alternative communication (AAC) systems*. Augmentative and alternative communication is any method that assists or supplements speech and language (augmentative communication), or, in some cases, replaces speech as the primary communication system (alternative). Examples of AAC include sign language, photo and picture cards, communication boards, and electronic or non-electronic communication devices.

Chapter 5 discusses using AAC with young children with Down syndrome to help them make the transition to speech. This chapter discusses additional reasons that AAC might be useful, as well as types of AAC systems, considerations for selecting, programming, and training in using AAC systems, and information on how to find professionals who have the expertise and experience to design appropriate and useful communication systems.

General Reasons to Consider AAC

In general, AAC systems are used as transitional, supplementary, or alternative means of communication.

Using AAC as a Transition to Speech. A transitional system is typically used as a bridge between language and speech. Transitional augmentative systems are appropriate for children who are not beginning to use speech by twelve to eighteen months of age and who are becoming frustrated by their inability to be understood by parents, siblings, and others. This includes the majority of children with Down syndrome. As discussed in Chapter 5, many children with Down syndrome use sign language or communication boards as transitional communication systems. The systems will be used to communicate their needs and desires until they are able to speak.

Using AAC to Supplement Speech. A supplementary system adds to a child's communication abilities by providing vocabulary, sentence structure, and comments that are new or too difficult for her to produce by herself. Sometimes, signs, communication boards, or electronic devices are also used to supplement speech when intelligibility is a problem for the older child or adolescent who has a lot to say, but is hard to understand.

Using AAC Instead of Speech. An alternative communication system serves as a child's primary method of communicating when she is unable to use speech to get her messages across. These systems are usually provided for older children, beyond first grade. But, they can be provided for younger children, as needed. These systems are often the most complex and time consuming to design, because they need to meet all of the child's needs for communication at home and in the community. If the child is of school age, they must also be designed to meet her needs for learning and communication at school.

Does Your Child Need AAC?

Currently, Total Communication (a type of AAC) is recommended for most young children with Down syndrome to help them make the transition to speech (see Chapter 5). Once children with Down syndrome begin to use speech to communicate, they still often rely quite a bit on gestures, facial expressions, and pointing to get their messages across. Often when their speech is difficult to understand or produce, people with Down syndrome are very creative at using alternative methods of getting their message across. For instance, a child who wants some ice cream but cannot use the words in a way that is understandable may take you by the hand and pull you over to the freezer, open the door, and point to the ice cream sandwiches.

Using augmentative and alternative communication adds to the choices of communication methods available, expanding the ways in which a child can send messages. For instance, if that same child used sign language for "ice cream" at the freezer door, she would be using AAC. If she has a communication board with snack choices, she may point to a picture of ice cream as well as a glass of milk on her communication board, expanding her message to "milk and ice cream sandwich." Or, she may have a voice output communication device with snack choices programmed on it. With this device, she could tell you, "I want milk and an ice cream sandwich, please," in a recorded voice from the device. Her message is the same, but using the AAC device enables her to build a sentence using "I want" and "please." With any of these AAC methods, she may or may not also use her own speech at the same time.

In general, if your child has reached kindergarten age, and speech and/ or sign are not meeting her needs to communicate effectively, other alternative communication systems should be considered. It should also be considered at any time when your child is frustrated and unable to communicate to meet her needs on a regular basis. All children have moments when they cannot be understood or can't get their message across, but if this is occurring on a daily or very frequent basis, AAC support may be needed. When children do not have a communication system that is adequate to meet their daily needs, they sometimes just give up and stop trying to communicate. We certainly don't want that to happen!

In addition, it may be appropriate to consider AAC support at an earlier age if your child has a dual diagnosis of autism and Down syndrome or has been diagnosed with childhood verbal apraxia. Having autism in addition to Down syndrome usually compounds communication delays, and learning a system other than speech to communicate can help a great deal. Children who have difficulties in motor planning for speech (apraxia) may be difficult to understand when they speak, so they may need assistive or alternative communication systems to communicate. Children with severe speech intelligibility problems may need an alternative communication system at all times for daily communication, or they may need it only when they are interacting with people outside of their immediate circle.

What Types of AAC Systems Are Available?

All of the AAC systems that were discussed in Chapter 5 for use as transitional communication systems may also be used with older children for supplementary or alternative communication systems. Options include:

- gestures/sign language systems,
- communication boards,
- communication books, including portable books and notebooks/large books,
- Picture Exchange Communication System (PECS), and
- electronic devices.

GESTURES/SIGN LANGUAGE SYSTEMS

By the age of five years, children with Down syndrome have usually outgrown the need to use signs as their primary communication system, but signs may continue to be helpful when a new language concept is introduced. For example, signs for prepositions such as in, between, or through are very visual and help children learn the concepts. Signs may also be useful as an adjunct to speech at times when it is hard for your child to get her message across verbally, such as when she is angry or tired, and may be used to cue words or actions. Signs may also be used when your child really wants to be understood clearly.

If your child has childhood verbal apraxia, it may be appropriate to continue using signs to communicate in daily life while she works in therapy on the motor planning movements needed for clear speech. For example, here is a description written by the parents of a little boy with Down syndrome and apraxia who used signs as a transition to speech:

> *Before Jordan was 11 months old, he was signing "more" and "all done." Soon many more signs followed. He was very adept at picking up new signs; often, he needed to see it only once and it became part of his repertoire. At two and a half, he said his first word, "apple." By the time he started school at three, he was using a hundred signs on a regular basis. He could ask for just about anything he wanted. He could also show us how much he was learning. At four he was making vowel and some consonant sounds and we kept thinking he would be talking within six months (and then within the next six months). Then at four and a half, Jordan was diagnosed with apraxia. It was devastating! Not only did he have speech delay secondary to Down syndrome, he now had this other obstacle to overcome.*
>
> *But recognizing that he had apraxia was the turning point for Jordan. His therapy was tailored to overcome the problems with motor planning that children with apraxia have. By five, Jordan*

was making sounds with almost every sign he used. At five and a half, some words became intelligible. He would use "daaahh" to express pleasure and grunt to show his displeasure. Every morning, we would ask Jordan how he was and he would say, "daaahh." Jordan was six when he began to transition from mostly signs to mostly words. Over the next six months he began dropping signs rapidly and picking up new words. One morning we asked Jordan how he was and he said "fine." And we knew he would be.

In general, signs are not usually the primary communication system for older children and adults with Down syndrome unless they have a significant hearing loss and are using signs the way any deaf person might. See Chapter 5 for more information on signing and Total Communication.

COMMUNICATION BOARDS

Communication boards are individually designed communication systems that may involve the use of pictures, photographs, rebus symbols or pictographs, alphabet letters, or words. The pictures may be mounted on paper, tag board, foam core board, flannel board, magnetic board, or other surfaces. The usual purpose of a communication board for children with Down syndrome is as a transitional system to promote the use of language while the child is not yet ready to use speech.

A communication board may also be used as a supplement to speech. For instance, if your child's speech can be understood by family but not others, she might use speech at home and a communication board at school. If she frequently communicates with people in the community, such as day care workers or bus drivers who do not know sign language, or if she has difficulty with the motor skills needed to sign, communication boards offer another channel for communication.

Communication boards are inexpensive, adaptable, and easy to change and update, as well as easy for the communication partner to decode. Communication boards may range from the simple to the complex, and the system may not even involve a "board." Some examples of communication boards are:

- photos of containers of orange juice, apple juice, and milk mounted on magnets on the refrigerator door so that your child can indicate her drink preference;
- line drawings of your child's favorite toys so that she can indicate her play preferences;
- small photos of relatives and line drawings of basic needs (bathroom, glass of water) inserted in the plastic pockets of a board book so that your child can call someone for help;
- symbols or alphabet letters painted onto a wooden board;
- commercial pictures of fast food items laminated and hung from a small key chain to enable an older child or adult to order food independently at her favorite fast food restaurant;
- a topic board that shows choices of preschool activity centers, so that your child can choose the center of choice. At each center, a topic board can show the choice of activities (e.g., at the music center: tape recorder with story, CD with music, "Eensy Weensy Spider" and other finger play songs on tape);

- topic boards in specialized areas at home (such as the kitchen or bathroom) with vocabulary and requests appropriate for those areas.

The best communication boards are developed to meet the unique needs of a specific user. Pictures included on your child's board should be geared to her interests and vocabulary and should be updated frequently as her needs change. As a parent, you may develop a communication board for your child to use at home, or you may serve as a major source of information for the speech-language pathologist designing the communication board.

There are many materials available commercially that simplify the actual production of communication boards. These range from laminated folders to albums to plastic key chain tabs. There are photos, line drawings, and symbols that can be purchased in different sizes, shapes, and colors. The wide variety available makes it possible to meet the specific needs of any communication board user. You and the speech-language pathologist can work together to design the best system for your child. The Picture Communication Symbols© made with Boardmaker™ software (Mayer-Johnson, Inc.) are the most widely used pictures for developing communication boards. Sources for pictures and symbols that may be used on communication boards are provided in the Resource Guide at the back of the book.

COMMUNICATION BOOKS

Instead of a communication board, some children use notepad- or pocket-sized books that have pictures, symbols, or words on the pages. Portable books may also be wallet type, credit card case, mini photo album, or plastic cards on a key chain. Any of these systems can serve as communication systems for a child or adult. Sometimes, separate books, albums, or key chains are used for different domains and situations. For example, a child may use one book for lunch and a separate book for reading and circle time. Portable books or cards may be attached to belt loops using a coiled, phone-cord-like key chain, or hung around a child's neck on a lanyard.

Notebooks or photo albums are larger-sized communication books. These are often used in specific situations, where they can stay in one place. For example, a communication notebook can be available in the kitchen, in the bedroom, or in the playroom. Since they are larger, they are a bit less portable, but they can hold more pictures, photos, symbols, or words.

PICTURE EXCHANGE COMMUNICATION SYSTEM (PECS)

The Picture Exchange Communication System was originally developed by Andy Bondy and Lori Frost to help children with autism learn to initiate communication. Using the system, communication partners physically exchange communication symbols such as photographs or line drawings as the basis for communication. In early exchanges, pictures are chosen to help the child get her immediate and most desired needs met—for instance, by requesting a pretzel or a favorite toy. PECS is especially useful for children who are not using natural gestures or pantomime to get their needs met. It often works well for children who have the dual diagnosis of Down syndrome and autism spectrum disorder. PECS helps teach communicative intent and turn-taking. It not only provides pictures for the concepts, but it actually teaches the child how to communicate. As the PECS program is implemented, children learn to build sentences using a combination of symbol or photo cards, to express desires, comments, and answer questions.

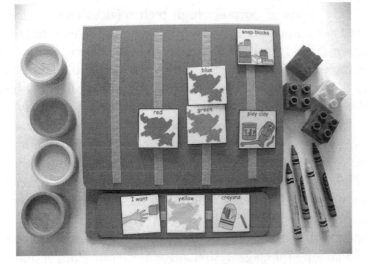

Studies have shown that PECS does not discourage children from going on to develop speech, and may actually encourage speech. As with Total Communication, the communication partner models correct speech when responding to the child. For example, if the child hands her mother the "I want" and "apple" symbols, the mother reads the child's message aloud ("I want apple") before responding to the message. For further information on PECS, see Chapter 5, as well as the Resource Guide and References and Suggested Reading section.

ELECTRONIC DEVICES

A variety of technologically based communication systems can enable children to communicate through speech, pictures, or writing. These "high tech" devices may be large and computer-based or smaller, more portable electronic devices. There are many good choices available from a variety of companies. The most important consideration is that the electronic device matches your child's skills and needs, so it is usable by your child. A system that sits on a shelf is useless. The only valuable communication device is one that is used constantly and meets your child's communication needs.

Computer-based communication devices are expensive and are more typically used with older children when speech is not a viable option, but they can also be used with younger children to provide a transitional system to speech. For children who have a great deal to communicate, but have difficulty learning sign language, a computer-based communication system that uses synthesized speech can enable them to communicate by "speaking electronically." Computers using synthesized speech can be helpful because:

1. They can provide a voice when the child is not able to speak.
2. They can provide consistent stimulation for speech. That is, when your child accesses a word or phrase, the computer produces it the same way each time. So, your child hears it said the same way each time.
3. Synthesized speech is slower than natural speech. For children with auditory processing difficulties or with speech production difficulties such as apraxia, slower speech is easier to process.
4. Synthesized speech can be repeated as many times as needed.
5. The computer gives the child control.
6. Using synthesized speech and text writing can help children develop literacy skills. Written language can also help children learn meaning directly without speech. Children can learn concepts and the label for the concept (word) without saying the word.

Not all high tech devices use synthesized speech. Smaller, less expensive, and more portable devices are often tried before a computer with a speech synthesizer. Or other devices may be used in conjunction with a synthesizer.

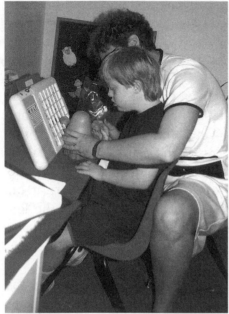

Many types of portable high tech devices can be used to help children communicate. For example, parents can use "talking" picture frames or "talking" photo albums to record messages appropriate for a specific place or activity, similar to the way topic boards are used. Along the same lines, the BigMack Communication Aid (AbleNet) is a small electronic recording device that can record and play back messages from twenty seconds to one minute long. If your child has a classroom aide, she can record messages right before your child needs to use them. For instance, she might record morning greetings for your child to play back when she sees her friends, or a repetitive line from a book the teacher is reading to the class. Partner One (Mayer-Johnson, Inc.), One-Step Communicator (AbleNet), Chipper (Adaptivation), and Full Moon Talker (Empowering Resources Inc) are similar one message systems. Partner Four (Mayer-Johnson) and Go Talk 4 (Attainment Co.) are easy-to-use systems that play up to four different pre-recorded messages.

There are many more complex devices that enable children to communicate by using preprogrammed messages spoken via a synthesized electronic voice, including the Alpha Talker II and ChatBox (Prentke Romich), Digivox, DynaMyte (DynaVox), Easy Talk (The Great Talking Box Company), Go Talk (Attainment Co.), Hawk and SuperHawk (ADAMLAB), VoicePal Max (Adaptivation), Macaw (Zygo Industries), and Tech/ Talk (AMDI - available through Mayer-Johnson). Speaking Dynamically (Mayer-Johnson) is software that attaches to your computer to enable the child to use her computer as a communication system.

Designing an AAC System

As you can see, a wide variety of augmentative communication systems are available today to enable a child or adult to communicate. All of these systems can be customized to meet the needs of their users, as well as to capitalize on their strengths. That is why we refer to *designing* an AAC system, rather than choosing one.

Once it has been determined that your child "needs" an augmentative communication system, and is "eligible" for a system through the school, there are many pertinent issues to be considered. (See the section on "AAC Evaluation and Eligibility" on page 206 for information on eligibility.) An evaluation must be conducted to determine an appropriate and effective communication system for your child. In some school systems, the evaluation is conducted by an augmentative communication team; in other school systems, by a speech-language pathologist. In addition, you, as a parent, should be involved by providing information on your child's communication needs at home and in different settings. And, once your child is using the system, you can provide important feedback on its effectiveness.

Larger school systems, or consortia composed of several school systems working together, are more likely to have an augmentative communication team. These teams are set up to evaluate whether your child is eligible to receive equipment and services through the schools. They are also set up to evaluate which systems will meet your child's needs, and to order, program, and service the equipment. Investigate whether there is an augmentative communication team available to you through your local school system.

Designing AAC systems requires expertise and daily experience. The technology changes rapidly and there are frequent upgrades in products. The professional evaluating your child not only needs up-to-date knowledge, but also must have a variety of equipment to try with your child to determine which system is most effective. If the equipment is not available, it is difficult to evaluate your child and determine what will work best. If the equipment is limited, there is a tendency to try to prescribe the available equipment, instead of looking for the equipment that meets the child's needs.

There are specialized centers in most states that can conduct in-depth evaluations to develop an appropriate communication system. Under the mandates of The Technology Related Assistance to Individuals with Disabilities Act of 1988, technology centers have been developed throughout the country. For a complete listing of centers, contact RESNA or see the Resource Guide at the end of the book. There is also a network of augmentative communication provider centers known as the Alliance for Technology Access (ATA). For a complete listing of ATA centers, contact ATA or see the Resource Guide. These centers can provide a variety of assessment services. Some centers are involved in the development of personal communication systems for children, and some centers lend equipment to families. Many have staff who can help you learn more about funding the devices. The services vary, so be sure to check the websites for RESNA and ATA and contact several centers to seek more information.

ISSUES TO CONSIDER

Some of the questions that the communication team can answer include:

1. How can your child best respond or activate the system (pointing, pushing a switch)?
2. What methods does your child currently use to communicate?
3. What should the content of the communication system be? What does your child want to "say"? (See "Selecting a Vocabulary" below.)
4. Where will your child use the communication system—in one setting, such as in preschool, or in many settings? Needs may be different in different settings (school or home).
5. Will the system or device be moved from place to place? Will it be used outdoors as well as indoors?
6. With whom will your child use the communication system? Will she use the system with the same few people or many different people (parents, day care providers, teachers, bus driver, siblings, friends)?
7. What type of symbols will be used—pictures, photos, line drawings, words? See "Symbol Systems" on page 201.
8. How many symbols will be used? Can your child choose from three symbols or can she choose among twenty symbols?
9. How will the system be organized? For instance, how many symbols will there be per page and how will they be arranged on the page?

10. How will your child select the language components to use them for communication? Will she use direct selection (see below) or will a light scan all choices until she stops the system at the choice she desires?
11. How simple or complex are your child's language needs and language capabilities?
12. How will the "listener" receive the message? What kind of output system (synthesized voice, printout on screen, typed message on paper) will be used?
13. What considerations are there relative to the size, portability, and durability of the communication board or device?
14. Will there need to be different communication boards for different settings? Or can different overlays be used for different settings, with your child carrying the system from place to place?
15. How much training does your child need to effectively use the system?
16. How much training is needed for significant people who interact with your child to learn to interact with the system?
17. Who will provide training for your child? the teachers? the family?
18. When and where will the training occur?
19. What is the plan for follow-up to determine whether the communication system is working effectively?
20. What is the plan for keeping the information current?
21. What is the plan for maintenance of the system? What if the system breaks down?

INDICATING A RESPONSE

How will your child indicate which symbols, words, or other language elements she wants to use from her communication system? For children from birth to six years, there are generally two appropriate options:

1. *Direct selection*—Your child indicates the desired item from a selection set by pointing, hitting a switch, using a mouse, etc.
2. *Scanning*—Items are presented one at a time and your child stops the system when it has reached her desired choice. This option benefits children with limited motor skills who cannot directly select an item but can push a large switch to stop the system at the right item.

Another option, called *semantic encoding,* is most often used by people who have physical difficulties producing speech but need to be able to communicate complex messages because they are at a high level cognitively. For instance, the Minspeak semantic encoding approach uses multiple-meaning small pictographs on the keys which can be combined to call up prerecorded sentences and can be customized for various environments or domains (home, school). This type of system is not typically used for children with Down syndrome.

SYMBOL SYSTEMS

What types of symbols can be used to represent language concepts and enable your child to communicate?

- Objects
- Photographs
- Colored pictures
- Black and white line drawings
- Abstract symbols
- Alphabet letters (for older children)
- Words (for children who can read)

Objects. Objects are the most direct and the least abstract way to identify the language concept. Instead of using the word or symbol for "cup," the child points to a cup. In many cases, miniaturized versions of the objects (such as a car or train) will be used instead of the actual objects. The objects must always be available to the child in order for communication to occur. Sometimes miniature objects are hung on a key chain and attached to the child's belt loops or put in the child's pocket. A fanny pack can also be used to hold the objects. Objects are most useful for very young children or children who do not understand that a picture can represent an object.

Photographs. Photographs may be taken in color or black and white. Generally, colored photographs are preferred because the color provides additional cues for the child and corresponds more closely to what the child sees when she looks at the object. The greatest benefit of photos is that they look like the actual objects—that is, they are specific rather than general. So, if your child wants to say "I," she can point to a picture of herself, rather than a generic picture of a girl. If she wants to say, "Go home now," she can use a photo of her own house rather than a generic photo of a house that may not look like her house. Not all of the concepts children want to communicate involve objects. Photographs can also show people, events, seasons, and holidays.

Photographs are very useful for communication boards. Using digital cameras and scanners, photos can be easily transferred into the computer and then onto a communication board.

Colored Pictures. Colored pictures may be cut from magazines or picture dictionary books, or may be printed out using software packages. Although the pictures are representational, the colors provide additional cues that help a child identify the object from the picture. Most standardized language and intelligence tests use colored pictures or black and white drawings. So, using pictures helps children learn skills that they will need for test taking. There are many software programs that provide printable small colored pictures that can be used for communication boards. See the Resource Guide for information.

Black and White Line Drawings. Black and white line drawings can be hand drawn or computer generated. They are inexpensive, can be easily copied, and can be easily enlarged or reduced in size to fit on any size communication board. Since many tests use black and white drawings, children need to be able to respond to this type of drawing. There are many software programs that provide printable small drawings or pictures that can be used for communication boards. See the Resource Guide for information.

Abstract Symbols. Abstract symbol systems are closer to language than pictures because symbols may not look like the objects they stand for. Whereas a picture of a glass of milk looks like an actual glass of milk, a rebus, bliss symbol or other symbol does not necessarily look like the actual object. Abstract symbols are useful for representing ideas or other words that might be difficult or impossible to take a picture of (for example, truth, happiness, fear). A drawback of using this type of symbols is that people who are unfamiliar with the system would not be able to figure out what your child is trying to communicate.

Alphabet Letters. Alphabet letters may be used for direct selection or for various types of scanning. If an older child has the ability to choose letters directly and to spell words, she can point to or type the appropriate letters. Sometimes, this is done with a communication board. At other times, a computer with a voice synthesizer is used. This system can only be used for older children who can use spelling to communicate. Thus, it is probably not an appropriate option for children six years and under.

Words. Words may be used as individual words or as triggers for phrases or sentences. For example, a communication board or computer system may have the individual words for "thank you," which the child points to whenever she wants to communicate "thank you." The child may also point to a word such as "please" to activate the phrase, "May I please have" or use one word to access a frequently used phrase such as "Let's order pizza." Some children with Down syndrome are able to read some words as early as three years of age, but many more children are not able to read until ages five to six or later, making this an option mainly for older children.

SELECTING A VOCABULARY

The size of the vocabulary included in your child's communication system will be determined, in part, by the type of system chosen, as well as your child's cognitive and language abilities. But, within that framework, how do you choose the vocabulary that will be part of the system? What vocabulary will be input into the high tech system or depicted through pictures or symbols to enable her to communicate? When selecting appropriate categories, the following should be considered:

1. What are your child's preferred activities? What does she most want to communicate?
2. What vocabulary is needed in each of her daily environments? What are her communication needs at home? at preschool or kindergarten? in the community?
3. What functions will the vocabulary play?
   - to initiate conversation
   - to make requests
   - to ask questions
   - to ask for help
   - to give answers and respond
   - to communicate socially
   - to share information
   - to express basic needs

4. How will vocabulary allow her to influence her environment (for example, "I want more"; "I don't want to do this anymore"; "I don't like this")?
5. Which expressions of emotion and colloquial expressions can enable her to participate with peers ("That's awesome"; "No way"; "That's super"; "Give me five")?
6. Which vocabulary is appropriate to the age and sex of your child (would "hi" be better than "good morning")?
7. Which carrier phrases, such as "I want to," are used often in conversation?
8. What messages can enable your child to participate in all settings? At home, they might include phrases such as "Wow!" or "Way to go!" as well as comments on favorite family hobbies, TV programs, or trips. In school, messages might include a repetitive phrase from a book that is read at circle time; a phrase such as "Me too"; a protest such as "Not me" or "I don't want to do that"; and requests such as "Help" or "Want to play with me?"

Vocabulary selection is an ongoing process. At some point, you may take a trip to the beach, and your child will want to communicate terms related to that experience, such as "sand," "waves," "pail," "shovel," "pour," "splash." Or you may notice that your child needs a way to ask for a break when she is feeling overwhelmed. Parents, teachers, speech-language pathologists, day care providers, and most important of all, your child herself (if she is older) can provide suggestions on an ongoing basis to ensure that the vocabulary is useful in meeting current needs. See the box on the next page for suggestions on how families can help.

Using AAC to Assist Language Learning

The primary purpose for using an AAC system is to enable someone to communicate effectively in a variety of situations. Another important objective is to enable the child to continue to develop language. Mary Ann Romski and Laura Meyers have both conducted research that has demonstrated that AAC can help children with Down syndrome progress in language learning. Meyers believes that the use of written language (through the computer) enables the child to progress more rapidly overall in language learning. This learning strategy is generally used with older children. Romski has had success in using sign language and other AAC systems to enhance language development.

Computers can be especially helpful learning tools for children with Down syndrome for the following reasons:

- Computers provide a visual display and visual reinforcement, which capitalizes on the visual strengths in children with Down syndrome.
- Computer graphics provide visual cues that can reinforce the visual message and help teach a concept.
- Auditory stimulation is usually accompanied by visual cues. For instance, when instructions are given verbally, there is

How Can Families Help?

When the communication system is being designed, families can provide important information. Once the system is designed, the need for family involvement continues. Some ways your family can help once a system has been designed include:

- Learn to use the augmentative system.
- Use the system consistently with your child. Make sure the system is available everywhere your child goes if it is designed to be used as her primary system throughout the day. Teach her to take it with her or have supporting people (classroom aide, peer buddy) who will be sure that the system is available when needed.
- If the system is being used as a transitional system, always use speech simultaneously with the sign or picture board, to encourage your child to make the transition to speech.
- Treat the augmentative system as a valid means of communication. Respond to the augmentative system as you would to speech. Have spirited conversations that interest your child to increase her motivation to use the system.
- Be a good communication partner. Reward your child's communication attempts by listening and responding. Do not interrupt. Teach familiar people how to be good communication partners.
- Be patient! Using an AAC system is often slower than speech, but your child's message will be worth waiting for. Be a good listener. Don't finish sentences for her or try to rush the process.
- Encourage grandparents, day care staff, friends, siblings, and others in your child's daily environment to learn the augmentative communication system and use it with your child
- Provide feedback to the SLP or the augmentative communication team regarding how well the system is working with different people in different settings as a communication system.

usually something on the screen that can help the child understand what she is supposed to do.

- Computers can provide instant feedback so that the child knows whether she has correctly answered the question. If she is incorrect, the computer can be programmed to provide the correct response, and then re-ask the question, providing an additional opportunity to learn. Errors can be handled in a positive manner, which can help self-esteem.
- Computer work can be highly individualized. Many programs can be modified for learner differences.
- Computers with speech synthesizers can provide verbal stimulation and verbal reinforcement that is slower than typical speaking rate, reliable (e.g., volume will not vary), and can be repeated. Regular speech is fleeting and may not be exactly the same when it is repeated each time. Synthesized speech will be the same and can be repeated over and over.
- The whole language approach to teaching language involves speaking, understanding, and concept experiences that help children learn vocabulary and meaning. Computer software

can help practice skills in these areas, especially in the areas of reading and language arts.

- On the computer, your child usually can control which activity she chooses and the number of repetitions for an item or a program. Control can help develop feelings of mastery and self-esteem.
- Most children love computers, talk about them, and compare and trade software. Computers have high interest for children and they view their time on the computer as fun, rather than work.

Of course, computers can't replace hands-on situational learning, nor can they replace SLPs or teachers. They cannot prescribe therapy or establish goals. But, they do provide a very effective means for teaching and reinforcing concepts and can serve as a strong support to learning. With early exposure to computers, many children feel comfortable and are advanced in using computers. What seems awkward to us as adults seems natural to children who are familiar with computers. A

computer system that includes a speech synthesizer that converts computer commands into artificial speech, a touch window that allows your child to respond by pressing on the screen, or a Power Pad (an alternate keyboard) can provide most of the support needed for the most frequently used software.

There is a vast array of educational and language software available that can be helpful to all children with Down syndrome, not just those who use AAC. Software is especially helpful for practicing specific concepts (*First Verbs, Stickybear Opposites*). For example, a bear that is "near" and a bear that is "far" away on the screen help teach or reinforce those specific concepts. You can then reinforce this learning through other experiences, such as on the playground. Once your child is able to use the programs in therapy, she should be able to use the same programs at home because most are very user friendly. The SLP, educators, and other parents can advise you on which programs are most appropriate for your child's learning needs and capable of engaging her interest.

Laureate and Edmark are two companies that provide software that addresses language concepts and that often works well for children with Down syndrome. (See the Resource Guide.) These companies have a strong tradition of customer service, and have technical representatives who can be of assistance to families and professionals. Software that we have used successfully with children with Down syndrome in this age range include *First Words, First Words II, First Verbs, Talking Nouns, and Talking Verbs.*

There are also centers dedicated specifically to the use of computers to enhance learning. Some centers are linked to a comprehensive Down Syndrome Center. For example, the center at Hope Haven in Jacksonville, Florida, is in the same facility as the Down Syndrome Center. Staff at these centers have a high level of expertise and knowledge concerning technology and software, as well as the learning needs of children with Down syndrome. Other centers are part of a national network of centers that specialize in computers and learning and computers and communication (for instance, the LINC center in Baltimore, Maryland, which is part of the Alliance for Technology Access network). (See Resource Guide.) These centers typically have a variety of computer-based communication devices, and can provide evaluation services. Some centers will prescribe software that will meet your child's needs or lend software and computers. Some of the centers are directly funded by the Tech Act. A list of these centers can be found on the RESNA website. Other centers are members of a national network known as the Alliance for Technology Access. Information on contacting both agencies is listed in the Resource Guide.

Low tech AAC devices such as communication boards can also assist in language learning. For example, children who previously could not make requests verbally can learn to do so with a communication board, and, of course, they can learn new vocabulary when new words are added to their board. In addition, the picture symbols used on communication boards can be used in a variety of ways for language learning. For example, picture symbols can be used to design early readers for children. Books such as *Hands-On Reading* (Mayer-Johnson Company) are designed to be used with picture symbol based-activities. Picture symbols can be used to help your child organize a language activity (such as using pictures to help her follow directions for a cooking or craft activity), and can be used to assist a speaking child in retelling a story or relating an experience. How technology can contribute to literacy and language learning is discussed in greater detail in Chapter 14.

AAC Evaluation and Eligibility

In the United States, each time an IEP or IFSP is developed for your child, the Individuals with Disabilities Education Act (IDEA) requires that her team consider whether she would benefit from assistive technology. (See Chapter 13 for information about IEPs and IFSPs.) Assistive technology is defined as "*any tool or item that increases, maintains, or improves functional capabilities of individuals with disabilities.*" This includes not only computer-based language devices, but also communication boards, switch-activated toys that prepare a child for communication, and communication device adaptations as the child grows and matures.

An AAC evaluation can determine whether an AAC system would benefit your child. An evaluation can be requested by the family, IEP team (especially the special educator, classroom teacher, or SLP), developmental pediatrician, or other specialists at a comprehensive Down Syndrome Center that follow your child on a regular basis. Based on the evaluation results, the IEP team should consider whether your child needs AAC as a transitional, supplementary, or alternative system.

If this team determines that your child might benefit from AAC, she will qualify for *Assistive Technology Service* on her IEP. This is defined as any service that directly assists a child with a disability in the selection, acquisition, or use of an assistive technology device. Assistive technology services include:

    (A) The evaluation of the needs of such child, including a functional evaluation of the child in the child's customary environment.

    (B) Purchasing, leasing, or otherwise providing for the acquisition of assistive technology devices by such child. (That is, your child's AAC system must be provided at no charge to you, the parents, if the IEP team determines she needs it.)

(C) Selecting, designing, fitting, customizing, adapting, applying, maintaining, repairing, or replacing of assistive technology devices. The selection of an appropriate device should be made with the consultation and guidance of a school AAC team, or a center that is a statewide technology center, or a participating member of the Alliance for Technology Access. The major consideration is that the center must have a wide variety of devices and equipment, and expertise and experience to enable them to determine what equipment is the best match for your child's needs and abilities (motor and language abilities).

(D) Coordinating and using other therapies, interventions, or services with assistive technology devices, such as those associated with existing education and rehabilitation plans and programs. For example, the SLP will help choose vocabulary but the OT may need to work on fine motor skills to help the child access the system with switches.

(E) Training or technical assistance for such child, or where appropriate, the family of such child. (That is, the school must teach your child and your family to use her AAC device.)

(F) Training or technical assistance for professionals (including individuals providing education and rehabilitation services), employers, or other individuals who provide services to, employ, or are otherwise substantially involved in the major life functions of such child. (That is, the school must provide training for school personnel who will need to communicate with your child.)

If your child is not found eligible for AAC or you are otherwise dissatisfied with the results, you can request an independent evaluation at the school district's expense. It would be wise to request that the new evaluation be completed by an AAC specialist, if your child has not previously been seen by one.

If your child is found eligible for AAC, the IEP team should focus on ways that AAC can be used to help her participate in and progress in the regular education curriculum (and when she is older, to make the transition to adult life). Your child's IEP/IFSP should spell out:

- How your child will be trained to use the AAC system;
- How the classroom teacher and others who interact with your child will be trained to "listen" to her;
- How AAC will be introduced to other children in the class to ensure that they will interact with your child when she is using her AAC device;
- The follow-up that will ensure the AAC is an effective communication system in all settings where it is needed;
- Who will be responsible for keeping the system current;
- Who is responsible for maintaining the equipment in good working order.

Again, it is important that parents be regarded as vital members of the team discussing your child's needs for AAC—not just at the first meeting where her AAC system is discussed, but at every IEP/IFSP meeting. Input should also be sought from every other member of the team, including: the assistive technology specialist, speech-language pathologist, special education teachers, and early intervention specialist or classroom teacher, as appropriate. AAC specialists have information about equipment. Speech-language pathologists have information about organizing language for communication interaction. Teachers have information about educational needs and classroom needs. Families have information about the communication needs of the child at home and in the community. Together, they can function as a team to design, train, and implement the use of augmentative communication systems.

Augmentative and assistive communication is dynamic and subject to change as a child's abilities change. Because a two-year-old uses sign language, it does not mean that the same child, at five years of age, will not be able to use speech. Or because a communication board with colored pictures is determined to be the best communication system for a child at age five, it does not mean that a high tech speech synthesizer will not be a better option when she is older. Just as a young child uses single words and an older child can have a conversation, AAC should keep up with your child's communication needs as she grows. A worksheet to help in designing an AAC system can be found on page 210. The need for and the effectiveness of augmentative, alternative, and assistive devices should be evaluated on a regular basis—at least once a year, during IEP development.

Conclusion

Augmentative and alternative communication can be used to make the transition to speech, or to provide a communication mode for children who cannot speak. For children with Down syndrome, AAC can be very empowering, unlocking doors to interactions at home, at school, and in the community that were previously blocked by difficulties with speech. In addition, technological advances have made it possible to use computers to assist language learning, and, if necessary, to augment or substitute for speech. There is a wealth of software that can engage your child in learning and can assist the professional with providing learning experiences outside of school hours. Professional expertise is available through your speech-language pathologist, educator, media specialist, and specialists at local, state, and regional technology centers. There is a rich resource network. At the back of the book, you will find lists of organizations and companies that specialize in AAC, sources for picture symbols, and a selected bibliography of books and research. Working together, we can help maximize the communication abilities of individuals with Down syndrome.

AAC and Speech-Language Pathology Services

AAC devices can give a child a means of communicating, eventually replacing or supplementing speech. But, they do not instantly provide language. Children must be taught to use the systems, and those systems must be used as part of a language development program. The system should be used *in* therapy, not *instead* of therapy. It is not uncommon to hear about children who have been provided with a communication aid and then removed from speech and language therapy, since they "now have a way to communicate." This would be equivalent to providing someone with a car and then not providing driving lessons since she now has the ability to drive. Or giving a child a clarinet, but not teaching her how to play it. It is very important to continue treatment in order to use the augmentative communication device to help your child progress in language.

What should you do if you are told that your child does not need speech-language therapy now that she has an AAC system? Let's look at two different approaches you could take for two different types of situations:

1. The IEP team insists that an aide or another staff member without speech-language training can teach your child to use her AAC device. In this case, the best response would be to find out more about the IEP team's proposal. If the aide has worked with many children with AAC devices, and has experience programming and maintaining systems, it may be appropriate for the SLP, teacher, and family to choose the vocabulary and to have the aide program, maintain, and help your child learn to use the system. But, a typical aide would not be acceptable because she would not have that experience.

2. The IEP team claims that there is nothing to teach your child about her AAC system since there are only six pictures on your child's communication board and she knows when to press each. To respond to this kind of argument, observe your child at home (and in school, if possible) and check off how many times she uses the system. Does she use it each time that it would be appropriate for her to "speak"? Does she become frustrated when using it? Does it enable her to communicate about everything she needs to or would like to? Tally up the data and bring it to the IEP team. Or ask them to keep data on how and when she uses the AAC device and whether it is meeting her needs.

WORKSHEET FOR DESIGNING AN AUGMENTATIVE COMMUNICATION SYSTEM

Name: _____   **Age:** _____

Current Needs:

❑ Transitional Pre-Speech System   ❑ Supplementary Learning System   ❑ Alternative Communication System

Team Members:

Type of System:

Unaided: *Sign Language*   Aided: Communication board ❑

SEE (Signed Exact English) ❑   Communication notebook ❑

ASL (American Sign Language) ❑   Picture Exchange System (PECS) ❑

Other ❑ _____   Electronic device (specify) ❑ _____

Other ❑ _____

Symbol System:

Objects ❑   Photographs ❑   Pictures ❑   Line drawings ❑

Letters ❑   Words ❑   Other ❑

Number of Symbols Used:

Content of System:

Sources for Pictures:

Settings:

Classroom ❑   Home ❑   Day care ❑   Community ❑   Other ❑ _____

Purposes:

Social communication ❑   Language learning ❑   Behavior prompts ❑

Other ❑ _____

Organization of Information:

Training Needed:

Child ❑   Parent ❑   Day care ❑   Teacher ❑   Other ❑ _____

Maintenance of System:

Funding of System:

_____

CHAPTER 12

Understanding Speech and Language Evaluation

In order for your child to receive the best, most targeted assistance in overcoming or compensating for his speech and language difficulties, he needs to be evaluated. Speech and language evaluations, or assessments, are the best way to identify the specific speech or language problems that may affect your child. That is why, for most parents and professionals, an evaluation is the first step in treatment.

Speech and language evaluation is a process that can give you a realistic picture of your child's current speech and language skills and how he uses them. Different terms may be used to describe a speech and language evaluation such as *assessment, diagnostic evaluation,* and *testing.* The terms often cause anxiety for parents because testing involves scores, comparisons, and judgments about their child. It helps, however, to keep in mind that testing also opens the door to treatment.

Evaluation and therapy are part of the same process leading to more effective functional speech and language skills. Evaluation provides information for treatment, and treatment results in changes in how your child communicates, which in turn affects his next evaluation. It is useful to regularly update evaluations so that the picture of your child's communication skills and your treatment plan stay current.

Why Evaluate?

Evaluations may be performed for a variety of reasons and may occur at many different times throughout your child's life. Reasons include:

- Child Find
- Screening
- Eligibility for services
- IEP/IFSP development
- Baseline testing
- Pre-testing and post-testing
- Specialized treatment
- Consultant/second opinion

EVALUATING CHILDREN UNDER AGE THREE

Your infant or toddler's first evaluation may be through your local school district or through an agency such as Child Find. Child Find programs (the name may vary from state to state) try to locate and identify children who have, or are at risk of developing, developmental delays and therefore need services to reduce or prevent delays. The purpose of a Child Find evaluation is to document your infant's or child's present skills in order to determine whether he is eligible for speech therapy, physical therapy, or other services according to the state guidelines. It is the evaluation that brings him into the early intervention or special education system.

The Child Find evaluation may be a brief screening or an in-depth evaluation. The purpose of a screening is to determine whether your child needs further evaluation. Screenings may take place at any age.

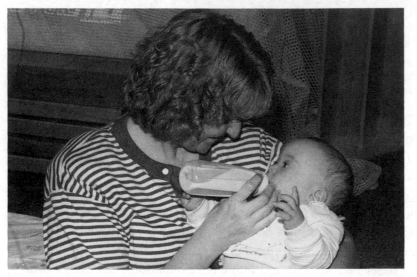

They may be the first step in getting you into the treatment system when a problem is suspected, or they may be routinely given at a specific age or at a specific point in your child's school career. For example, some HMOs screen hearing at well baby visits; some at six-month or annual intervals. Some school systems perform speech and language screenings before children enter kindergarten. Some preschools schedule screenings before children start preschool. Screenings are generally shortened versions of tests that sample a variety of skills. They do not provide detailed descriptions or profiles of your child's skills; rather they are a means of determining which children do not require further testing and which children do require further testing.

Your child's first diagnostic evaluation may be long and complex, or it may be a short intake interview. If your local early intervention system automatically provides services to babies who have been diagnosed with Down syndrome, the first evaluation may be just a formality, and consist more of filling out forms than actual evaluation. In that type of situation, the actual evaluation is carried out by the professionals during the first few sessions of therapy. They talk with you, observe your child, meet as a team, and try to develop a clear picture of how your child responds to his environment, how he learns, and what services he needs.

In your early intervention program, speech-language pathology evaluation and treatment services may or may not be routinely provided to all infants. You may need to request feeding and speech-language evaluations. These evaluations can determine your child's level of skill in various areas of speech and language and can then serve as a baseline to compare how much progress your child makes in the future. For example, initial testing may show that your child relies on pointing and pantomime to make his needs known. Future testing will document when he starts to make sounds and to use words. Or testing for an older child may document that he uses the /b/, /d/, /p/, /r/, and /m/ sounds. Future testing will document the new sounds your child adds to his repertoire.

If your infant or toddler is found eligible for speech-language therapy, information about his needs in this area, as well as the types and amounts of therapy he will receive, will be written down in an Individualized Family Service Plan (IFSP). See Chapter 13 for information about IFSPs. Remember that your child's needs and eligibility must be individually determined. Many parents have told me that their school systems have said, "We do not provide speech therapy for infants." This is a statement that goes against the spirit and letter of the Individuals with Disabilities Education Act and its amendments. Your child's needs are the basis for determining eligibility for services and this must be determined on an individual basis.

EVALUATING CHILDREN AGE THREE AND OLDER

An evaluation may also be conducted to determine whether your child is eligible for services in a particular setting (such as preschool or kindergarten) or from a particular agency. For example, at age three, children become ineligible for early intervention, whether or not they have mastered their IFSP goals. In order to continue receiving services such as speech-language therapy, they must be found to be eligible for special education services (generally available for children aged three to twenty-one). The local school system (often referred to as the LEA, or local education agency) will usually conduct an evaluation. This evaluation will determine whether your child is eligible to receive special educational services, including speech-language therapy, through the school system. Although most children with Down syndrome are found to need at least some special education services, they do not always qualify for speech-language therapy. See the section called "Who Is Eligible for Speech-Language Services?" in the next chapter for reasons this might happen.

Before the school can find your child eligible for speech-language therapy, your child's speech and language abilities must be evaluated, and the following questions must be answered:

1. Is there a communication disorder affecting your child's speech and language?
2. Is the communication disorder affecting your child's ability to learn in the classroom?
3. Is your child eligible for related services (therapies such as speech-language therapy necessary to help a child with disabilities learn) according to the guidelines of the local educational agency (LEA)?

The Individuals with Disabilities Education Act (IDEA), the federal special education law, stipulates that when a child is first being considered for special education services, he must be evaluated "in all areas of suspected disability." This statute should ensure that speech and language are always tested in children with Down syndrome since communication can certainly qualify as an "area of suspected disability" for children with Down syndrome. Parents should not be told that "in our district, we don't test speech until the child is talking," or "in our district, we test speech at age three for all children with Down syndrome." Since most children with Down syndrome are delayed in speech development, communication should always be considered an area of "suspected disability."

OTHER REASONS FOR EVALUATION

There are other reasons for evaluation, including:

1. To determine whether a specific treatment program you are considering, such as myofunctional therapy, would benefit your

child. If you were curious, you could request an evaluation for that specific program.

2. To obtain a second opinion (for example, about whether sign language use should be considered).

3. To get a more independent evaluation (for example, if the school does not have the equipment to test your child for an AAC device, or if you think the school is claiming your child does not need AAC because they do not want to provide an AAC system).

4. Because your pediatrician referred your child for a speech and language evaluation.

Requesting an Evaluation

The first thing you should know is that you, the parent, can request a speech-language evaluation for your child for any of the reasons above. If you are asking that the school system or early intervention agency evaluate your child, the evaluation will be at no charge to your family. You can also request a private evaluation from a speech-language pathologist at any time, provided you or your insurance company is willing to pay for it. Some states have funds that can be used by families for services such as evaluations. You do not need a medical referral or a referral from a school speech-language pathologist to qualify for an evaluation. Speech-language pathologists can accept referrals directly from parents.

If you think your child might benefit from speech-language therapy, you should not hesitate to request an evaluation. Studies have shown that parents are often as reliable as professionals in judging whether a child needs referral for evaluation. In addition, there is a high correlation between parental reports of vocabulary and syntax level and what the results of formal evaluation subsequently show.

How do you request a speech-language evaluation? If your child is in an early intervention program, ask the case manager/service coordinator how to request an evaluation. You can request a feeding evaluation or a hearing evaluation when your baby is an infant. Early language evaluations can be done before your child is speaking. You may find out that the early intervention program conducts ongoing evaluation as part of the treatment program, so they may have information regarding your child's language and speech progress that they can share with you.

If your child is under three but is not receiving early intervention, you can talk with parents in the local Down syndrome family group. They will often have names of speech-language pathologists who have worked with children in the group. In our center at Loyola College, that's how most of our families find us, through recommendation of professionals or other families. You can also ask your pediatrician about speech-language pathologists he has worked with in the area. If your child is seen regularly at a comprehensive Down syndrome center, the physician, therapists, and administrators will often be able to refer you to SLPs in your area. You can request an evaluation by contacting the SLP directly.

If your child is older than three, ask the SLP at the neighborhood elementary school how to set an evaluation in motion. If your child is already receiving services, ask what the schedule is for evaluations. Often they are done every three years. But, if you have concerns about speech and language, you can request an evaluation at any time.

If you cannot locate the agency or program responsible that can tell you how to get the evaluation process started, you can contact the National Information Center for Children and Youth with Disabilities (NICHCY) at 800-999-5599 or visit their web site at www.nichcy.org. Request a free copy of the *State Resource Sheet* for where you live. This sheet will list names and addresses for the agencies providing information about services under IDEA in your state.

Before the Evaluation

Once an evaluation is scheduled, ask lots of questions and offer information about your child so that you and the speech-language pathologist can plan for everything to go as smoothly as possible. Where will the evaluation be conducted? How long will the testing last? Will it be done in one session or several? Can you bring your child to the place where he will be evaluated a day or two before the evaluation to help him feel comfortable there? Suggest books that your child loves or songs that your child knows finger plays or dances for. Suggest toys or topics for

play and conversation that will interest your child. If food rewards will be used, suggest favorite snacks and let the SLP know about any food allergies or food preferences. Plan to bring favorite toys or stuffed animals to help your child feel comfortable.

Because the purpose of the speech and language evaluation is to get an *accurate* picture of your child's communication skills, ask if you can observe the evaluation session. (This will probably not be possible when an older child is being evaluated during the school day by the school speech-language pathologist, but should be permissible in most other situations.) Many diagnostic centers are set up to permit observation. Research has shown that children generally use longer phrases and sentences at home. So, if your observations of your child at home don't agree with the test results, you should talk with the speech-language pathologist and help her get a clearer picture of how your child usually communicates.

Tests of communication depend on your child's cooperation and comfort level during the testing. An unfamiliar setting, fatigue, an ear infection, or a cold may alter your child's performance. It is very frustrating to observe an evaluation and know that your child is capable of understanding language, saying words, and completing a task, but is not performing at that level during the test. Speak up! Any diligent professional is interested in getting accurate results, and you can greatly help by providing information. If your child is not identifying colors during the testing session, and you know that he can do this, talk with the SLP and suggest some activities that may enable your child to show that he has that skill.

What Happens During Evaluations?

The process of diagnostic evaluations, especially the initial evaluation, may vary greatly depending on who is performing the evaluation and where it is performed.

SCHOOL EVALUATIONS

When initial evaluations are performed at public expense by the school system to determine eligibility for early intervention or special education services, they are usually *multidisciplinary* evaluations. That is, professionals with many different areas of expertise evaluate your child separately, in all suspected areas of difficulty. Over the course of several days, your child will be seen not only for speech-language evaluation, but also for evaluation by a psychologist, occupational therapist, physical therapist, and perhaps a social worker.

School systems may use home-based or center-based (school or central office) evaluations. When the school system uses home-based evaluations, the SLP evaluates your child at home in his natural setting. The evaluation may be completed in one or several sessions. The professional will bring the testing materials to your home, and will meet with you at home or in the center office for a follow-up session to share the results of the evaluation.

PRIVATE EVALUATIONS

Private evaluations performed in university-based settings or sometimes in an SLP's office usually take place over more than one session. The SLP may even suggest a one-month period of diagnostic therapy for your infant or toddler to get a true picture of your child's typical speech and language skills over an extended time. This means that different therapy methods will be used, and the SLP will observe your child's reactions, play, and learning styles to get a picture of his typical functioning. At the end of that time, the SLP will develop a comprehensive treatment plan based on what she has learned while working with your child during that first month.

Private practitioners and SLPs in hospitals use many different models for evaluating speech-language skills. Feel free to talk to the SLP before the evaluation to find out exactly what to expect.

HELPING YOUR CHILD PERFORM WELL

If possible, speech and language evaluation should be conducted over several sessions in a familiar environment with familiar people. Studies have shown that children with communication difficulties perform more poorly with unfamiliar examiners than with familiar examiners (Fuchs et al. 1985). A one-session evaluation in an unfamiliar setting with unfamiliar examiners is unlikely to give an accurate picture of your child's typical language performance. This is frustrating for parents and professionals. Often, professionals are allowed a limited amount of time (two hours or one day) to conduct an evaluation, score the test batteries, and present the results to the family. This situation is most likely to occur with the first evaluation or if your LEA uses a county diagnostic center for testing than when the evaluation is conducted by the speech-language pathologist in the neighborhood school who knows your child.

If your child must be evaluated by unfamiliar people in an unfamiliar setting, then supplement the evaluation with videotapes (preferable) or audiotapes of your child at home, with siblings, friends, and grandparents engaged in communication. This can become part of the evaluation portfolio and can be available to the speech-language pathologists to help document your child's communication abilities. And be sure that observations and insight are provided by the early intervention, preschool, or regular or special education classroom teacher. IDEA allows for material provided by the parents and teachers to be included in the evaluation. This information is most difficult to have included at the initial evaluation, because you, your child, and the testers are all new to each other.

Regardless of whether the purpose of an evaluation is to assess many areas of development or just speech and language skills and regardless of where the evaluation is held, all evaluations follow certain general procedures. For example, they usually include a written and/or oral case history interview with you, and include a variety of different kinds of formal and informal tests. Tests might involve asking your child to identify pictures, repeat sounds, and follow spoken directions. (See the section on "Formal and Informal Evaluation.") In addition, the SLP will probably observe your child and how he communicates with you, and will take some time to play with your child, talk with him, and establish rapport.

Areas Evaluated

What is included in a speech-language evaluation will depend on the age and developmental level of your child. For infants and toddlers, evaluation should include language and speech *precursor* skills—that is, imitating sounds, or responding when you call his name. (See Chapter 4 for a complete discussion of communication, language, and speech precursor skills.) For a preschool, kindergarten, or school-age child who is using speech, a comprehensive speech and language evaluation should include assessment of:

- **speech:** your child's verbal output (how your child sounds when he speaks);
- **oral motor:** the strength and coordination of muscles in the mouth area used for speech;
- **receptive language:** your child's understanding of language through hearing and reading;
- **expressive language:** what your child says or expresses through speech and writing; and
- **pragmatics skills:** social interactive language including nonverbal communication.

For school-aged children, evaluation should also include language and literacy skills (reading), and curriculum-based language skills (that is, does he know the words and concepts that he needs in order to learn what the teacher is expecting him to learn). It is important to explore how your child's communication skills affect his ability to function in the classroom setting.

In addition, referrals should be made for audiological (hearing) evaluation and otolaryngological (ear, nose, and throat) evaluation unless you have records of recent audiological and ENT examinations. Children with Down syndrome are at high risk for ear infections and middle ear fluid and hearing problems, and research has demonstrated that hearing ability affects success in the classroom. Hearing testing should include:

- assessment of middle ear function and fluid in the ear;
- pure tone testing (to determine how well your child hears a variety of sound frequencies or pitches);
- speech reception (to determine how loudly words need to be spoken for your child to identify them accurately);
- speech sound discrimination (testing the ability to distinguish between different speech sounds, such as light, might, tight, sight), and
- central auditory processing (testing the ability to understand and make sense out of what is heard).

Referrals for neurological evaluation and evaluation of sensory integration skills should be made as needed. Remember that speech and expressive language are output systems based on input from vision, hearing, and touch as well as integration of that sensory information so that your child can make sense out of what he receives from the environment. So, if your child is having difficulty processing information from the environment, a neurological evaluation can pinpoint the difficulty and suggested treatments. Likewise, a sensory integration evaluation can describe and provide a treatment plan if your child craves or avoids certain sensory experiences (touch, spinning, high places) or seems to have sensory overload or difficulties processing sensory information.

THE CASE HISTORY

Before a scheduled evaluation, most SLPs, school districts, or centers will want to gather background information about your child. They will likely do this by a written questionnaire. The purpose of this form is to provide background information for the SLP as she prepares for the evaluation. Questions usually address medical history, developmental history, social and family history, educational history, and behavioral history. The SLP may also ask for suggestions on how best to approach your child. For example, if your child is shy in new situations: would it help for your child to have a favorite stuffed animal with him or to talk with him first; would it help to begin with a play activity? The case history form will also request information regarding his favorite books, toys, and foods. This form will be carefully read by the professional planning the evaluation, so if you have any specific suggestions that will help in planning, be sure to include them when you return the form. Sometimes a comment, such as "My child loves Big Bird" or "My child will talk about Spiderman," will greatly assist the professionals whom your child is meeting for the first time.

FORMAL AND INFORMAL EVALUATION

Speech and language evaluations generally include both formal and informal evaluations. In formal evaluations, your child's performance on standardized tests is compared to the performance of other children; his performance is quantified and measured. During informal evaluation, observation and conversational samples are used, among other techniques, to broaden the picture of your child's communication skills. Informal evaluation attempts to describe rather than measure your child's communication skills. In the U.S., IDEA requires that all testing be done in your child's usual mode of communication, which may include sign language or augmentative communication.

FORMAL TESTS

Standardized Tests. Standardized tests are often used in evaluating speech and language abilities. When a test is standardized, it means that the test has:

- *validity* (it measures what it is supposed to measure),
- *reliability* (scores are consistent),
- a standard set of instructions and standard administration procedures, and
- standard scoring (explicit instructions are given as to how to score responses, and a scoring system must be followed).

Standardized tests present some difficulties for children with Down syndrome, because standard instructions mean that the examiner may not be able to repeat the instructions, or rephrase them, or allow extra time. Psychologists tell us that you cannot violate the rules of standardized tests, so if adaptations are made, the scores are no longer considered valid. And, as explained below, if the *norms* with which your child's scores are being compared are not norms for children with Down syndrome, the scores may not be meaningful.

Standardized tests may be norm-referenced or criterion-referenced. **Norm-referenced** tests compare your child's performance to the performance of between five hundred and fifteen hundred other children who were tested to establish the test norms. Comprehensive tests that sample a wide range of expressive and receptive language skills are usually norm-referenced. Scores can be presented in several different ways, depending on the test. Sometimes, you will be told that your child answered as many items correctly as the average child of a particular age, such as three years, six months. Other times, you will be given percentage or percentile scores (comparing your child to other children who took the test).

The major problem with norms is that they are scores of typically developing children, not children with Down syndrome. So, when the examiner compares your child's scores (a child with Down syndrome) with the norms (scores for children with typical development), the test result may or may not be relevant. Although we have some physical development norms (height, weight, and head circumference) for children with Down syndrome, we do not, at this time, have norms for psychological, educational, and speech-language tests for children with Down syndrome.

This explains why the test results that you, as parents, are given often seem so out of sync with your child's performance in daily life. For example, you may be told that your five-year-old's scores are at the level of a three-year-old. On the surface, this means that although your child has had five years of living and experiences, his language output and speech, or ability to verbalize similarities and differences are at the level of a typically developing three-year-old. But what does that really mean, how does it really affect his ability to get along in daily life?

Criterion-referenced tests measure how your child performs on a specific set of skills. A criterion-referenced test might tell you which word endings your child has mastered and which word endings he has not yet mastered, or tell you how well he can identify nouns or the number of syllables in a word. Tests in speech and language for syntax, morphological skills, or auditory memory are typically criterion-referenced. A criterion-referenced test usually provides a list of the skills to be mastered in developmental order, so that the test can also be used over time to measure your child's progress in specific skill areas.

Criterion-referenced tests are helpful in educational planning because they usually document which skills your child has mastered as well as which skills need to be mastered. If we describe the results on a criterion-referenced test, rather than just giving a score, these results can be meaningful. So, criterion-referenced tests can often serve as guidelines for not only what skills your child has, but what he needs to learn next. The results can help in planning treatment.

INFORMAL EVALUATION

The purpose of informal testing is to observe and evaluate what your child actually does to communicate. Here is where observations and videotapes can be used to provide a picture of your child's skills in his natural environment. The SLP will talk with your child at play, observe him interacting with you, and try to obtain a language sample to determine his usual communication patterns. If your child is speaking, she may read a book with your child, and then ask your child to retell the story. Informal evaluation can also be used to evaluate your child's attention and on-task behavior. Early intervention programs often use observations of your child and parent checklists to assess functional level. Many school systems rely more heavily on formal tests, while others emphasize actual performance.

There is growing recognition that formal testing does not always provide an accurate picture of a child's actual daily communication skills. In a testing situation, children with Down syndrome may respond inconsistently, shift their attention rapidly, or be difficult to motivate. Their responses may also be affected by problems with memory, hearing, vision, or motor skills. Also, as mentioned earlier, they generally do not do their best when testing is conducted by unfamiliar examiners in unfamiliar surroundings. And, even familiar examiners are caught in a difficult situation when test results and their real-life observations do not agree. For examine, the test results might show that your child cannot identify the color green, but the SLP knows that he just identified "green" when they were reading *Green Eggs and Ham* in his preschool classroom.

Parent-Child Observation. When a parent and child arrive for the diagnostic evaluation in a diagnostic center, hospital-based center, or private practice, the first step is usually for the speech-language pathologist to observe them playing and talking together through a one-way mirror. In this setting, the child is usually most relaxed, so the SLP is more likely to get an accurate view of his communication pattern. Many times, SLPs have observed through the mirror an animated, talkative child having fun with his mother or father, but when they come into the room and try to interact with him, they may get nowhere. Had they not observed the parent and child initially, they would have had an inaccurate impression of the child's communication skills.

During the observation, SLPs are particularly interested in observing the verbal and nonverbal interactions between you and your child, as well as turn-taking, questions and responses to questions, how your child gets attention, and how he gets his needs met through communication. Parents of young children need information on how to enhance communication; therefore it is essential for the SLP to know how parents are currently interacting with their child and reacting to his communication.

The observation is usually videotaped and then used to evaluate conversation skills, pragmatics, and nonverbal communication skills. The professional might look at the length of phrases and sentences, whether your child initiates conversation or only responds to your questions, and whether he uses specific morphological endings such as plurals or specific terms such as pronouns. The observation, combined with information from a conversational sample in older children (an actual transcript of your child's conversation), will also provide information on how intelligible your child's speech is, and whether his communication partners have difficulty understanding his speech.

If your child is not communicating as he usually does during this observation session, speak up! This happens a lot and is very frustrating for parents. Consider making a video tape of your child at home and sending it to the SLP if you haven't already done so. If your child is using single words or two-word phrases, try to keep a running list of words your child says and share it with the SLP.

If your child is receiving speech-language services at home as part of his early intervention program, there probably will not be a formal parent-child observation session. Instead, the SLP will most likely informally observe you communicating with your child, over time. Her observations will be written up as an informal kind of evaluation. You will probably not be present at all if your child's SLP evaluates him at school during the course of the school day. You may receive the results months later at the next regularly scheduled IFSP or IEP planning meeting.

Dynamic Assessment or Diagnostic Therapy. In dynamic assessment, your child is seen by the SLP for multiple sessions for a short trial period of therapy. This trial period is designed to determine whether your child improves after guided learning and what methods will be effective for him.

Portfolio Assessment. Portfolio assessment is a way of documenting your child's progress over time. Rather than use one testing session to evaluate your child's skills, a folder is maintained with samples of his work in language and speech. Other terms used to describe this method are *authentic assessment* or *the new assessment*. (Assessing real samples of the child's skills *is* authentic assessment, but in popular usage, this type of evaluation, which usually includes portfolio assessment, is referred to as portfolio assessment.)

Portfolio assessment involves collecting and evaluating multiple representative samples of the child's work. It is similar to the portfolios that artists and advertising specialists have always carried to interviews to demonstrate their skills, and to the manila folders that teachers use during school meetings to show parents examples of their child's academic performance. Portfolios contain authentic examples of the child's communication abilities in various situations, and also show problems encountered and progress over time.

The specific samples to be included in the portfolio may be specified by the school system, the speech and language or special education program, or may be individually designed. Video or audio tape recordings of the student speaking or reading, logs and journals of observations by the SLP and teacher, anecdotes from the parent, and other information may be part of the portfolio. Portfolios may also include results of formal and informal tests.

Checklists and Developmental Scales. Finally, a recognition is emerging that parents know a great deal about their child's communication and that speech and language evaluation is a collaborative effort. Tests that include parents' evaluation of their child's language as an integral part of the test include:

- *Environmental Language Inventory* (MacDonald and Horstmeier),
- *Communication & Symbolic Behavior Scale* (Wetherby and Prizant),
- *Learning Accomplishment Profile* (Sanford and Zelman),
- *MacArthur Communicative Development Inventories* (Fenson et al.),
- *Language Development Survey* (Rescorla), and
- *Sequenced Inventory of Communication Development* (Prather et al.).

Checklists and observation forms that are developed by the teacher and/or speech-language pathologist can also be used by parents to provide feedback regarding their child's speech and language and educational functional level. In addition, they can be used to document the progress that occurs with speech-language treatment and with progress in the classroom. For example, parents may be able to report that their child is using longer sentences at home, or is indicating that he doesn't know what to do when he does not understand the instructions that have been given.

As a parent, you should request the opportunity to fill out a checklist if you are not sure that the rest of the evaluation is providing an accurate picture of your child's communication abilities.

What Is Evaluated?

A comprehensive diagnostic evaluation should assess all speech and language skills appropriate to your child's age and developmental level. Most evaluations, however, will target only those skill areas being tested for. If the evaluation is for pre- or post-testing while your child is in therapy, it may sample only one skill, such as the ability to use plural word endings or the ability to produce the /g/ sound. Annual IEP or IFSP testing may target the speech and language goals from the last IEP or IFSP to determine how much progress has been made. All this means that if you never seek an evaluation outside of the school system, your child may only receive a truly comprehensive speech-language evaluation several times over the course of his school years.

This section will address the areas of speech and language that are likely to be assessed at some point in your child's development. It will describe how each of the areas are generally evaluated, and provide insight into what the results mean. A separate section at the end of the chapter will discuss understanding evaluation results.

Can Children Who Are Not Speaking Be Evaluated?

Sometimes early intervention programs or schools will say that they can't evaluate your child's communication skills if he doesn't have any speech. This is nonsense!

True, speech (including articulation, voice, loudness, etc) cannot be evaluated until your child is speaking. However, the precursors to speech (respiration skills, sound production skills) and factors that contribute to speech and language development, such as hearing and strength of muscle activity during feeding, can be evaluated for any child. Other factors such as articulation or intelligibility cannot be evaluated until later in development. In addition, there is a difference, as we have previously discussed, between speech and expressive language. If your child is using sign language or an augmentative system, testing can be done using those systems. In fact, IDEA mandates that testing be conducted in your child's usual mode of communication. The goal is to describe how your child communicates and how successful he is with using expressive language. So, language output can be evaluated as long as your child has a functional language system.

Even if a child has little or no expressive language, it is still possible to evaluate his receptive language (or ability to understand what he hears). Receptive language tests (such as the *Peabody Picture Vocabulary Test* and the *Receptive One-Word Picture Vocabulary Test* can be used if the child can understand and follow the instructions. The SLP can also glean important information about a child's communication abilities and needs by observing him.

Do not allow your child's early intervention program or school to delay an evaluation on the grounds that they cannot evaluate him until he is speaking. Evaluations open the door to treatment and it is often those children with Down syndrome who are more difficult to evaluate who are most in need of therapy. See pages 237-40 for an example of an evaluation that was completed for an eleven-month-old boy with Down syndrome, before he was using true words in speech or sign.

LANGUAGE EVALUATION

During the language evaluation portion of the evaluation, the SLP may just test specific language skills, such as auditory processing of commands (following spoken directions) or the use of morphological word endings, such as plurals and possessive. Or the SLP may give your child a comprehensive battery of tests designed to get a complete picture of his language abilities. Examples of comprehensive batteries include the *Sequenced Inventory of Communication Development, Test of Early Language Development, Rossetti Infant Scale,* or *the Communication and Symbolic Behavior Scales.* These tests are frequently revised and there are different versions for children at different age and skill levels. Whether your child is given a comprehensive battery or is just assessed in certain areas will depend on the purpose of the evaluation, as discussed at the beginning of the chapter.

Evaluation is usually accomplished through both formal and informal testing. Informal evaluation allows the SLP to get another view of your child's communica-

tion ability. This portion of the evaluation is usually audiotaped or videotaped so that it can be analyzed. With an infant, toddler, or younger child, toys and activities that are above, below, or at age level will be presented to analyze the language skills your child has mastered or that are emerging. With older children, the informal evaluation would include a conversational sample. The SLP and your child might discuss a favorite activity, or a favorite television program, movie, video, family event, or vacation trip. It is important for you to provide information to the SLP regarding topics that will be of interest to your child, and you may want to bring photos to help your child remember details of a trip or event.

Formal evaluation of language skills is accomplished through the use of standardized tests. These may be tests of specific skills such as expressive single-word vocabulary (*Expressive One Word Picture Vocabulary Test, EOWPVT*) or following verbal directions (*BOEHM-3*), or they may be comprehensive language batteries that sample a wide range of language skills (*Sequenced Inventory of Communication Development, SICD-R*, or *Preschool Language Scale, PLS-4*).

On tests of receptive language, the SLP may ask your child to point to pictures ("Show me wheel"); point to objects ("Show me your shoes"); or point to body parts ("Point to nose"). On tests that involve following directions and comprehension, the SLP might ask your child to touch the small yellow circle, put the green block in the box, or to point to the star on the bottom of the page. On tests of expressive language, the SLP may ask your child to say the word that describes a picture or to imitate a word.

The sections below discuss some areas of language that may be evaluated in your child.

Language Evaluation

- Language precursors
- Level of play and attention
- Phonology
- Semantics
- Pragmatics
- Nonverbal communication
- Social interactive communication
- Expressive ability
- Comprehension ability
- Vocabulary comprehension
- Ability to follow instructions

LANGUAGE PRECURSORS

In Chapter 4, the language precursors are discussed in detail. We usually test the precursors informally by observation and through play. But, there are tests that involve parent checklists of their observations, as mentioned above.

LEVEL OF PLAY

Why do SLPs evaluate your child's play skills during a language evaluation? Evaluation of play tells therapists a lot about your child's cognitive level and his readiness for certain pre-language and language tasks. Observing your child's play provides a window into his developmental level. It also provides information crucial to planning therapy activities that are at the appropriate play level for your child. For example, in working on turn-taking, would rolling a ball back and forth be more effective than pretend play with a toy farm?

Play is usually evaluated by using an observation scale that lists different levels of play, from *exploratory play,* in which infants use their senses to explore an object by looking, touching, and mouthing, through the level of *pretend play* with objects, and up to the level of complex games with rules and socio-dramatic play. During the evaluation, the examiner will engage your child in play.

LEVEL OF ATTENTION

This evaluation determines how long and how intensely your child focuses on toys or objects he is playing with. The purpose of evaluating your child's level of attention is to determine how best to present stimuli during therapy in order to maximize your child's learning. For example, will having all of the items for a therapy session in the room distract your child? Should there be only one toy in the room at a time? Can stations be set up around the room with your child and therapist moving from activity to activity? Can your child focus on a toy, object, or activity for seconds or minutes? What does he do to indicate that he is finished with the object and wants to move on to another activity? For older children, what is the length of a story that can be used in therapy? How long can your child focus on an activity or a conversation?

RECEPTIVE LANGUAGE SKILLS

Your child's receptive language skills will be evaluated to determine what he can understand. This includes both receiving and interpreting spoken messages. The SLP will test understanding of sign and pictures, as well as your child's ability to follow short and longer directions. For preschool-aged children, she might read a book with your child and observe his ability to point to pictures to show his comprehension. ("Where is Spot?" Or, "Show me the cat.") When receptive language skills are tested informally, the SLP may observe your child's play and his ability to follow instructions. For toddlers, this will involve simple directions. For preschool-aged children, she will be looking for the answers to questions such as whether he can follow one-stage commands but not two-stage commands, whether he can follow longer more complex instructions, and whether he understands "wh-" questions.

Formal receptive language tests range from single-word vocabulary tests to tests that assess your child's ability to follow complex directions. Examples of tests commonly used for children with Down syndrome in the area of single-word vocabulary are the *Peabody Picture Vocabulary Tests (PPVT)* and the *Receptive One-Word Picture Vocabulary Test.* Other tests target specific receptive language skills such as the ability to follow more complex instructions. They would be used for preschool, kindergarten, or older children. For example, *The Boehm Test* includes instructions along the lines of "Point to the fish on the plate," and *The Token Test for Children* includes instructions along the lines of, "Touch the small green square."

EXPRESSIVE LANGUAGE SKILLS

Evaluation of expressive language skills examines everything your child does to communicate. This includes how he expresses himself through speech, as well as through gestures or an augmentative communication system.

During an informal language evaluation, the SLP might observe how your baby points to a bottle to indicate that he wants it or how he lifts up his hands to indicate that he wants to be taken out of his crib. If your child is older, his use of Total Communication would be considered, including any signs or gestures he uses to communicate. For preschool-aged children, expressive testing might involve identifying objects or pictures, answering questions such as "What is it?" or "What do you do with it?" Once your child reaches school age, the SLP may assess the appropriateness of his vocabulary and level of syntax (grammar) and morphology (word prefixes and suffixes) by asking him to describe pictures and line drawings, and by taking conversational samples while he is playing with you.

Formal tests of expressive language will assess your child's speech and language output. They may range from tests of single-word vocabulary such as the *Expressive One Word Picture Vocabulary Test* to tests such as *CELF-Preschool (CELF-P)* or *The Preschool Language Scale (PLS-4)* that test ability to use concepts such as the words for colors and shapes. Criterion-referenced tests may evaluate your child's skills in a specific area of language usage such as syntax. Your child may be asked to repeat a sentence (e.g., "The boy is sleeping"), formulate sentences (e.g., by answering, "What is the boy doing?") or describe what is happening in a picture.

Another measure often used is MLU, or "mean length of utterance." MLU represents the average number of morphemes (words or word parts) your child uses in his speech. For example, the SLP may report that your child has a MLU of 2.0. This means that the average length of your child's phrases and sentences is 2.0 morphemes, as in "get coat," "go now," "want cheese," "railroad," and "birthday." Remember that possessive and plural word endings count as morphemes, too, so a phrase such as "John's bike" would include three morphemes (John + 's + bike) and "Joy's books" would contain four (Joy + 's + book + s).

Receptive-Expressive Gap. As part of your child's language evaluation, the SLP should consider whether he has a receptive-expressive gap. This means that he understands more language than he expresses. This is one of the most important findings that an evaluation can yield, and is very common in children with Down syndrome, as discussed in Chapters 2 and 7. This information may be very helpful in documenting your child's need for therapy in the area of expressive language because testing will show a discrepancy between understanding and speaking, documenting that your child needs help in the areas of expressive language and speech. Make sure your child's evaluation results provide this information.

Pragmatics Skills. Pragmatics is language in daily use. Informal language evaluations evaluate pragmatics in younger children by observing what they do to get their message across, including using pantomime or pointing. In addition, pragmatics evaluations will examine the use of pre-linguistic skills such as turn-taking and communicative intent. In older children, the pragmatics evaluation would look at primarily conversational skills by evaluating a videotaped conversation for turn-taking, topic maintenance, topic introduction, and awareness of listener needs for information. It would also include an analysis of nonverbal communication skills such as eye contact. Pragmatics skills are usually evaluated using observations and checklists. See Chapter 10 for more information on pragmatics and Chapter 4 for information on early nonverbal and pragmatics skills in infants and toddlers.

SPEECH EVALUATION

Because speech evaluations assess your child's verbal expression, you cannot evaluate speech until your child is actually speaking. There are, however, other developmental items to assess. Evaluations of infants and toddlers may include an evaluation of the muscles for feeding or certain pre-speech skills, such as the ability to make a kissing sound, elevate the tongue, and close the mouth. The speech evaluation will also assess the structure and function of the muscles of the face, larynx, and pharynx. Depending on the purpose of your child's speech-language evaluation, the SLP may do some, many, or all of the evaluations described below.

The Speech Evaluation

- Assessment of orofacial structure and function
- Voice evaluation
- Resonance evaluation
- Fluency evaluation
- Articulation/phonological evaluation
- Stimulability testing
- Diadochokinesis testing
- Intelligibility evaluation

OROFACIAL STRUCTURE AND FUNCTION

A comprehensive speech evaluation should include an oral peripheral examination (sometimes called the oral facial or oral motor examination). This usually includes assessment of the structure and function of the *orofacial muscles* (the muscles in and around the mouth and face), voice and resonance, and the respiratory (breath) support for speech. The purpose of this part of the evaluation is to determine whether any physical factors are making it difficult for your child to speak clearly.

The SLP will observe your child's facial structure. She will comment on facial symmetry, on the appearance of the lips, and on the relative size and positioning of the maxilla (upper jaw) and mandible (lower jaw). She will examine the size of the tongue and its relative size compared to the mouth. She will examine the relationship of the upper and lower teeth, and any space (*diastema*) between the teeth. She will observe the length of the soft palate, and will look for any signs of cleft palate or sub-mucous cleft palate (a cleft that occurs beneath the skin in the muscles of the soft palate so it is not visible). She will then focus on how your child's lips and tongue work. Your child will be asked to smile and to pucker up for a kiss so the SLP can observe lip retraction and protrusion.

To evaluate your child's control of his tongue muscles, he will be asked to stretch his tongue toward his nose and toward his chin, put his tongue behind his teeth, touch the outside corners of his lips with his tongue, lick his lips as if licking off ice cream, and move his tongue toward a spot on each cheek after the examiner points to that spot. This allows the examiner to observe your child's tongue mobility and tongue control. If your child cannot understand the instructions, the SLP will model the movements and ask your child to imitate them or use a prompt such as "Smile" or "Throw me a kiss."

During this part of the evaluation, the SLP will also note any involuntary movements (tics) or drooling. She will be interested in your reports of any breathing difficulties, moaning or vocal grunts, tooth grinding, or other habits that involve the mouth.

Voice and Respiration Evaluation. The SLP will ask your child to make the "ah" and "ee" sounds and hold them for as long as he can. The examiner is interested in listening to volume, clarity, voice quality, and the ability to sustain a vocal tone. She will also listen for hoarseness, breathiness, huskiness, pitch, and other vocal qualities. She may use a Visipitch speech-viewer or other technology that displays vocal output on a screen. She will also assess the respiratory support for speech—that is, does your child's voice appear to be weak because there is insufficient breath? She will notice whether your child breathes from the stomach area, chest, or shoulders or whether he elevates his shoulders in a shallow breathing pattern.

Resonance Function. The SLP will also evaluate your child's oral-nasal balance and velopharyngeal closure ability (ability to close off the nasal area with the soft palate and throat muscles for sounds that should not go through the nose). She will try to determine whether sounds are produced through the nose or through the mouth. To evaluate resonance, the SLP may ask your child to say "ah" or "ee" and to hold the sound for as long as he can. She will observe the movement inside your child's mouth and evaluate the mobility of the velum (soft palate) and the effectiveness of the velopharyngeal closure. The SLP may hold a mirror under your child's nose or use the "see scape," a device that displays how air is emitted through the nasal cavity for nasal sounds.

If your child's voice sounds too nasal (hypernasal) or not nasal enough (hyponasal), follow-up evaluation may include more formal resonance testing, using equipment such as a spirometer or a manometer to measure the effectiveness of the velopharyngeal closure, or more advanced technology such as videofluoroscopy or dynamic MRI studies. See Chapter 8 for more information about resonance.

FLUENCY EVALUATION

The SLP will also be interested in evaluating the fluency of your child's speech, or how smoothly his speech flows. She may ask you to fill out a questionnaire about situations in which fluency is a problem for your child, or ask if you have noticed any stuttering (difficulty on certain sounds, in certain parts of sentences or conversations, or in certain situations.) Stuttering is not common in children with Down syndrome from birth to six years, but more common in older children. She will try to determine whether there is difficulty with the smoothness of the airflow and whether there is muscle tension in various articulators. The evaluation will also assess your child's rate of speech. Is the rate slow, fast, or appropriate to the person and the situation?

If the speech evaluation does not find a fluency problem, but *you* hear a problem with stuttering, especially in conversations, make sure that you tell the SLP, and, if possible, audiotape or videotape a situation where the fluency problem is likely to occur.

ARTICULATION EVALUATION

One of the goals of the speech evaluation is to describe the sounds your child uses for speech and to identify any speech sound errors. Three general approaches are used:

1. the articulation approach,
2. the distinctive features approach, and
3. the phonological process approach. These approaches are used once your child is using a fair number of sounds. If he is only using a couple of sounds, his articulation would be documented by listening, observing, and then writing up the sounds produced. For example: "Your child makes the /p/, /b/, and /d/ sound consistently and combines then with the vowels /a/ and /u/."

The Articulation Approach. Using this approach, the SLP will systematically examine your child's production of each sound presented, usually in single words. For example, pictures of the words "<u>b</u>ox" and "ba<u>b</u>y" and "bi<u>b</u>" may be used to examine your child's production of the /b/ sound when it is at the beginning, in the middle, or at the end of words. In professional lingo, this is referred to as the sound in the initial, medial, and final position. This type of test may also include a conversational sample to evaluate how your child produces sounds in connected speech.

Based on the articulation test, you may be told that your child has difficulty with specific sounds and you will be told in which positions these errors occur. An example of a test result is: "C.P. has difficulty with the /s/ in the initial and final position, /l/ in the medial and final position, /r/ in the initial and final positions, and /g/ in the final position."

Along with these formal test results, you may also be given information about how your child stacks up developmentally compared to other children—or how he compares to the *norms*. For example, you may be told, "Your child has difficulty with the /s/ sound in initial and final position, but you don't need to worry because that sound is typically not developed until age eight." In my opinion, this does not mean that you should forget about therapy for /s/ until age eight, because developmental articulation data may be misleading when applied to articulation in children with Down syndrome. See "The Pitfalls of Using Articulation Norms" below for more reasons that using norms is not particularly helpful with children with Down syndrome.

The Pitfalls of Articulation Norms

There are a number of reasons why using developmental norms to determine whether your child needs therapy for articulation problems may not be helpful. They include:

1. There is no one standard set of articulation norms, even for typically developing children. That is, there is not total agreement about the ages at which specific sounds such as /f/, /s/, or /r/ are learned. Further, some norms consider a sound to be "acquired" if a child can produce it 75 percent of the time, while other norms require 90 percent. So, it is possible that one SLP will say that your child's sounds are age appropriate while another will say that your child's sound production is delayed. (See pages 148-49 for one set of norms that may be used.)

2. The norms were set based on a sample of typically developing children, not on a sample of children with Down syndrome. Consequently, factors like low muscle tone and hearing were not considered when setting the norms.

3. Most norms for articulation were developed based on single-word tests. While typically developing children may have no more difficulty with a sound in a word when it is part of conversation, children with Down syndrome may be able to make sounds in single words, but may have much more difficulty in speech and conversation. For example, your child may say the word "cake" correctly when looking at a picture or reading the single word, but have difficulty saying the word in a sentence such as, "I want a chocolate birthday cake." This makes it important for the SLP to test connected speech as well as single words in your child, especially if he has childhood verbal apraxia.

4. Test results will likely vary a great deal depending on whether norms for children of your child's chronological age or his mental age are used. In evaluating your child's speech, the SLP may use either type of norms. For example, if your child is five but has a mental age of three, the SLP may compare his speech with the norms for a typically developing five-year-old or a typically developing three-year-old.

When mental age comparisons are made, children with Down syndrome often lose out on valuable speech-language services. This is because some early intervention and special education programs deny children speech therapy unless their speech skills are significantly below the norm. Clearly, if the norm used for your child is the norm for someone of his mental age, not chronological age, it will be harder for him to qualify. Your child's overall mental age is, after all, based on the age level at which he functions in many developmental areas, including speech. So, if your child has a mental age of two, he is likely to have speech skills at about the two-year level, and can therefore be denied speech therapy. But if the norm for someone of his chronological age of five is used, he is much more likely to be found eligible. Your school system may mandate that mental ages be used, but it never hurts to ask the SLP whether she can use chronological ages instead.

The Distinctive Features Approach. The distinctive features approach to articulation evaluation looks at the sounds your child makes *incorrectly* and determines what features these sounds have in common. This testing looks at the pattern of errors that your child makes. For example, does your child have difficulty with all sounds that involve lifting the tongue tip or all sounds that involve puckering and rounding the lips? This is a good system for evaluating sound making for children who have low muscle tone, because difficulty with a specific movement may affect more than one sound. For example, if your child has difficulty lifting his tongue, it will affect /t/, /d/, /l/, and /n/ sounds. And if treatment can help him learn to lift his tongue, the result may be that several sounds will improve. Likewise, if your child has difficulty with sounds that require closing the lips tightly, he will have difficulty with all sounds that involve closing the lips tightly.

As Chapter 9 explains, all the sounds of English are produced:
- using specific articulators (place of production);
- emitting air in a certain way (manner of production); and
- either vibrating or not vibrating the vocal cords for the specific sound (voicing).

For children with Down syndrome, using the articulation approach described above cannot usually describe problems as clearly as a distinctive feature analysis can. When you are given the results, you will be told something along the lines of:
- "Your child has difficulty with plosive sounds," or
- "Your child has difficulty with lingua-alveolar sounds (sounds made with the tongue tip on the gum ridge in back of the teeth)."

Treatment will then focus on the specific distinctive features that are difficult for your child. Then, when he masters the distinctive feature (e.g., tongue elevation), the skill that he has learned will carry over to all sounds that have that distinctive feature as part of the sound production. Distinctive features therapy is discussed in Chapter 13.

STIMULABILITY TESTING

Once the SLP has catalogued your child's articulation sound by sound, stimulability testing will be performed. This is a brief examination of whether your child can imitate a sound correctly even though he cannot yet produce the sound correctly in his own speech. For example, can he say /s/ in imitation, even if he does not use the sound in his own speech? Stimulability testing provides the SLP with information about which sounds are emerging in your child's speech and which sounds may be easy to teach in therapy. Some therapists wear a clown's hat and tell your child that they are going to make some funny sounds. Then they produce the sound and ask your child to repeat it. Others simply ask your child to repeat the sounds after them. Usually, only sounds your child was *not* able to produce on the articulation test are tested for stimulability, but some professionals test all consonant and vowel sounds for stimulability. The results will usually be reported to you in the following form:
- "Your child is stimulable on three of his error sounds"; or
- "He is stimulable on the /p/, /k/, and /f/ sounds, but not on the /s/ and /r/ sounds."

When your child is able to imitate a sound, you may be able to stimulate that sound at home, using some of the suggestions provided in Chapter 9.

DIADOCHOKINESIS TESTING

Diadochokinesis (pronounced die-adoe-ko-ki-knee-sis) means the ability to make rapid alternating movements of the articulators, such as those needed for longer words and phrases. For example, words like "cheeseburger" and "French fries" require diadochokinetic ability. These skills are based on muscle strength, accuracy, and coordination. As part of the evaluation, the SLP will look at your child's ability to make the rapid movements needed for speech. This is often a complex task for children with Down syndrome because they have difficulty in coordinating the rapid movement of the articulators. This is one of the reasons your child may be able to pronounce a sound in a single word, but have difficulty when it appears in a conversation.

Usually, this skill will be tested by asking your child to repeat the following syllables as fast as he can until the SLP says stop:

- <u>puh</u> as in putt;
- <u>tuh</u> as in tuck; and
- <u>kuh</u> as in cup.

The SLP will count the number of times your child is able to say each syllable in a five-second period. Your child will then be asked to repeat what the SLP says. She will combine the syllables—puhtuhkuh, and ask him to say this "silly word" as quickly as he can for five seconds. If your child has difficulty with puhtuhkuh, she may instead ask him to say "buttercup," "peanutbuttercup," or "prettykitty" as quickly as he can. These syllables test the ability to rapidly move the articulators for front, middle, and back sounds. You will be told that your child is able to or has difficulty with making rapid alternating movements. Oral facial therapy techniques (both oral sensory and oral motor) and treatment for childhood verbal apraxia are discussed in Chapter 13.

INTELLIGIBILITY EVALUATION

How is intelligibility judged? There are some individual factors that we can objectively measure—such as loudness of the voice or strength of a muscle. However, what we are generally measuring in intelligibility is very global—that is, your child's overall understandability. As discussed in Chapter 8, this is affected not only by the speaker, but also by the familiarity of the listener, the hearing and attentional abilities of the listener, the content of the message, and the situation. Therefore, evaluation of intelligibility is very subjective. You cannot accurately determine intelligibility by counting the number of sounds or words produced correctly or by coming up with a percentage or comparison of sounds or words produced correctly and incorrectly.

Probably the most widely used method of judging intelligibility is a numerical or descriptive rating scale. Often, subjective terms on a scale of goodness are used, ranging from "unintelligible" to "completely intelligible." Descriptive judgmental terms such as "good," "fair," "poor," or "unintelligible" are also sometimes used.

The scale of goodness may also include more specific markers such as:

- Completely intelligible;
- Some sound errors, but intelligible;
- Many sound errors, but usually intelligible;
- Speech is partially intelligible;

- Speech is sometimes unintelligible;
- Speech is completely unintelligible.

If a numerical scale is used instead of descriptive terms, intelligibility may be rated on a 7-point scale ranging from highly intelligible to highly unintelligible, with 1 being completely unintelligible and 7 being completely intelligible. Or your child's intelligibility may be expressed as a percentage such as "50 percent intelligible."

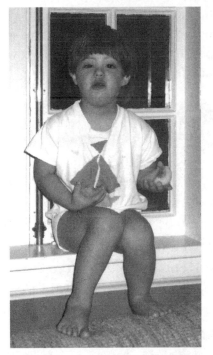

Another scaling method is to describe the situations in which your child is more and less intelligible. For example, you can understand your child, but his aunt cannot, or you can understand your child when you know the situation he is trying to tell you about, but not when the topic is unfamiliar. This approach can be helpful in describing the communication situations in which children have more or less difficulty, in order to provide information for writing goals and objectives for treatment.

Since we know that there are listener variables and environmental factors that can affect intelligibility, we should consider asking not just one listener to "judge" or describe your child's speech intelligibility, but several individuals who regularly interact with him in different ways to evaluate his intelligibility. This may include the parents, preschool or kindergarten classroom teacher, day care person, bus driver, friends, and siblings.

Phonological Process Analysis. Another approach to evaluating the sound-making abilities of your child is through phonological process analysis. This is a method of analyzing sound errors in speech by looking at the sound simplification rules or the substitution patterns your child uses. A phonological process analysis might look at, for example, whether your child makes all sounds in the front of the mouth, reduces all consonant blends to single sounds (pronouncing "sprinkle" as "finkle"), or whether he leaves off all of the final sounds in words.

Suppose that your child can produce the /p/ sound and the /t/ sound, but he says /ca/ for "cat" and /ca/ for "cap." What if he also says /sto/ for "stop" and /po/ for "pot"? The problem here is *not* that he is incapable of producing a correct /p/ or /t/ sound. He says the /p/ sound correctly in "pot" and says the /t/ sound correctly in "stop." The problem is that he leaves out the sound whenever it is at the end of words. These types of errors are described as phonological process errors.

Several types of tests are commonly used to evaluate phonological processes:
- Picture- or object-naming tests such as the *Bankson-Bernthal Test of Phonology;*
- Tests that analyze conversational samples such as the *Shriberg and Kwiatowska Natural Process Analysis;*
- Analyses that take the results of standard articulation tests and re-analyze the results to discover the phonological process rules your child is using (such as using the *Khan-Lewis Phonological Analysis* based on the results of the *Goldman-Fristoe Test of Articulation*).

See Chapter 9 for more information about phonological processes.

To sample your child's speech and language, a sample of your child's conversational speech is usually used. This is sometimes known as a spontaneous language sample. Your child may be asked to retell a favorite story, or to describe a picture which has a lot going on, such as a picture of a child's birthday party. The SLP may read a story to your child and then ask him to tell her the story, or she may ask him about his favorite video or a family vacation. She may have a variety of toys on a table, and talk with your child while he is playing. What she is trying to determine is his usual way of speaking, including vocabulary, morphosyntax, speech sounds, voice, resonance, and intelligibility. So, if you think that the sample she is getting is not typical of your child's speech, tell her. Offer to tape your child at home so that she can analyze his typical conversation.

Toward More Meaningful Intelligibility Testing

Many of the intelligibility tests currently in use rely on the child to read words or to produce connected speech samples of 50 to 100 utterances. This may not be possible for some children with Down syndrome under age six, who may have limited speech. And even if a child is able to complete intelligibility testing, the tests do not analyze what physical, neurological, speech, language, nonverbal, or external environmental factors are the basis of any difficulties in producing understandable speech. Basically, the tests describe the extent to which speech is understandable. For these reasons, current measures of intelligibility do not contribute much towards developing a treatment plan.

My opinion is that what is needed, in addition to a global description of intelligibility, is a clear analysis and description of the factors that may be contributing to your child's difficulties in producing understandable speech. I have developed two forms designed to make intelligibility testing of children with Down syndrome more meaningful. One form outlines the areas needed for comprehensive evaluation of intelligibility and the other provides room for summarizing the results of the speech-language pathology and related evaluations (e.g., hearing evaluation). This will enable the speech-language pathologist to record, describe, and summarize a child's skills in the areas that frequently have an impact on intelligibility of speech. See the forms on pages 324-26 in the Appendix. Based on these results, a comprehensive and individualized treatment program can be designed.

Understanding Evaluation Results

Once the speech-language evaluation has been completed, the SLP may discuss the results of the evaluation with you in person or may send a written report. (If the evaluation was performed through the school system, IDEA requires that you be given a written copy of evaluation results.) It is best if you not only can review the report, but also can ask questions, ask for further information, and provide input about your home observations that may add important information to the evaluation. For example, it is never too late in the evaluation to tell the SLP that your child's voice is hoarse at the end of the day or that he stutters in new situations. It is also important to provide information about speech and language skills that your child uses at home but did not demonstrate during the evaluation.

The meeting may be held at the end of the evaluation, but will more likely be held at least a week afterwards. During the meeting, you will discuss the results of the diagnostic evaluation. The parent-child observation will be discussed, formal speech and language test results will be provided and explained, and the informal language evaluation will be summarized.

At the end of the chapter, examples of written evaluation reports for a boy with Down syndrome receiving services through the Loyola College Speech & Language Center are presented. If you read these over before your child's evaluation results are reported to you, you should have an idea of the scope of information that could be part of a detailed report of a comprehensive speech-language evaluation.

UNDERSTANDING TEST SCORES

As a parent, you have specific needs for information. You will undoubtedly have questions you want answered. "What do these test results mean? What information can the results provide about my child's speech and language skills? For what purposes will the test results be used? What services will be provided based on these results?" You, your child's SLP, and your early intervention program or local school district will want to use the results to plan a specific speech and language intervention program. Be sure you understand clearly what the test scores and the results mean, and do not be shy about asking enough questions for you to understand the information.

When you are given the test results, scores may be reported in many different ways. You may be told how many questions your child answered correctly, how many he answered incorrectly, the percent of questions correct or incorrect, the percentile rating (how he compared with others taking the test), developmental age scores or language age equivalent scores (e.g., he scored at the 4 year level receptively and the 2 year 6 month level expressively), or standard scores or scaled scores.

How test results are reported depends on how the specific test is scored and how the results are calculated. Ask questions like: "What does this test measure? What does a specific score mean? Does an Expressive Language Quotient Score of four years mean that my child performed at the level of a four-year-old? Does a 60th percentile score mean that he answered 60 percent of the questions correctly, 60 percent incorrectly, or that he performed better than 60 percent of the children on whom the test results were based?"

When evaluation results are expressed developmentally, ask questions to ensure that you understand exactly what the results mean for *your* child's speech production. Ask whether your child's performance is being compared to norms for chronological or for mental age. Other questions you might want to ask to help you better understand what the test results mean include:

- What is the format of the test?
- What do the different parts of the test cover? How many sections and different types of questions are asked?

- Can you show/tell me examples of each type of question asked?
- What problems do the test results highlight?
- Do you think the results represent my child's best efforts or typical performance? Or did he seem tired, distracted, ill, etc.?
- If your child uses AAC to communicate, how was AAC used to enable him to participate in the evaluation?
- What therapy, supports, modifications follow from the results?

What Next? Results, Referrals, and Service

The purpose of speech and language evaluations varies in different situations. If the purpose was to determine eligibility for speech and language services, the results will be reported back to you as a decision whether your child is eligible for services through the schools. If the evaluation was to determine what type of speech and language services are needed, the evaluation should provide information that can be used directly to design an appropriate treatment plan. Testing can pinpoint areas in which your child needs help, and areas of strength that can be used to help him develop good speech and language skills. If the evaluation was done to evaluate your child's progress in a therapy program (pre- and post-testing), the therapy program will already be in place and the evaluation will provide information on how to modify that therapy program. The evaluation may also point out the need for referrals to other specialists, such as a developmental pediatrician, otolaryngologist (ear, nose, and throat specialist), audiologist, neurologist, occupational therapist, pedodontist (children's dentist), or orthodontist.

If it is determined that your child does not qualify for services, the speech-language pathologist may suggest re-evaluating your child in six months or one year. Eligibility for free public services through your local school district depends on the evaluation. Your child may not be "eligible" for services, but may still "need" services. These tricky eligibility and need issues are discussed in Chapter 13.

Evaluation can be very confusing and can be emotionally exhausting for both you and your child. However, if you remember two facts, evaluation can be a more positive experience for everyone involved. First, always remember that you know your child best; you have much to contribute to a realistic understanding of your child's speech and language skills and needs. Second, remember (and make sure the testers remember, too) that the goal of evaluation is not endless data collection (I recently reviewed an evaluation that included 32 tests that were given to the child). Instead, the goal is to come up with useful, practical information and insight into your child. You and the professionals need information that can be put to use to help your child's speech and language skills develop and improve. Good evaluations provide this. Settle for nothing less.

SAMPLE DIAGNOSTIC REPORTS OF
COMPREHENSIVE SPEECH-LANGUAGE EVALUATIONS
Completed at Loyola College, Speech & Language Center

DIAGNOSTIC REPORT FOR ALEX, AGE 11 MONTHS

Identification

Alex is the eleven-month-old son of _____. He was referred to this clinic by his parents. He began diagnostic therapy at the Loyola Speech and Language Center on January 21, 1997. Alex is scheduled to receive one 30-minute session of therapy per week this semester for the remediation of speech and language delays secondary to Down syndrome.

Alex is currently receiving special instruction once a month from the Maryland Infants and Toddlers Program at _____. His service profile is as follows: monthly special instruction, monthly occupational therapy, monthly physical therapy through the Kennedy Krieger Institute, and weekly physical therapy.

Medical History

According to the case history completed by his parents, Alex was born following a 40-week pregnancy. The delivery was described as "normal" and Alex's health at the birth was reported to be "good." A hearing test done by his infants and toddlers program on 5/2/96 demonstrated he has hearing within normal limits.

Developmental History

During the first three sessions, Alex demonstrated the ability to sit by himself, to prop himself up on his arms when lying face down, to roll over, and to reach across the midline (when sitting).
According to the case history and parental report, Alex's eating habits have always been good. He currently breastfeeds, and eats baby food and table food.

Parent Child Interaction

The interaction between Alex and his mother was observed during a 15-minute portion of the initial therapy session. Mrs. _____ displayed pleasure while playing with Alex, gave specific praise often, and demonstrated excellent face-to-face interaction when possible. Alex was allowed to lead the interaction and initiate as Mrs. _____ followed his eye gaze and joined in his attention. Her utterance length ranged appropriately from one to three words and included many explotives and interesting prosodics. In addition, she was observed to provide hand-over-hand assistance for pointing and signing ("more" and "all done").

Behavioral Observations

Alex presented as a happy and friendly child who easily separated from his mother. According to Blackstone's Levels of Play, Alex demonstrated age appropriate exploratory play. He changed activities quickly and demonstrated pleasure with motor activities (bouncing). Along with visual inspection and "mouthing" of objects (i.e., the stacking rings, the book), Alex demonstrated manipulative exploration with his hands (e.g., Tangiball).

Based on Reynell's Levels of Attention, Alex demonstrated level one skills. These skills are age appropriate. He attended to a given activity, but was distracted by any new object, person, or event.

Test Results

Information regarding Alex's receptive and expressive language skills was obtained during the first three sessions through the administration of the *Rossetti Infant-Toddler Language Scale*, informal observation of play, and parental report.

Interaction-attachment

The interaction-attachment subtest assesses the caregiver's ability to respond in ways "that reflect a reciprocal relationship" (Rossetti, 1990). Alex is considered to have mastered all skills at the 6-9 month level, although his mother did not report his aspect of "smiling while playing alone" with absolute confidence. Alex showed an obvious confidence. Alex showed an obvious desire to be with people as it was reported that he cries for attention, and clings to the individual with whom he is playing. Alex also responded to his mother's enthusiasm over toys (i.e., the <u>Peek-A-Boo</u> book) with laughs, smiles, and enthusiasm.

Alex's skills in this area were indicative of a mild delay. Areas in need of remediation included requesting assistance from an adult, and performing for social attention.

Pragmatics

Pragmatics abilities include "the way the child uses language to communicate with and affect others" (Rossetti, 1990). Alex mastered all skills at the 6-9 month level and demonstrated emerging skills from the 9-12 month level. During the initial three sessions, Alex indicated a desire to change activities by shifting his eye gaze to a different toy and occasionally reaching for it. An example of emerging level skills was when Alex rolled the ball to the clinician in response to a verbal cue (i.e., "Give ball, please").

During the initial sessions, it was noted that Alex frequently watched the clinician and his mother during play interactions and maintained eye contact. He used his eye gaze and reaching out to request toys or people. Alex demonstrated protesting by making a discomforted facial expression and an occasional "whined" vocalization. A mild delay in pragmatic skills was indicated by the skills he demonstrated. Areas in need of remediation included vocalizing in response to someone calling him, and the exchange of a greater variety of gestures.

Gesture

Gesture skills, according to Rossetti (1990), are defined as "the child's use of gesture to explore thought and intent prior to the consistent use of spoken language." Alex demonstrated emerging skills at the 9-12 month level. The test does not assess skills below this age range for this developmental area. During the initial three sessions, Alex leaned into the clinician and pulled himself toward her to indicate he wanted to be held. He also extended his arms upwards to be picked up. This arm extension was reported to be the only intentional gesture in his repertoire.

His emerging repertoire indicated a mild delay in the area of gestures. Alex's limited gesture repertoire has influenced his ability to use pragmatics appropriately. Therefore, the use of gesture will be targeted in therapy. Such gestures will include pointing, reaching, and the use of functional signs.

Play

According to Rossetti (1990), "changes in a child's play reflect the development of representational thought." Alex mastered all skills at the 6-9 month age range. During the initial three sessions, Alex smiled and laughed while playing games with adults (i.e., peek-a-boo). He searched for hidden objects (i.e., pulling the blanket off the ball), reached for himself in the mirror, and interacted with an object with his hands as opposed to only mouthing it (i.e., handling and rolling the ball). Emergent characteristics of the 9-12 month level included resisting the removal of a toy.

To master this next level, functional play skills must be demonstrated such as pretending to stir with a spoon, and pushing a car. His limited vocal output has limited this progression as well, as it requires that he participate in speech routine games. Such examples of play development will be targeted in therapy. Alex was considered to be mildly delayed in this area.

Language Comprehension

This section assesses the child's ability to understand verbal language. Alex mastered all skills at the 3-6 month level. He moved in response to a voice (i.e., turning his head, shifting his eye gaze), and attended to the speaker's mouth.

Emerging skills are scattered from the 6-9 month through the 9-12 month level. At the 6-9 month level, Alex responded to sounds other than voices, and searched for a noise when it was not in his view (i.e., the clinician shaking a rattle behind him). For the 9-12 month level, he looked at the person saying his name and looked at the ball when it was named.

Alex demonstrated a moderate delay in the area of language comprehension. Areas in need of remediation overlap those discussed in the areas of gesture and pragmatics. Examples include using gestures in response to verbal commands (e.g., learning Total Communication), waving in response to bye bye, and looking for particular objects when they are named.

Language Expression

This test portion assesses "the child's use of preverbal and verbal behaviors to communicate with others" (Rossetti, 1990). Alex has mastered all of the skills at the 0-3 month level. During the initial sessions, Alex cooed, whined, vocalized /ə /, /a/, and /u/, and laughed to express pleasure.

Emerging skills were scattered from the 3-6 month to the 6-9 month level. At the 3-6 month level, Alex attempted to interact with an adult (i.e., playing with the ball), laughed, and whined to show displeasure. According to parental report, Alex produces the following sounds /ba/, /da/, and /na/. At the 6-9 month level, Alex occasionally vocalized during play, shouted to get attention (parental report), and vocalized a two syllable combination. He demonstrated a moderate delay in the area of language expression. Areas in need of remediation include sound play, taking turns vocalizing, imitating sounds, producing strings of varied consonant-vowel (CV) syllables, and vocalizing to objects that move.

Receptive and Expressive Language

Informal baseline information concerning receptive and expressive language was obtained through play, clinical observation, and parental report. During the initial three sessions, Alex vocalized /ə /, /a/, /u/, and produced raspberries. He used the signs for "more" and "all done" with hand over hand assistance. He also laughed occasionally and whined.

Information regarding his level of receptive language is limited by his motor skills, use of gesture, and vocal expression. These aspects are utilized as measures of comprehension by the Rossetti Infant and Toddler Scale. Parental report indicated that acknowledgment of "no" is beginning to arise, but name recognition of family members is difficult to determine. Alex did look at the ball when it was named, and looked at the speaker when he heard his name.

Oral Motor Skills

During mirror play, Alex imitated some facial expressions when given adequate time to respond, but did not demonstrate the imitation of tongue movements. Alex displayed adequate lip rounding when making a "surprised" or "confused" facial expression. Parental report indicated that Alex demonstrated normal feeding habits and did not indicate a concern for swallowing difficulties. At rest, Alex demonstrated an open mouth posture with tongue protrusion and minimal (if any) drooling noted.
The oral normalization sequence, mirror play, and feeding activities will be attempted in therapy to encourage development of his oral musculature.

Summary

Alex is an eleven-month-old child with Down syndrome who was brought to this center for a diagnostic evaluation because of parental concerns about stimulation of speech and language development. Results from the Rossetti Infant-Toddler Language Scale indicated that Alex had some age appropriate skills emerging. Based on the skill levels he has mastered, the following diagnosis is given.

Diagnosis/Prognosis

The results of the assessment indicated a mild delay in the areas of interaction attachment, pragmatics, gesture and play. Alex demonstrated a moderate delay in the areas of language comprehension and expression.
With speech and language therapy and parental support, the prognosis for improvement of speech and language skills is considered to be good.

Recommendations

It is recommended that Alex continue to receive one, 30-minute therapy session per week for the remediation of speech and language delays. In addition, home activities will be provided.

Therapy Goals

Long Term: To increase expressive and receptive language skills to a more age appropriate level.

Short Term:
1. To improve expressive and receptive language skills in the following areas using a Total Communication approach:
    a. use of one word functional signs (e.g., more, want, please)
    b. following one-step directions (e.g., "give ball")

2. To increase the frequency and variety of Alex's vocalizations:
    a. /p, b, n, m, k, g/
    b. /ae, ɛ, ə, o, u/

3. To evaluate and increase the awareness and strength of Alex's oral musculature through the use of the NUK oral massage brush, mirror play, bubbles, and feeding exercises.

4. To develop the following skills:
    a. referential gaze (e.g., looking at the toy that an adult is looking at)
    b. requesting assistance from an adult (e.g., holding out a jar for an adult to open)
    c. increased repertoire of gestures (e.g., reaching, pointing, waving)
    d. functional play skills (e.g., pushing a car)

5. To improve motor planning and imitation skills through structured play.

6. To provide Alex's parents with information concerning speech and language development and to provide activities for language stimulation at home.

DIAGNOSTIC REPORT FOR ALEX, AGE 5 YEARS, 7 MONTHS

Identification

Alex is the five-year-old son of _____. He has been receiving therapy at the Loyola College Speech and Language Center since January of 1997 for the remediation of speech and language delays secondary to Down syndrome. This semester Alex is scheduled to receive one, 45-minute session of therapy per week.

Alex is currently in kindergarten at _____ Elementary School. He receives occupational therapy 60 minutes per week and speech therapy 60 minutes per week in the classroom.

Behavioral Observations

Alex presented as a happy, friendly child. He separated easily from his mother. Alex participated in all of the therapy activities presented to him by the clinician. He especially liked book time (i.e., Clifford and Arthur books) and snack time (i.e., chocolate milk and pudding). A schedule board was used to help Alex remain on task. Alex attended well to the schedule board and easily followed clinician directions (i.e., "Alex, take mouth time off."). Each activity lasted for approximately ten minutes.

According to Reynell's Levels of Attention, Alex demonstrated level three skills. His attention was single channeled in that he did not attend well to auditory and visual stimuli from different sources. He did not listen to the clinician's directions while playing, but his whole attention could be shifted from the speaker back to the game with the help of the clinician. For example, while reading Clifford Alex wanted to read it first himself and did not focus on the clinician's directions until after numerous attempts to regain his attention. Alex concentrated on activities for approximately 10 minutes.

According to Blackstone's Level of Play, Alex demonstrated simple symbolic play skills. He included other actors and receivers of actions in his play. For example, while playing in the motor room, he told the clinician, "You be the mommy." He also offered the clinician toy food as he was pretending to eat. He played make believe games in the motor room (i.e., he pretended to be going somewhere in the truck in the motor room). Alex was also able to follow simple sequences (i.e., making chocolate milk and pudding).

Assessment Results

The *Goldman Fristoe Test of Articulation – 2 (GFTA2)* was administered to assess Alex's current level of performance in the area of articulation skills. This test assessed Alex's production of 23 phonemes and 12 blends in the initial, medial, and final positions of words through the naming of familiar pictures. Sounds in words and one section of sounds in sentences was administered. Stimulability was not assessed. The following results were obtained (— indicates sound omission; NA indicates not attempted):

Sounds in Words:

Errors in Words

PHONEME	TARGET WORD	INITIAL	MEDIAL	FINAL
/g/	girl	/d/		
/k/	cup/monkey	/t/	/g/	
/y/	yellow	/l/		
/ʃ/	shovel	/sl/		
/ʧ/	chair	/kl/		
/ʤ/	jumping, pajamas	/dr/	/s/	
/θ/	thumb, bathtub, bath	/t/	/t/	/t/
/v/	vacuum, shovel	/b/	/f/	
/s/	house			/θ/
/z/	zipper, scissors	/s/	/s/	
/ð/	this, feather	/d/	/d/	

Errors in Blends

BLEND	TARGET WORD	PRODUCTION
/br/	brush	/pl/
/dr/	drum	/w/
/fl/	flowers	/θ/
/gl/	glasses	/l/
/kl/	clown	/kw/

Results of the Goldman Fristoe 2 Test of Articulation indicated sound substitutions in the initial, medial, and final positions of words. Alex made 23 errors and is in the 12th percentile in relation to children of the same age and sex. This indicates that his performance is equal to or better than 12 percent of the boys in his age group.

The results of The Goldman Fristoe 2 Test of Articulation revealed a number of substitutions of consonants. These rule-based errors are phonological deviations. The data obtained from the Sounds in Words subtest was assessed through the Khan-Lewis Phonological Analysis. This analysis provides a means for assessing fifteen phonological processes of children ranging in age from 2.0 through 5.11. It was designed to supplement the baseline data derived from The Goldman Fristoe Test of Articulation. Each process is given a severity rating between 0 and 4; 0 being insignificant and 4 as excessive. Alex scored the following developmental phonological processing ratings:

> Deletion of final consonants: 2
> Syllable reduction: 3
> Velar fronting: 3
> Consonant harmony: 4
> Stridency deletion: 2
> Stopping of fricatives and affricates: 2
> Cluster simplification: 2

Alex demonstrated minimal to excessive use of the above-mentioned phonological processes.

Deletion of final consonants occurs when the speaker omits a consonant in the final position of words. An example of this omission is /ple/ for plane.

Syllable reduction occurs when the speaker omits a syllable from a word. An example of this is /ʤæməz/ for pajamas.

Velar fronting occurs when a back or velar consonant (e.g., /g, k/) is replaced with a consonant made at or in front of the alveolar ridge (e.g., /p, b, t, d/). An example of velar fronting is /tærɪt/ for carrot.

Consonant harmony occurs when one of the contrasting consonants of the target word takes on features of another consonant in the same word. An example of this is /ɛ/o for yellow.

Stridency deletion occurs when a speaker's production of strident consonants (e.g. /f, v, s, z, t, ʧ/) is deleted or replaced and therefore, not strident. This usually occurs in conjunction with other processes. An example of stridency deletion is /ha/ for house.

Stopping of fricatives may result in an affricate or a stop, and stopping of affricates may result in the production of a stop consonant. An example of stopping of fricatives and affricates is /dɪs/ for this.

Cluster simplification is the process in which combinations of two or more consonants are reduced by at least one. Alex simplified the cluster /lz/ to /l/ and /dr/ to /d/.

Receptive Language

During a variety of therapy activities, Alex demonstrated comprehension of various items by pointing to them in response to a verbal command (matrix size 4-6).

Alex approached or pointed to the following animals when directed by the clinician:

> Horse (object)   Dog (picture)
> Ducks (picture)

Alex approached or pointed to the following objects in the motor room when directed by the clinician:

> Car   Tunnel
> Swing   Trampoline

Alex approached or pointed to the following objects in the therapy room when directed by the clinician:

> Trashcan   Chair
> Bubbles   Table

Alex pointed to the following pictures in books when directed by the clinician:

> Money   Zoo   Bed
> Grass   Sun   Police car
> Ice cream

Alex pointed to the following body parts when directed by the clinician:

Ears (on self, clinician, and horse)   Eyes (on self, clinician, and horse)
Mouth (on self)   Nose (on self)

Alex demonstrated comprehension of the following verbs by completing the action described in response to a verbal command:

Sit (sit down)	Stand (stand up)	Turn (turn the page)
Drink (drink the milk)	Eat (eat the pudding)	Open (open the milk)
Push (push the button)	Close (close the door)	Slide (slide down)
Read (read a book)	Blow (blow the horn)	Look (look around)

Alex demonstrated comprehension of the following concepts by completing the action described in response to a verbal command:

Up (go up the stairs)	Down (sit down)	Next (what do we do next?)
Out (go out of the room)	In (go in the tunnel)	Off (take off picture)
Under (put it under)	On (put picture on the board)	

Alex demonstrated the ability to follow two-three step commands in the initial three sessions. For example, Alex would "go to the schedule board, take off mouth time, and put it in 'all done' column." Alex also demonstrated the ability to sequence 3-4 step goal-oriented activities during snack time. While making chocolate milk and pudding. Alex used pictures and verbal prompts provided by the clinician to complete the activity. Upon completion of the activity, Alex had a difficult time retelling the steps in the sequence but was able to with prompting from the clinician.

Alex demonstrated comprehension of the following functional words by nodding his head and verbalizing in response to the clinician using them:

More (more pudding?)   All done (all done with mouth time?)   Want (want to swing?)

Alex demonstrated comprehension of the following wh-questions by pointing to a picture, answering the clinician's question or finding the desired object:

What "What do we need?"   Who "Who is that?"   Where "Where is the horse?"

Expressive Language

Alex communicates primarily through vocalizations. During the initial session, Alex named the following items either spontaneously (S) or imitatively (I):

Food Items: [report includes phonetic spellings of Alex's pronunciations]
Pepperoni (S)   Pizza (S)   Hot dog (S)   Milk (S)

Animals:
Horse (S)   Puppy (S)

Motor Room Items:
Blocks (S)   Playground (S)   Tunnel (S)   Swing (S)

Other Items:
Spoon (S)   Cup (S)   Mailman (S)   Car (S)   Book (S)   Eye (S)

Alex expressed the following verbs both imitatively (I) and Spontaneously (S):

Tickle (S)	Stop (S)	Eat (S)	Drink (S)	Go (S)	Push (I)
Read (S)	Blow (S)	Pour (I, S)	Stir (I, S)	Add (I, S)	

Alex expressed the following concepts either imitatively (I) or spontaneously (S):

All done (S)	All finished (S)	More (S)	Please (S)
Want (S)	Up (S)	Down (S)	In (S)

Alex's intelligibility was excellent within context and good when out of context. During the initial three sessions, the clinician used motokinesthetic (MK) cues for the phonemes /t, d, k/ and /g/. Alex used the cue for /k/ imitatively. When doing so he inconsistently produced the phoneme correctly. He did not use the cues for /t, d/ and /g/.

In analyzing Alex's spontaneous speech sample from the initial three sessions, several articulation errors and phonological patterns were noted. He substituted /f/ for the voiceless "th" sound and /d/ for the voiced "th" sound. He also deleted final consonants (i.e., /ri/ for read). Alex also demonstrated difficulty with /r/ and /l/ blends in the initial position (i.e. / w ^ m / for drum).

Length of Utterance

Alex's spontaneous length of utterance was at the 3-5 word level. A pacing board was used to help him increase his length of utterance to a more consistent four and five word level. The following is a sample of Alex's spontaneous (S) and imitative (I) utterances:

One word utterances [report includes phonetic spellings of Alex's pronunciations]

Flag (S)	Heavy (S)	McDonald's (S)	Trampoline (I)
Tire (S)	Baseball (S)	Basketball (I)	Tunnel (S)
Stop (S)	Upstairs (S)	Playground (S)	Dirt (S)
Book (S)	Whistle (S)	Pepperoni (S)	

Two word utterances

This way (S)	The stairs (S)	Count twenty (S)	Horsey ride (S)
That mouth (S)	No lips (S)	Up here (S)	All finished (S)
More, please (I)	Water fountain (S)	Like that (S)	No pictures (S)
Let's eat (S)	The mailman (S)		

Three word utterances

Push me please (I)	I want that (S)	I all done (S)	This is downstairs (S)
No, too high (S)	I want drink (S)	I have snack (S)	Open the door (S)
It's my turn (S)	Help me please (I)	I going leave (S)	

Four word utterances

Tire swing right here (S)	We do a book (S)	I'm going read it (S)
No, I read it (S)	Yes, it's snack time (S)	We going this way (S)
I want drink it (S)		

Five word utterances

I want to go down (S)	I want to get off (S)	I want to sit yellow (S)
Not that one, this one (S)	To the blocks over there (S)	See in a little bit (S)

Six word utterances

I want to go in here (S)

Seven word utterances

I want to play hide and seek (S)

Eight word utterances

No I want to sit in my chair (S)

The following grammatical structures and parts of speech were observed in Alex's spontaneous language:

Pronouns (I, we, me)	Contractions (let's, it's)	Demonstrative pronouns (this, that)
Negatives (no)	Article (the, a)	Copula (This is downstairs.)
Infinitive (I want to go in here)		Present progressive verb (I going leave)
Action + article + object (Open the door)		Pronoun + action + object (I want drink)

The following grammatical structures were not consistently observed and may be in need of remediation:
    Pronoun (you)
    Pronoun + action + article + modifier + object (I see a big dog.)
    Pronoun + auxiliary + verb + ing + adverb (He is jumping high.)
    Pronoun + action + recurrence + modifier + object (I want more big balloons.)

Oral Motor Skills

Alex demonstrated a slight open mouth posture at rest. No tongue protrusion or drooling was noted at rest. During each session Alex participated in oral normalization. He tolerated the NUK oral massage brush only after he had a turn to use it first. Facial massage and the Beckman facilitation techniques were also used during the initial sessions. Beckman facilitation techniques used included nasal bridge stretch, upper and lower lip stretches, mini "C" stretch, and upper and lower cheek stretches. Alex was reluctant to allow the clinician to complete these at first, but he gradually became more tolerant of them. Alex's oral motor skills were also informally assessed using the Sara Rosenfeld-Johnson horn program and Mr. Tongue's House. During the third session, Alex blew horn number two 25 times with appropriate breath support and lip rounding, but his posture was inconsistent (i.e., he used his arms to stabilize himself by grasping the sides of the Rifton chair). He was resistant to change his posture with cues from the clinician (i.e., "hands on lap"). Alex completed almost all activities from "Mr. Tongue's House" successfully. The clinician verbally explained each activity. Alex responded to the following without further cuing from the clinician:
    Stick tongue out and up toward nose
    Stick tongue out

Alex followed a model from the clinician to complete the following:

Tongue clicks	Tongue in right cheek
Tongue in left cheek	Sweep roof of mouth front to back with tongue
Blow 2-3 times	Stick tongue out and down toward chin
Tongue side to side	Sweep tongue between lower lip and teeth
Lick upper teeth	Lick lower lip

Alex did not use lip rounding when asked to "kiss the cat" (pucker lips), and would not stick his tongue out and down as far as possible when asked to and given an example by the clinician.

Pragmatics

At the beginning of each session Alex spontaneously greeted the clinician with a smile and "hi." At the beginning of the third session, Alex ran up to the clinician and gave her a hug. Alex also responded to various people in the clinic by saying, "hi" when they said hi first. Alex had a very difficult time parting at the end of each of the initial sessions. He did not want to leave. He often stated he wanted to stay and read a book. He only said bye to the clinician after much prompting from his mother. Alex spontaneously established and maintained eye contact throughout the entire session. He requested desired objects by pointing to them, labeling them, or asking for them. For example, when Alex entered the therapy room, he spontaneously said, "snack " or "block" to indicate what he wanted to do. He also requested by asking the clinician to do what he wanted. For example, when Alex wanted the tunnel in the motor room to be stood up, he stated, "do up." Alex initiated activities by pointing to specific activities on the schedule board (i.e., snack time), going to a specific object (i.e., rocking horse), or by telling the clinician what he wanted to do. For example, while playing in the tunnel in the motor room, Alex initiated a game of hide and seek by saying, "I want to play hide and seek," and by telling the clinician to count to 20. Alex protested activities by saying "no." For example, during mouth time, Alex protested facial massage by saying, "no cheeks." Alex demonstrated appropriate turn-taking skills. He did so while taking turns with the clinician using the NUK brush. Alex often stated, "my turn" and correctly answered when the clinician asked, "Whose turn?"

Recommendations

It is recommended that Alex continue to receive one, 45-minute therapy session per week for the remediation of speech and language delays secondary to Down syndrome. Home activities will be provided.

Long Term: To increase Alex's receptive and expressive language skills to a more age appropriate level.

Short Term
1. To increase Alex's awareness and strength of his oral musculature through the use of oral normalization, Beckman facilitation techniques, the Sara Rosenfeld-Johnson horn program, and oral motor activities and exercises specific to target phoneme production.

2. To increase Alex's receptive and expressive language skills in the following areas:
   a. Vocabulary through the use of thematic units (clothing, fruits, and vegetables)
   b. Spatial concepts (next to, in front of, behind)
   c. Use of modifiers (big/little, fast/slow)
   d. Colors (purple, pink)

3. To increase Alex's ability to follow 3-4 step directions in goal-oriented activities with visual cues.

4. To eliminate the following phonological processes at the word level with 80% accuracy through the use of motokinesthetic cues and the pacing board:
   a. final consonant deletion
   b. weak syllable deletion
   c. velar fronting

5. To increase Alex's spontaneous length of utterance to a consistent 4-5 word level.
   Targets include:
   Pronoun + action + object + courtesy (I want chocolate please)
   Pronoun + action + article + modifier + object (I want the big ball)
   Pronoun + auxiliary + verb + ing (He is jumping)
   Pronoun + action + recurrence + modifier + object (I want more red balls)
   Modifier + object + copula + modifier + adverb (Tire swing is right here)

6. To increase Alex's literacy skills targeting the following areas:
   a. Identification of title/author
   b. Identification of characters
   c. Identification of setting
   d. Sequencing of three events (beginning, middle, end)

7. To improve Alex's pragmatic skills in the areas of greetings, farewells, turn taking, requesting, initiating, and protesting.

8. To provide Alex's parents with information concerning Alex's speech and language development and to provide activities for language stimulation and oral motor strengthening at home.

CHAPTER 13

Understanding Speech and Language Treatment

Children with Down syndrome have complex speech and language difficulties. Although most children with Down syndrome face significant obstacles in mastering speech and language skills, all of the speech and language difficulties that occur in children with Down syndrome can also occur in other children. This means that there is a great deal of knowledge and experience that can be applied to helping your child with Down syndrome with her specific areas of challenge. Some of the knowledge and experience that applies to children with Down syndrome in general is collected in this book. However, because your child has her own unique pattern of communication, she will need a speech-language treatment plan individualized to her strengths and needs in order to make the most progress.

In general, a speech-language treatment plan for children with Down syndrome consists of one or more of the following:

- *Consultation between parents and a speech-language pathologist.* Parents may need advice about whether their child is ready to use sign language or what evaluations are appropriate at what ages or levels of development, but their child does not require ongoing SLP services at present.

- *Collaborative consultation between the speech-language pathologist and teachers.* For example, the SLP may work with the preschool or kindergarten teacher to help provide appropriate language experiences. The teachers can provide information on the concepts the child will learn in the curriculum, and the SLP can educate the teacher about what the child is able to do, in what ways the child can respond, etc.

- *Support from a speech-language pathologist.* For example, families may request information from the SLP or ask for help in creating a home program.

- *Direct treatment from a speech-language pathologist.* This involves ongoing services in which the speech-language pathologist works directly with the child or models for the parents what to do in the upcoming week, providing training, models, and home exercises.

Parents should always be an integral part of the treatment plan (although this does not always happen in practice). This is because at some stages (such as early infancy) and for some areas (such as social language interaction and conversation practice), assistance with communication is best carried out within daily life at home and in the community. In addition, some types of treatment (such as work on oral motor skills or motor planning skills) require daily practice. That practice cannot be provided solely through therapy sessions, because they are not scheduled seven days a week. For help with language development, the SLP can demonstrate what needs to be done, but she is not there each day throughout the day to implement the plan. She can suggest that bubble blowing can be a good activity during bath time, and that the mirrors in the bathroom will promote sound making, but she will not be there while you give your child a bath.

I really believe that parents make the difference; they make the changes happen. The SLP provides information, resources, and demonstrates what needs to be done. But, the parents are the ones who carry out the plan. With typically developing children, parents feel confident to work with their child. With children with Down syndrome who have greater needs for assistance in learning to speak, many parents do not initially feel well equipped to work with their child. SLPs can provide guidance and can demonstrate techniques. They can provide information and can explain how to proceed. They can use their knowledge to create an organized intervention plan to help children learn to speak and they can use their training and experience to access methods and materials that will facilitate improved speech and language skills. But, they are not the ones, on a daily basis, making the change happen. Parents are! Speech and language consultation, support, and direct treatment may be needed not only in the early years, but on an ongoing basis throughout the life cycle.

At some points in development, working on language development and language skills will take priority; at other stages, speech skills will take priority. In the early years, therapy addresses communication and pre-language skills. The speech-language pathologist can work with you to help facilitate your infant or toddler's language development. In preschool and kindergarten, treatment will focus on speech skills, as well as language skills. Older children often need help in the areas of speech intelligibility and conversational skills. They may also need help with following instructions in school, language comprehension, and vocabulary related to their school subjects. At some points in development, your child will need direct services, but at other points, she just may need to be monitored regularly by a professional SLP who can provide help as needed.

Your child's communication development and needs should always guide you in determining whether a specific treatment option is appropriate. Evaluation, including family input, should provide the information to design appropriate treatment.

Although your child's speech-language treatment program must be individually designed, this chapter presents some general guidelines for speech and language treatment to help you know what to expect and ask for. This discussion will describe possible communication needs at different ages and stages, some treatment options available to meet those needs, and family participation during treatment programs.

What to Expect from Speech-Language Therapy

Ideally, every child with Down syndrome should have a *comprehensive speech-language treatment program*—that is, an individually designed program that meets all of the communication needs for that specific child. A comprehensive program should consider your child's present needs and plan for her future needs. Family and community input (from teachers, scout leaders, skating, swimming or other sports instructors, religious leaders, and any other important people in your child's life), as well as test results, should be used to design this individualized treatment plan. See the box on the next page for an example of a comprehensive speech-language treatment program.

Treatment must relate to daily life. Communication goes on outside of therapy sessions, as well as inside the sessions. During infancy, activities may be involved with feeding and tactile experiences such as expanding the food textures that your child will eat and massaging her lips and tapping on her tongue. In early childhood, play will form the basis for speech-language treatment, since play is the child's work and is at the core of her daily experience. Before and during preschool and kindergarten, concepts of size, shape, colors, letters, numbers, and sounds must be part of treatment. They will form the basis for later school-based learning.

During the school years, speech-language treatment must relate to your child's educational setting, and the communication needs of the classroom and the curriculum. Speech-language treatment should also consider your child's needs related to community activities such as religious groups and scouting.

Let's examine some of the areas that could be targeted in a comprehensive program at different speech and language learning stages.

THE BIRTH TO ONE-WORD PERIOD

This period may last approximately one to four years. Until your baby is about eight to ten months old, the most important speech-language intervention occurs at home. Families need to be the focus of the treatment program because babies cannot be expected to pay attention to an SLP for a given period of time just because it's the time that has been scheduled for therapy. Regular direct therapy sessions are therefore not possible on as frequent a schedule as the child needs. Parents, however, are with their child throughout the day and can capture optimal moments for learning, when the child is awake, attending, and interested.

During these very early months, your early intervention program may not provide any formal speech-language therapy, or may only provide an evaluation of speech-language skills. Even so, the infant educator from the early intervention program will be working with your child on important skills that lay the groundwork for communication. He or she will also be advising you about ways you can work with your child on these skills.

For infants, one focus of the treatment program will be on *sensory stimulation*—providing activities and experiences to help your baby develop auditory, visual, and tactile skills, including sensory exploration and sensory feedback and memory. Language development is based on what the child hears and sees in her environment. Your child needs to experience what a bell sounds like, or feel the difference between touching velvet or sandpaper. During this time, it is also es-

Alex's Speech-Language Treatment Program

Here is an example of a comprehensive speech-language treatment program developed for Alex, a six-and-a-half-year-old-boy with Down syndrome who was receiving private speech-language pathology services through the Loyola College Speech and Language Center. The goals were jointly arrived at by his parents and SLP and individualized to his unique needs at the time, as determined through formal evaluations and ongoing observation and informal evaluation by his speech-language pathologist.

Treatment Goals:

1. To increase Alex's awareness of his articulators for speech production and strengthen his oral motor skills through the use of oral massage, the Sara Rosenfeld Johnson horn hierarchy, and oral motor activities and exercises to target specific phoneme production.

2. To increase Alex's receptive and expressive vocabulary skills in the following areas:
   a. unit vocabulary (e.g., clothing, fruits, and vegetables)
   b. spatial concepts (e.g., next to, in front of, behind)
   c. modifiers (e.g., big, little, slow, fast)

3. To increase Alex's spontaneous length of utterance to a consistent 4-5 word level. Targets include:
   a. pronoun + action + object + please (e.g., I want purple please)
   b. pronoun + action + article + modifier + object (e.g., I want the small crayon)
   c. pronoun + auxiliary + verb + ing (e.g., He is sliding down)
   d. modifier + object + copula + modifier + adverb (e.g., Tire swing is right here)
   e. interrogative + auxiliary + article + object (e.g., Where is the dog?)

sential to monitor your baby's hearing status and to provide assistive listening devices as needed.

Another focus of treatment for infants may be sensory integration. Many infants and toddlers with Down syndrome are very sensitive to touch (*tactilely defensive*). They do not want to be touched, don't want their teeth brushed, don't like their hair shampooed or cut, and do not like certain textures of foods. We have found that by using oral massage (first with a gloved finger) and a sensory normalization program, infants and toddlers are able to increasingly tolerate touch in the lip and tongue area. The massage program begins with the arms and legs and gradually moves toward the face and inside the mouth. For the oral normalization program, we use the Infadent (a bumpy latex finger cover that can be used to massage and stimulate) and then the NUK massager (a rubbery toothbrush with bumps instead of bristles) to help provide stimulation and experience with being touched around and in the mouth. (See photo on page 249.) We find that babbling and sound making increase after the oral normalization activity. It helps children develop feedback loops—that is, to know when they are touched and where. I believe it also helps later with sensory awareness when children begin to learn the sounds of speech.

4. To eliminate the following phonological processes at the word level through the use of Jelm's visual tactile cues and the pacing board:
    a. final consonant deletion
    b. weak syllable deletion
    c. velar fronting
5. To increase Alex's precision and accuracy of production of /θ/ and /ð/ at the syllable level with 80% accuracy.
6. To increase Alex's ability to follow 3-4 step directions in goal-oriented activities with visual cues (e.g., making pudding).
7. To increase Alex's literacy skills targeting the following areas:
    a. identification of the title/author
    b. identification of the characters
    c. identification of the setting
    d. sequencing of three events (e.g., beginning, middle, and end)
    e. response to "Wh" comprehension questions
8. To improve Alex's pragmatic skills in the following areas:
    a. greeting
    b. parting
    c. conversational turn-taking over 4-6 exchanges
    d. requesting
    e. initiating
    f. protesting
9. To provide Alex's parents with information concerning his speech and language development and to provide activities for language stimulation at home.

Once your child can tolerate touch, it is important to help her learn to *dissociate,* or separate, the movements of the lips, tongue, and jaw. This is a prerequisite for making speech sounds. Specific exercises can help accomplish this task.

One of the goals of early oral motor treatment is to help infants learn to freely move the articulators. Once that is accomplished, the oral motor skills program might progress to include blowing whistles, blowing bubbles, making funny faces, and sound imitation activities. Generally, the SLP will imitate the child rather than providing a model to imitate. Feeding or activities with food may be used to practice various oral movements, with the expectation that these movement skills, once mastered, will transfer into movement skills for speech.

The basis for communication is social interaction, and certain conversational skills such as turn-taking can be developed at a very young age through play. Peek-a-boo games and handing a toy or musical instrument back and forth or rolling a beach ball back and forth are ways of developing turn-taking. These social interactive communication skills are known as pragmatics. Many pre-language skills can be addressed in treatment before your child is able to talk, so therapy should begin early, before your child speaks her first word.

By eight months to one year of age, babies with Down syndrome have a great deal to communicate with the people around them. Once they have developed the desire to communicate, they begin making attempts to influence their environment through communication. They might point or make sounds, or drag you over to what they want. If they do not have an effective way of communicating their messages, young children become frustrated by their inability to be understood. For this reason, one of the first areas that we usually address when we begin treatment is to evaluate what type of transitional communication system will work best for the child.

As Chapter 5 discusses, providing a transitional communication system is very important until your child is neurophysiologically able to speak. The transitional communication system we most often recommend during this age range is Total Communication because it is closest to speech. Your child needs to learn signs and spontaneously generate those signs to express her messages and she doesn't need to carry anything with her to express herself. Other systems such as a communication board may be used if your child has difficulty making signs but is ready to communicate. Chapter 11 discusses the pros and cons of different communication systems in great detail.

THE ONE-WORD TO THREE-WORD PERIOD

Once your child begins to use single words (in sign or speech), treatment will proceed to stimulate both horizontal and vertical growth in language. By horizontal growth, we mean learning more concepts and vocabulary at the one-word level. By vertical growth, we mean combining words into two- and three-word phrases.

Treatment may address increasing your child's single-word vocabulary (semantic skills) in many thematic and whole language activities, such as cooking, crafts, play, and trips. So, there may be a great deal of horizontal vocabulary growth—learning new concepts and the words that go with them. Treatment will also target increasing your child's *mean length of utterance* (MLU)—the length of phrases or combinations of words she can use. We often use a pacing board during this stage to help children expand the length of their utterances. The pacing board is usually a rectangular piece of tag board with separate circles that represent the number of words in the desired utterance. ("Throw ball" would have two dots.) As Chapter 6 explains, there are many meaningful relations that children can make with two-word phrases (e.g., agent-action, possession, negation), before they move on to three-word phrases.

Pragmatics skills such as making requests and using greetings, as well as conversational skills, are also taught during this period. Vocabulary, pragmatics, and other language activities are generally approached through play activities. Play is also used to increase listening skills (*auditory attending*) and on-task attention skills. Appropriate computer activities to help your child learn language skills may be introduced, and she will begin to work on pre-literacy skills such as matching shapes, letters, and words and perhaps identifying single-word labels.

Also during this period, sensory integration and oral motor skills therapy are used to strengthen the muscles and help your child progress in speech. This therapy will be similar to that used at earlier ages, but progressively more difficult.

PRESCHOOL THROUGH KINDERGARTEN

Preschoolers and kindergarteners with Down syndrome are usually far more advanced in receptive language skills than in expressive language skills, but both areas are targeted in therapy. During this stage, receptive language work may focus on auditory memory and on following directions, which are important skills for the early school years. The SLP may work with your child on strategies to help her learn to follow longer instructions. The SLP may also provide visual or sign cues to help your child process longer instructions. Additionally, therapy will focus on concept development such as learning about colors, shapes, directions (top and bottom), and prepositions (with, in, from, to) through practice and play experiences. Reading is often introduced during this stage, if not earlier.

As before, expressive language therapy will include semantics and expanding the MLU. It will also begin to include grammatical structures (word order) and word endings (such as plural or possessive)—if the child is ready for these skills. Pragmatics skills such as asking for help, appropriate use of greetings, requests for information or answering requests, and role playing different activities of daily living may be addressed.

Again, play activities such as dressing and undressing a doll, crafts activities such as making a card, or cooking activities such as making cupcakes may be used in therapy. The same activity may target semantic, syntactic, and pragmatics skills. For example, answering questions such as "What color should we make the Valentine's Day card?" and "How many hearts should we use?" require semantic (vocabulary) skills and are good ways to teach children how to answer "wh-" questions. And following the directions to make the valentine requires language comprehension, and is a good way to practice auditory memory and processing skills.

During this stage, sounds and specific sound production would be targeted and articulation therapy could begin (see below). But the therapy would also include oral motor exercises and activities on an ongoing basis to strengthen the muscles and improve the coordination of muscles. Maximizing intelligibility is the goal of the speech component of therapy.

Understanding Speech Treatment

As mentioned above, sometimes the focus of your child's speech-language treatment will be on speech skills, sometimes on language skills, and sometimes on a combination. The purpose of speech therapy is to help your child learn new speech skills, to resolve any problems with her current speech skills, or to practice skills she will need to prevent problems from occurring (for instance, helping her learn to include the final /s/ sound because the class will be working on plurals). Speech and language therapy may be provided individually or in small groups, in your home, in the SLP's office, or within the classroom as part of the school program. The following sections discuss various areas that may be addressed through speech therapy.

ORAL MOTOR TREATMENT

For children with Down syndrome, therapy for speech should not only teach sounds, but should also strengthen the muscles used to make the sounds through an oral facial exercise program. This type of program strengthens the muscles in the facial area (lips, tongue, cheeks) that are used to make all speech sounds.

For children with Down syndrome, it is important to evaluate what anatomical and physiological factors and combinations of factors are contributing to speech difficulties. Does the child have low tone or weak muscles? Then therapy must work on strengthening the oral facial muscles.

The specific exercises and activities will be based on the specific difficulties that your child is having. For example, does she have difficulty moving the tongue muscles separate from the lips and jaw? Then therapy must work on separating tongue movement so that she can move her tongue independently. Bite blocks or foods such as pretzels or licorice sticks might be used to stabilize the jaw, and specific tongue exercises would be used to practice moving the tongue independent of moving the jaw. Does your child have trouble rounding or closing her lips? Then horns and straws such as those available from Sara Rosenfeld-Johnson can be used to target your child's lip development. (See Resources.)

ARTICULATION THERAPY

The goal of articulation therapy is to remedy problems your child has in producing specific sounds. Depending on your child's speech development, he may or may not be ready for direct articulation therapy before the age of five or six, but therapy that focuses on the underlying movements (oral motor skills) or on sequencing sounds (apraxia) can begin before articulation therapy. So this section will cover the basics of articulation treatment and a later volume on communication skills in older children will address articulation in greater detail. The therapy approaches typically used to improve articulation include the traditional articulation approach, distinctive features approach, phonological processes approach, and coarticulation approach. In each of these approaches, the SLP focuses on helping your child learn to produce speech sounds; what differs is the sounds targeted in treatment, how many sounds are worked on simultaneously, and how she focuses on the sounds (for instance, whether the focus is on certain sound contexts, on learning to control, move, and use the articulators, or on certain patterns such as including final sounds in words).

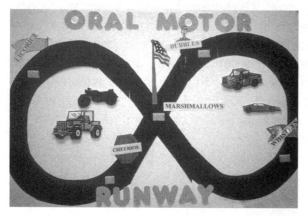

TRADITIONAL ARTICULATION THERAPY

Traditional articulation treatment focuses on one or more sounds your child does not produce accurately and works on each in the different positions (beginning, middle, end) it appears in words. Examples of some goals of articulation therapy using the traditional approach are:

- Your child will be able to identify the /f/ sound when it is heard in the initial position in words 90 percent of the time (<u>f</u>un, <u>f</u>ive).
- Your child will be able to produce the /s/ sound in the initial position in words 90 percent of the time (<u>s</u>un, <u>s</u>ix).

- Your child will be able to produce the /k/ sound in the final position in words 90 percent of the time (bi<u>ke</u>, li<u>ck</u>).

In the traditional approach, your child's errors will be identified according to the sound in error, such as /s/, the type of error production, such as "omission," and where in words the error occurs, such as the final position. Examples of descriptions of error sounds are:

- Your child substitutes /th/ for /s/ in the initial and final positions in words (she says "<u>th</u>un" for "sun" and "i<u>th</u>" for "ice").
- Your child omits the /l/ in the initial position in words (she says ight for light).
- Your child distorts the /s/ sound in all positions in words (she produces the /s/ incorrectly in <u>s</u>un, ba<u>s</u>eball, and i<u>ce</u>)

If your child has quite a few speech errors, the SLP will first focus on sounds that occur frequently in English or in your child's personal speech. For example, the /n/ and /t/ sounds are often used in English, so they are generally important to work on. The /v/ and /ch/ sounds are not used as often. However, if your child's name is Vivian Vo, she will be saying the /v/ sound frequently, so working on that sound would probably be a higher priority than for a child named Tammy Thomas.

With the traditional approach, your child will first be taught to listen for and identify the correct sound production when she hears it, then she will be taught to produce the sound through *phonetic placement*. In phonetic placement, your child is taught *how* to produce the sound correctly in isolation, such as /p/. Then she is taught to produce the sound in nonsense syllables in a specific position, such as "poo"; then in a specific position in words, such as "pie"; then in the same position in phrases, such as "lemon pie"; then in the same position in sentences, such as "I want lemon pie please"; and then finally in conversation. This process is followed for each sound in error in each position in which it occurs; this makes the traditional approach slow and tedious.

AUDITORY DISCRIMINATION

Another method widely used is the auditory discrimination method. This therapy concentrates on helping your child hear the difference between correct and incorrect sound productions—for example, the difference between "too<u>f</u>" and "tooth"). With children with Down syndrome, however, the problem is usually *not* that they cannot hear the difference between two sounds. Instead, the problem may be that they do not know *when* to make a particular sound.

Traditional articulation therapy and auditory discrimination are slow and tedious and do not remedy the underlying movement or perception problem; they merely address the symptoms of the problem. In my professional experience, I have found that ***traditional articulation treatment or the exclusive use of auditory discrimination do not work well for children with Down syndrome.***

DISTINCTIVE FEATURES APPROACH

With the distinctive features approach, the sound errors your child makes are categorized according to whether they are errors in the place of production, the manner of production, or voicing (discussed in Chapter 9). For example, does your child have difficulty raising her tongue tip to produce sounds such as /t/, /d/, /n/, and /l/, or making a plosive sound such as /p/, /b/, /k/, and /g/, or making a voiced sound such as /d/, /v/, and /z/? Therapy then focuses on teaching your child that specific skill, such as raising the tongue tip.

The basis of distinctive features therapy is the *generalization hypothesis*. According to this theory, if your child masters the skills needed to make a sound in a specific place, manner, or voicing pattern, she will be able to use the same place, manner, or voicing in making other sounds. She will be able to generalize the skill that she has learned. Let's say, for example, that your child learns in therapy to raise her tongue tip and to correctly make the /t/ sound. If she generalizes, she will be able to elevate the tongue tip when she produces other sounds that involve the tongue tip, such as /d/, /l/, and /n/.

Therapy might also focus on manner of articulation, such as by teaching how to valve (hold) and then release a puff of air for stop sounds. Again, the expectation is that when the child learns to hold and explode the air for one sound, such as /t/, it will carry over to all other stop sounds.

The distinctive features approach is a very logical, organized way of teaching sounds when the errors are based on neuromuscular problems such as low muscle tone. It works well for children who have oral motor difficulties that underlie articulation difficulty. I have found it to be a better approach for children with Down syndrome because it teaches a movement or placement that can help your child produce more than one sound correctly. It makes sense that if your child cannot raise the tongue tip for /t/, she probably won't be able to raise the tongue tip for /l/. Targeting a feature in therapy is also usually a more rapid method for achieving results than a sound-by-sound approach.

PHONOLOGICAL PROCESS APPROACH

Your child may be able to produce a sound correctly in isolation, or when the sound appears in certain words or in certain parts of words but not in others. For example, if your child says /ba/ for both "bat" and "ball," but can say "take" and "lake," she may not need to specifically work on how to produce the /t/ and the /l/ sound in the initial position in words. She knows how to make the sound but she needs to work on including the final sounds in words so that, for example she says "ball" instead of /ba/. Testing can determine whether your child has difficulty producing these sounds, or whether the difficulty occurs because those sounds are in the final position in words.

Identifying the phonological process patterns used by children with Down syndrome is important because there are therapy methods that can help with the problems. Therapy for phonological processes works on increasing your child's awareness and use of sounds that she can make in some contexts but not in others. Through games and activities, therapy teaches your child when to make a selected phonological process, such as producing a final sound in a specific word. For example, treatment for final consonant deletion will focus on helping your child understand that final consonants affect meaning and that she is leaving off those final consonants. This therapy approach might use "minimal pairs," words that differ by only one sound in the final position in words, such as "cat," "cap," and "can." The approach in treatment would be first to illustrate through games such as Go Fish,

Simon Says, or Lotto that there is a difference in meaning between the /ca/ words with different sounds at the end. Then, treatment would provide practice in saying the words with the different sound endings.

Chapter 9 discusses phonological processes in more detail and includes descriptions of activities you might do at home.

COARTICULATION

In this therapy approach, the SLP looks not only at the sounds your child has trouble with, but also at the contexts in which the errors occur and the contexts in which your child can make the sound easily. For example, it is often easier for a child to produce an /s/ sound when it is followed by a /t/ sound, such as "stoop" rather than "soup." Instead of teaching your child how to produce a sound, coarticulation therapy tries to find a context in which your child is already producing the sound correctly. Then, through therapy, your child learns to transfer that correct sound production to other word contexts in which she was not making the sound correctly. For example, if your child can say "stop," the SLP will work with her on combining that word with other "s" contexts she cannot say, such as "stop soon," "stop soap," "stop bus."

THE BEST APPROACH FOR YOUR CHILD

The goals for treatment and the benchmarks to measure progress must be individually designed to target the specific problems affecting your child's articulation. Therapy may be provided individually, in a small group, in a separate room, or in the classroom. But, the approach used should be based on what your child needs to help with her particular articulation difficulties, not a general approach for all children in a group who have the same sound problem—for example, difficulty with making the /s/ sound. Therapy needs not only to target the /s/ sound, but also to target where your child is having difficulty. Is your child protruding her tongue? Is she sending air over the side of her tongue? Is she closing her lips and pressing them together? What is she doing to make the /s/ sound and why is she having difficulty? So, several children may have difficulty saying /s/ but the underlying causes of that difficulty could be different for each child. And you can request a home practice program for /s/ so that you can help your child at home.

Once your child is able to make the sound correctly, it is especially important to practice at home. Articulation is a motor skill that should feel automatic. Your child should not need to consciously think about each sound when she is talking. When she is not saying a sound correctly, she is actually practicing saying it incorrectly every time she says it. So, once she learns to say it correctly, she needs a lot of practice in order to be able to automatically and unconsciously say the sound correctly.

SPEECH INTELLIGIBILITY TREATMENT

As Chapter 8 explains, intelligibility is affected by many factors intrinsic to the person and by some factors external to the person, and the specific factors that influence intelligibility in any one person may be different from those that affect intelligibility for another individual. Therefore, the most important first step in planning treatment is to obtain a comprehensive evaluation of the factors affecting intelligibility in your child.

Therapy for Childhood Verbal Apraxia

If your child has the motor planning difficulties of childhood verbal apraxia, the problem is not that she cannot physically make the movements needed to produce particular sounds. Instead, as Chapter 8 explains, the problem is that she cannot reliably produce and sequence the movements needed to make the sound combinations in words. Although she may also have articulation problems in addition to apraxia, merely using one of the treatment methods for articulation described above is not going to improve her apraxia.

Instead, a treatment program for childhood verbal apraxia (also known as pediatric verbal apraxia, and developmental apraxia of speech) must be used to help her learn to produce sequences of speech sounds. Usually, such a treatment program will involve using a visual/motor cueing system to help your children learn to produce and combine speech vowel and consonant sounds. One approach (*Easy Does It for Apraxia—Preschool*) involves using visual cue cards that show turtles making movements such as stretching the arms out wide or putting the arms over their head. Different movements correspond to different vowel sounds and children are taught to make the movements and vowel sounds when cued with the cards. Consonant production cue cards may also be used, but consonant cues usually take the form of a finger pointing to the articulator or facial area where the sound is made. For example, a prompt for making the /t/ sound involves pointing to the middle over the upper lip, the general area of tongue elevation for the /t/, while the /p/ prompt points to the cheeks near the lips where air is held and exploded for the /p/ sound. Children are taught these prompts in therapy, and the SLP uses the prompts, as well.

Once your child has been evaluated, treatment should then target the specific intelligibility factors affecting her. For example, if she has difficulty with the /r/ sound, articulation therapy will focus on the /r/ sound. If she uses the phonological process of deletion of final consonants, therapy will address the use of that process. If low muscle tone is a factor, therapy will focus on strengthening the muscle tone in the face, lips, and cheeks through practice with whistles, blowing bubbles, and lip and tongue exercises. If your child does not look at the speaker's face, therapy will focus on eye contact. If staying on the topic is a problem, language therapy will focus on topic maintenance.

If there are underlying physical or sensory problems contributing to intelligibility problems, other specialists in addition to the SLP will need to be involved in treatment. For example, hearing loss would be tested by an audiologist (hearing specialist) and treated by an otolaryngologist (physician specializing in ear, nose, and throat). Malocclusions would be diagnosed and treated by a dentist. Sensory processing or sensory integration difficulties can be treated by physicians and occupational therapists (OT). Parents have reported wonderful treatment sessions in which the SLP and OT collaborate and the child is swinging while she is practicing sounds, or beating out the number of syllables in words with percussion instruments.

If many or all of the factors affecting your child's intelligibility can be improved, the overall intelligibility of her speech will increase.

In short, there is no specific treatment plan recommended for intelligibility treatment. Indeed, because SLPs formerly concentrated mainly on language, rather than speech problems in individuals with Down syndrome, "As of 1999, there are no intervention programs or guidelines to assist speech-language pathologists in developing integrated approaches to meet both the speech intelligibility and language communication needs of this population [children with Down syndrome]" (Rosin & Swift, 1999). Rather, the treatment plan should include objectives to address each factor that is affecting your child's speech intelligibility, and benchmarks to measure progress for each factor. A treatment program planning form can be found in the Appendix.

VOICE AND RESONANCE THERAPY

Voice and resonance therapy is used to correct voice and resonance problems identified during your child's evaluation. The most common voice problems are:

- conditions affecting the larynx (such as laryngeal webbing),
- conditions related to allergies (such as hyponasality, hypernasality, or hoarseness),
- conditions related to mouth breathing (such as hyponasality or hypernasality),
- damage (such as vocal nodules) from vocal abuse such as shouting.

Before any speech treatment for voice or resonance difficulties is begun, your child should be seen by the pediatrician and otolaryngologist. Medical evaluation is critical and medical treatment may include surgery, medication, or a speech appliance. The most common resonance problems include hyponasality and hypernasality, often related to allergies and mouth breathing. See Chapter 8 for an explanation of these problems.

Therapy for voice and resonance problems includes exercises involving the mouth and facial muscles, the larynx, or pharynx (throat) to strengthen the muscles used for voice and resonance. Specific exercises may focus on strengthening the palate muscles in order to decrease hypernasality or strengthening the adductor muscles that adjust (tense and relax) the vocal bands of the larynx in order to reduce breathiness. Equipment such as the Visipitch™ or the IBM Speech Viewer™ may be used to give your child feedback as she does the exercises.

RATE THERAPY

Rapid rate of speech is common in children with Down syndrome and it contributes to intelligibility problems. The SLP may work on rate using demonstrations and material such as drums, a metronome, table-tapping, or rhythm added to speech. She may also use a musical melody to accompany speech (*melodic intonation therapy*), a pacing board, or a model that shows your child her rate of speech, such as a slow and fast moving toy truck. These methods are described further in the Home Activities for rate in Chapter 8. Once your child is taught the concept of slow and fast speech and uses a slower rate, practice in using the new slower speech pattern will help to incorporate the slower rate into everyday speech.

Understanding Language Treatment

Children with Down syndrome receive language therapy for the same types of reasons they receive speech therapy: to help them learn language skills and to reduce problems with language development. Virtually any person with Down syndrome—from birth through adolescence and beyond—can benefit from language therapy.

Because language is so critical to your child's future success, it is important to monitor her language development closely. In the early years, therapy may focus on prelinguistic skills. Chapters 3 and 4 discuss language therapy and home activities for the precursors to spoken language. Therapy during the birth to three-word period usually focuses on training you to facilitate your child's language development and on changing your child's environment so that there are many opportunities for learning and using language skills. Early language therapy usually uses Total Communication to help your child make the transition to speech while providing a viable communication method to express her new language skills.

Language therapy for children beyond the three-word stage is generally aimed at remedying specific language problems that have been identified during an evaluation. Often therapy is designed just to solve one "problem" at a time. For some children with Down syndrome, this remediation approach is adequate. For most, however, it is best to be proactive. It is preferable to determine what language skills your child needs now and what language skills she will need to be successful as an adolescent and adult, and then work on those skills in an organized, sequential manner.

The SLP will provide language therapy. The areas of language development that will be addressed—depending on your child's needs—include phonology, morphology, syntax, semantics, pragmatics, and nonverbal communication. Phonology is discussed in Chapter 9, since it is closely linked to articulation. Morphology and syntax are often addressed together and jointly called morphosyntax. The areas are discussed below.

MORPHOLOGY

As you may recall, morphemes are the smallest unit of meaning in words. For example, in the word "cowboys," "cow" and "boy" are morphemes, since they are both words in their own right, and the "s" is also a morpheme, since it changes the meaning of the word as a whole from singular to plural.

Morphemes are most often worked on in therapy through the use of "pattern practice" or repetitive practice exercises. For example, if your child is working on "-ing," she will name groups of pictures of people jump*ing,* runn*ing,* or walk*ing.* Or two therapists might work together and model the responses for your child. "What is Anna doing? She is jump*ing.*" In group therapy, children might take turns running, jumping, or walking, while the other children describe what they are doing. "Cory is jump*ing,* Becky is hopp*ing,* Elizabeth is walk*ing.*" Morpheme practice lends itself to home practice, so be sure to ask which morphemes are currently being targeted in therapy.

Examples of treatment goals for morphology include:

- Sarah will be able to use the /s/ ending to designate plurals in spontaneous speech 80% of the time.

- Brian will be able to use correct verb tense markers for past and present 90% of the time in spontaneous speech.

SYNTAX

Syntax (grammar) is frequently worked on in therapy through pattern practice and through play activities using manipulative toys such as a play farm or schoolhouse. For example, toy people may be moved around to practice the concepts of "in front of" and "in back of." The SLP may ask, "Where is Grover?—In front of the line." "Where is Grover now?—In back of the line." Syntax also includes word order, so one activity might be learning the difference between "The man hits the ball" and "The ball hits the man." For older children, action figures can be used in the same way, or dolls, stuffed animals, or trucks. Syntax is also worked on in therapy through the use of published books or computer programs that provide structured practice materials.

Once your child can read, reading can be used to teach and reinforce syntax. For example, if your child cannot hear the word endings for past tense, seeing the "–ed" ending on words may help her understand how to put verbs into past tense.

Examples of sample goals and objectives related to syntax include:

- Abigail will use correct negative forms in sentences 80% of the time.
- Bernie will use phrases of at least 2 morphemes spontaneously 70% of the time.
- Bernie will use phrases of at least 3 morphemes through imitation at least 90% of the time.
- Denise will increase correct use of interrogative forms in spontaneous speech to 80% of the time.
- Tyler will use copula verbs (is, am) correctly in sentence practice 90% of the time.

SEMANTICS

As you may recall from Chapter 7, semantics is concerned with your child's ability to grasp the meaning of language and is intimately related to your child's vocabulary skills.

As your baby develops and grows into a child, the goals for semantic treatment proceed from enriching vocabulary development to more complex tasks. Early on, treatment might focus on one-word vocabulary in certain categories—for example, teaching the names of colors, sizes, and shapes, or teaching words that go with seasons or clothing or food. Later therapy might focus on word definitions, synonyms and antonyms, and learning vocabulary that will help your child follow directions, such as "line up," "underline," "circle," "match," etc.

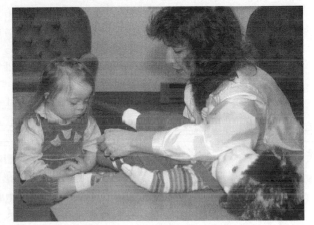

Therapy usually includes completing an activity, such as a food or craft activity, or an experience, such as going to the post office, and reading books about specific topics. Vocabulary will be taught as your child experiences the concepts, activities, and events. For example, making a holiday card or dressing a toy doll are good bases for language activities. Vocabulary, syntax, and other goals can be made part of the session. For example, how do you ask for crayons for the card or specify the colors you need? Which prepositions do you need to use when talking about dressing the doll?

Language experience activities are useful in teaching children new words and concepts. For example, your child's SLP may plan language activities around a class field trip to the bakery. All of the vocabulary, such as "oven," "bread," and "baker" would be taught before the field trip. Your child would see what a bread oven, dough mixer, cookies, cake, and cash register are. After the trip, your child could write or dictate a story about the trip. In subsequent therapy sessions, she might re-read the story or act out the trip to the bakery. This is an excellent way of making language learning concrete and real for your child.

Computer software such as *First Words I, II, III, First Verbs, Talking Nouns,* and *Talking Verbs* (Laureate Software) can assist vocabulary development. Laureate Software and Mayer-Johnson Company are good sources for language software. Other software programs that you may find useful are listed in the box below.

Following are some examples of semantic treatment goals, beginning with simpler goals and progressing to more complex goals:

- Claire will be able to point to five familiar objects when they are named.
- Bruce will be able to point to family members when they are named.
- Kristen will be able to say the names of family members.
- Bob will be able to use two-word phrases for location ("in box"), possession ("Bob's book"), and recurrence ("more music").
- Natalie will understand words for color and size.
- Natalie will use words for color and size.
- Sam will demonstrate understanding of same and different.
- Ruth will be able to give examples of words in categories.
- Allan will be able to describe the functions of objects.
- Becky will be able to define familiar words from the environment.
- Matthew will be able to identify synonyms and antonyms for common words.

PRAGMATICS

Because pragmatics skills involve social interaction, these skills are best taught in small group therapy. Pragmatics therapy can cover the many different conversational skills your child will need. For example, she may need help learning the social situations in which informal and formal language should be used, how to ask for help, and how to start and end conversations.

In teaching pragmatics, the SLP will probably use role playing, simulations, games, and activities. Peers, cousins, siblings, and friends can practice pragmatic skills together; pragmatics is more realistic with another child, adult, or a group. Stuffed animals, dolls, and puppets can be used for practice, as well.

Some Suggested Software

Commercially available software is being used successfully with children with Down syndrome both at home and in school. Some programs that are well designed and help with learning vocabulary, phonological awareness, other pre-reading skills, and preschool and kindergarten concepts such as colors, numbers, and shapes are listed below. Titles listed were available as of 2003.

- *Reader Rabbit Preschool*
- *Millie's Math House*
- *Reader Rabbit Learn to Read with Phonics*
- *Jumpstart Preschool*
- *Sesame Street Toddler Deluxe*
- *Disney Winnie the Pooh Learning Series*
- *My First Reading Adventure*
- *My First Incredible Amazing Dictionary*

- *Bailey's Book House*
- *Living Books Library*
- *Jumpstart Toddler*
- *Leap Frog Imagination Desk*
- *The Playroom*
- *I Love Phonics*
- *My First CD-ROM Toddler*
- *My First CD-ROM Preschool*

Dr. James MacDonald advocates that SLPs use a conversation model for language intervention. MacDonald believes that all behavior communicates, including eye contact and gestures, and that movements communicate messages. He further believes that we should always interpret child behavior as communicative. MacDonald suggests that teaching must be at the level at which each child can succeed. SLPs should only expect the child to express herself on her level, but they should provide models and expansions slightly more complex than the child's current skill level. MacDonald believes that the key to language success is a great deal of practice in social interactions in real situations. Thus, home practice must support the pragmatics skills being worked on in therapy.

MacDonald advocates working extensively on imitation and turn-taking from a very early age. For example, if your toddler bangs her doll on the table by accident, you might say, "My turn" and bang the doll once before giving it back to your child. You can also initiate interactions well before your child is verbal. For instance, you might give her a "high five" sign while you are both standing in line, waiting. If she doesn't respond, do the "high five" again. Eventually, she might initiate the "high five." You could then take turns giving each other "high fives".

Here are some sample goals for pragmatics:

- Sherry will use greetings consistently with peers.
- Sherry will use greetings with adults 80% of the time in school.
- Blair will take three conversational turns consistently.
- Fiona will stay on topic in conversation 80% of the time.
- Julio will use appropriate eye contact 90% of the time when talking with peers.

OTHER AREAS
OF LANGUAGE
INTERVENTION

There are other language skills beyond morphology, syntax, semantics, or pragmatics that SLPs can work on with your child. These goals can include increasing your child's receptive language skills, enhancing her auditory memory, or improving her listening skills. Therapy might also seek to help your child learn to follow instructions of increasing length. This material might be taught through drills, word games, role playing and simulations, and reading and discussing a story. Therapy to improve expressive language skills might involve increasing the length of utterance or the number of turns in a conversation.

There are many other approaches to speech and language therapy that your child's SLP may suggest. For example, some authorities use reading and writing to teach language, as discussed in Chapter 14. Knowledge about how best to teach communication skills to children with Down syndrome is still growing, and eventually, we may know the solutions to problems that perplex us now.

Be sure to ask the SLP for regular feedback on what your child is doing in therapy. Request a home activities program to reinforce the material being learned in therapy. If possible, observe your child's therapy sessions frequently, so that you can apply the language learned into your child's daily life.

The Parent's Role in Speech-Language Therapy

Your role in speech and language development is critical. Ideally, you and a speech-language pathologist will work together as partners to address the speech and language needs of your child with Down syndrome.

While your child is in early intervention, it will probably be easier to be directly involved in her speech-language treatment program. In early intervention, speech-language therapy is either home-based or center-based. In most centers, parents are observers and/or participants and know what is going on in therapy. They may observe through a one-way mirror or be in the treatment room. In home-based therapy, the parents may try to stay out of the child's sight, but they nevertheless can hear what topics are being used and what is going on in therapy. When your child transitions to preschool and school-aged services, you are less likely to observe and be part of the speech and language sessions. Your child may receive some of her therapy in the classroom or as a member of a small group, or part of her therapy may consist of consultation between the SLP and classroom teacher.

COMMUNICATING
WITH THE SLP

If you observe your child's therapy regularly or are present in the therapy room, you and the SLP will probably communicate regularly. If you bring your child to a private practitioner or a rehabilitation center, ask that the SLP leave some time after each session to talk with you. You need to be updated after each session to stay abreast of the goals, your child's progress, and the activities of each session, as well as what home activities you might try that week. Even if the SLP shortens the therapy session to talk with you, it is worth the time; you will be able to follow through on the therapy goals for that week and will gain knowledge that can help your child.

The lesson plan for Alex (shown on the next page), aged three years and ten months, shows how SLPs at Loyola College communicate in writing on an ongoing basis with parents about what is being worked on in therapy and what should be

LESSON PLAN	SPEECH/LANGUAGE LOG

Client's Name: Alex

Clinician's Name: Julie

Date: 1/19/00

Session: Spring Session 1

Objectives for this Session	Procedures and Materials	Clinical Observations

1. To increase Alex's receptive and expressive language skills in the following areas using a Total Communication approach:
  a. vocabulary through thematic skills
  b. following one- to two-step directions
  c. spatial concepts (on/off, up/down, in/out)
  d. use of modifiers (big/little, fast/slow)
  e. colors (green, yellow, red, blue)
 	
2. To increase Alex's awareness and strength of his oral musculature through the use of the NUK brush, mirror play, bubbles, whistles, and Beckman Oral Motor Interventions
 	
3. To improve Alex's pragmatic abilities in the areas of greetings, farewells, turn-taking, requesting, initiating, and protesting
 	
4. To increase Alex's spontaneous length of utterance to a consistent 2-4 word/sign level
 	
5. To increase the frequency of Alex's vocalizations through the use of motokinesthetic cues
	1. Body Time
	  • Gross Motor Room
	
	2. Mouth Time
	  • NUK brush
	  • *Bubbles*
	  • Horn Program
	
	3. Art Time
	  • Paint a snowman
	
	4. Story Time
	  • *How's the Weather?*
	  • *I Love Snow*
	
	5. Snack Time
	  • Make hot chocolate
		Welcome back! I hope you had a great holiday and a happy new year. I am really anxious to start working with Alex again this semester. Today we are going to paint a snowman and try to read the books *How's the Weather?* and *I Love Snow*. We are going to make hot chocolate for snack time. I'd like to continue the horn program. Were you able to work with the horn program over break? I'm sending home the little book *I Love Snow*. Please read this with Alex at home and we will definitely read it next week if we don't get to it today.

worked on at home (see below). At the Loyola College Speech and Language Center, therapy sessions are conducted in a two-room suite with a one-way mirror. This allows parents and significant others (including grandparents, day care providers, SLPs, friends, and siblings) to observe all therapy sessions. The Clinical supervisory faculty member observes with the parents and provides explanation and commentary, so that the parents will be able to work on the targeted skills at home throughout the week with their child.

If you are not having regular face-to-face meetings with your child's SLP, you and the SLP will still need to work very closely to help your child achieve maximum success in communication. It is essential for you to have information about therapy sessions so that you can follow through at home. The lines of communication need to be open and used on a regular basis. You need to be able to ask questions and feel that the SLP is well trained to answer those questions.

The most important factors in communication between parents and SLPs are honesty, a willingness to share information, and frequent contact. If meetings are infrequent, they are likely to be more formal and less open. Infrequent communication usually focuses on problems, not triumphs. A common concern of parents is that, with only annual meetings to evaluate the IEP, these meetings tend to focus on problem areas and how therapy will remedy the problems. More frequent meetings are more balanced between successes and difficulties, and may even help prevent problems.

From the very beginning, discuss with the SLP the best way to communicate. Some parents and therapists send a notebook, log, or journal back and forth from each session. This provides information to parents and lets them give the SLP feedback and suggestions. Other parents and professionals prefer to communicate by phone, email, weekly or monthly progress reports, or periodic meetings.

Beginning with your child's first IFSP or IEP, it is a good idea to include a specific goal to promote parent-professional communication and cooperation. The IFSP/IEP can include specific plans for how communication will occur between teachers and related services personnel and others in school and between the school and home. A suggested goal would be:

- To provide a means for speech-language pathologist-parent communication on a regular basis.

The short-term objectives might be:

- The SLP and parents will communicate through a written journal notebook at least once weekly.
- The SLP will provide information on the child's sessions and home activities.
- The parents will provide feedback on home practice, progress, and problems and report on family activities that might serve as the basis for conversations in therapy sessions.

See the section on "Speech-Language Services and the IFSP/IEP" for more information about IFSPs and IEPs.

WORKING ON A HOME PROGRAM WITH THE SLP

If your child is in early intervention or is receiving private speech-language therapy, the SLP should be suggesting follow-up activities and activities for you to do with your child at home. Once your child is in preschool or elementary school, you may need to ask that a home program be specified in her IEP if you want to ensure that the SLP suggests home activities.

If a home program is specified in your child's IEP, there should be a means of school-to-home communication so that you can give the SLP feedback on your child's progress at home. An example of a home activity might be to find pictures that represent one, two, and three of the same objects, then practice labeling them and saying "one, two, three" with your child. On the home-to-school log, you would report back to the SLP regarding your child's progress in labeling the pictures with the numbers.

Legislation and Speech-Language Pathology Services

In the United States, the Individuals with Disabilities Education Act (IDEA) and its amendments require each state to provide services to meet the special educational needs of children with disabilities. Under the law and regulations, these services must include speech and language therapy, as well as assistive technology such as augmentative and alternative communication (AAC), when needed. Speech and language services, as well as other services intended to help children with disabilities make progress in the curriculum, are referred to as "related services." Most children with Down syndrome qualify for special education (or early intervention) services, but not all qualify to receive speech-language therapy through the schools. The next section explains why.

WHO IS ELIGIBILE FOR SPEECH-LANGUAGE SERVICES?

There are two primary reasons that speech and language services may be beneficial for infants and children with Down syndrome:
1. to prevent speech and language problems, and
2. to remedy speech and language problems.

While your child is in early intervention, either one of these reasons is considered a valid reason to declare your child eligible for speech-language therapy. That is, your infant or toddler will probably qualify for speech and language services simply because she has Down syndrome and is considered to be at risk of speech and language delays. Once your child begins receiving preschool or elementary special education services, however, she may be eligible for speech-language services only when problems that need "fixing" have been identified. IDEA allows states to provide services merely because a child is *at risk* of delays from age three until age nine, but it is left to the states to make that decision. The services are not mandated.

Early speech and language intervention for infants and toddlers is usually intended as prevention. Early language stimulation and techniques such as Total Communication may prevent some communication problems. For example, in speech therapy, the prevention approach would teach your child to round her lips (perhaps by practice with blowing bubbles) on the "oo" vowel sound even before she shows difficulty producing that sound. In language therapy, the prevention approach would teach your child greetings when they are appropriate for her to use, but before they have become a problem.

Once speech and language problems have developed, an approach called "remediation" is generally used. Speech and language problems are documented, then therapy is designed to "remedy" those problems. For example, if your child substitutes /d/ for /g/ (as in the words "do," and "go"), speech therapy works on teaching the /g/ sound. In language therapy, the remediation approach would teach your child the proper pronoun form and the correct verb ending for the word "runs" if she says "him run" instead of "he runs."

Since almost every child with Down syndrome is delayed in speech and language skills by the time she reaches school age, you would think that schools would routinely provide speech and language services for all students with Down syndrome. Unfortunately, that is not the case. School speech and language services are designed to help children with communication problems that have an adverse affect on progress in the "regular education curriculum." School services are not designed to help your child reach her maximum communication potential or to prevent problems that might develop down the line. So, it is possible that your child needs speech-language pathology services, but is not eligible to receive them through the school if her communication problems are not considered to affect her progress in the regular education curriculum.

ELIGIBILITY CRITERIA

The Developmental Model. If your child is three or older, a variety of criteria will be used to determine whether she is eligible for speech and language therapy. The developmental model for evaluation and intervention is most commonly used for determining eligibility. This model looks at the age at which typical children develop speech and language skills. These ages, or "norms," are then used to evaluate your child's development. If your child's speech and language development is slower than the "norms," therapy is considered.

This method puts parents of children with Down syndrome in a Catch-22 situation. If your child has been doing well in speech or language development for the past several months, she may score "at age level." That is, her speech and language skills may match her chronological age (C.A.) or mental age (M.A.) level. Based on her scores, speech and language services will be denied. The services may only be reinstated a year or two later, when she may be far enough below the developmental norm, and can qualify for services. Parents certainly want to hear that their child's speech and language are developing well, but if therapy has helped her progress and it is then discontinued, is this really a helpful course of action? Do not assume that your child does not need services just because the services are not being provided through the school system. Seek another evaluation if you're in doubt. Comprehensive Down syndrome clinics, university programs in speech-language pathology, and private practitioners can provide this service.

Disparity between Cognitive and Language Abilities. Another eligibility criterion sometimes used for children with developmental disabilities, including Down syndrome, is to require that their language scores be at a certain level below their cognitive scores in order to qualify for language services. If your child's language and cognitive scores are at approximately the same level, you may be told that her language level is commensurate with her intelligence or overall cognitive level, and that services will not be provided.

This creates another Catch-22 situation. Because most intelligence and cognitive testing is based on language ability (both to understand and follow the instructions and to answer questions), standardized test results may show that language and cognitive abilities are at the same level. The *real* question of whether your child needs language therapy is not answered. This criterion should not be used as a reason to declare your child ineligible for speech and language services.

You can ask that your child be given a nonverbal intelligence test that will not penalize her for language delays. The tests most widely used by psychologists are the Leiter International Performance Scale and the Comprehensive Test of Nonverbal Intelligence (CTONI). These scores can then be compared with your child's language scores. Often, in children with Down syndrome, the scores indicate that the child has more difficulty with language skills than would be predicted by IQ score. This finding may help your child qualify for free speech-language services through the schools.

SEEKING PRIVATE THERAPY

If you have concerns about your child's articulation or language development and feel that she "needs" services, seek an evaluation from an SLP outside of the school system. You may also want to contact a private SLP if you would like your child to receive more therapy than provided through her early intervention program or school.

Many speech-language pathologists are in private practice. Comprehensive Down syndrome centers, health departments, private practitioners, and university training programs are all possible providers of speech-language services. Often, services provided through the health department or university training programs are subsidized and are provided at low cost to the family. Scholarships or sliding scale payment schedules may also be available. The SLP in the local school, the chairperson of a local university training program, the administrator or developmental pediatrician at a comprehensive center, or your local parent support group may be able to recommend speech and language professionals in your area who have experience in working with children with Down syndrome.

Some health insurance policies cover speech-language pathology services, but others will only pay for an evaluation and will not cover ongoing services. But even if you can only afford to go once a month, private speech-language therapy can be very beneficial for your child if the SLP gives you a home program.

Qualifying on the Basis of Developmental Delay

In some, but not all states, children aged three to nine may be found eligible for special education and related services, including speech-language therapy, solely on the basis of having a "developmental delay." IDEA allows, but does not *require*, this provision. In school districts that allow this provision, children qualify for services if they are found to have a developmental delay in physical, cognitive, communication, social or emotional, or adaptive development. In states that use this eligibility criteria, it is usually easy for children with Down syndrome to qualify for speech-language therapy, since most have at least some developmental delay at this age. To find out whether your state allows young children to qualify for services under the developmental delay criteria, ask for a copy of your state's special education regulations from the State Department of Education. Libraries, especially law libraries, should also have copies of the regulations.

SPEECH-LANGUAGE SERVICES AND THE IFSP/IEP

Under IDEA, children who qualify for early intervention or special education are given written contracts stating what the early intervention program or school system agrees to do to help them learn. For children in early intervention, the contract is called an Individualized Family Service Plan (IFSP). For children aged three and older, the contract is called an Individualized Education Program (IEP).

If your child qualifies for speech-language services, her IFSP or IEP should spell out when and where she will receive the services, what goals will be worked on in therapy, and other details that will enable you and the school system to make sure that speech-language therapy is benefiting your child. Below are some of the important issues your child's IFSP/IEP should address related to speech-language services (as well as other related services she qualifies for). For more detail about writing good IFSPs or IEPs, you may wish to refer to my book *Classroom Language Skills for Children with Down Syndrome* (Woodbine House, 2001).

HOW MUCH THERAPY, WHERE AND WHEN?

Your child's IFSP or IEP should spell out what services your child will receive, where, and when. For example, for a child in early intervention, the IFSP might specify whether services will be provided at home or in a center, in individual or group sessions, for how long, how frequently, and by whom. Sometimes in early intervention, one professional provides SLP, OT, and PT services (sometimes known as integrated treatment) in consultation with other therapists. The specialist is usually chosen based on which area is most difficult for your child or which area is developmentally most important at that point in her development. For an older child, the IEP might specify individual speech-language therapy, provided twice a week for thirty minutes at a time, once in the classroom and once in the therapy room.

The scheduling and frequency of services must be keyed to your child's unique needs. It should *not* be based on some arbitrary formula such as "We provide thirty minutes of speech therapy twice weekly in groups for children with Down syndrome." Likewise, putting your child in group therapy because the SLP says, "I don't have time in my schedule to see children individually" is not a legitimate reason. However, if your child is in early intervention, it may be legitimate for them to say that your child will receive individualized therapy rather than group therapy because they provide all early intervention services at home.

Following are the models for providing therapy that are generally used for children in school-based programs beginning with kindergarten and beyond. If your child's preschool is located within an elementary school setting, the same models are often used. Variations of these service delivery models are used for early intervention. A combination of these types of models may be appropriate for your child at some times. At other times, one model may be better for your child, depending on the goals she is working on. Your child's goals should determine what model is used for her.

Pull-Out Therapy. In the past, therapy was almost always done outside of the classroom, in separate sessions. This method for service delivery is now referred to as "pull-out therapy." For children with Down syndrome, individual pull-out therapy works best when working on muscle exercises and oral skills, articulation, and intelligibility. Classroom-based therapy, below, works well for semantic and pragmatic skills. For children in early intervention, home-based therapy may be seen as a kind of pull-out therapy, because it is provided on an individual basis outside of a classroom.

Classroom-Based Therapy. With classroom-based therapy, the therapy might involve the entire class or may be conducted with a small group within the classroom. Classroom-based therapy may also be viewed in another way—not as therapy held in the classroom setting, but as therapy that is applicable to what goes on in the classroom. This may involve learning to follow rules or how to ask for help or using the curriculum as the material for speech-language pathology sessions. The expectation is that progress that results from treatment will be seen as improvement in the classroom situation. In early intervention, center-based group therapy is a type of classroom-based therapy.

Curriculum-Based Therapy. A recent trend is to coordinate therapy with your child's academic curriculum. That is, vocabulary taught in therapy would be based on the material in the educational curriculum. For example, if your child is learning about transportation, the SLP might help her learn such words as "train," "airplane," "automobile," "truck," "ship," "ferry," etc.

Collaborative Consultation. Another recent trend is for the classroom teacher and the SLP to collaborate to help the child succeed. This is referred to as the collaborative consultation model. In this method, the SLP might help the classroom teacher learn how best to give instructions to your child, or help the preschool and kindergarten teacher learn how to adapt language on written worksheets or design visual cueing instruction sheets that can help your child complete written work or follow classroom instructions. The SLP and the teacher might work together with a behavioral specialist to determine what your child might be communicating through behavior and come up with a positive behavior intervention plan that will consider the relationship between communication and behavior for your child.

The Whole Language Model. Yet another trend is called the "whole language model." Speaking, listening, reading, and writing are viewed as integrated skills that make up the overall communication skill that your child needs to learn, rather than as separate and discrete skills. The classroom teacher, reading specialist, and SLP all work together to plan curriculum units that use all communication skill areas to help your child learn. For example, your child's class may be learning about bears. The class would read books about bears, talk about bears, go to the zoo, see a video about bears, sing a song about bears, write a story about bears, and make teddy bear cookies.

WHAT WILL YOUR CHILD LEARN IN THERAPY?

You need to be directly involved in developing communication goals with the SLP so that the skills taught will be useful in your child's daily life. You also play a key role in helping your child achieve the goals.

Each time an IFSP or IEP is developed for your child, you should have the opportunity to suggest speech-language goals for your child. And if you don't have any to suggest, you should be asked to look at the SLP's proposed goals and accept, reject, or ask for changes to them. If your child is seeing a private SLP, you will also be involved in setting goals, but the goals are not always written down. Since you will likely be transporting your child to therapy, you will be able to have ongoing and informal discussions with the SLP about your child's goals and progress toward them.

The SLP will most often base her goals on the results of your child's evaluation or on problems she sees in therapy sessions. But parents should also feel free to suggest goals to help with communication problems they observe at home, in school, or during daily living. Parental input is especially crucial during the early intervention period.

If there is a home-to-school communication book, send feedback to the SLP about situations that come up at home or in daily life where your child has difficulty. Are there names or words that are difficult for your child? Let the SLP know. Also send feedback regarding situations where your child is successfully using the strategies that are being targeted in therapy.

Look at things that make your child frustrated at home and ask the SLP if this area can be targeted in treatment. Don't worry about whether you are phrasing your goal "correctly." Just describe what the difficulty is.

Let the SLP know what is going on in your child's life. Are there upcoming events for which your child needs certain skills? Is your child going to be a flower girl or ring bearer? Has she been asked to sing a song at a family event? Is there a family visit, vacation, or large dinner where certain skills might be helpful? Send information to the SLP, along with words or phrases or social skills that will be needed for the event.

Under IDEA, you must be informed about your child's progress toward meeting IEP goals at least as often as students at the school are given reports about their progress in academics. In other words, whenever your child gets a report card, she should also get a report detailing her progress on IEP goals. If you want more frequent communication about your child's progress, you may want to request a home-school log to keep you informed about progress. See below for a weekly form that focuses on IEP goals.

Beth's Progress for the Week of _____

Beth answered to her name.   yes ❑   no ❑

Beth stayed on task.   yes ❑   no ❑

Beth said "hi" to 2 other students.   yes ❑   no ❑

Beth participated in the opening exercises.   yes ❑   no ❑

Beth stayed in line.   yes ❑   no ❑

Beth followed classroom rules.   yes ❑   no ❑

Beth participated in circle time.   yes ❑   no ❑

Beth participated in centers.   yes ❑   no ❑

Beth identified initial sounds in words in a book.   yes ❑   no ❑

Beth answered who and where questions based on a book.   yes ❑   no ❑

DOES YOUR CHILD NEED AAC OR OTHER SUPPORTS?

If your child needs assistive technology, including augmentative and alternative communication (AAC), that must be addressed in her IFSP/IEP. The IFSP/IEP should specify what AAC device/strategy will be used, who will provide it, and how your child and others will be trained to use it. See Chapter 11 for more information on AAC.

In addition, if your child has hearing impairments, her IEP or IFSP should specify whether she needs any supplementary aids to help her function in the classroom. For instance, she might need a classroom amplification system such as is described in Chapter 2.

HOW WILL THE PROGRAM BE MODIFIED FOR YOUR CHILD?

Your child's IEP needs to address how teaching methods, curriculum, classroom setting, or other elements need to be adapted to help her succeed in reaching her goals in the classroom. For instance, when your child is in early intervention or preschool, teachers may need to use sign or PECS in order to communicate instructions to her. And when your child is older, the classroom instructions may need to be written out, the number of items on a test may need to be reduced, or other modifications may be needed. For detailed information about making these types of adaptations, see *Classroom Language Skills for Children with Down Syndrome.*

WHAT SUPPORTS DO SCHOOL PERSONNEL NEED?

Sometimes teachers or other professionals will need training or other assistance to help your child meet her speech-language goals. For example, teachers and aides may need in-service classes to learn sign language or the Picture Exchange Communication System (PECS), or they may need a resource library of books and materials. If your child will be using an AAC device, staff members may need to learn to operate it, as well as troubleshoot when it stops working. Your child's IFSP or IEP needs to identify what types of supports staff members need and how they will be provided.

HOW WILL YOUR CHILD'S PROGRESS BE MONITORED?

Your child's IFSP/IEP should stipulate how her ongoing progress will be determined once she has begun a treatment program. This often involves informal observations and tests. It may also involve more formal evaluations sometimes referred to as "pre-testing" and "post-testing." Your child would first be tested on a specific skill, such as her ability to produce the /p/ sound correctly. Then treatment would be given, followed by a post-test to determine whether she has mastered the /p/ sound in treatment. This gives precise information about the effectiveness of a treatment approach or therapy.

| ENSURING SLP INPUT AT YOUR CHILD'S IEP MEETING |

If you want to make sure that your child's IFSP or IEP provides the communication support she needs in the inclusive classroom, it would be logical to expect the SLP to attend the IEP planning meeting, wouldn't it? However, under IDEA, the SLP is not ordinarily required to be on a child's IEP or IFSP team.

If your child's primary disability is a speech-language impairment and the only special education service she receives is speech-language therapy, then the SLP might be expected to attend. In kindergarten and the primary grades, some children with Down syndrome receive speech-language services as their only special education service. In that case, the SLP should be the special educator to attend IEP meetings. Otherwise, the speech-language pathologist is not required by federal law to attend the IEP meeting. But if the SLP is not present, how can the meeting be a team planning meeting?

If your child receives speech and language services through the school, it is your right to specifically request that the SLP attend your child's IEP meeting, and be an integral part of the planning process. If this is not possible, the SLP should submit your child's speech and language goals to the team before the meeting. You should also try to talk with her before the meeting. It is especially important to try to get the SLP to attend the IEP planning meeting if you expect the team to object to any communication-related services you will be requesting at the meeting. It may be difficult to reschedule a meeting, but is definitely worth trying to have the SLP in attendance if she will help advocate for your child.

Controversial or Alternative Treatments

Working on speech and language through traditional speech-language therapy is a slow process. This can make new or alternative treatments that promise quicker fixes seem highly attractive. Often, these new approaches to treatment are rolled out with great fanfare but are not proven. Some alternative treatments are based on research, but many only offer anecdotal reports of their effectiveness. Many are very costly, and are provided only at specific centers or by practitioners who hold the certification to provide that specific treatment approach. The certification training for a specific approach might involve hundreds of hours of training or might involve a single two-hour training session. For example, auditory integration therapy, Samonas sound therapy, or dolphin-assisted therapy may cost thousands of dollars. School systems rarely cover the costs of these treatments, so the expenses are paid by the family.

How does a parent know whether an alternative therapy might help their child? Or whether it could hurt their child? For example, if the treatment involves listening to sounds, could the sound be presented at levels loud enough to damage your child's hearing? Here are some questions to ask when considering any alternative therapy:

- What problems does the treatment approach target?
- Does my child have that problem or is she at high risk for developing it?
- Where can I find out more about the treatment?
- Has the treatment been used with children with Down syndrome?
- Is there data on the effectiveness of the treatment with children? With children with Down syndrome? Is there research data, in addition to anecdotes and testimonial information, that demonstrate the effectiveness of the treatment?
- Who provides the treatment? What kind of training does the provider have?
- Can you talk with families who have tried the treatment? What has been their experience?

- What are the conventional treatment approaches that target the same problem?
- Does the alternative treatment provide a better approach? An approach based on sound theory? A proven approach?

Be cautious! A new or alternative approach does not necessarily mean a better approach. If in doubt, talk to your child's SLP about the pros, cons, and possible risks of trying the approach. Remember that speech and language treatment needs to be comprehensive, touching on all areas that present difficulties for your child. It is probably not wise to put all your eggs in one basket, especially where unproven therapies are concerned.

Conclusion

Your child has a great deal to gain from working with a skilled, committed SLP. As her parent, so do you. A speech-language pathologist can guide you in working with your child in the ways that best nurture her speech and language development, and can make your daily communication with your child easier. If you and your child's SLP have frequent and open communication about problems and solutions, your child stands to get the most out of the services she receives.

Speech-language therapy is not easy and there are no instant "cures," but hard work and perseverance usually pay off. Learn as much as you can about how your child's SLP works with your child, and you will learn how better to work with your child yourself. Ask for a home program so that you can practice the skills being addressed in treatment with your child at home. And always remember that your child's SLP relies on you to tell her how to best work with your child. The insight and personal knowledge of your child that you contribute to the SLP is absolutely critical to the success of therapy. Work as a team.

Chapter 14

Literacy and Language

Literacy—the ability to read—opens many doors for any child. Children with Down syndrome may reap even more benefits from learning to read. In fact, reading can be a very successful route to assist children with Down syndrome in learning language. Reading can enable children with Down syndrome to learn language concepts through their strong visual channel, circumventing any difficulties they have with auditory processing and speech. Sue Buckley at the Down Syndrome Educational Trust in the United Kingdom has found that reading training has positive effects on spoken language, receptive vocabulary, and memory tasks. She advocates using visual processing and visual memory skills to support all learning (Buckley, 2001).

Some parents and professionals advocate teaching children with Down syndrome to read as early as possible. Buckley, for example, believes that children with Down syndrome are able to learn to read at two to three years and has done research documenting that children who are introduced to reading in the preschool years reach the highest levels of literacy in adolescence and adulthood. Others advocate taking a more relaxed approach and teaching reading and pre-reading skills using the same timeline most children follow (starting at about age six).

My view is that specific difficulties in learning speech should not be allowed to hold back your child's language progress. I believe that language learning can often proceed more quickly when signing and reading are used and that one or both should be used in a comprehensive treatment program for young children with Down syndrome. Visual learning can be an effective way to help children with Down syndrome learn about the world, expand their vocabulary, help with memory, and prepare them for independent living in the future. Street signs, bus schedules, recipes, instructions, and job applications all involve reading. If a child can read at the eight- to nine-year-old level, he can sound out words and read newspapers, books, and magazines. Recent research involving young adults with Down syndrome in Australia found that 60-70 percent of adults with Down syndrome can read at the eight- to nine-year-old reading level (Bochner, Outhred & Pieterse, 2001). Helping children learn to read provides them with skills that increase their chances of achieving independence and success in the future.

Regardless of when you choose to start teaching your child to read, there are activities and experiences you can do with him from an early age to help lay the foundation for reading skills. This chapter explores those early reading experiences and also describes some approaches that work well in teaching children with Down syndrome to read.

Preparing Your Child to Read

Many different methods can be used to teach reading, but there are certain basic experiences that form the groundwork for later teaching. These skills can be developed by professionals and parents working together in early intervention. They can be practiced at home as part of daily life. Many of these pre-reading experiences are the same experiences that young children need to be ready to learn language. They are also known as pre-literacy or early literacy skills.

Teach Turn-Taking. Reading and all communication are interactive, participatory experiences. Learning to take turns is important and can be fostered through games such as peek-a-boo, rolling a ball back and forth between two people, and transferring the wand for a xylophone or a musical toy from one person to another. Chapters 4 and 10 offer additional suggestions for teaching turn-taking.

Observe Learning Styles. Study your child to learn how he takes in information and learns best. Does he prefer loud or soft noises? What type of music does he like? Does he enjoy touching different textures? Does he prefer to watch first or to get right in there and participate? What is the best time for him to focus on a task? What helps him focus? Determining your child's learning style will help you choose an appropriate method for helping him learn to read.

Provide Sensory Experiences. Seeing, hearing, tasting, smelling, and touching are the sensory channels through which infants and toddlers learn about their world. And understanding about the world is a prerequisite for reading. Provide your child with many sensory experiences, such as hearing music, smelling flowers, and feeling different textures. Allow him time to focus on a sense and direct his attention to interesting sensory experiences in the environment. For example, let him discover what sand feels like, how his toes feel when they are in water, how different family members' voices sound, what blueberry muffins smell like when they are baking. When he reads about the beach, voices, and baking, the words will be better understood if he has had the experiences. Many children's books focus on children's experiences.

Integrate Sensory Experiences with Language. Integrating, organizing, associating, and interpreting information from the environment are tasks that are basic to language and to literacy. Focus your child on the connections between senses. For example, point out, "Sandpaper feels scratchy and looks rough"; "Cotton feels soft and looks soft and fluffy." Give him the words to describe his experiences. Or on a more advanced level, "Hear that thunder? It's going to rain. Look outside, it's getting dark and cloudy. Do you see the trees blowing? The trees are blowing because it's windy."

Increase Attention. In order to learn to read, you need to be able to focus and attend for a period of time. In infancy, visual and auditory stimulation can be used to increase the length of time that your child can focus. For

example, hold his face close to yours and get his attention. Then, make funny faces and funny sounds that engage his interest. Or, sing a favorite song such as "The Eensy Weensy Spider." Then, once your child learns to enjoy the movements and the song, sing a few more verses. Your goal is to teach your child to focus for increasing periods of time.

Create an Environment That Fosters Literacy. We tend to think of reading as a specific skill to be mastered. But, we are now becoming more aware of the role of the environment in fostering literacy. Children need to get to know about books. When an infant turns the pages of a vinyl book in the bathtub, this helps to foster a culture of reading. Children need to see books, magazines, and other reading matter at home and in early school settings. They need to be read to and to have time to explore books. Children may turn the pages and look through the pictures in a book well before they are actually able to read the book. When adults and children read a book together, children learn many pre-literacy skills, such as how to hold a book, reading from top to bottom and left to right, recognizing that printed words have a regularity and differ from marks or scribbles on a page, and progressing from page to page. Children also gain practice in hearing language as you read to them.

The factor that has been found to relate most highly to learning to read is that the child has been read to. Reading together and sharing storybooks, on a regular basis, provides positive pre-literacy experiences. In addition, some professionals feel that besides reading books with your child, it is also important to embed reading experiences in everyday life activities. For instance, read the cartoons in the newspapers to your child or read recipes aloud while making dinner. Read menus when you go out to eat. And read signs at the supermarket. You might even want to make a picture shopping list. Your child will get experience in visual matching and will be able to find the products on his own shopping list.

Before your child can actually read, books can be used to stimulate language growth. Point out the characters in the book, then have your child point to the characters as you talk about them. Talk about what is happening (the plot), and describe the action. Your child can demonstrate comprehension by pointing or by pantomime or pretending, even before he can speak. Pointing to the words while you are reading gives your child practice in visual scanning from left to right and in moving down the lines.

Children love to read books about themselves and their own experiences. Use photos to make personalized books that relate directly to your child's daily experiences. Now that computer technology enables us to scan pictures, it is easy to create personalized books that help a child relive his daily experiences.

Teach Visual Matching. Visual matching is an early skill that helps children practice a skill that will be needed for reading. In order to learn to read, you need to be able to recognize visual similarities. You need to have experience with the letter shapes to be able to recognize letters. Shape boxes and puzzles in which one wooden shape fits into an identically shaped space provide practice in matching pictures.

Lotto games can also be used to teach and to practice visual matching skills. It is easy to make lotto games that are personalized to your child's interests, making them more motivating to play. One low-tech way is to take photographs of objects or people in your child's environment and have double prints made. Glue four to six photos on a piece of construction paper or poster board and have your child match the duplicate photos to the board. You can also purchase software such as *Picture This!* (listed in the Resource Guide), which enables you to choose photos from many categories and print out lotto boards and pieces. Or you can use Boardmaker™ software to print out thousands of Picture Communication Symbols©.

Emergent Literacy Skills

Emergent literacy focuses on helping children learn how to experience books and act like readers even before they can actually read. Here are some pointers to help your child enjoy learning these skills.

Choose Appropriate Books. One way to help young children experience books is to choose books that are appropriate for them. Select books that have bold graphics and interesting pictures. Board books, flap books, and touch and feel books (such as *Pat the Bunny*) help children learn to explore and manipulate books. Books with few words per page (one to four words) are appropriate for children at the emergent literacy level. Or you can use books with more words per page, but adapt the text to your child's level as you are reading. Be careful not to choose books with too many words and visual things going on per page, however, as in some Richard Scarry books.

Adapt Books for Easy Handling. It is also important to make sure that your child can handle the books you choose for him. In infancy, a baby is not able to turn the pages of a regular book, but plasticized books or adapted books can make it possible for him to participate in reading. Here are some ideas to help slightly older children learn to turn the pages, some of them adapted from the work of Patti King-DeBaun. (See References.)

- Adapt sturdy board books by placing foam rubber pads (sold for stabilizing and positioning picture frames), rubber furniture bumpers, or Velcro tabs at the top or bottom of each page. Packing popcorn can also be glued to the corner of each page, but be sure your child can't peel it off and eat it. This will keep the pages slightly apart and make them easier to turn.

- Use chip bag clips, clothespins, or bulldog clips on each page as page turners, but be sure your child has sufficient motor control so that he will not hit himself in the face with the clips.
- Books can also be taken apart and reassembled. Place each page in a plastic page protector envelope that is already three-hole-punched (available at office supply stores). Put all of the book pages in order in a loose leaf notebook. These pages will be easy for your child to turn and will be waterproof.

Help Your Child Participate in Reading. Before your child can read, and even before he can speak, you can help him be a vital part of the reading process. One simple way to help your child participate in reading is to copy some of the pictures in the book you will be reading. You can scan pictures from existing books or create your own books using Picture Communication Symbols from Mayer-Johnson or photographs from software such as *Picture This!* (See the Resource Guide for suggestions for software packages for pictures for storybooks.) Make one extra copy of the picture. Laminate the picture and back it with Velcro. On or next to the picture in the book (depending on what else in on the page and how much white space there is), mount the other part of the Velcro circle, square, or strip. Show your child how to match the extra picture to the one in the book. Label the picture by saying, for example, "Where's the duck? Here's the duck. Duck."

Once your child has experience turning the pages, she may attempt to make speech sounds, as if she is reading. I have seen many children turning the pages, and making babbling sounds as if reading. Sometimes, they have appropriate intonation, rhythm, and rate patterns and you have to listen hard to realize that they are not really reading the book.

Another suggestion is to tape record a recurring phrase from a book on a single channel recorder or other taping device. Many books have what are known as predictable phrases—phrases that are repeated many times in the book and which your child can anticipate. Some books have repeated lines, although their placement cannot be predicted. An example is in the *Three Little Pigs:* "I'll huff and I'll puff and I'll blow your house in." Whenever that phrase comes up in the book, your child just needs to press the switch to activate the taped message. Then, your child is the one saying, "I'll huff..." and is able to participate in the story even though he cannot yet read or speak the words. Likewise, for the *Three Billy Goats Gruff,* you could record the question "Who's crossing my bridge?" and let your child provide the voice for the troll.

Other examples of predictable stories include:

- Campbell, Rod. *Dear Zoo*. New York, NY: Little Simon, 1986.
- Carle, Eric. *The Very Hungry Caterpillar*. New York, NY: Putnam, 1983.
- Galdone, Paul. *Henny Penny*. Boston: Houghton Mifflin, 1984.
- Hutchins, Pat. *Good Night, Owl*. New York, NY: Simon & Schuster, 1972.
- Martin, Bill. *Brown Bear, Brown Bear, What Do You See?* New York, NY: Henry Holt, 1992.
- McGovern, Ann. *Too Much Noise*. Boston: Houghton Mifflin, 1967.

- Numeroff, Laura Joffe. *If You Give a Mouse a Cookie*. New York, NY: Harpercollins, 1985.
- Peck, Merle. *Mary Wore Her Red Dress and Henry Wore His Green Sneakers*. Boston: Houghton Mifflin, 1988.
- Sendak, Maurice. (1962). *Chicken Soup with Rice*. New York, NY: Harpercollins.
- Sendak, Maurice. *Where the Wild Things Are*. New York, NY: Harpercollins, 1988.

Incorporate Reading Activities into Daily Life. Activities of daily living lend themselves to learning print, and since they occur frequently, they provide opportunities for repetitive practice.

- Use sign-in and sign-out charts at home. On the "in" chart, place laminated name cards with Velcro on the back. When family members go out, they move their name card to the "out" chart. When they come home, they move their name to the "in" house chart. That way, your child learns to recognize his name through daily practice.
- Use chore charts, with your children's names and a pictured or word list of chores to be done.
- Use calendar charts with stickers for the weather conditions and any special events.
- Create word and picture schedules for the activities your child needs to complete each day.

Teaching Children with Down Syndrome to Read

Until quite recently, most professionals believed that only an exceptional child with Down syndrome would be able to learn to read. This view prevailed even though many parents succeeded in teaching their children with Down syndrome to read without benefit of professional expertise, and several accounts of the literary skills of children with Down syndrome were published in the 1960s, including *The World of Nigel Hunt* and *Yesterday Was Tuesday All Day and All Night*. That professional perception began to change in the 1970s when Dr. Valentine Dmitriev and Patricia Oelwein began routinely teaching reading to young children with Down syndrome who were enrolled in the Program for Children with Down Syndrome and Other Developmental Delays at the University of Washington.

Currently, professionals and parents agree that many, if not most children with Down syndrome can learn to read. Some are able to learn to read using the same approaches used to teach any other child; others require more specialized approaches, as discussed below in "Specially Designed Methods and Materials for Children with Down Syndrome."

For some children, learning to read may be easier than learning to speak. Many children with Down syndrome learn more easily through the visual channel—through seeing rather than through hearing. The written word, in a book or on the computer screen, stays there for the child as long as it is needed, and the child can look back at the word, while speech is rapid and fleeting. In many children with Down syndrome, middle ear fluid and fluctuating hearing loss are problems that interfere with reliable hearing and with learning solely through hearing. Because of these factors, children with Down syndrome may be able to learn to read words before they can say the words, and may be able to learn and understand concepts more easily through reading than through hearing.

Sue Buckley and her colleagues at the Down Syndrome Educational Trust in Portsmouth, England have conducted a great deal of research into the benefits of reading for children with Down syndrome. They believe that we need to make literacy and effective literacy instruction a priority for children with Down syndrome. Buckley begins teaching reading to children with Down syndrome when they are two years, six months. She feels that it is appropriate to begin training when the child has a single-word vocabulary of forty to fifty words and can match and select pictures. See below for more information.

Specially Designed Methods and Materials for Children with Down Syndrome

There are three reading programs that provide "how to" information and materials specially designed to teach children with Down syndrome to read:

- *Love and Learning* by Joe and Sue Kotlinski,
- *Teaching Reading to Children with Down Syndrome* by Patricia Logan Oelwein, and
- The approach used by Sue Buckley and her colleagues at the Sarah Duffen Centre in England.

Sometimes parents or teachers choose to use these programs with children with Down syndrome only if they do not succeed in learning to read using another conventional method. Other times parents or teachers begin using one of these methods early, before any other method has been tried. See the "Strategies for Learning a New Skill" for guidance in choosing the right approach for your child.

LOVE AND LEARNING

Love and Learning is a multisensory system for teaching reading developed by Joe and Sue Kotlinski to teach their daughter, Maria, to read. There are six learning kits available that gradually progress from learning the alphabet and the corresponding sounds to advanced conversational skills. Each kit teaches the child between 50 and 150 new words. Each learning kit has three parts:

1. An audiotape lets the child hear the sounds and words spoken in a clear, slow manner. The tape is played at bedtime or playtime on a regular basis to increase the child's familiarity with how the words sound.
2. A videotape shows how each word is spelled and pronounced and also provides clear and colorful video action examples. For example, the letter "b" (visual) is shown and pronounced (phonetic), then the word "bus" appears and is pronounced, then we see a bus, and finally Maria appears and gets on the school bus.

3. Specially designed books accompany the audio- and videotapes and provide for reinforcement and reading practice for the new words. The material on the video is the same material that the child has heard on the audiotape and the same material that is included in the specially designed books.

Each videotape also has a teaching section in which Joe Kotlinski shares insights on how to use the materials most effectively. This is a relaxed, loving approach that has worked well for many children with Down syndrome. The audiotapes can be played at bedtime starting at an early age (twelve to eighteen months) and the method can be used through adolescence and adulthood for new readers.

For more information:
Love and Learning
Joe and Sue Kotlinski
P. O. Box 4088
Dearborn, MI 48126-4088
313-581-8436
www.loveandlearning.com

TEACHING READING TO CHILDREN WITH DOWN SYNDROME

Teaching Reading to Children with Down Syndrome: A Guide for Parents and Teachers by Patricia Logan Oelwein (Woodbine House, 1995) is a step-by-step guide to using a language experience approach to teach reading skills to children with Down syndrome. This individualized, functional reading program is based on the author's years of experience in working with children with Down syndrome at the University of Washington.

Parents and professionals develop individualized teaching materials for a child using photos and objects in his own environment. Pictures of family members, trips, activities, and games are all used to

teach language and reading. The system is visually based, and begins with teaching sight words. For each activity, children learn to match, select, and then name (read the written word) the word. For example, they learn to match a card with the word "cat" printed on it to another card printed with the word "cat"; then, when presented with a choice of two cards, select the one with the word "cat"; and finally read the word "cat."

The child can use Total Communication and signing to "read" the word if he cannot yet speak or cannot speak understandably. So, he can read the word by giving the sign to demonstrate his ability. When the child is able to read two or more words, discrimination tasks can be used in which the child matches and then reads the two different words.

The system uses flashcards developed based on the child's interest. The cards are gathered into a word bank which the child can use for further practice and review. After teaching some functional sight words, the program then introduces phonics through rhyming words, word bingo, and a word family approach. These activities are fun for children with Down syndrome and move them along in learning the skills. The Appendices include a typical sequence for teaching reading from the pre-primer level to the level at which the child has a sight reading vocabulary of 500 words, learns common prefixes and suffixes, and identifies number of syllables. The appendices also include basic sight vocabulary words and materials and illustrations for games.

The book is available from:
Woodbine House
6510 Bells Mill Road
Bethesda, MD 20817
800-843-7323
www.woodbinehouse.com

READING PROGRAM AND RESEARCH OF SUE BUCKLEY AND COLLEAGUES

As mentioned earlier, Sue Buckley believes that children with Down syndrome should be taught to read before three years of age. She believes that reading will help language develop, and that the child does not need to be able to say words in order to learn their meaning. Some of the language-learning benefits Buckley and her colleagues have documented in children with Down syndrome include:

- When children learn to read new vocabulary words, they soon start using the new words in their speech.
- Practicing reading two- and three-word phrases accelerates the appearance of two- and three-word phrases in speech.
- When children practice reading grammatically correct sentences, it leads to better grammar and syntax in their own speech.

Buckley believes that "the brain can go straight from print to meaning without changing the visual image of the word to its spoken form first and then accessing the meaning" (Buckley, 1996). In other words, before a child with Down syndrome even learns to speak, he may be able to look at a word such as "dog" and see a picture of a dog in his mind without saying or even being able to pronounce the word in his head.

Buckley believes that there may be several routes to facilitate reading in children with Down syndrome:

1. Build up a large sign vocabulary and large spoken vocabulary.
2. Teach sight vocabulary first ("logographic" strategy).
3. Establish phonological patterns (letter to sound correspondence).
4. Teach children how to sound out words (alphabetic strategy).
5. Teach children to use context and meaning to help reading. For example, "door is sh__." If you can't read the word, the phonological context (the cue of "sh") will help you to guess the word "shut" rather than "closed" or "open."

Typically, when Buckley and her colleagues are teaching a young child to read, they begin by teaching him a small sight word vocabulary. They make flash cards with the names of family members or other very well-known words written in lower case, without pictures. Then, using "errorless learning," they teach the child to match, select, and name the words, as described above. Errorless learning means

guiding the child through each step correctly with prompts, not allowing him to make wrong guesses or to fail. Later, they introduce new words and phrases using flash cards and use games and activities to motivate the child to practice the words. Eventually, staff and parents write sentences and personalized stories for the child, using grammar and syntax at his level and begin pointing out which sounds correspond with which letters (Buckley & Bird, 1993).

Since 1980, Sue Buckley and her colleagues have been researching and documenting reading success in children with Down syndrome. Until the early 1990s, most studies relied on case studies and anecdotal reports of reading success. Beginning in 1993, Buckley began a longitudinal study of reading progress of twenty-four children with Down syndrome in inclusion. She found a wide range of individual differences in reading abilities, but all twenty-four students showed progress in reading. Reading test scores showed that reading ages were consistently ahead of language and number (math) age scores. Many of the children were reading at the same level as other typically developing children in their classes. When children were able to read at the seven- to eight-year-old level, they began to use phonics knowledge to sound out unfamiliar words in books and to spell words.

In 1995, Buckley reported on the skills of two groups of children with Down syndrome, who were at the same cognitive level at the beginning of the study. One group was taught to read and the other was not. Results demonstrated that at the end of the study, the readers had more advanced language and memory skills than the nonreaders. Furthermore, she has found that children with Down syndrome who begin to read early are more advanced in speech, language, and educational progress by age ten to eleven.

Strategies for Learning a New Skill

Here are some do's and don'ts that can help make it easier for children with Down syndrome to learn language and reading skills:

1. *Make sure learning is pleasurable.* Do not put pressure on your child to learn to speak or read at home or in therapy. Provide opportunities, but allow him to move at his own pace.
2. *Break new skills into smaller steps.* This way, your child can be successful in mastering each small step.
3. *Don't get stuck on having your child master "prerequisite" skills.* For example, many authorities believe that phonemic awareness (knowing the relationship between each sound and its letter and being able to sound out words) must be mastered before a child can read. But, some children may not master this skill. Instead, they may be able to learn to read through a visual or whole language approach.

4. *Provide experiences at your child's current level.* If he can turn the pages, then that can be his participatory role. When he can answer questions about what is happening in the book, he can participate at a higher level. When he can read the book, he can participate as a reader. But, he should not have to wait to be a reader in order to be able to participate.

5. *Try to choose a teaching approach that matches your child's learning styles.* There are many pathways to learning a new skill such as reading.

6. *Follow your child's interests.* Choose books that are interesting for him, as well as on the appropriate reading level.

7. *Provide many opportunities for practicing a new skill.* When your child knows the letter "c," choose books that have many "c's" in them. When your child knows the word "hop," read books such as *Hop on Pop* that include the word.

8. *Follow your child's timetable.* Children with Down syndrome may need more practice and may take longer to master a specific skill. Don't get discouraged. Try to provide a variety of materials and practice, so that your child doesn't get discouraged and continues to move forward.

9. *Provide many opportunities for repetition and practice.* Research has shown that children will choose the same book to read over and over. Children use the repetitions to master the story, and then try to become more participatory in reading the book. At first, they may recognize words and say them; later, they may remember lines and repeat them verbatim.

10. *Reinforce the new skill and show pleasure in your child's accomplishments.*

11. *Provide experiences that will help your child generalize the skills learned.* You don't want him to only be able to read the word "red" when it is written beneath a colored square on an index card or on a red crayon. Provide multisensory experiences and many different experiences to help him master the concept of "redness" as it relates to a variety of experiences.

Other Literacy Experiences That Can Reinforce Reading Skills

In daily life, literacy involves a lot more than reading books. In the course of his day, a six-year-old might encounter:

- newspapers and magazines,
- words on the television screen,
- advertisements,
- words on the computer screen,
- words on menus or lists of food choices,

- recipes and instructions on food boxes,
- street and highway signs,
- directional and informational signs (Exit, Rest Rooms, Telephone).

Help your child notice all the ways that words and print are used during real-life activities. When you go for a walk, comment on and read the street signs. When you go to the supermarket, read the signs for fruit and vegetables and discuss what "produce" means. Read the labels on food boxes and discuss what you can make from that food when you get home.

The basic survival language skills can be part of a speech-language therapy, school, and a home program in childhood. They can then be refined and learning can continue up to a more advanced level as your child grows into an adult. The following sections offer some suggestions for using daily life activities to work on literacy skills.

FOOD ACTIVITIES

Activities surrounding food make up a major area of independent living. Making lists, shopping for food, putting food away in the appropriate place, using recipes, and following instructions for food use are all part of daily life.

There are many language and reading activities you can do when your child is young to help lay the foundation for handling these food-related chores independently in adulthood. For example, for young children, we often use food categorization or food shopping activities as part of language therapy. We use toy food, a small shopping cart, a toy cash register, and lots of props such as hats and aprons from supermarkets. These lessons are reinforced in real life by trips to the supermarket. I would suggest taking photographs of a supermarket trip and using those as the basis for writing a personalized story based on your child's experiences (known as a language experience story).

SHOPPING LISTS

Even young children can create picture shopping lists from discarded food labels and boxes from their favorite foods. Print "Shopping List" at the top of the page, and provide lots of labels and box parts with the names of products for your child to glue to the list. Then he can choose the cereals (Cheerios), candies (Hershey's chocolate), condiments (ketchup), and grains (macaroni) that he would like to purchase on your next trip to the supermarket.

For items that don't have labels (such as fruits and vegetables), you can obtain pictures from sale advertisements, use small pictures from computer clip art collections or coloring books, or take photos.

Once your child is reading, he can progress to using a list with pictures and names. Worksheets can help him practice the names of the foods. One suggested practice sheet might have four food names. Three belong in the same category; one does not. Your child needs to cross out the one that doesn't belong. Here are some examples:

- apple, peach, grape, sweater
- lettuce, carrots, soap, green pepper
- bread, hot dog rolls, ice cream, sub rolls

Another activity might be to divide your shopping list into categories: *fruit, vegetables, frozen foods, meat, cleaning items*. Then put the names or pictures of items you want to buy on sticky labels. Let your child stick the labels in the correct category.

SHOPPING FOR GROCERIES

To shop efficiently, you need to know how the food is organized in your store. Either you need to be able to read the signs in the aisles or to read the chart-like list that gives that information (e.g., Soup, Aisle 6). If you cannot read the signs, you may need to walk each aisle to find the items that you need. So, what can you do to

help your child learn the skill? Make a cue card for just one aisle sign. Have your child find that aisle. You might choose the aisle for cereal or another favorite food. Walk across the store as you begin the shopping trip, and look only for that sign with your child. Once your child can correctly match the sign, work on recognition of the sign without the cue card. After he has found "his" aisle, continue on your regular shopping trip, walking each aisle in sequence.

Survival reading is important for reading food labels. Many household products look very similar. Pine Sol, Mr. Clean, and apple juice are similar in color and in similar large plastic containers. Lemon Palmolive and Sunlight detergent have lemons on the label and could easily be mistaken for lemonade and juices. Tuna fish and cat food are in similar size and shape cans. Sometimes, the packaging is changed for the *new, improved* versions of products or for a holiday (such as Christmas packaging), so it looks different from the packaging that you are used to seeing on the shelf. As an adult, you know that the only reliable way to get the products that you want is to be able to read the labels. When your child is a pre-reader, it's helpful to bring those shopping lists with actual labels glued to them and talk about why the label of the product in the store does or does not look exactly the same as the one on your list—point out that the *name* of the product is still on there, even if the background design has changed.

When you go to the checkout and choose a line, there may be separate lines, marked by signs, for "10 Items or Under" or "Cash Only." Being able to read will help you choose the appropriate line. Before your child can read, make a point of showing him the signs, seeing if he can pick out the number 10 on the sign and help count the items in your cart to see if you have 10 or less.

RECIPES

Preparing food and using recipes involves reading and understanding instructions. For some recipes, children can help and can read the recipe—for instance, pouring a cup of milk into pudding, or stirring Jello with a spoon.

Before your child can read, look for cake mixes that have the rebus style instructions on the back and let your pre-reader "read" them to you—show him how the picture of two eggs means you need two eggs and the picture of a full cup of water means you fill the measuring cup to the one-cup line. You can also write your own simplified recipes for your child, using words and pictures he can read. When your child is helping you, introduce vocabulary words such as "beat" and "whisk" when you are doing those actions to help him later comprehend those words when he's reading them.

We use recipes a great deal in language therapy sessions, beginning with simple sequential picture recipes, such as making lemonade or popcorn or peanut butter and jelly sandwiches.

SCHEDULES AND CHARTS

In childhood, charts are often used at home and at school to list chores and jobs, and to track behavior. Children can be taught to read charts so that they know if this is their week to load the dishwasher or take out the trash, or if they are the classroom aide who will hand out scissors or collect test papers. Charts are also used with stars or smiling or frowning faces to track behavior, rewards, and punishments.

In school, schedules are used in many ways. For preschool children, the schedule might tell in what order story time, snack time, and play time occur. For school-age children, schedules might be used to write down short-term homework assignments and long-term project assignments. Schedules are used, for all ages, in summer camps. Each group has a schedule that lists what time they have lunch, arrival, and dismissal, and what times and which days they have activities such as swimming, baseball, and arts and crafts.

The skills learned in reading schedules can then be used in adulthood when using public transportation. Schedules for different lines will need to be consulted. Schedules will let you plan the time that you can take the bus or train. Signs on the street or track will indicate where you wait for the bus or train.

Some ways to help your child be able to "read" and understand the purpose of charts and schedules include:

- Use stickers on a calendar to help your child know when important events will be occurring (e.g., a picture of a birthday cake to indicate a party; a picture of an airplane to indicate the start of a family trip).
- If you use a chore or reward chart at home, glue photos of each child in the family next to his name on the chart; take photos of your child doing the chores on tasks to indicate what he needs to do.
- To help your child remember or learn routines at home, make picture activity schedules. Take pictures of him doing each step in the routine (such as brushing his teeth) and glue them in order, either from left to right or top to bottom, on a large piece of paper. Write short directions next to each photo: "Turn on water." "Brush top teeth."
- Use small picture schedules in the car that match a larger date book or wall calendar at home. This gives him experience in following shorter schedules. When he gets home, he can take the schedule with him, and use it as a visual cue for telling his older sister or dad about what he did today.

■ Make an in- and out-board as described earlier in the chapter. You can use photos of family members at first, but also print names on strips of paper (laminated and with Velcro backings) so everyone can indicate their whereabouts when entering or leaving the house.

MAPS AND SIGNS

As adults, we need to read store signs (Push, Exit), directories and maps (Dr. Jones, Suite 416), and traffic signs (Bus Stop, Caution, Railroad Crossing). We can start teaching children these skills at a young age.

To introduce your child to maps, consider making a map of your neighborhood out of a large piece of paper, felt, or fabric. Include landmarks important to your child, such as the library, mall, fast food restaurant, supermarket, school, etc. You can use photos or pictures that your child draws and you then label. Take the map outside and walk or drive the route. Then use the map during play with toy cars, bikes, and toy people. Talk about where they are going and how they are going to get there.

When you are out with your child in public, make a habit of pointing out informational signs. For example, when you are on an airplane or in a movie theater, have your child help you locate the nearest exit sign and explain that that is how you would go out in an emergency. When you need to use the restroom, show your child how you know which door to go in, and how you know whether to "push" or "pull" a door. Show him signs such as "Danger" or "Watch Your Step" that let you know you should use caution. At Loyola College, our center is currently located on two floors connected by an elevator. The children love to push #2 as they go upstairs and #1 on their way down. It has been a learning experience, because the emergency buzzer button is red and large and placed lower than the numbers for the floors. So each child has to learn not only to push the correct number, but not to push the red emergency button.

In general, help your child learn that signs are important to pay attention to and that you think he is capable of understanding them.

Conclusion

Reading is an important skill that can enhance the quality of your child's life. The ability to read opens up many more opportunities for jobs and a greater range of independent living and recreational opportunities in the community. To be independent and safe in adulthood, you need to be able to read signs and instructions. In addition, reading is an enriching hobby that many people with Down syndrome enjoy. Furthermore, reading can provide a strong channel through which your child can learn more advanced language skills such as word endings and word order in sentences.

Whether or not your child is an early reader, you should make literacy activities a regular, enjoyable part of his life. You want him to learn that reading is an important, empowering skill so that when the time comes for him to read, he will be motivated to learn. He may learn to read at a slower pace, but helping him learn to read is an effort that will have great rewards.

CHAPTER 15

Communication Needs in School and the Community

Communication does not occur only in therapy sessions or during assessments. Your child communicates in her world. Two critical parts of that world are your child's school and community. The speech and language skills and problems discussed in earlier chapters all are factors at school and in the community. In addition, these two settings each have their own speech and language demands that challenge all children to learn and adapt. Many of the skills needed in the two settings, such as conversational skills, are similar, but there are also differences between the skills needed for academic success and those needed for interpersonal or social success. This chapter provides a brief overview of the communication skills needed for success in school and the community.

Language and Speech Needs in the Preschool Years

While your child is in early intervention, the emphasis of instruction and therapy is on helping her function as well as possible in *her own world*. The SLP works closely with your family and other members of the early intervention team to help your child learn the speech and language skills *she* needs to make her needs and wants known and to make progress in the areas that you identify as being the most important for her. Once your child enters preschool, however, she will have to fit into a larger world. There will be school routines to learn, a curriculum to master, and other children she will need to get along with. You will not have direct knowledge of everything that goes on in her day, so there will be a greater need for you to be able to find out what happened during the day through a home-school communication program. This will give you a frame of reference so that you can understand what your child is trying to tell you about her day.

Clearly, school places new demands on children with Down syndrome. The skills that have been mastered through the joint efforts of your child, you, and the speech-language pathologist (SLP) have built the foundation for successful communication in school, but with each year, there will be new academic language skills for your child to master. Language is the foundation for educational success, because language is the basis for learning in school.

To continue to progress in speech and language skills in preschool and beyond, your child needs:

- a reason to communicate,
- strong communication models,
- opportunities to practice communication skills, and
- a system with which to communicate.

This makes it essential for your child to be placed in a school setting that will be responsive to her needs.

CHOOSING A SETTING THAT WILL FOSTER COMMUNICATIONS GROWTH

A Reason to Communicate. In a responsive school environment, there are reasons to communicate. The classroom setting is designed so that there are real needs to communicate and opportunities for communicating with teachers, other children, and school personnel. For example, if your child signs or says "juice," she gets a response. Perhaps that response is, "We're not ready for juice now. But we will have our snack in a little while." The response need not be positive, but it does need to be responsive and recognize what your child requested. If a child does not get responses to her communication, she will communicate less.

Scheduled events such as circle time, story time, and show and tell offer built-in reasons to communicate. When the teacher reads a story and asks questions, she is promoting communication. If your child cannot answer the questions verbally, she may be able to respond using signs, a communication picture board, PECS, or an electronic communication device (with voice). Or she can use gestures. For example, when asked, "Show me how strong the lion is," she can flex her muscles or growl.

Strong Communication Models. Children with Down syndrome often have excellent imitation skills. If they are around other children with good communication skills, they may learn skills just by playing and interacting with the other children. For this reason, it is often a good idea for children with Down syndrome to attend preschool in inclusive environments—that is, in settings that include typically developing children as students. In inclusion, there are good communication models for children with Down syndrome.

Many children attend two preschools—a special education preschool within the local school system where they can get services such as speech and physical therapy, and a private preschool where they have strong communication models as they interact with typically developing children. Available preschool opportunities vary from city to city. Your child may be welcomed by a school that has had successful experiences including young children with Down syndrome. Or you may encounter prejudice. You may be the first person in your area to "integrate" a preschool, thereby making it easier for the children and families who follow.

If your child is in a special education preschool, you want to be sure that language and communication are focused on. Most children with Down syndrome will use speech as their primary communication system, and they need to hear speech and practice speaking in their school environment. They need models, whether peers or adults, who are using speech.

Opportunities to Practice Communicating. In school, your child will ideally develop some friendships that provide communication opportunities both inside and outside the classroom. When you observe, investigate whether this is a verbal, active classroom. Are teachers and children reading, singing, making sounds? You don't want your child in a very quiet classroom; that may be helpful for attention and behavior difficulties, but it does not promote conversation.

Look for a program where teachers allow times for students to talk to each other. Observe whether the classroom is set up to encourage kids to communicate. Are they sitting in clusters or at tables facing each other? Are kids talking with each other during the day, not just on the playground? When teachers come over to groups of children, do you notice that they are encouraging children to talk with each other? Or is the conversation primarily teacher-student? Is there a lot of communication interaction, or are the children mostly listening or focusing on finishing their assigned work throughout the day?

A Communication System That Works. Most children with Down syndrome will communicate using speech as their primary communication system. If speech is not a viable system for your preschooler, the speech-language pathologist, teachers, and family need to work together to ensure that your child has an effective communication system: sign language, communication board, PECS, or computer-based communication system. And, just as importantly, staff should be eager to use that system with your child all the time. The IEP can include training for staff to learn to use the system that your child is using. AAC training is funded under IDEA.

There should always be at least one person in the classroom who can communicate with your child using her system, so if the main teacher or aide is out one day, your child just won't be ignored that day. This should be spelled out in the IEP. The IEP should also note who will be responsible for updating your child's AAC system—teaching her more signs or PECS symbols, adding new pictures to her communication board, etc.

When you observe possible programs, note how teachers use AAC with the students. If you don't see them using AAC with anyone, ask them whether they have ever used AAC with children and what kinds of systems they are acquainted with.

FINDING A GOOD MATCH FOR YOUR CHILD

When considering where your child should go to preschool or kindergarten, it is a good idea to think about whether her speech and language skills are a good match for the new situation. There are published lists of school survival skills that shed light on which specific communication skills are believed to be important for early school performance. The skill that appears on each list and seems to be considered paramount by teachers for early school success is "Follows general rules and routines." Other communication skills that have been identified as important to school success in the early years are:

- Expresses wants and needs.
- Understands and complies with specific directions given by an adult.
- Takes turns.
- Interacts verbally with peers.
- Interacts verbally with adults.
- Focuses attention on speaker/makes eye contact and listens.
- Knows and recognizes her name.

In considering whether your child has a skill such as following rules, it helps to examine what that skill includes. For instance, the ability to follow rules may involve communication skills such as understanding what is being asked, or the ability to do what is being asked, but it may also involve behavior. The ability to complete a worksheet may involve understanding the instructions and having the skills to complete the task, but may also involve having the attention skills to stay on task and the motivation and desire to complete the worksheet

Helping Your Child Learn about Rules

Being able to follow rules is important to school success, and the first step in learning to follow rules is understanding the concept of a "rule." How can you help? Most families have definite rules, and it is essential that the child understand that these are "rules." Discuss your rules frequently and be sure to label them as rules. For example, "We don't go in the street. That's the rule," or "We don't eat food in the living room. That's the rule." Whenever someone in the family breaks a rule, note that fact, by saying, for example, "Jacob, you shouldn't be eating pretzels in the living room. We don't eat food in the living room. That's the rule."

When your child is enrolled in a play group or preschool program, find out what the rules are and reinforce those school rules at home. For example, "Brian, at school, you have to stand in line to go to the bathroom. That's the school rule. At home, you can go in if no one else is using the bathroom." If there are a limited number of rules, and your child has difficulty learning them, you can make a chart. Use photographs or line drawings (such as Picture Communication Symbols©) to illustrate the rules and briefly list the rules. Place a smiley face or a star on the chart each time your child remembers to follow the rule.

The communication skills cited by preschool teachers happen to be the very skills that are usually addressed in early language intervention programs, and are usually part of the follow-up activities SLPs suggest for parents to do at home. Many of the home activities suggested in earlier chapters focus on the communication skills important for school. Your child will probably have mastered many of these general skills. But, it is most important to determine whether the *specific* level of skill required in a *specific* school is a good match for the level of your child's communication abilities. For example, if the school promotes the individual child working alone on tasks, would this be a good match for your child's skills and needs, or would a social-interactive environment better meet her needs?

In exploring the best speech and language match for your child with Down syndrome, there are many things you can do:

- *Talk with the early intervention specialists in your area.* They probably have experience with the local preschool and elementary school programs in the area. They can provide direction and advice.
- *Talk to parents who have had children in different programs in your area.* Ask them how the programs met or failed to meet their children's needs. You can also talk with parents who have had children in a specific program recently, and inquire about the director and specific teachers.
- *Observe in the school, and, if possible, in the specific classroom.* Observe inclusion preschool programs, special education service programs, and any other appropriate program for your child in your geographical area. Determine whether the programs would provide good models and language stimulation for your child. Some programs may not allow interaction, but may instead focus on completing a motor, sorting, or pre-math task, and then going on to the next task without talking. Some programs have playtime and a social interaction time; other programs do not.
- *Ask the program director if you can bring your child to visit the class.* Observe the communication interaction between the teacher and your child.
- *The SLP who knows your child may be able to observe a particular program with you to determine whether the program would be a good match with your child's communication abilities.* Then, consult with your early intervention team so that they can help you make an informed decision.

Many children with Down syndrome attend both a regular preschool and a special education program. They may attend one program for three mornings and another program for two full days, or some similar combination. The decision will depend on the resources and the people available in your area, as well as your child's needs. Some children cannot tolerate a long day or a long bus ride to school. Other children take awhile to get into a routine, and two different placements with different rules may not work for them.

SHOULD SPEECH INTELLIGIBILITY BE A FACTOR?

Sometimes parents wonder whether they should consider their child's speech intelligibility when choosing a preschool program. Will their child be at a disadvantage in an inclusive program if her speech is not easily understood outside her family? Usually, decisions about inclusion should *not* be based on whether your child's speech is understandable.

The fact is, many *typically developing* preschoolers have intelligibility problems and dysfluencies between the ages of three and five. In addition, preschool activities are often structured so that much of the action focuses on the here and now. Because of this, teachers, parents, and other children can focus on the context of the communication and can frequently figure out what your child is trying to say. At this age, your child's communication partners are more patient and more willing to try to figure out what she is saying. Remember, too, that by law in the United States, your child must be provided with an augmentative and alternative communication system (including sign language) and encouraged to use it in the classroom if her IEP team determines that she needs one. If your child has the language needed for her school setting and can follow the rules and routines, she will generally do well even if it is difficult to understand her speech.

Language and Speech Needs in Kindergarten and Beyond

The communication skills needed for successful communication in kindergarten are more complex than those needed for preschool success. Children are expected to perform academically in kindergarten, learning letters and early math skills. Other expectations include:

- Understands and follows classroom routines.
- Follows the teacher's instructions.
- Listens to a story and answers questions about it.
- Shares a story or toy in a "show and tell" time.
- Uses greetings appropriately.
- Interacts socially and communicatively with the other students in the class.

In addition, during the elementary school years, your child spends much of her day listening to the teacher talk. This differs greatly from life outside of school, where there is a more even distribution between listening and talking. Listening, remembering, and following verbal instructions are major parts of school. Auditory skills are stressed. This may be difficult for children with Down syndrome, who often learn better visually or with a multisensory approach.

UNDERSTANDING AND ADAPTING LANGUAGE DEMANDS

By kindergarten or early elementary school, many children with Down syndrome are lagging in speech and/or language skills compared to typically developing children. This means that for your child to succeed, the language demands in the classroom need to be adapted in some way. She will also probably need the assistance of a speech-language pathologist in learning general skills such as following directions and giving responses, requesting clarification and further information, and interacting on the playground. She may also need help with some specific skills, such as understanding and using the language of the curriculum—that is, the content vocabulary for the subjects your child needs to learn. In addition, the teacher will likely need assistance from the SLP in modifying the curricular materials or how she gives directions to your child.

Before you can understand how the language demands at school can best be adapted for your child, you must first understand what those demands are.

In regular classroom inclusion settings, there are six types of language demands:

1. Language of the curriculum;
2. Language of instruction in the classroom;
3. Language of the hidden curriculum;
4. Language of testing;
5. Language of classroom routines;
6. Social interactive communication.

LANGUAGE OF THE CURRICULUM

What is the language of the curriculum? This area focuses on the vocabulary and language level of the material included in the curriculum for each subject. That is, what specific language concepts does your child need to know to master the objectives for each subject during that academic year? Does she need to learn names of colors, shapes, or letters; to identify initial sounds in words; how to sound out words, etc.? We can describe the language of the curriculum for a specific grade in a specific subject by answering the following questions:

- What books are being used in class?
- What vocabulary words are used?
- What concepts are included in the subject area?

Sometimes, you will see the curricular goals for your child's grade on hand-outs at open school night or at kindergarten orientation for parents. Even if they are not readily offered, you can usually ask the classroom teacher for information

about what will be covered for each subject. Ideally, you and your child's IEP team will discuss the curricular goals and how they should be adapted for your child before the school year starts, and the changes will be implemented from the beginning of the school year. Sometimes, the school will be willing to provide information regarding the curriculum for the next year before summer vacation. That will enable you to plan trips and local visits, have experiences, and read books and see videos that relate to the curriculum for the next year throughout the summer.

You can work with the SLP and the classroom teacher to help your child learn the language concepts demanded by the curriculum. Try to be proactive; that is, plan ahead for what your child will need to learn. If you know that your child's class will be talking about community workers, plan family trips to the post office, the fire house, and the library. Take out videos and library books on the topic. If your child's class is learning about rooms in a house, furniture, and household objects, take a field trip to a furniture store, play with dollhouses and toy furniture, or look through magazines and cut out pictures of objects that would go in each room in your house. Then, put them in a photo album as a "book" about your house. There is an almost unlimited variety of "whole language" activities. Your child may need additional experience to learn, but your child can be a successful student.

For specific suggestions about adapting the language of the curriculum and other types of school language demands, you may wish to refer to my book *Classroom Language Skills for Children with Down Syndrome* (Woodbine House, 2001).

LANGUAGE OF INSTRUCTION

The language of instruction is the language used to teach and learn within the classroom. It includes factors such as:

- What channels does the teacher use to get information across? Does the teacher provide oral instructions only? Does the teacher provide pictured or diagramed instructions?
- What terms are used in teaching and in learning in that classroom? In the primary grades, terms used for instruction might include "underline," "circle," "match," and "draw a line." These terms can be taught and practiced so your child can answer the questions that are being asked in class. Otherwise, even if your child knows the answer, she may not get credit for what she knows. For instance, she may know which word begins with a /b/, but not understand the instructions to circle that picture or underline that word.
- How does the teacher give instructions? In short or long strings of instructions? Slowly or rapidly? If your child cannot follow the instructions, does she need more models and examples? Does she need help doing the task several times before she is ready to do the task independently? Visual cues and samples of questions and correct answers can be used to help your child understand what is being asked.

The ability to listen attentively and process instructions is a skill that is needed in many different classroom situations. Children with Down syndrome may have difficulty following long and complex directions, especially those presented verbally, so you and the SLP can work with your child's classroom teacher to use shorter directions and to provide visual cues whenever possible.

LANGUAGE OF THE HIDDEN CURRICULUM

The hidden curriculum is never explained to children or parents. It is not purposely hidden; it is largely unconscious and out of our awareness, and even out of the conscious awareness of the teachers themselves. The hidden curriculum is what you need to do in a specific class with a specific teacher to be a successful student. Just as students are different, teachers are different, too. They have certain expectations of students and of what they consider below average, acceptable, or above average work. This is especially true in higher grades, but it is even true in preschool or kindergarten.

Some teachers consider behavior to be most important. If a child is compliant, they consider that child to be doing well. Some teachers prefer enthusiastic students who bubble with excitement; other teachers prefer quiet children who do not talk unless they are asked to participate.

Sometimes your child can listen and clearly know what the expectations are for a task, but at other times, the requirements are not clearly stated. Teachers often make judgments and grade students on "hidden requirements." For example, is a one-word answer sufficient when asked to define "cat"? When the speech-language pathologist and the classroom teacher collaborate, they can search out the stated and hidden language requirements of each lesson, and help your child know what is expected so that she can succeed. Children with Down syndrome may have the skills to answer a classroom question adequately and appropriately as long as they understand what they need to include in the answer.

LANGUAGE OF TESTING

There may be some overlap between the language of instruction (how the child is taught) and the language of testing, especially in the lower grades. The major difference is that the language of testing is often highly *decontextualized*. That is, there are few, if any cues in the context to help you figure out what the material is about. On tests, there are generally few illustrations and no manipulatives. The questions and the words stand alone, and you need to interpret and respond to those words with no cues.

The language of testing includes classroom tests that the teacher designs and administers, as well as district-wide and state-wide standardized tests. On classroom tests, the teacher should be willing to adapt the language to your child's needs, if this adaptation is spelled out in your child's IEP. For example, suppose your child is given a picture of a cow. She is asked to underline the one picture (out of four choices) that begins with the same letter as the sample. An adaptation might be to write the word "cow" next to the picture, and underline the c. On another test item, your child may be asked to use the spelling word that fits best in a sentence. The list of spelling words could be at the top of the page as a word bank.

On standardized tests, few if any adaptations may be allowed without invalidating the test. The rule generally is that instructions cannot be modified without invalidating the results. Sometimes, adaptations are allowed as long as the adaptation does not directly affect the specific skill being tested.

LANGUAGE OF CLASSROOM ROUTINES

Classroom routines might include arriving on time; sitting in your seat ready to work; beginning a task, staying on task, and completing a task; shifting tasks as indicated by the teacher; lining up and dismissal procedures; and lunch, assembly, and fire drill procedures. The language of classroom routines includes not only the language that the teacher and school staff use to teach routines, but also the language comprehension involved in following instructions and learning routines. For example, all students need to learn how to respond to a teacher's request, when and how to ask for help, how to indicate that they don't understand the task or the instructions, when to talk and when not to talk, and how to work in cooperative learning groups.

The language of classroom routines will be most difficult for children at the beginning of the school year. Routines often involve long strings of instructions that may be difficult for children with Down syndrome to follow. But, routines are repeated frequently, so there are visual models and many opportunities for practice.

One of the goals of preschool is to teach children how to follow classroom routines. By kindergarten, children are expected to follow the routines, to line up, and transition from one classroom activity to another. Sometimes, a buddy system works well when routines are first being learned. For example, someone who sits near your child would be asked to keep an eye on her and be her partner in line. By giving her visual or verbal prompts and walking with her, the classmate would help her line up correctly. Classroom aides can also be of great assistance in helping children with Down syndrome master the routines. If routines are difficult for a child because she has difficulty making transitions, a visual schedule can be used to help her prepare for what comes next and get ready to make the change.

To understand the language of routines in a class, some questions that need to be asked may include:

- With which routines is your child successful?
- Which routines are difficult for your child?
- How is communication ability related to behavior for your child? For example, does she only have difficulty when the instructions are given verbally? When the instructions are more than five words long?
- What would enable your child to communicate her needs effectively when she is frustrated or unable to verbally communicate those needs? For example, how can she ask for help when she does not understand what to do? How can she ask for a break when the sounds and demands are overwhelming her sensory system? (Also see the information on functional behavioral assessments on pages 304-305.)

Some parents find that it is beneficial for their child to spend two years in kindergarten. In the first year, the child acclimates to the class, teacher, and other students and masters the classroom routines, while in the second year, the focus is on the academic learning.

SOCIAL INTERACTIVE COMMUNICATION

Social interactive communication includes communication with peers and all school personnel (including teachers, therapists, aides, and bus drivers) in the classroom, at lunch, recess, and on the school bus.

To help determine what assistance or adaptations your child may need for social communication, some questions that need to be answered are:

- How does your child interact with peers?
- What communication system does she use?
- What maximizes communication? (e.g., physical movement? walking next to another child?)
- What interferes with communication? (e.g., not knowing when speaking is allowed in class?)

- Does your child use social greetings or start conversations?
- Does she take turns in conversations? stay on topic?
- Where does she communicate best? with whom?
- Where does she have difficulty? with whom?
- Does your child use eye contact? appropriate gestures? appropriate facial expressions? maintain appropriate distance between people?

Social interactive communication is a vital part of your child becoming a real member of her class community. Especially at younger ages, classmates are more likely to want to be friends with your child if she can communicate with them at lunch, recess, and at the school bus stop about things they care about like TV shows, music, and the latest new toy that everyone wants. So, talk about those things at home. Children communicate about the things they enjoy.

Fortunately, social interaction skills can be a real strength for children with Down syndrome. Children with Down syndrome generally want to communicate. Often, however, they need help figuring out how to say the things that they want to say. See Chapter 10 for information on helping your child with social interactive communication.

Communication Skills in the Community

Communication is interacting with people in real life. Life in the community is life with your family, your neighbors, your friends, the kids in Cub Scouts and Brownies, the children and adults in your church or synagogue, the people in the supermarket. This is your child's world, made up of the people who surround her.

The speech skills that your child needs in her community are similar in some ways to those she needs for school. As in school, people in the community need to be able to understand your child to interact directly with her. In many situations, in both school and in the community, understandable speech or an AAC communication system that can be easily understood is extremely important. Speech and language also need to be appropriate. For example, it would be inappropriate to shout in church, or to use very formal speech in Cub Scouts or Brownies with your friends.

In some respects, it may be easier for your child to communicate in the community than at school. There are actually many acceptable varieties of speech and language for interaction in the community. For example, if you ask a child with Down syndrome if she would like to go for pizza, she can flash a smile and give you the high five sign and you will know that the answer is yes, just as if she had said the word. In the neighborhood, appropriate responses may be gestures, such as shaking the head or shrugging the shoulders, or may be single words or sentences.

Functional Behavioral Assessments

If your child is acting out in class, running out of the room, or not following routines, it is important to determine why the behavior is occurring. The system that is used to figure out the reasons for behavior difficulties at school is a *functional behavioral assessment*. A functional behavioral assessment is an evaluation of the causes and functions of a student's behavior. It looks at what the student gets or avoids as a result of the behavior. It tries to understand and document the relation between problem behavior that is occurring and events during the child's school day. It also seeks to develop a treatment plan that addresses the reasons a student misbehaves, and effectively helps her change the behavior patterns through modifying the behavior and/or the environment. The treatment plan is known as a *positive behavioral support plan or a positive behavioral intervention plan.*

Functional behavioral assessments are usually conducted by a psychologist or behavioral specialist. The classroom teacher, special educator, speech-language pathologist, and family should be consulted. They can provide input regarding behaviors that they have observed. The SLP can analyze the situations to determine whether communication difficulty appears to be related to the behavior, and can suggest appropriate alternative ways in which the child can communicate her needs. The goal, if possible, is to prevent problem behaviors in the classroom, rather than to punish the problem behaviors.

Ideally, the support team should be made up of people who know the child well, are open and willing to share ideas, and have the power to change the environment and access resources to support the child. Positive behavior support is a collaborative effort which cuts across disciplines and across settings.

When developing a functional behavior assessment in which the misbehavior is related to speech, language, and communication difficulties, it is important to clearly identify multiple examples of the inappropriate behaviors. Then, for each instance, we must determine:

- the antecedent (i.e., what precedes the behavior),
- the behavior, and
- the consequent (i.e., what follows the behavior).

Your child may have more difficulty, however, communicating with people she does not know well in the community. At school, there is a small and stable group of people who regularly interact with your child. Staff members and students are accustomed to her style of communication or AAC system. But out in the community, shopkeepers, waiters, etc. may not immediately be able to figure out what your child is saying. They may look to you for a "translation" if you are around. For the age group that we are focusing on in this book, this is customary. But, as much as possible, you will want to prepare your child for independence. You may need to translate longer messages, but it is important for your child to learn to greet people and make brief social conversation as she grows. This can be difficult if your child uses sign language or another form of AAC. Work with the SLP to make sure your child has an AAC system (if she needs one) that strangers can understand. Many times, though, the school will not allow the child to take the AAC device home. They sometimes stipulate in the IEP that the communication device is to be used at school. This does not help when your child is trying to communicate in the community.

When describing the antecedent event, consider the specific activities, events, and classroom subjects that occur right before the behavior occurs. In what settings does the behavior occur (classroom, therapies, when removed from the classroom, lunchroom, playground, school bus)? Are there certain times of the day or week when the behavior is more likely to occur (morning, before lunch, Fridays)? Who is present when the behavior occurs? Who is absent when the behavior occurs?

Clearly describe the behavior, providing any details that are observed. Then, describe the consequences. What happens immediately after the misbehavior? What result does the behavior have? Does this result serve a purpose for the child (gaining attention for the child, helping her avoid a task she does not want to do)? The function of that behavior must be understood so that a replacement behavior that will accomplish that same purpose for the child can be taught. For example, if the behavior results in gaining the teacher's attention, teach the child to raise her hand or to hold up an "I need help!" sign to get attention. If the behavior helps her avoid or escape a task, teach her ways to request a break from her work or to ask for help rather than running out of the classroom into the hall.

Sometimes the behavior does not appear to be under the child's control. Dr. Daniel Crimmins believes that behaviors such as self-injury, socially stigmatizing rituals, aggression, tantrums, and destruction of property can still serve a purpose for the child, even though they are not under her conscious control. Crimmins suggests translating the behavior into an "I" message. For example, screaming may mean "I'm confused by what I hear"; running away may mean "I feel scared when my world is not predictable and I am not able to tell you what I need"; repetitive behaviors and self-stimulation may mean "I need to do this over and over to block out a confusing world" (Crimmins, 1996).

Different responses and educational interventions are needed depending on the purpose the behavior is serving for your child. Everyone on your child's team needs to work together to determine the function of the behavior.

BUILDING YOUR CHILD'S VOCABULARY

Once your child is past the early intervention stage, the school speech-language therapy will focus on vocabulary needed at school. Parents can work with the SLP to suggest vocabulary that your child needs in daily life, but there may not be time at school to work on that. For the most part, it will be basically up to you to teach your child the vocabulary she needs in the community.

How can you work on vocabulary in the community? Many times, you can predict vocabulary needs based on what is going on in your child's life. Are you going to visit grandparents out of state? Is there a major family event such as Thanksgiving dinner or a wedding? Is there a religious event or a life cycle event? If your child is going on a family trip to Disney World, the names of the Disney characters will be a natural part of the experience. If you are taking an airplane, the vocabulary of the airport, luggage, terminal, gate, and airplane will be a part of the experience. You can talk about the event and even rehearse what will happen. Read books with your child before or after the event that relate to the experience. Take photos and discuss them after the event. Make a personalized book to help retell the story of the event. If your child uses signs or an AAC device, make sure you learn the signs for new things you will encounter or bring a sign language dictionary along on excursions so you can talk about new experiences with your child while you're there.

We know that vocabulary acquisition is driven by your child's interests. If your child likes to swim, the vocabulary of the sport will interest her. Baking, cooking, and crafts projects all have their own vocabularies. Consult Chapter 7 for home activities for vocabulary building.

Research tells us that children with Down syndrome continue to add words to their vocabularies well into adulthood and that children with Down syndrome have larger functional vocabularies than children with other developmental disabilities, matched for mental age level. For example, a child with Down syndrome with a mental age of seven usually has a bigger vocabulary than a child with autism or pervasive developmental disability with the mental age of seven. Vocabulary, then, can continue to increase if it is fueled by interests and experiences. Experiences in the community with family and friends provide an excellent basis for learning many new vocabulary words.

ROUTINE COMMUNICATION

In daily life, much communication in the community is repetitive and routine, such as greetings, good-byes, and questions directed toward children. These can be practiced as routines so that your child will be familiar with these situations. If your child learns the "script" for greeting people, she can use that script over and over again.

Greetings are social rituals and aren't expected to be different or unique each time. "Hi," "hello," and "How're you doing" are all fine greetings. "See you later," "great to see you," and "bye-bye" are all fine departures. They don't need to vary, and your child will have the chance to practice them repeatedly so that these social routines will feel very comfortable. In general, people greet children, ask how they are, how old they are, where they go to school, what grade they are in, and perhaps what subjects they like best. These questions are meant to be answered briefly and routinely. When someone asks, "How are you," they are not asking for a medical report, they are merely greeting you and touching base. So, if your child answers these general questions well, she will certainly hold up her end of the social greeting ritual.

Conversational skills are more complex and thus are more challenging for children with Down syndrome. These are the skills that children need and use regularly in daily life. The grammatical skills needed for longer phrases and sentences are discussed in Chapter 7 and pragmatics and conversational skills are explored in Chapter 10. The goal is effective communication, and in the community, all communication systems (such as speech, gestures, facial expressions) can contribute to having your message understood.

Conclusion

Communication can either be your child's door to opportunity and experiences or it can be a barrier. Understanding the different demands that your child's school and community place upon her communication skills can help you focus your work with your child, her SLP, and her teacher.

Recently, there have been dramatic changes in the participation of children with Down syndrome in school and in the community. There are now real opportunities for children to learn and play in the real world. And what has fueled this change has been parent advocacy and the ever-increasing abilities of people with Down syndrome, including their communication abilities. As more is learned about how to tap their potential (and just what the full extent of that potential is), people with Down syndrome will become even more integrated into their schools and communities. How you and your child's teachers and SLP work with your child will go far to opening the doors to inclusion throughout life for your child.

Concluding Thoughts

We all use communication to navigate our way through each day. Without a communication system—be it speech, sign language, communication board, or electronic communication device, we are locked inside ourselves. Communication enables us to interact, to reach out, and to send our own personal message to people in our world.

Children with Down syndrome, like all children, have a wide range of communication abilities. Communication skills are very difficult for some children, and relatively easy for others. Some children progress steadily in communication and language development but experience more difficulty when they begin to speak. Communication, language, and speech abilities will often progress at different paces, but we want to help children continue to move forward in all three areas. In my experience, communication skills, especially speaking skills, are one of the most difficult areas of learning for children with Down syndrome—but also one of the most important areas. That is why I have written books and articles on the subject and devoted my professional life to helping children with Down syndrome learn to communicate better.

One of the best gifts parents can give their child with Down syndrome is to assume that he will need extra help in mastering communication skills and become actively involved in his communication learning. Speech and language cannot be learned in a one-hour session once a week. Communication is best learned in real-life situations. SLPs can help you learn how to best teach language. They can model techniques and provide information, but you, as parents, are the ones who make the change happen, on a daily basis. You are the ones who can seize the appropriate moment to teach language skills. You can provide the practice when and where it best fits, working on oral facial muscles while feeding, body part names while bathing, verbs and prepositions while moving around in the playground. Parents need information, and that's what this book can provide.

Your child may learn language and speech skills slowly, but he will learn, and each step forward will be a momentous achievement. Language and speech development in typically developing children occurs so rapidly that often we don't even notice the small steps. In children with Down syndrome, we have the time to notice the small steps. We can be mindful of the progress, and savor each advance. With children with Down syndrome, speech and language development takes time, effort, practice, and patience. We need to enjoy the journey and celebrate each milestone.

The previous fifteen chapters provide a detailed plan for helping your child learn to communicate from birth on. Hopefully, you will have the time to read the chapters that are relevant to your child's developmental stage and make use of the suggestions that are right for him at present. But if you are pressed for time, or need an "executive summary" of the highlights, here are the eleven most important things to remember in helping your child learn to communicate:

1. Try to find a local speech-language pathologist who is experienced in working with young children and their families on developing language. Read books, attend workshops, and learn as much as you can about early communication skills.

2. Communicate regularly with the SLP and ask for a home activity program. The SLP can teach you about language, but real life provides the best opportunities for communication development and practice.

3. Provide many experiences for your child. He needs something to communicate about. Use these real-world experiences to boost communication skills, such as going on errands for learning vocabulary, and making recipes and crafts for practicing sequencing.

4. Provide many models, frequent opportunities for practice, and a lot of feedback. If you say, "Where's the doggy?" and your child points to the dog, comment, "Doggy, yes, that's the doggy."

5. Don't focus on therapy—focus on communicating. Don't set aside a therapy time. Incorporate activities where they fit into daily life.

6. Help your child compensate for sensory, motor, or cognitive difficulties that make it harder for him to learn language from his environment. Try to structure the environment so that the language stands out—so that it is more visible to your child. Get your child's attention with interesting sights and sounds before you start talking to him; turn off the TV so he can focus on speech sounds. Language needs to pop out of the background noise so that your child can notice the language, see it, hear it, and learn it.

7. Your child needs a communication system that effectively meets his needs at each stage of development. The system may be signs, PECS, pictures on a communication board, an electronic system, or speech, as appropriate to your child's needs and abilities. His needs and skills will change over time. But, he must be able to communicate at every age.

8. Find your child's passion. If he is interested in toy cars, bugs, dolls, fuzzy things, follow his interest. Your child learns the most when you encourage him to learn about things that interest him.

9. Support any areas of difficulty. You may need to work on sensory difficulties, practice exercises for the lips and tongue, and check

hearing on a regular basis. Speech, language, and communication are broad areas with many sub-skills and supporting skills needed to maximize your child's communication potential.

10. Remember that it may take a long time to see results, but the goal is worth the effort. Celebrate each success along the way.

11. Strive to surround your child with people who have high expectations, who believe that he has something important to communicate. The community that surrounds your child is crucial to fostering communication growth.

This book has provided many ideas for helping your child master communication skills. We have talked about early sensory stimulation, early communication, precursors to language, prerequisites for speech. We have talked about transitional communication systems that enable your child to continue to learn language and "speak" to you before he is ready to actually use speech. We have talked about semantics, syntax, articulation, phonology, and pragmatics. We have talked about improving vocabulary, speech intelligibility, and conversational skills. Every journey begins with a single step, and it is time for you to get started walking down the path of communication development. I hope you will consider this book my way of walking beside you so you do not ever have to walk that path alone.

Appendices

Comprehensive Communication Evaluation Guidelines for Children with Down Syndrome

Evaluation is the beginning of the treatment cycle. This is a guide to evaluations typically needed at each stage of speech, language, and communication development for children with Down syndrome. A comprehensive individualized language and speech treatment plan is developed based on the evaluation results.

NEONATAL: BIRTH-1 MONTH

Laying the framework for communication in the neonatal period involves ensuring that the baby has a hearing screening and a feeding evaluation. The audiologist and otolaryngologist will be involved in the hearing screening. A feeding evaluation may be done by a feeding team, or by a speech-language pathologist who has completed advanced training in feeding.

1. Hearing screening (from Medical Guidelines)
   - Auditory Brain Stem Response (ABR) or
   - Evoked Otoacoustic Emissions Testing
2. Feeding/Oral Motor evaluation
   - feeding evaluation in first month if difficulty is noted
   - coordination of suck-swallow-breathing synchrony

INFANCY: 1-12 MONTHS

1. Hearing evaluation (from Medical Guidelines)
   - auditory Brainstem Response Testing
   - Evoked Otoacoustic Emissions Testing
   - hearing testing every 6 months
2. Feeding/Oral Motor evaluation
   - feeding evaluation
   - muscle strength, range of motion, coordination
3. Pre-language evaluation
   - pragmatics, language, and cognitive precursors
   - Total Communication and/or augmentative communication system (evaluate at 8-12 months of age)

CHILDHOOD: 1-3 YEARS

The following evaluations should occur once yearly. If the child is in ongoing treatment, annual evaluation can be part of treatment sessions:

1. Oral motor and oral sensory evaluation
   - to develop pre-speech treatment plan: consider muscle strength, range of motion, oral sensory sensitivities, tactile defensiveness
2. Feeding evaluation
   - food texture progression
3. Language evaluation
   - evaluate progress on pragmatics, language, and cognitive precursors
   - evaluate use of Total Communication or other AAC system as transition to speech

- develop treatment plan to stimulate early vocabulary
- involve family in treatment plan

4. Development of IFSP to include speech, language, oral motor, and feeding therapies as appropriate
5. Hearing evaluation (every 6 months) (from Medical Guidelines)

CHILDHOOD: 3-5 YEARS

The following evaluations should occur once yearly unless the child is in ongoing treatment:

1. Oral motor evaluation
    - speech evaluation
    - oral motor skills evaluation
    - childhood verbal apraxia evaluation
2. Language evaluation
    - receptive and expressive language
    - preschool language concepts
    - consider beginning reading training
3. Hearing evaluation (at least once yearly) (from Medical Guidelines)
4. Development of IEP to include speech, language, oral motor, and apraxia treatment as appropriate, plus evaluation of need for augmentative communication.

CHILDHOOD: 5-12 YEARS

The following evaluations should occur once yearly unless the child is in ongoing treatment:

1. Speech evaluation
    - oral motor
    - intelligibility
    - childhood verbal apraxia
    - dysarthria (oral motor function)
    - tongue thrust
2. Language evaluation
    - school language
    - narrative language
    - conversational language
    - social interactive language
    - modality specific language abilities (e.g., auditory memory, comprehension)
    - reading
    - writing/word processing language
    - impact of communication difficulties on behavior
3. Hearing evaluation (at least once yearly) (from Medical Guidelines)
    - evaluate impact of OME and hearing loss on language
    - consider supports and modifications in the IEP (e.g., hearing aids, preferential classroom seating)
4. Development of IEP to include speech, language, and oral motor therapies as appropriate, plus evaluate need for augmentative communication. Consider communication difficulties when conducting a functional behavior assessment and when writing a positive behavior support plan.

Speech & Language Referral Guidelines for Pediatricians

These guidelines summarize important issues in a child's medical and developmental history, as well as findings in physical examinations that may affect speech and language development at different ages. They note consults that may be needed and recommendations for referrals to be shared with the family.

NEONATAL: BIRTH-1 MONTH

1. History
   - Was hearing tested using Auditory Brain Stem Response (ABR) or Evoked Otoacoustic Emissions Testing?
   - Any difficulties with feeding?
2. Exam
   - Weakness in lips?
   - Difficulty with coordination of suck-swallow-breathing synchrony?
3. Consults
   - ENT
   - audiology
   - hearing evaluation
   - feeding evaluation
4. Recommendations
   - Feeding therapy as needed
   - Information for family about early pre-speech vocalizations, and pre-language skills
   - Information on how to encourage sound making and language development at home
   - Refer to local parent support group

INFANCY: 1-12 MONTHS

1. History
   - Parental concerns regarding hearing, vision, tactile skills, and feeding.
   - Parental report of sound making and responses to sound and words. Does the child respond to his name, environmental sounds? Does he appear to understand relationship between a word and its referent object? Will he look at the ball when you say "ball"?
2. Exam
   - Informal evaluation of pre-language skills such as reciprocal gaze, referential gaze, visual exploration, auditory attending, auditory localization, tactile sensitivities, tactile exploration including mouthing, cognitive skills such as object permanence, cause and effect, and means-end.
   - Informal evaluation of pragmatics skills such as turn-taking, appropriate facial expressions, use of gestures and body language, and social interaction.

- Informal evaluation of respiration, voice, and strength and range of motion of oral muscles, and oral structures for speech.

3. Consults
   - Hearing testing every 6 months.
   - Speech-language pathology evaluation at 6-12 months to:
   - evaluate oral motor skills
   - evaluate pragmatics, language, and cognitive precursors for speech and language
   - design Total Communication program

4. Recommendations
   - Refer for early intervention program
   - Provide resources and information on early speech and language developmental milestones
   - Ongoing family involvement in speech-language pathology program
   - Begin to facilitate Total Communication beginning at 8-12 months as appropriate

CHILDHOOD: 1-3 YEARS

1. History
   - According to parental report, is the child using speech? How many single words? Is the child using multi-word combinations? What length phrases?
   - Does the child appear to have difficulty hearing? Understanding language? Following simple directions?
   - If the child is not using speech, how is he communicating? Gestures? Grunts? Does he have a usable communication system? Is he frustrated?

2. Exam
   - Interact with the child. Is the child socializing using gestures, facial expressions, and smiles?
   - Check respiration, voice, oral-motor strength, and range of motion.
   - On observation, is the child using speech? How many single words? Is the child using multi-word combinations? What length phrases? Does the child appear to have difficulty hearing? Understanding language? Following simple directions? If he is not using speech, how is he communicating? Does he have a usable communication system? Does he appear frustrated? (Children with Down syndrome may begin to use speech to communicate between ages 2 and 4 years, but there is a wide range. They will usually understand far more than they can verbalize. Child's intent to communicate and production of a variety of sounds should be noted.)

3. Consults (The following evaluations should occur once yearly unless the child is in ongoing treatment. If the child is in treatment, data on progress can be ongoing.)
   - Hearing evaluation (every 6 months)

- Oral motor and oral sensory evaluation (pre-speech characteristics, posture, respiratory support for speech, oral sensory issues, tactile defensiveness, muscle strength and coordination, speech sound development)
- Feeding evaluation (food texture progression)
- Pre-language evaluation
    - o progress on pragmatics, language, and cognitive precursors
    - o effectiveness of Total Communication
    - o develop treatment plan with family participation in treatment
- Reading evaluation by age 3 years

4. Recommendations

- Development of Individualized Family Service Plan (IFSP) to include speech, language, oral motor, and feeding therapies, as appropriate
- By 1 year, use of Total Communication program, which may include sign language, communication board, PECS (Picture Exchange Communication System), and/or synthesized speech (voice output) communication device to provide communication system until child starts to use speech
- Speech-language pathology treatment including oral-motor therapy, speech therapy, and language therapy
- By age 3, start to teach reading to support development of language

CHILDHOOD: 3-5 YEARS

1. History

- According to parental report, what is the size of the child's vocabulary? How is the child communicating? With speech, signs, other communication system, or a combination of systems? Is he using multi-word combinations? Ask for an example of how the child would ask for a cookie, or would ask to go out to play. Can he effectively make his needs known?
- Does the child appear to have difficulty hearing? Understanding language? Following directions? Ask for an example of an instruction that he can follow at home. Is he frustrated?
- Is he in pre-school? How does he communicate in preschool?

2. Exam

- Interact with the child. Is he socializing using gestures, facial expressions, and smiles? Is he speaking? Are respiration, voice, oral motor strength, and range of motion adequate to support speech? What does he say to you? To family member present? If he is not using speech, how is he communicating? Is the child using multi-word combinations? What length phrases?
- Does the child appear to have difficulty hearing? Understanding language? Following directions? Can he respond to yes/no or "wh-" questions? ("What is your name? How old are you?")

3. Consults (The following evaluations should occur once yearly unless the child is in ongoing treatment. If the child is in treatment, data on progress can be ongoing.)
  - Hearing evaluation (at least once yearly)
  - Oral motor evaluation
    o speech evaluation
    o muscle strength and coordination
    o difficulties in ease and clarity of speech production
  - Language evaluation
    o receptive and expressive language
    o preschool language concepts
    o referral to an augmentative communication team when present communication system is not meeting the child's needs
    o reading training

4. Recommendations:
  - Development of Individualized Education Program (IEP) to include speech, language, and oral motor therapies as appropriate
  - Provide resources for information on speech and language development, preschool concept development (e.g., colors, shapes), and literacy development
  - Evaluate need for augmentative communication. Services outside of school should be considered if school therapy is not provided, or is not meeting all communication needs

CHILDHOOD: 5-12 YEARS

1. History
  - Discuss parental concerns regarding speech, language, and hearing. Has there been steady progress? Sudden regressions? How is the child communicating? At home? At school with teachers and peers? Are there communication needs that are not being met? How would the parent rate comprehension skills? Expressive language skills? Speech sounds and articulation? Can child's speech be understood by family? By teachers, peers, and strangers?

2. Exam
  - Talk with the child; ask about a favorite television program or video. Note whether child is able to answer questions and have more complex and longer conversations. Does he use greetings and closings? Observe whether speech is intelligible. Note if he can identify objects, retell a story, and read a story or a sign. By the end of this period, some children are using advanced language skills, and can talk about academic subject material, as well as family trips, while others are using single words or short phrases.

3. Consults (The following evaluations should occur once yearly unless the child is in ongoing treatment. If the child is in treatment, data on progress can be ongoing.)

- Hearing evaluation (at least once yearly)
  - ▫ Evaluate impact of OME and hearing loss on language development and performance
  - ▫ Consider supports and modifications in the IEP (e.g., hearing aids, preferential seating)
- Speech evaluation: determine skills and the need for therapy in each of the following areas:
  - ▫ intelligibility
  - ▫ motor planning abilities (childhood verbal apraxia)
  - ▫ oral motor abilities (dysarthria)
  - ▫ tongue thrust/deviate swallow
- Language evaluation
  - ▫ school language
  - ▫ narrative language/discourse skills (telling a story, telling about an event)
  - ▫ conversational language
  - ▫ social interactive language
  - ▫ modality specific language abilities (e.g., auditory memory, comprehension, expressive skills)
  - ▫ reading/literacy skills
  - ▫ writing/word processing language
  - ▫ impact of communication difficulties on behavior

4. Recommendations
   - Development of IEP to include speech, language, and oral motor therapies as appropriate
   - Major emphasis on speech and language skills needed for success in school and in community activities
   - Evaluate need for augmentative communication (AAC)
   - Services outside of school should be considered as needed

Comprehensive Speech & Language Treatment Guidelines for Children with Down Syndrome from Birth to Six Years

I. Birth—One Word Period
- A. Sensory Stimulation
  - 1. Auditory
  - 2. Visual
  - 3. Tactile
- B. Hearing/Assistive Listening
- C. Sensory Integration
- D. Feeding Therapy
- E. Oral Motor Skills
- F. Pragmatics Skills
- G. Pre-Language Skills
- H. Transitional Communication System Evaluation
  - 1. Total Communication
  - 2. Communication Boards
  - 3. Picture Exchange Communication System
  - 4. High Tech Communication Systems

II. One Word—Multiword Utterances
- A. Sensory Integration
- B. Attending and Play Skills
- C. Pragmatics Skills
- D. Semantic/Vocabulary Skills
- E. Increasing Mean Length of Utterance/Pacing Board
- F. Oral Motor Skills
- G. Computer Support
- H. Early/Pre-Literacy Skills

III. Preschool—Kindergarten
- A. Receptive Language Skills
  - 1. Comprehension
  - 2. Semantics/Concept Development
- B. Expressive Language Skills
  - 1. Semantics
  - 2. Morphosyntax
  - 3. Mean Length of Utterance
- C. Pragmatics Skills
  - 1. Social Interactive Skills
  - 2. Communication Activities of Daily Living
  - 3. Requests
- D. Classroom Language Skills
- E. Speech Skills
  - 1. Articulation
  - 2. Intelligibility
  - 3. Oral Motor Skills
  - 4. Motor Planning Skills
- F. Literacy Skills

EARLY INTERVENTION SPEECH & LANGUAGE TREATMENT PROGRAM PLANNING FORM

Name: _____ Date of Birth: _____

Goal: Master prerequisite skills for speech and language including sensory, oral motor, pragmatics, and cognitive skills.

I. Pragmatics/Language Level
- A. Communicative intent ❑
- C. Engaging ❑
- E. Protesting ❑
- B. Turn-taking ❑
- D. Requesting ❑
- F. Social communication ❑

II. Sensory Input/Integration Skills
- A. Visual skills ❑
- C. Tactile skills ❑
- E. Motor skills ❑
- B. Auditory skills ❑
- D. Imitation skills ❑

III. Cognitive/Linguistic Skills
- A. Cognitive skills ❑
- B. Referential knowledge ❑

IV. Pre-Speech Skills
- A. Respiration ❑
- C. Tactile skills ❑
- E. Oral motor skills ❑
- G. Sound production skills ❑
- B. Feeding skills ❑
- D. Imitation skills ❑
- F. Motor planning skills ❑

V. Transitional System/Assistive Technology Needs
- A. Sign language
- C. PECS ❑
- E. Assistive listening devices ❑
- B. Communication board
- D. High tech speech output device ❑
- F. Other ❑ _____

VI. Family Supports Needed _____

_____

VII. Referrals Needed
- Ophthalmologist ❑
- Feeding Specialist ❑
- Sensory Integration Spec. ❑
- Special Educator ❑
- Pediatrician ❑
- Physical Therapist ❑
- Otolaryngologist (ENT) ❑
- Audiologist ❑
- Psychologist ❑
- Occupational Therapist ❑
- Neurologist ❑
- Other ❑ _____

SPEECH & LANGUAGE TREATMENT PROGRAM PLANNING FORM: FIRST WORD TO AGE 6

Name: _____   Date of Birth: _____

A comprehensive speech and language treatment plan should target the following areas, as needed. Treatment plans are individualized to meet the strengths, learning styles, challenges, and needs of the child.

One Word - Multiword Utterances
   Sensory Integration ❑
   Attending and Play Skills ❑
   Pragmatics Skills ❑
   Semantic/Vocabulary Skills ❑
   Increasing Mean Length of Utterance/Pacing Board ❑
   Oral Motor Skills ❑
   Computer Support ❑
   Early/Pre-Literacy Skills ❑

Preschool - Kindergarten
   Receptive Language Skills
      Comprehension ❑
      Semantics/Concept Development ❑
   Expressive Language Skills
      Semantics ❑
      Morphosyntax ❑
      Mean Length of Utterance ❑
   Pragmatics Skills
      Social Interactive Skills ❑
      Communication Activities of Daily Living ❑
      Requests ❑
      Classroom Language Skills ❑
   Speech Skills
      Articulation ❑
      Intelligibility ❑
      Oral Motor Skills ❑
      Motor Planning Skills ❑
      Literacy Skills ❑

SPEECH INTELLIGIBILITY EVALUATION SUMMARY FORM FOR CHILDREN WITH DOWN SYNDROME

Name: _____   Date of Birth: _____

1. Anatomical/structural factors (from oral peripheral examination)

2. Physiological/functional factors (from oral peripheral examination)

3. Oral Motor component (describe nature of impairment)

4. Childhood verbal apraxia (list characteristics)

5. Swallowing pattern/Feeding pattern (describe)

6. Hearing test results (from ENT and audiology reports)

7. Articulation
      number of sounds in error _____
      list sounds in error:

8. Phonological Processes (list processes used)

9. Voice
      Volume
      Too soft ❑   Too loud ❑   Inconsistent ❑   Inappropriate ❑

      Pitch

      Voice Quality (describe)

10. Resonance (Oral/Nasal balance)
      Hyponasal ❑   Hypernasal ❑   Other ❑ _____

11. Rate

        Too slow ❏   Too fast ❏   Combination ❏   Uncontrolled ❏

12. Fluency Pattern (describe)

13. Prosody (describe)

14. Pragmatics factors

        topic introduction ❏   topic maintenance ❏   uses changing topic markers ❏

        social language skills ❏   conversational skills ❏   narrative discourse skills ❏

        other pragmatics factors ❏ _____

15. Nonverbal factors

        eye contact: appropriate ❏   looks away ❏ other ❏ _____

        gestures: appropriate ❏   inappropriate ❏

        facial expressions: match message - appropriate ❏   do not match message - inappropriate ❏

        proxemics: too close ❏   too far ❏   other ❏ _____

16. Language message factors (describe)

        Greetings

        Routine/automatic verbalizations

        Longer verbalizations

        Complex messages

17. External/environmental factors (see examples provided in Chapter 9)

        visual

        auditory

        listener variables

18. Other factors

SPEECH INTELLIGIBILITY TREATMENT PROGRAM PLAN FOR CHILDREN WITH DOWN SYNDROME

Name: _____   Date of Birth: _____

A comprehensive treatment plan for an individual with Down syndrome may include any of the following. IEP goals can be written for each of these areas, as needed.

Exercise Programs
Oral motor muscle strengthening ❏   Intervention for feeding problems ❏
Intervention for tongue thrust/swallowing problems ❏

Muscle Programming and Coordination Level
Intervention for childhood verbal apraxia ❏   Intervention for oral apraxia ❏

Speech Production Level
Treatment for articulation ❏   Treatment for phonological processes ❏
Treatment for volume and loudness ❏   Voice therapy ❏
Treatment for resonance (oral/nasal balance) ❏   Rate control ❏
Treatment for prosody ❏   Fluency therapy ❏

Pragmatics/Language Level
Treatment for nonverbal factors ❏   Language skills that affect intelligibility ❏
Conversational skills ❏   Narrative discourse skills ❏

Assistive Technology Needs
Augmentative communication for classroom use ❏   Augmentative communication for general use ❏
Assistive listening devices ❏

Supports and Modifications Needed
Staff training in using/programming assistive technology ❏
Staff training in using visual tactile cues for apraxia ❏

Other staff training: _____

Modifications of classroom speech demands needed (list): _____

_____

Referrals Needed
Otolaryngologist (ENT) ❏   Audiologist ❏
Neurologist ❏   Psychologist ❏
Feeding specialist ❏   Other ❏ _____

Resource Guide

Canadian Down Syndrome Society
811 14ᵗʰ St. NW
Calgary, AL T2N 2A4
Canada
800-883-5608; 403-270-8500
www.cdss.ca

Disability Solutions Website
www.disabilitysolutions.org
    Disability Solutions is a free, bimonthly newsletter that often examines issues related to communication or education of people with Down syndrome. Issues can be downloaded from the website.

Down Syndrome Education Information Network
www.downsed.org
Website of the Down Syndrome Educational Trust in Portsmouth, UK.
    Extensive information on cognitive development, memory, reading, and communication is available on this website. Current and past research findings of Sue Buckley and colleagues and journal articles from *Down Syndrome Research and Practice* are available.

Down Syndrome: Health Issues
www.ds-health.com
    Award-winning website related to medical and developmental issues in children with Down syndrome developed by Dr. Len Leshin. Dr. Kumin's chapter on comprehensive speech and language intervention is on this website.

Down Syndrome Quarterly
www.denison.edu/dsq
    The website for the journal posts position papers, research articles, and the DS health guidelines.

Down Syndrome Research Foundation
1409 Sperling Ave.
Burnaby, BC V5B 4J8
Canada
604-444-3773
888-464-DSRF (in Canada)

Healthcare Guidelines for Individuals with Down Syndrome
www.denison.edu/dsq/health99/shtml and www.ds-health.com
Guidelines were developed by physicians from the Down Syndrome Medical Interest Group (DSMIG) and are updated periodically. The guidelines address hearing testing, as well as health and medical issues. Excellent guidelines to share with your pediatrician or family doctor.

National Association for Down Syndrome (NADS)
www.nads.org
Website has current information on a variety of issues important to individuals with Down syndrome.

National Down Syndrome Congress (NDSC)
1370 Center Drive
Suite 102
Atlanta, GA 30324
800-232-NDSC (6372)
www.ndsccenter.org
The NDSC provides information on all issues affecting children with Down syndrome. It also provides information and referral to local parent groups and comprehensive Down syndrome centers.

National Down Syndrome Society (NDSS)
666 Broadway
New York, NY 10012
800-221-4602
www.ndss.org
The NDSS provides information and publications relating to all areas of Down syndrome. Publications are available on medical and educational issues, research, and the use of computers. There is information on the website on speech and language developed by Dr. Kumin.

DEVELOPMENTAL DISABILITIES

The Arc
1010 Wayne Avenue, Suite 650
Silver Spring, MD 20910
301-565-3842
www.thearc.org
National advocacy organization of and for people with mental retardation and related developmental disabilities and their families.

NICHCY
P.O. Box 1492
Washington, DC 20013-1492
800-695-0285; 202-884-8441 (fax)
www.nichcy.org
The National Information Center for Children and Youth with Disabilities (NICHCY) has many publications on special education issues and other disability issues available. They can be downloaded free from the website or ordered for a nominal fee by phone or mail. Website information and some publications available in Spanish.

AUTISM

Autism Society of America
7910 Woodmont Avenue, Suite 300
Bethesda, MD 20814-3067
800-3AUTISM
www.autism-society.org
Information is available from this national organization on conferences, local chapters, research findings.

SENSORY INTEGRATION

Sensory Integration International
http://home.earthlink.net/~sensoryint/
Organization founded to advance the pioneering work of Jean Ayres on sensory integration. Provides information, publications, testing, and training for parents and professionals.

Sensory Integration Resource Center
www.sinetwork.org
Informative website with many links to organizations and companies concerned with sensory integration. Provides resources for families, teachers and therapists

SPEECH AND LANGUAGE

Advance for Speech-Language Pathologists & Audiologists
www.advanceforspanda.com
Homepage for ADVANCE magazine allows you to search for articles online including an article on early intervention for children with Down syndrome by Dr. Kumin, oral-motor articles, and articles on children and adults with Down syndrome.

American Speech-Language-Hearing Association
10801 Rockville Pike
Rockville, MD 20852-3279
800-638-8255
Web site: www.asha.org
The ASHA is the national professional association for speech-language pathologists and audiologists. It has a toll-free information line that can provide information and resources, especially related to how to find services in your area.

Apraxia- Kids
www.apraxia-kids.org
A comprehensive website on Childhood Verbal Apraxia which includes expert articles, research findings, a discussion list, and other pertinent information. It does not have information specifically on apraxia in children with Down syndrome.

Center for Speech, Language and Learning
www.centersforspeech.com
This website has a list of frequently asked questions and has a kids only link that has practice sheets and games for language practice.

Childhood Apraxia of Speech Association of North America (CASANA)
www.apraxia.org
Family support association for children with apraxia.

Hanen Centre
1075 Bay St., Ste. 515
Toronto, Ontario
Canada M5S 2B1
416-921-1073
www.hanen.org
Source for information and materials on early language intervention. Hanen provides training for parents and professionals working with children who have speech and language delays.

STATE SPEECH AND HEARING ASSOCIATIONS

Most states have associations for speech and language professionals. If you need information about how and where to find appropriate services in your state, you may contact your state professional association. State associations may provide resources, referrals, information, pamphlets, and possibly speakers for your parents' group. The address and phone number of your state speech and hearing association is usually available from directory assistance or by calling the American Speech-Language-Hearing Association. For example, ask for the "New Jersey Speech-Language-Hearing Association."

SPECIAL EDUCATION/ DISABILITIES

ERIC Clearinghouse on Disabilities and Gifted Education (ERIC EC)
Council for Exceptional Children
1110 N. Glebe Rd.
Arlington, VA 22201-5704
800-328-0272
ericec@cec.sped.org
http://ericec.org

Offers many fact sheets and digests on the education of children with disabilities. Many publications available in Spanish. Documents may be downloaded free of charge from the website. If you do not have Internet access, you may write or call for documents in print form. One copy of each document is available free of charge; additional copies of most publications cost $1.00 each. Website provides access to the ERIC database of publications on disabilities.

Family Village
www.familyvillage.wisc.edu

Informational website designed for families of people with mental retardation and other disabilities. Designed and updated by the Waisman center at the University of Wisconsin.

Office of Special Education Programs Website
www.ed.gov/offices/OSERS/OSEP

Fact sheets and other online publications about U.S. special education regulations and laws are available here.

SERI Website
http://seriweb.com

SERI (Special Education Resources on the Internet) provides many links to sites with information on special education laws, inclusion, and the education of children with specific disabilities.

Wrightslaw Website
www.wrightslaw.com

Website offers a great deal of information for parents interested in being their child's educational advocate. Website includes many informative articles on IEPs, inclusion, etc., and the option to subscribe to a free online newsletter.

TOYS/PLAY (INCLUDING ORAL MOTOR EQUIPMENT)

Crestwood Company
6625 N. Sidney Place, Dept. 21F
Milwaukee, WI 53209
414-352-5678
www.communicationaids.com

An excellent source for voice-activated and switch-activated toys to teach cause and effect.

Dragonfly Toys
www.dragonflytoys.com
800-308-2208

Toys for children with sensory and motor disabilities. Website contains articles, suggestions, and a product catalog.

National Lekotek Center
2100 Ridge Ave.
Evanston, IL 60201
847-328-0001
800-366-PLAY (Toy Resource Helpline)
www.lekotek.org

A national center for information about play and learning in children with special needs. This is a national network with many local affiliates. Services include workshops, materials, and a lending library of toys. The Lekotek Center has free publications on a variety of aspects of play and toys for children with disabilities, including an information packet on adapting toys.

New Visions
www.new-vis.com
Website that focuses on feeding, sensory, and oral motor development. Website has articles by Suzanne Evans-Morris. It also is the company through which you can purchase Mealtimes feeding, oral-sensory and oral motor toys, materials, and equipment.

PDP Products
14524 61ˢᵗ Street Ct. N.
Stillwater, MN 55082
651-439-8865
www.pdppro.com
Source of MORE whistles.

Sara Rosenfeld-Johnson's Website
www.oromotorsp.com
Informational articles regarding oral motor intervention. Whistles, horns, straws, bite blocks, books, and other materials for working on oral motor skills.

Sammons Preston Rolyan
4 Sammons Ct.
Bolingbrook, IL 60440
800-323-5547
http://ecom1/sammonspreston.com
Adaptive toys and equipment, including "Nosey Cut-out Tumblers" in 3 sizes.

Therapro
225 Arlington St.
Framingham, MA 01702-8723
800-257-5376
www.theraproducts.com
A source for oral-sensory and oral motor toys and practice materials including whistles, blow toys, feeding tools, and chewing tools.

THERAPIES

American Occupational Therapy Association
4720 Montgomery Lane
P.O. Box 31220
Bethesda, MD 20824-1220
301-652-2682
www.aota.org

American Physical Therapy Association
1111 North Fairfax St.
Alexandria, VA 22314-1488
800-999-APTA
www.apta.org

SOFTWARE

Here are some companies that produce software helpful for early language learning. Also see the section on AAC below.

Broderbund
www.broderbund.com
Distributes a variety of software including language and educational software by Edmark and Riverdeep.

Edmark
P.O. Box 97021
Redmond, WA 98073-9721
800-362-2890
www.edmark.com

Laureate Learning Systems
110 E. Spring St.
Winooski, VT 05404
800-562-6801
www.laureatelearning.com

Optimum Resource
18 Hunter Rd.
Hilton Head Island, SC 29926
843-689-8000
www.stickybear.com
   Offers the Stickybear line of software, including *Stickybear ABC, Stickybear Opposites,* and *Stickybear Shapes.*

AUGMENTATIVE & ALTERNATIVE COMMUNICATION (AAC)

ORGANIZATIONS

AAC Institute
338 Meadville St.
Edinboro, PA 16412
814-392-6625
www.aacinstitute.org
   A nonprofit organization dedicated to the most effective communication for people who use AAC.

AbleData
www.abledata.com
   A federally funded project that provides information on assistive technology and rehabilitation equipment

Alliance for Technology Access
217 East Francisco Blvd., Suite L
San Rafael, CA 94901
415-455-4575
Web site: www.ataccess.org
   This national network of technology resource centers provides information and resources and demonstration. Some centers will analyze your child's computer needs and provide free or low-cost evaluations. Others will lend or provide computers and software. On the Internet, you can find a complete list of all centers affiliated with ATA organized by state.

Apple's People with Special Needs Website
www.apple.com/disability
   Has a searchable database of hardware, software, and other products for people with disabilities that are compatible with Apple computers. Also links to helpful organizations.

Center for Special Education Technology
1920 Association Dr.
Reston, VA 22901
703-620-3660
   Publishes a monthly newsletter about technology and children with special needs.

Closing the Gap
P.O. Box 68
Henderson, MN 56004
612-248-3294
Web site: www.closingthegap.com
    Resource center for technology information; publishes bimonthly newsletter and holds annual conference. Website provides library resources, article summaries, and a list of upcoming conferences.

IBM Accessibility Center
www-3.ibm.com/able
    The website has links to information on AT products (IBM) and solutions for people with disabilities.

International Society for Augmentative and Alternative Communication (ISAAC)
49 The Donway West, #308
Toronto, ON M3C 3M9
Canada
416-385-0351
www.isaac-online.org
    ISAAC's mission is to improve communication and quality of life for people with communication impairments. They have publications, conventions, and, on the website, links to resources.

National Easter Seal Society
230 W. Monroe St., #1800
Chicago, IL 60606
312-726-6200
www.easter-seals.org
    Among services offered by local chapters is assistance with assistive technology, including computers.

IBM Independence Series Information Center
1000 N. W. 51st St.
Boca Raton, FL 33432
800-426-4832; 800-426-4833 (TT)
    Resource center for information about IBM products for individuals with disabilities.

RESNA (Rehabilitation Engineering & Assistive Technology Society)
1700 N. Moore St.
Arlington, VA 22209-1903
703-524-6686
www.resna.org
    Information on state Technology Assistance Projects that will provide hardware and software support. The RESNA website provides a complete list of state centers that are funded under the Technology-Related Assistance for Individuals with Disabilities Act of 1988 and 1998.

TASH
29 W. Susquehanna Ave.
Baltimore, MD 21204-5201
410-828-8274
www.tash.org
    This organization, which advocates for "equity, quality and social justice for people with disabilities," has information and an annual conference.

Trace Research & Development Center
University of Wisconsin-Madison
5901 Research Park Blvd.
Madison, WI 53719-1252
info@trace.wisc.edu
www.trace.wisc.edu
This website provides information about assistive technology, including augmentative and alternative communication.

United Cerebral Palsy
Assistive Technology Funding and Systems Change Project
1660 L Street, NW, Suite 700
Washington, DC 20036
202-7765-0406
www.ucp.org
UCP's website includes articles on assistive technology, on topics such as choosing AT and finding funding sources.

The U.S. Society for Augmentative and Alternative Communication
P.O. Box 21418
Sarasota, FL 34276
941-312-0992
www.ussaac.org
Information and resources regarding augmentative communication, hardware, and software. It is the United States chapter of ISAAC.

SOURCES OF EQUIPMENT AND SUPPLIES

These companies can provide information on hardware and software to support assistive technology. Many design and sell augmentative communication devices. Some also provide picture symbols or picture systems for communication. Picture symbols can be used for communication boards, notebooks, and other communication systems. They are also helpful in creating adaptive materials such as learning worksheets for classroom inclusion. The picture symbols are often used in language therapy. The major products that could be helpful in assistive technology for children with Down syndrome are noted.

For information and catalogs, contact these companies directly, or contact CAMA (The Communication Aids Manufacturers Association) or ATIA (The Assistive Technology Industry Association), the associations which include the major companies.

ATIA holds an annual conference where you can learn about communication devices, software, and learning aids. Speakers address a wide range of topics on assistive technology equipment, techniques, and research intiatives.

ABLENET
1081 Tenth Ave. SE
Minneapolis, MN 55414
800-322-0956
www.ablenetinc.com
Resources include *Language Master* (card replay system); *Let's Go Activity Pack; Can Do Recorder; Quick Start Communication Kit; Big Mack* recorder switch; *TalkTrac; Step by Step Communicator; One Step* and *All Turn It Spinner.*

Academic Software
331 W. Second St.
Lexington, KY 40507
859-233-2332
www.acsw.com
Specializes in AT and computer access for individuals with disabilities.

Adaptivation
2225 W. 50th St., Suite 100
Sioux Falls, SD 57105
800-723-2783
www.adaptivation.com

VoicePal Max; switches and interfaces to create activities; *Recipes for Success, Volumes 1 and 2.* Website includes links to sites with information on AT.

AlphaSmart
973 University Ave.
Los Gatos, CA 95032
888-274-0680; 408-355-1000
www.alphasmart.com

The *AlphaSmart* is a portable keyboard that stores typed information and then easily sends it to any type of computer. Simple editing and printing may be done directly from the *AlphaSmart.*

Assistive Technology, Inc.
7 Wells Ave.
Newton, MA 02459
800-793-9227; 617-641-9000
www.assistivetech.com

They sell the *Freestyle,* a tablet-type Macintosh computer with a touch window and companion software. They also sell the *LINK,* a "smart" keyboard that talks; *EvaluWare,* assessment activities for augmentative communication; *Emerging Language Software* (cause & effect, language readiness, early concepts, advanced concepts); Assistive technology photos for daily life; Computer funding guide; *Gemini* computer.

Attainment Company
504 Commerce Parkway
Verona, WI 53593-0160
800-327-4269
www.attainmentcompany.com

They sell *Go Talk-36* message voice output communication system; *Teaching Social Competence; WordWise* (functional literacy program); *Picture Cue CD; Writing with Symbols; Ready Set Read.*

CAMA
P.O. Box 1039
Evanston, IL 60204
800-441-CAMA (2262)
www.aacproducts.org

CAMA holds conferences for professionals and/or families throughout the country where you can learn about various communication devices.

Cole Educational
P.O. Box 1717
Pasadena, TX 77501
713-944-2345; 800-448-COLE
www.edumart.com/teacherstore

They sell the *EIKI Portable Card Reader, the Language Master,* and blank cards.

Communication Skill Builders
313 North Dodge Blvd., Box 42050-H
Tucson, AZ 85733
602-323-7500
www.psychcorp.com/catg
　　　Picture Symbol Systems including *Peel and Put, Pictures Please Stickers, Communicards, Photo Sticks, Photo Cue Cards*.

Consultants for Communication Technology
508 Bellevue Terrace
Pittsburgh, PA 15202
412-761-6062
www.concommtech.com
　　　Equipment for turning a laptop into a communication device in British English, American English, Spanish, and German.

Crestwood Communication Aids
6625 North Sidney Place
Milwaukee, WI 53209
414-352-5678
www.communicationaids.com
　　　Speaking aids such as *The Crespeaker* and the *Crespeaker MAXX* use alphabet letters. Talking picture frames and recorded card machines are excellent for practice. Talking pictures and passports can be used as picture communication systems including *Passport to Independence, School Passport*, and *Sign Language Pictures*.

Developmental Equipment
P.O. Box 639
Wauconda, IL 60084
800-999-4660
　　　They sell *Picsyms, Oakland Picture Dictionary*.

Don Johnston, Inc.
26799 West Commerce Dr.
Volo, IL 60073
847-740-0749; 800-999-4660
or
Don Johnston Special Needs Ltd
18 Clarendon Ct., Calver Rd.
Winwick Quay, Warrington
England WA2 8QP
info@donjohnston.com
www.donjohnston.com
　　　Talking word processor (*Write:Outloud*) and word prediction software. Adapted as well as other Macintosh and Windows products and a variety of other communication and computer products, including books and other resource materials: *Core Picture Vocabulary; PixWriter; Clicker 4* (writing software with picture support); *Discover Literacy; Start-to-Finish Book Club; Discover Board, Switch, and Screen; PCA Checklist; ATI Assessment*.

DynaVox Systems, Inc.
2100 Wharton St.
Suite 400
Pittsburgh, PA 15203
888-697-7332
www.dynavoxsys.com
　　　Communication devices in English and Spanish: *DynaMyte 3100; Dynamo-digitized; DynaVox 3100*.

Edmark
P.O. Box 97021
Redmond, WA 98073-9721
800-362-2890
www.edmark.com

Software for typical and special-needs learners available in English and Spanish. Critical thinking, early learning, language arts, math, science, and social studies software. Website has curricular correlations which match curriculum objectives with Edmark software products. Curricular objectives and the matching products are provided for each state, and for curricular programs that may be used in more than one state, such as the Stanford 9 Instructional Objectives and the Texas Essential Knowledge and Skills. Company has excellent customer support.

Educational Resources
1550 Executive Dr.
Elgin, IL 60123
708-888-8300
www.edresources.com

A discount supplier of software and hardware from many companies.

Electronics Technology Group
9333 Penn Ave.
South Bloomington, MN 55431-2320
800-480-4384; 612-948-3100

A discount supplier of software and hardware from many companies.

Enkidu Research
247 Pine Hill Rd.
Spencerport, NY 14559
800-297-9570
www.enkidu.net

They sell portable *IMPACT* dynamic display augmentative communication devices that come in three different hardware versions: The Palmtop, the Handheld, and the Tablet. Also, *DeCtalk,* speech synthesis, letter-based and symbol based communication systems.

Feelings, Inc.
P.O. Box 574
Virginia Beach, VA 23451
757-363-9585

Communication vests and toys made from Tempo Loop Display fabric.
Use for visual supports for communication.

Frame Technologies
W681 Pearl St.,
Oneida, WI 54155
414-869-2979
www.frame-tech.com

Inexpensive digitized voice-output devices: *Voice-in-a Box, TalkPad, Book Talker,* and *MicroVoice.*

Free Foto
www.freefoto.com

Free collection of photographs that can be downloaded or copied and used to create visual supports and practice materials. Photos are available in over 50 categories.

Freedom Scientific Learning Systems Group
480 California Ave., Ste. 201
Palo Alto, CA 94306
888-223-3344
www.freedomscientific.com
   WYNN (text to speech software). They have an online newsletter.

The Great Talking Box Company
2245 Fortune Dr., Suite A,
San Jose, CA 95131
408-456-0133; 877-275-4482
http://greattalkingbox.com
   They sell the *E-Talker, Dynamic Display Augmentative Communication Device,* the *EasyTalk,* and *Digicom-2000.*

Gus Communications
P.O. Box 4362
Blaine, WA 98231-4362
604-279-0110
www.gusinc.com
   They sell a dynamic display communication software for IBM compatibles.

Imaginart
307 Arizona St.
Bisbee, AZ 85603
800-828-1376; 520-432-5741
www.imaginartonline.com
   They sell Pick 'N Stick Fast Food, Pocket Picture Holder, Touch 'N Talk Communication Board/ Notebook, Pick 'N Stick Color Packs, as well as language books and materials.

IntelliTools, Inc.
1720 Corporate Circle
Petaluma, CA 94954
800-899-6687; 707-773-2000
www.intellitools.com
   They sell *IntelliKeys* (specially designed limited choice and adaptable multiple choice programmable keyboards); keyguards; *Overlay Maker; IntelliTalk II* communication system; *IntelliPics* picture library; *Access Pac* (curriculum adaptation tool). They also have an activity exchange on their website.

Laureate Learning Systems
110 E. Spring St.
Winooski, VT 05404
800-562-6801
www.laureatelearning.com
   Extensive variety of well-designed language software for learners with special needs, including *First Words I & II, First Verbs, Exploring First Words I & II, Talking Nouns, Talking Verbs, First Categories. Simple Sentence Structure, Early Emerging Rules: Plurals, Negations, Prepositions, Adjectives & Opposites, Words & Concepts I-III, Language Activities of Daily Living: My House, My Town, My School,* the *Sentence Master 1-4.*

Mayer-Johnson Company
P.O. BOX 1579
Solano Beach, CA 92075
800-588-4548
www.mayer-johnson.com

Mayer-Johnson sells a wide variety of AAC systems and tools, including *Picture Communication Symbols,* which can be photocopied or printed by computer with *Boardmaker* software (available in ten languages). Mayer-Johnson also sells *Speaking Dynamically Pro,* an AAC software program; inexpensive digitized voice output devices; curricula augmented by symbols and other resources; *Communication Board Builder; Print 'n Communicate; Print 'n Learn Thematic Units for Boardmaker; Print 'n Learn Community Units for Boardmaker; Speaking Dynamically Pro; Speaking Academically; TALK Boards; Language Exercises for You and Me; Hands On Reading; Curriculum Experiences for Literacy, Learning and Living.*

Pyramid Educational Consultants
226 West Park Place, Suite 1
Newark, DE 19711
888-PECS INC (888-732-7462)
www.pecs.com
This company, founded and run by the developers of PECS, offers training and sells products to assist with the Picture Exchange Communication System (PECS).

Prentke-Romich Company
1022 Heyl Rd.
Wooster, OH 44691
800-262-1984
www.prentrom.com (in the U.S.)
www.prentromint.com (outside the U.S.)
Offers a wide variety of augmentative communication devices, and have extensive customization options and customer support services. Website includes links to summer camps for people who use AAC.

Saltillo Corporation
2143 Township Rd., #112
Millersburg, OH 44654
800-382-8622; 330-674-6722
www.saltillo.com
They sell the *ChatPC,* the *ChatBox, Message Box, VocaFlex,* and a variety of other AAC devices.

Sammons Preston
AbilityOne Corp.
4 Sammons Ct.
Bolingbrook, IL 60440
800-323-5547 (in U.S.); 800-665-9200 (in Canada)
www.sammonspreston.com
They sell *Communication Sheets;* many self-help daily living aids.

Silver Lining Multimedia
P.O. Box 2201
Poughkeepsie, NY 12601
845 462 8714
www.silverliningmedia.com
Produces the *Picture This* CD-ROM, which can be used to print out clear, photo-quality images of hundreds of common objects, actions, people, etc.

Slater Software
351 Badger Lane
Guffey, CO 80820
719 479 2255
www.slatersoftware.com
AT for pre-readers and beginning readers, such as *Picture It, Tool for Teachers; PixReader; PixWriter; T.A.L.K. Take Along Language Kits; Interactive Book Kits.* Information on computers and literacy.

Softtouch
4300 Stine Rd., Suite 401
Bakersfield, CA 93313
877-763-8868
www.funsoftware.com

Software for children with special needs, including: *Teach Me to Talk; Companion Activities for curriculum adaptation; Learning software;* overlays for *IntelliKeys; Picture This: Nouns & Sounds, Learning for Teens; Concepts on the Move; Print, Play & Learn; Teach Me Phonemics.*

Synergy
68 Hale Rd.
East Walpole, MA 02032
508-668-7424
www.synergy.qpg.com

They sell Macintosh PowerBook and Windows systems with built-in touch screens for use as a portable communication devices and other AAC devices.

Technology for Education
1870 E. 50th, Suite 7
Inver Grove Heights, MN 55077
800-370-0047
www.tfeinc.com

They sell AT and learning products from a variety of manufacturers.

Turning Point Therapy and Technology
P.O. Box 310751
New Braunfels, TX 78131-0751
877-608-9812; 830-608-9812
www.turningpointtechnology.com

They sell custom keyguards and protectors for computer keyboards.

USDA Photography Center
Room 1544-S
Washington, DC 20250
202-720-6633
www.usda.gov/oc/photos/opclibra.htm

Photos of food and plants available in the photo library.

Words+
1220 West Avenue J
Lancaster, CA 93534
800-869-8521
www.words-plus.com

They sell communication software, communication systems, speech devices. Website has online newsletter with news about AAC issues.

Zygo Industries
P.O. Box 1008
Portland, OR 97207-1008
800-234-6006; 503-684-6006
www.zygo-usa.com

Specializes in high-tech AAC systems: *Optimist* (augmentative communication device); *Winspeak* (symbol based communication system); *PICTOCOM SE*; software programs; *MACAW* communication device.

References and Suggested Reading

CHAPTER 2

REFERENCES

Buckley, S. & Bird, G. (2001). *Speech and language development for infants with Down syndrome.* Portsmouth, UK: Down Syndrome Educational Trust.

Buckley, S. & Sacks, B. (2001). *An overview of the development of infants with Down syndrome.* Portsmouth, UK: Down Syndrome Educational Trust.

Cohen, W. (Ed.)(1999). Healthcare guidelines for individuals with Down Syndrome. *Down Syndrome Quarterly, 4* (3).

Marder, E. & Dennis, J. (1997). Medical management of children with Down's syndrome. *Current Paediatrics, 7,* 1-7.

Roberts, J., Wallace, I. & Henderson, F. (Eds.)(1997). *Otitis media in young children.* Baltimore, MD: Paul H. Brookes Publishing.

Rosenfeld-Johnson, S. The oral-motor myths of Down syndrome. *ADVANCE magazine,* August 4, 1997.

Rosenfeld-Johnson, S. (1999). *Oral-motor exercises for speech clarity.* Tucson, AZ: Innovative Therapists International.

Rosenfeld-Johnson, S. & Money, S. (1999). *The homework book.* Tucson, AZ: Innovative Therapists International.

Shott, S.R., Joseph, A. & Heithaus, D. (2001). Hearing loss in children with Down syndrome. *International Journal of Pediatric Otolaryngology 1:61 (3):* 199-205.

SUGGESTED READING

Disability Solutions: A Resource for Families and Others Interested in Down Syndrome and Related Disabilities
9220 SW Barbur Blvd., Ste. 119,
Portland, OR 97219.
www.disabilitysolutions.org
    A bimonthly newsletter. Each issue typically examines one issue related to Down syndrome in depth. Subscriptions are free or the newsletter can be read online.

Hanson, Marci (1987). *Teaching the infant with Down syndrome.* Austin, Texas: Pro-Ed.
    Provides many ideas in all areas of development.

Healthcare Guidelines for Individuals with Down Syndrome
www.denison.edu/dsq/health99/shtml and www.ds-health.com
    Guidelines were developed by physicians from the Down Syndrome Medical Interest Group
(DSMIG) and are updated periodically. The guidelines address hearing testing, as well as health and
medical issues. Excellent guidelines to share with your pediatrician or family doctor.

Segal, M. and Masi, W. (1998). *Your child at play: Birth to one year.* 2nd ed. New York: Newmarket Press.

Stray-Gundersen, Karen (Ed.) (1995). *Babies with Down syndrome: A new parents' guide.* 2nd ed.
    Bethesda, MD: Woodbine House.
    The classic overview for new parents about raising a child with Down syndrome, this book
covers developmental, medical, educational, legal, family, and emotional issues.

Van Dyke, D.C., Mattheis, P., Eberly, S.S. & Williams, J. (Eds.) (1995). *Medical and surgical care for
    children with Down syndrome: A guide for parents.* Bethesda, MD: Woodbine House.

Winders, Patricia C. (1997). *Gross motor skills in children with Down syndrome: A guide for parents
    and professionals.* Bethesda, MD: Woodbine House.

CHAPTER 3

SUGGESTED READING ON SENSORY INTEGRATION

Anderson, Elizabeth & Emmons, Pauline (1996). *Unlocking the secrets of sensory dysfunction: A
    resource for anyone who works with, or lives with, a child with sensory issues.* Ft. Worth, TX:
    Future Horizons, 1996.

Kranowitz, Carol Stock & Silver, Larry (1998). *The out of sync child: Recognizing and coping with
    sensory integration dysfunction.* New York: Perigee.

Kranowitz, Carol Stock (2003). *The out of sync child has fun: Activities for kids with sensory
    integration dysfunction..* New York: Perigee.

Rosenfeld-Johnson, S. (1999). *Oral-motor exercises for speech clarity.* Tucson, AZ: Innovative
    Therapists International.

SUGGESTED READING ON FEEDING AND NUTRITION

Medlen, Joan (2002). *The Down syndrome nutrition handbook: A guide to promoting healthy
    lifestyles.* Bethesda, MD: Woodbine House.

Morris, S.E. & Klein, M.D. (2000). *Pre-Feeding skills: A comprehensive resource for mealtime
    development.* Tucson, AZ: Communication Skill Builders.

CHAPTER 4

REFERENCES

Ayres, A.J. (1980). *Sensory integration and the child.* Los Angeles, CA: Western Psychological
    Publishers.

Ayres, A.J. & Mailloux, Z. (1981). Influence of sensory integration procedures on language
    development. *The American Journal of Occupational Therapy, 35,* 383-390.

Buckley, S. (1996). *Reading before talking: Learning about mental abilities from children with
    Down's syndrome.* University of Portsmouth Inaugural Lecture, Portsmouth, England.

Cohen, W. (Ed.) (1999). Healthcare guidelines for individuals with Down Syndrome. *Down
    Syndrome Quarterly, 4 (3),*1-26.

Kumin, L., Councill, C. & Goodman, M. (1998). Expressive vocabulary development in children with Down syndrome. *Down Syndrome Quarterly, 3,* 1-7.

Kumin, L. & Bahr, D.C. (1999). Patterns of feeding, eating, and drinking in young children with Down syndrome with oral motor concerns. *Down Syndrome Quarterly, 4,* 1-8.

Medlen, J. (2002). *The Down syndrome nutrition handbook: A guide to promoting healthy lifestyles.* Bethesda, MD: Woodbine House.

Roizen, N. (1997). Hearing loss in children with Down syndrome: A review. *Down Syndrome Quarterly, 2,* 1-4.

Roizen, N., Wolters, C., Nicol, T., & Blondis, T. (1992). Hearing loss in children with Down syndrome. *Pediatrics, 123,* S 9-12.

Rosin, P. & Swift, E. (1999). Communication intervention: Improving the speech intelligibility of children with Down syndrome. In J. Miller, M. Leady & L.A. Leavitt. *Improving the communication of people with Down syndrome.* Baltimore, MD: Paul H. Brookes.

Rosin, M., Swift, E., Bless, D. & Vetter, D.K. (1988). Communication profiles of adolescents with Down Syndrome. *Journal of Childhood Communication Disorders, 12,* 49-64.

Shott, S. R. (2000). Down syndrome: Common pediatric ear, nose, and throat problems. *Down Syndrome Quarterly, 5,* 1-6.

SUGGESTED READING

Bruni, Maryanne. (1998). *Fine motor skills in children with Down syndrome: A guide for parents and professionals.* Bethesda, MD: Woodbine House.

Many fine motor skills, such as pointing and feeding, are intertwined with early communication skills, and this book does a fine job explaining the issues and suggesting activities to help with development of those skills.

Manolson, Ayala (1992). *It takes two to talk: A parent's guide to helping children communicate.* Toronto: Hanen Centre.

Schwartz, S. & Miller, J. *The new language of toys: Teaching communication skills to children with special needs.* 2nd edition. Bethesda, MD. Woodbine House, 1996.

CHAPTER 5

REFERENCES

Acredolo, L. & Goodwyn, S. (1996). *Baby signs.* Chicago, IL: Contemporary Books.

Buckley, S. (2000). *Speech and language development for individuals with Down syndrome: An overview.* Portsmouth, UK: Down Syndrome Educational Trust.

Buckley, S. & Bird, G. (2001). *Speech and language development for infants with Down syndrome.* Portsmouth, UK: Down Syndrome Educational Trust.

Buckley, S. & Sacks, B. (2001). *An overview of the development of infants with Down syndrome.* Portsmouth, UK: Down Syndrome Educational Trust.

Bondy, A. & Frost, L. (2001). *A picture's worth: PECS and other visual communication strategies in autism.* Bethesda, MD: Woodbine House.

Derr, J.S. (1983). Signing vs. silence, *Exceptional Parent, 13* (6), 49-52.

Gibbs, E.D. & Carswell, L. (1991). Using total communication with young children with Down syndrome: A literature review and case study. *Early Childhood and Development, 2,* 306-320.

Kouri, T. (1989). How manual sign acquisition related to the development of spoken language: A case study. *Language, Speech and Hearing Services in Schools, 20,* 50-62.

McVay, P., Wilson, H. & Chiotti, L. (2003). "I see what you mean!" Using visual tools to support student learning. *Disability Solutions, 5,* 1-15.

Strode, R. & Chamberlain, C. (1995). *Easy does it for apraxia and motor planning: Preschool.* Moline, IL: LinguiSystems.

Strode, R. & Chamberlain, C. (1993). *Easy does it for apraxia and motor planning.* Moline, IL: LinguiSystems.

SUGGESTED READING

Baker, P.J. (1986). *My first book of sign.* Washington, DC: Gallaudet University Press.

Bornstein, H., Saulnier, K. & Hamilton, L. (1983). *The comprehensive Signed English dictionary.* Washington, DC: Clerc (Gallaudet University).

Bornstein, H. & Saulnier, K. (1984). *The Signed English starter.* Washington, DC: Clerc (Gallaudet University).

Bornstein, H. & Saulnier, K. (1988). *Signing: Signed English basic guide.* New York: Crown Publishing.

Gibbs, B. & Springer, A. (1995). *The Early Use of Total Communication: An introductory guide for parents* (pamphlet and video). Baltimore, MD: Paul H. Brookes.

Simplified Signs Website: www.simplifiedsigns.org
    Website provides pictures of signs from this simple sign system which can be easily understood. The signs are designed more for the vocabulary used by adults with neurological disorders, rather than the signs needed by infants and toddlers.

REFERENCES

CHAPTER 6

Chamberlain, C. & Strode, R. (2000). *For parents and professionals: Down syndrome.* East Moline, IL: Lingui Systems.

Kumin, L., Councill, C., & Goodman, M. (1999). Expressive vocabulary in young children with Down syndrome: From research to treatment. *Infant-Toddler Intervention,* 87-100.

Kumin, L., Councill, C. & Goodman, M. (1998) Expressive vocabulary development in children with Down syndrome. *Down Syndrome Quarterly, 3,* 1-7.

Mervis, C. (1997). Early lexical and conceptual development in children with Down syndrome. Presented at the National Down Syndrome Society International Down Syndrome Research Conference on Cognition and Behavior, November, 1997.

Oliver, B. & Buckley, S. (1994). The language development of children with Down syndrome: First words to two-word phrases. *Down Syndrome Research and Practice, 2,* 71-75.

Rondal, J.A. (1988) Language development in Down's syndrome: A lifespan perspective. *International Journal of Behavioral Development, 11,* 21-36.

CHAPTER 7

REFERENCES

Barrett, M.N. & Diniz, F. (1988). Lexical development in mentally handicapped children. In Beveridge, M., Conti-Ramsden, G. & Leader, I. (Eds), *Language, communication and mentally handicapped people.* New York, NY: Chapman and Hall, 2-32.

Berglund, E., Eriksson, M. & Johansson, I. (2001). Parental reports of spoken language skills in children with Down syndrome. *Journal of Speech, Language and Hearing Research, 44,* 179-191.

Brown, Roger W. (1973). *A first language: The early stages.* Cambridge, MA: Harvard University Press.

Buckley, S. (1993). Developing the speech and language skills of teenagers with Down syndrome. *Down Syndrome Research and Practice, 1(2),* 63-71.

Buckley, S. et. al. (1986). *The Development of Language and Reading Skills in Children with Down's Syndrome.* Portsmouth, England: Portsmouth Polytechnic Institute.

Buckley, S. (1995). Improving the expressive language skills of teenagers with Down syndrome. *Down Syndrome Research and Practice, 3(3),* 110-115.

Buckley, S. (1993). Language development in children with Down's syndrome: Reasons for optimism. *Down's Syndrome: Research and Practice, 1,* 3-9.

Buckley, S. (1996). Reading before talking: Learning about mental abilities from children with Down's syndrome. University of Portsmouth Inaugural Lecture, Portsmouth, England.

Buckley, S. (2000). Speech and language development for individuals with Down syndrome: An overview. Portsmouth, UK: Down Syndrome Educational Trust.

Buckley, S. & Pennanen, T. (in press). Profiles of early language development for children with Down syndrome: The link between vocabulary size and grammar. Down Syndrome: Research and Practice.

Cardoso-Martins, C., Mervis, C.B. & Mervis, C.A. (1985). Early vocabulary acquisition by children with Down syndrome. *American Journal of Mental Deficiency, 90,* 177-184.

Fowler, A.E. (1995). Linguistic variability in persons with Down syndrome: research and implications. In Nadel, L. & Rosenthal, D. (Eds.) *Down syndrome: Living and learning in the community.* New York: Wiley-Liss, 121-131.

Gillham, B. (1979). *The first words language programme: A basic language programme for mentally handicapped children.* London: George Allen & Unwin.

Kumin, L., Councill, C., & Goodman, M. (1999). Expressive vocabulary in young children with Down syndrome: From research to treatment. *Infant-Toddler Intervention,* 87-100.

Kumin, L., Councill, C. & Goodman, M. (1998). Expressive vocabulary development in children with Down syndrome. *Down Syndrome Quarterly, 3,* 1-7.

Kumin, L., Goodman, M. & Councill, C. (1991). Comprehensive communication intervention for infants and toddlers with Down syndrome. *Infant-Toddler Intervention, 1,* 275-296.

Mervis, C. (1997). Early lexical and conceptual development in children with Down syndrome. Presented at the National Down Syndrome Society International Down Syndrome Research Conference on Cognition and Behavior, November, 1997.

Miller, J.F. (1995). Individual differences in vocabulary acquisition in children with Down syndrome. *Progress in Clinical and Biological Research, 393,* 93-103.

Miller, J.F. (1992). Lexical development in young children with Down syndrome. In Chapman, R. (Ed.), *Processes in language acquisition and disorders.* St. Louis, MO: Mosby Year Book.

Miller, J.F. (1988). Developmental asynchrony of language development in children with Down syndrome. In Nadel, L. (Ed.), *Psychobiology of Down Syndrome.* New York, NY: Academic Press.

Miller, J., Sedey, A. & Miolo, G. (1995). Validity of parent report measures of vocabulary development for children with Down syndrome. *Journal of Speech and Hearing Research, 38,* 1037-1044.

Oliver, B. & Buckley, S. (1994). The language development of children with Down's syndrome: First words to two-word phrases. *Down's Syndrome: Research and Practice,* 1-4.

Rondal, J.A. (1978). Maternal speech to normal and Down's syndrome children matched for mean length of utterance. In Myers, C.E. (Ed.), *Quality of life in severely and profoundly mentally retarded people: Research foundations for improvement.* Washington, DC: American Association on Mental Deficiency.

Rondal, J.A. & Edwards, S. (1997). *Language in mental retardation.* London: Whurr Publishers.

Rutter, T. & Buckley, S. (1994). The acquisition of grammatical morphemes in children with Down's syndrome. *Down Syndrome Research and Practice, 2,* 76-82.

Strode, R. & Chamberlain, C. (1995). *Easy does it for apraxia and motor planning: Preschool.* Moline, IL: LinguiSystems.

Strode, R. & Chamberlain, C. (1993). *Easy does it for apraxia and motor planning.* Moline, IL: LinguiSystems.

CHAPTER 9

REFERENCES

Bleile, K. (1982). Consonant ordering in Down's syndrome phonology. *Journal of Communication Disorders, 15,* 275-285.

Bleile, K. & Schwarz, I. (1984) Three perspectives on the speech of children with Down's syndrome. *Journal of Communication Disorders, 17,* 87-94.

Desai, S.S. (1997). Down syndrome: A review of the literature. *Oral Surgery Oral Medicine Oral Pathology, 84,* 279-285.

Dodd, B. (1977) A comparison of the phonological systems of mental age matched, normal, severely subnormal and Down's Syndrome children. *British Journal of Disorders of Communication, 1,* 27-42.

Hodson, B. & Paden, E. (1991). *Targeting intelligible speech: A phonological approach to remediation.* 2nd ed. Austin, TX: PRO-ED.

Kumin, L. (1999). Comprehensive speech and language treatment for infants, toddlers, and children with Down syndrome. In Hassold, T.J., *Down syndrome: A promising future, together,* 145-53. New York, NY: Wiley-Liss.

Kumin, L. (1996). Speech and language skills in children with Down syndrome. *Mental Retardation and Developmental Disabilities Research Reviews, 2,* 109-116.

Kumin, L., Councill, C. & Goodman, M. (1994). A longitudinal study of the emergence of pho-nemes in children with Down syndrome. *Journal of Communication Disorders, 27,* 265-275.

Kumin, L., Councill, C. & Goodman, M. (1998). Expressive vocabulary development in children with Down syndrome. *Down Syndrome Quarterly, 3,* 1-7.

Kumin, L. (2002a). Maximizing speech and language in children and adolescents with Down syndrome. In Cohen, W., Nadel, L. & Madnick, M. (Eds.), *Down syndrome: Visions for the 21st century,* 403-15. New York, NY: Wiley-Liss.

Kumin, L. (2002b). Why can't you understand what I am saying: Speech intelligibility in daily life. *Disability Solutions, 5 (1),*1-15.

Kumin, L. (2002c). You said it just yesterday, why not now? Developmental apraxia of speech in children and adults with Down syndrome. *Disability Solutions, 5 (2),*1-16.

Kumin, L. & Adams, J. (2000). Developmental apraxia of speech and intelligibility in children with Down syndrome. *Down Syndrome Quarterly, 5,* 1-6.

Kumin, L., Councill, C. & Goodman, M. (1995). The pacing board: A technique to assist the transition from single word to multiword utterances. *Infant-Toddler Intervention, 5,* 23-29

Mackay, L. & Hodson, B. (1982). Phonological process identification of misarticulations of mentally retarded children. *Journal of Communication Disorders, 15,* 243-250.

Moran, M.J., Money, S.M. & Leonard, D.A. (1984). Phonological process analysis of the speech of mentally retarded adults. *American Journal of Mental Deficiency, 89,* 304-306.

Rosin, M., Swift, E., Bless, D. & Vetter, D.K. (1988). Communication profiles of adolescents with Down Syndrome. *Journal of Childhood Communication Disorders, 12,* 49-64.

Smit, A., Hand, L., Freilinger, J., Bernthal, J., & Bird, A. (1990). The Iowa Articulation Norms Project and its Nebraska replication. *Journal of Speech and Hearing Disorders, 55,* 795.

Smith, B.L. & Stoel-Gammon, C. (1983). A longitudinal study of the development of stop conso-nant production in normal and Down's syndrome children. *Journal of Speech and Hearing Disorders, 48,* 114-118.

Sommers, R.K., Patterson, J.P. & Wildgen, P.L. (1988). Phonology of Down syndrome speakers, ages 13-22. *Journal of Childhood Communication Disorders, 12,* 65-91.

Stoel-Gammon, C. (1980). Phonological analysis of four Down's syndrome children. *Applied Psycholinguistics, 1,* 31-48.

Stoel-Gammon, C. (1997). Phonological development in Down syndrome. *Mental Retardation and Developmental Disabilities Research Reviews, 3,* 300-306.

Van Borsal, J. (1996). Articulation in Down's syndrome adolescents and adults. *European Journal of Disorders of Communication, 31,* 425-444.

SUGGESTED READING AND MATERIALS ON CHILDHOOD VERBAL APRAXIA

Marshalla, P. (2001). *Becoming verbal with childhood apraxia.* Kirkland, WA: Marshalla Speech and Language. Available through Super Duper Publications, 800-277-8737.

Strode, R. & Chamberlain, C. (1995). *Easy does it for apraxia and motor planning: Preschool.* Moline, IL: LinguiSystems.

Strode, R. & Chamberlain, C. (1993). *Easy does it for apraxia and motor planning.* Moline, IL: LinguiSystems.

Time to Sing. Available from the Pittsburgh Symphony, 412-392-3313, and Super Duper Publications, 800-277-8737.

  This is a CD of familiar children's songs played and sung more slowly than usual. This helps enable children with apraxia to sing along.

Velleman, S.L. (2002). *Childhood apraxia of speech resource guide.* New York: Singular Publishing.

SUGGESTED READING AND MATERIALS ON ORAL MOTOR SKILLS

Mackie, E. (1996). *Oral-motor activities for young children.* Moline, IL: LinguiSystems.

Oetter, P. & Richter, E. (1995). *Motor Oral Respiration Eyes (MORE) - Integrating the mouth with sensory and postural functions.* 2nd ed. Hugo, MN: PDP Products.

Rosenfeld-Johnson, S. (1999). *Oral-motor exercises for speech clarity.* Tucson, AZ: Innovative Therapists International.

Rosenfeld-Johnson, S. & Money, S. (1999). *The homework book.* Tucson, AZ: Innovative Therapists International.

CHAPTER 10

REFERENCES

Attwood, A. (1988). The understanding and use of interpersonal gestures by autistic and Down's syndrome children. *Journal of Autism and Developmental Disorders, 18,* 241-257.

Capone, G.T. (1999). Down syndrome and autism spectrum disorders: A look at what we know. *Disability Solutions 3:*8-15, 1999. Special issue devoted to dual diagnosis. (Can be downloaded from the website, www.disabilitysolutions.org)

Cullinan, D., Sabornie, E.J. & Crossland, C.L. (1992). Social mainstreaming of mildly handicapped students. *The Elementary School Journal, 92,* 339-351.

Gallagher, T. & Prutting, C. (Eds.) (1983). *Pragmatic assessment and intervention issues in language.* San Diego, CA: College-Hill Press.

Guralnick, M.J. (1995). Peer-related social competence and inclusion of young children. In Nadel, L. & Rosenthal, D. (Eds.), *Down syndrome: Living and learning in the community,* 147-53. New York: Wiley-Liss.

Leifer, J.S. & Lewis, M. (1984). Acquisition of conversational response skills by young Down syndrome and nonretarded young children. *American Journal of Mental Deficiency, 88,* 610-618.

Loveland, K.A. & Tunali, B. (1991). Social scripts for conversational interactions in autism and Down syndrome. *Journal of Autism and Developmental Disorders, 21,* 177-186.

Loveland, K.A., Tunali, B., McEvoy, R.E. & Kelley, M. (1989). Referential communication and response adequacy in autism and Down's syndrome. *Applied Psycholinguistics, 10,* 301-313.

MacDonald, J. (1989). *Becoming partners with children: From play to conversation.* Chicago: Riverside.

Mundy, P., Sigman, M., Kasari, C. & Yirmiya, N. (1988). Nonverbal communication skills in Down syndrome children. *Child Development, 59,* 235-249.

Patterson, B. (1999). Dual diagnosis: The importance of diagnosis and treatment. *Disability Solutions 3,* 16-17.

Wolpert, G. (1996). *The educational challenges inclusion study.* New York, NY: National Down Syndrome Society.

SUGGESTED READING ON AUTISM

Bondy, A. & Frost, L. (2001). *A picture's worth: PECS and other visual communication strategies in autism.* Bethesda, MD: Woodbine House.

Capone, George. T. (1999). Down syndrome and autism spectrum disorders: A look at what we know. *Disability Solutions 3,* 8-15.
    Special issue devoted to dual diagnosis. (Can be downloaded from the website, www.disabilitysolutions.org)

McClannahan, Lynn E. & Krantz, Patricia J. (1999). *Activity schedules for children with autism: Teaching independent behavior.* Bethesda, MD: Woodbine House.

Patterson, Bonnie. (1999). Dual diagnosis: The importance of diagnosis and treatment. *Disability Solutions 3,* 16-17. (Can be downloaded from the website, www.disabilitysolutions.org)

Powers, Michael D. (2000). *Children with autism: A parents' guide.* Bethesda, MD: Woodbine House.

REFERENCES

CHAPTER 11

Beukelman, D. & Mirenda, P. (1998). *Augmentative and alternative communication: Management of severe communication disorders in children and adults.* 2nd ed. Baltimore: Paul H. Brookes.

Blackstone, S. & Bruskin, D. (Eds.) (1986). *Augmentative communication: An introduction.* Rockville, MD: American Speech-Language-Hearing Association.

Bondy, A. & Frost, L. (2002). *A picture's worth: PECS and other visual communication strategies in autism.* Bethesda, MD: Woodbine House.

Burkhart, L. (1987). *Using computers and speech synthesizers to facilitate communication interaction with young and/or severely handicapped children.* Wauconda, IL: Don Johnston.

DeBruyne, S. & Noecker, J. (1996). Integrating computer into a school and therapy program. *Closing the Gap, 14,* 31-36.

Kefauver, L. (1998). Computer applications in speech-language therapy. *Advance, 25,* 23-25.

Light, J. & Binger, C. (1998). *Building communicative competence with individuals who use augmentative and alternative communication.* Baltimore, MD: Paul H. Brookes.

Meyers, L. (1988). Using computers to teach children with Down syndrome spoken and written language skills. In L. Nadel (Ed.), *The Neurobiology of Language.* Cambridge, MA: M.I.T. Press.

Meyers, L. (1994). Access and meaning: The keys to effective computer use by children with language disabilities. *Journal of Special Education Technology, 12,* 257-75.

Musselwhite, C.R. & Louis, K.W. (1982). *Communication programming for the severely handicapped: Vocal and non-vocal strategies.* San Diego, CA: College-Hill Press.

Reichle, J., York, J. & Sigafoos, J. (1991). *Implementing augmentative and alternative communication: Strategies for learners with severe disabilities.* Baltimore, MD: Paul H. Brookes.

Robinson, Jr., J. L., Cole, P.A., & Kellum, G.D. (1996). Computer information retrieval systems as a clinical tool. *American Journal of Speech-Language-Pathology. 5:3,* Aug. 1, 1996, 24-30.

Romski, M.A. & Sevcik, R.A. (1996). *Breaking the speech barrier: Language development through augmented means.* Baltimore, MD: Paul H. Brookes,

Steiner, S. & Larsen, V.L. (1994). Integrating microcomputers into language intervention. In Butler, K.G. *Best Practices II: The Classroom as an Intervention Context.* Gaithersburg, MD: Aspen Publishers.

SUGGESTED READING

Alliance for Technology Access (2002). *Computer and web resources for people with disabilities: A guide to exploring today's assistive technology.* 3rd ed. Alameda, CA: Hunter House Publishers.
   If you buy one book, this is the one. Excellent comprehensive discussions; extensive resource lists of organizations, conferences, publications, telecommunications resources, and databases.

Closing the Gap, P.O. Box 68, Henderson, MN 56004, 612-248-3294.
Web site: www.closingthegap.com
   Publishes a comprehensive annual directory and guide to the selection of microcomputer technology for children and adults with special needs in February/March. (See listing in Resource Guide.)

CHAPTER 12

REFERENCE

Fuchs, D., Fuchs, L. Powers, M. & Dailey, A. (1985). Bias in the assessment of handicapped children. *American Educational Research Journal, 22,* 185-197.

SUGGESTED READING

Anderson, W., Chitwood, S. & Hayden, D. (1997). *Negotiating the special education maze: A guide for parents and teachers.* 3rd ed. Bethesda, MD: Woodbine House.

Wright, P.W.D. & Wright, P.D. (1999). *Wrightslaw: Special education law.* Hartfield, VA: Harbor House Law Press.

CHAPTER 13

REFERENCES

Kumin, L. (2001). *Classroom language skills for children with Down syndrome: A guide for parents and teachers.* Bethesda, MD: Woodbine House.

Rosin, P. & Swift, E. (1999). Communication interventions: Improving the speech intelligibility of children with Down syndrome. In J. Miller, M. Leddy, & L.A. Leavitt (Eds.), *Improving the communication of people with Down syndrome,* 133-159. Baltimore, MD: Paul H. Brookes.

SUGGESTED READING

Kumin, L. (2002). Maximizing speech and language in children and adolescents with Down syndrome. In Cohen, W., Nadel, L. & Madnick, M. (Eds.), *Down syndrome: Visions for the 21st century,* 403-15. New York, NY: Wiley-Liss.

Kumin, L. (2002). Starting out: Speech and language intervention for infants and toddlers with Down syndrome. In Cohen, W., Nadel, L. & Madnick, M. (Eds.), *Down syndrome: Visions for the 21st century,* 391-402. New York, NY: Wiley-Liss.

Kumin, L. (1999). Comprehensive speech and language treatment for infants, toddlers, and children with Down syndrome. In Hassold, T.J.& Patterson, D. *Down syndrome: A promising future, together,* 145-53. New York, NY: Wiley-Liss.

Kumin, L. (1996). Speech and language skills in infants and toddlers with Down syndrome. New York: National Down Syndrome Society. Available on the NDSS website: www.ndss.org

Kumin, L., Goodman, M. & Councill, C. (1996). Comprehensive speech and language intervention for school-aged children with Down syndrome. *Down Syndrome Quarterly, 1,* 1-8.

Kumin, L., Goodman, M. & Councill, C. (1991). Comprehensive communication intervention for infants and toddlers with Down syndrome. *Infant-Toddler Intervention, 1,* 275-296.

MacDonald, J. (1989). *Becoming partners with children: From play to conversation.* Chicago: Riverside.

Manolson, A. (1992). *It takes two to talk.* Toronto: Hanen Centre.

Miller, J.F., Leddy, M. & Leavitt, L.A. (1999). *Improving the communication of people with Down syndrome.* Baltimore, MD: Paul H. Brookes.

Schwartz, S. & Miller, J. (1996). *The new language of toys: Teaching communication skills to special-needs children.* 2nd ed. Bethesda, MD: Woodbine House.

REFERENCES

Bochner, S., Outhred, L. & Pieterse, M. (2001). A study of functional literacy skills in young adults with Down syndrome. *International Journal of Disability, Development and Education, 48,* 67-90.

Buckley, S. (2001). *Reading and writing for individuals with Down syndrome: An overview.* Portsmouth, England: The Down Syndrome Educational Trust.

Buckley, S. (1995). Teaching children with Down syndrome to read and write. In Nadel, L. & Rosenthal, D. (Eds.), *Down Syndrome: Living and Learning in the Community,* 158-69. New York: Wiley-Liss.

Buckley, S. (1993). Developing the speech and language skills of teenagers with Down's syndrome. *Down's Syndrome: Research and Practice, 1,* 63-71.

Buckley, S. (1984). *Reading and language development in children with Down's syndrome: A guide for parents and teachers.* Portsmouth, England: Down's Syndrome Project.

Buckley, S. & Bird, G. (1993). Teaching children with Down's syndrome to read. *Down's Syndrome: Research and Practice, 1,* 34-41. Available online at www.down-syndrome.net/library/periodicals/dsrp/01/1/034/

Buckley, S., Bird, G. & Byrne, A. (1996). The practical and theoretical significance of teaching literacy skills to children with Down syndrome. In Jean Rondal and Juan Perera (Eds.), *Down Syndrome: Psychological, Psychobiological and Socioeducational Perspectives,* 119-28. London: Whurr Publishers.

Elkins, J. & Farrell, M. (1994). Literacy for all? The case of Down syndrome. *Journal of Reading, 38,* 270-280.

Fitzgerald, J., Roberts, J., Pierce, P. & Schuele, M. (1995). Evaluation of home literacy environment: An illustration with preschool children with Down syndrome. *Reading & Writing Quarterly: Overcoming Learning Difficulties, 11,* 311-334.

Fowler, A.E., Doherty, B.J. & Boynton, L. (1995). Basis of reading skill in young adults with Down syndrome. In Nadel, L. & Rosenthal, D. (Eds.), *Down Syndrome: Living and Learning in the Community,* 121-31. New York: Wiley-Liss.

King-DeBaun, P. (In press). *Baby's brain starting out smart! A parent's guide to the literacy and language connection.* Park City, UT: Creative Communicating.

King-DeBaun, P. (1999). *Storytime revised: Stories, symbols, and emergent literacy activities for young special needs children.* Park City, UT: Creative Communicating.

Laws, G., Buckley, S.J., Bird, G., MacDonald, J. & Broadley, I. (1995). The influence of reading instruction on language and memory development in children with Down's syndrome. *Down's Syndrome Research and Practice, 3,* 59-64.

Lorenz, S., Sloper, T. & Cunningham, C. (1985). Reading and Down's syndrome. *British Journal of Special Education, 12,* 65-67.

Love and Learning Series. P. O. Box 4088, Dearborn, MI 48126-4088. 313-581-8436. www.loveandlearning.com

Oelwein, P. (1995). *Teaching reading to children with Down syndrome: A guide for parents and teachers.* Bethesda, MD: Woodbine House.

ADDITIONAL SUGGESTED READING

Buckley, S. & Bird, G. (1993). Teaching children with Down's syndrome to read. *Down's Syndrome: Research and practice, 1,* 34-41. Available online at www.down-syndrome.net/library/periodicals/dsrp/01/1/034

Kelly, J. & Friend, T. (1995). *Hands-on reading.* Solano Beach, CA: Mayer-Johnson.

King-DeBaun, P. (1990). *Storytime.* Acworth, GA: Pati King-DeBaun.

Lockhart, B.M. (1992). *Read to me, talk with me.* Tucson, AZ: Communication Skill Builders.

Pleura, R.E. & DeBoer, C.J. (1995). *Story making: Using predictable literature to develop communication.* Eau Claire, WI: Thinking Publications.

Reading Together Red: Beginnings, Age 2+ (1999). Cambridge, MA: Candlewick Press.

Reading Together Yellow: First Steps, Age 3+ (1999). Cambridge, MA: Candlewick Press.

Reading Together Blue: Next Steps, Age 4+ (1999). Cambridge, MA: Candlewick Press.

Trelease, J. (2001). *The Read-aloud handbook.* 5th ed. New York: Penguin Books.

CHAPTER 15

REFERENCES

Crimmins, D.B. Positive behavioral support: Analyzing, preventing, and replacing problem behaviors. In Hassold, T. & Patterson, D., (Eds.), *Down Syndrome: A Promising Future Together* 127-32. New York: Wiley-Liss.

Kumin, Libby (2001). *Classroom language skills for children with Down syndrome: A guide for parents and teachers.* Bethesda, MD: Woodbine House.

SUGGESTED READING

Kliewer, Christopher (1998). *Schooling children with Down syndrome: Toward an understanding of possibility.* New York: Teacher's College Press.

Staub, Debbie (1998). *Delicate threads: Friendships between Children with and without special needs in inclusive settings.* Bethesda, MD: Woodbine House.

Children's Books for Language Stimulation

Listed here are books that you can use to help boost your child's expressive and receptive language skills. Books for stimulation of specific speech sounds can be found in Chapter 9.

Single Word Objects

Carle, E. *My Very First Book of Food.*
Day, A. *Good Dog, Carl.*
Girnis, M. *ABC for You and Me.*
Girnis, M. *123 for You and Me.*
Hutchins, P. *Rosie's Walk.*
McGuire, L. *I Know My Animals.*
McGuire, L. *I Know My Foods.*
Markes, J&J. *Sidewalk ABC.*
Markes, J&J. *Sidewalk 123.*
Ricketts, A. *Animals to Know.*
Ricketts, A. *Look and Listen.*
Ricklen, N. *Baby's Toys.*
Rockwell, A. *Planes.*
Seuss, Dr. *Mr. Brown Can Moo, Can You?*
Simon, L. *My Toy Box.*
Simon, L. *Things I Like to Wear.*
Slier, D. *Farm Animals.*
Wik, L. *Baby's First Words.*

Two Word Books

Gundersheimer, K. *Find Cat, Wear Hat.*
Gundersheimer, K. *Splish Splash, Bang Crash.*
Murphy, C. *Slide 'N Seek: Counting.*
Murphy, C. *Slide 'N Seek: Colors.*
Parr, T. *Big and Little.*
Parr, T. *Black and White.*
Pienkowski, J. *1, 2, 3.*
Seuss, Dr. *One Fish, Two Fish, Red Fish, Blue Fish.*

Manipulatives

Bland, S. *Phone Friends: Bedtime Bear.*
Gerth, M. *All About Me.*

Hood, S. *Teddy Bear, Teddy Bear, Turn Around.*
McCole, N. *Busy Block Books: Trucks.*
Murphy, C. *Slide 'N Seek: Colors.*
Pelham, D. *Sam's Pizza.*
Thorpe, K. *Bear's Breakfast Treat.*
Torres, L. *The Fantastic Foam Book.*

Finger Play
Archambault, J. *Here Are My Hands.*
Brown, Marc. *Hand Rhymes.*
Brown, Marc. *Play Rhymes.*
Carle, E. *From Head to Toe.*
Cauley, L.B. *Clap Your Hands.*
Christelow, E. *Five Little Monkeys Jumping on the Bed.*
Hoberman, M. *Miss Mary Mack.*
Raffi. *Songs to Read: Baby Beluga.*
Raffi. *Songs to Read: Five Little Ducks.*
Raffi. *Songs to Read: Shake My Sillies Out.*
Trapani, I. *I'm a Little Teapot.*
Trapani, I. *The Itsy Bitzy Spider.*
Zelinsky, P. *The Wheels on the Bus.*

Predictable Phrases
Ahlberg, J.A. *Peek-A-Boo!*
Boynton, S. *Blue Hat, Green Hat.*
Boynton, S. *But Not the Hippopotamus.*
Christelow, E. *Five Little Monkeys Jumping on the Bed.*
Hood, S. Teddy Bear, *Teddy Bear, Turn Around.*
Kirk, D. *Bus Stop, Bus Go.*
Lewis, K. *Chugga-Chugga Choo-Choo.*
Mother Goose & Grimm. *The Gingerbread Man.*
Mother Goose & Grimm. *Old MacDonald Had a Farm.*
Santomero, A.C., Smith, M., & Wilder, A. *Blue's Clues: Lights On! Lights Off!*
Sierra, J. *Preschool to the Rescue.*

TV Characters
Albee, S. *Sesame Street: Monsters Are Red, Monsters Are Blue.*
Awdry, W. *Thomas ABC Book.*
Bidwell, N. *Clifford's Family.*
Davis, E. *Barney's Musical Castle.*
Gold, B. *Phil and Lil Go to the Doctor.*
Nadeau, N. *Caillou: The Shopping Trip.*
Santomero, A.C. *Blue Goes To School.*
Shealy, D. *Buzz Lightyear of Star Command: The Good, The Bad, and the Robotic.*
Zoehfeld, K.W. *Winnie the Pooh: A Bear-y Good Neighbor.*

Colors
Burningham, J. *Colors.*
Carl, E. *My Very First Book of Colors.*
Fujikawa, G. *My Favorite Colors.*
Hill, E. *Spot's Book of Colors.*
Hoban, T. *Colors Everywhere.*
Hoban, T. *Tana Hoban's Red, Blue, Yellow Shoe*
Karas, Brian. *My Crayons Talk.*
Martin, Bill. *Brown Bear, Brown Bear.*

McGuire, L. *I Know My Colors.*
Murphy, C. *A Razzle-Dazzle Book: Colors.*
Murphy, C. *Slide 'N Seek: Colors.*
Pragoff, F. *What Color?*
Ricklen, N. *Baby's Colors.*
Seuss, G. *One Fish, Two Fish, Red Fish, Blue Fish.*
Seuss, G. *My Many Colored Days.*
Seuss, G. *Green Eggs and Ham.*

Semantics/Vocabulary

Barrett, Judi. *A Snake is Totally Tall.*
Barton, Byron. *Boats.*
Barton, Byron. *Trains.*
Barton, Byron. *Trucks.*
Base, Graeme. *Animalia.*
Brown, Margaret Wise. *Big Red Barn.*
Brown, Margaret Wise. *Goodnight Moon.*
Brown, Margaret Wise. *The Important Book.*
Brown, Margaret Wise. *The Runaway Bunny.*
Carle, Eric. *The Grouchy-Ladybug.*
Carle, Eric. *The Mixed-Up Chameleon.*
Carle, Eric. *The Secret Birthday Message.*
Carle, Eric. *The Very Busy Spider.*
Carle, Eric. *The Very Hungry Caterpillar.*
Carle, Eric. *The Very Noisy Cricket.*
Carlstrom, Nancy White. *Jesse Bear, What Will You Wear?*
Day, Alexandra. *Carl Goes Shopping.*
Day, Alexandra. *Carl Goes to Day Care.*
Day, Alexandra. *Carl's Afternoon in the Park.*
Day, Alexandra. *Carl's Masquerade.*
Day, Alexandra. *Good Dog, Carl.*
Ehlert, Lois. *Growing Vegetable Soup.*
Ehlert, Lois. *Nuts to You.*
Ehlert, Lois. *Planting a Rainbow.*
Gwynne, Fred. *A Chocolate Moose for Dinner.*
Gwynne, Fred. *A Little Pigeon Toad.*
Gwynne, Fred. *The Sixteen Hand Horse.*
Heller, Ruth. *A Cache of Jewels and Other Collective Nouns.*
Heller, Ruth. *Kites Sail High: A Book about Verbs.*
Heller, Ruth. *Many Luscious Lollipops: A Book about Adjectives.*
Heller, Ruth. *Up and Away: A Book about Adverbs.*
Hoban, Russell. *Bread and Jam for Francis.*
Hoban, Tana. *Exactly the Opposite.*
Hoban, Tana. *Is It Larger? Is It Smaller?*
Hoban, Tana. *Over, Under, and Through and Other Spatial Concepts.*
Krauss, Ruth. *A Hole is to Dig: A First Book of Definitions.*
Martin, Bill. *Brown Bear, Brown Bear, What Do You See?*
Martin, Bill. *Polar Bear, Polar Bear, What do You Hear?*
Sendak, Maurice. *Alligators All Around Us.*
Sendak, Maurice. *Chicken Soup with Rice.*
Sendak, Maurice. *Pierre: A Cautionary Tale.*
Sendak, Maurice. *Where the Wild Things Are.*
Shaw, Nancy. *Sheep, Help Me Fall Asleep.*
Shaw, Nancy. *Sheep in a Jeep.*
Shaw, Nancy. *Sheep on a Ship.*

Viorst, Judith. *Alexander and the Terrible, Horrible, No Good, Very Bad Day.*
Viorst, Judith. *Alexander Who Used to Be Rich Last Sunday.*
Viorst, Judith. *The Tenth Good Thing about Barney.*

Prepositions
Berenstain, S. & Berenstain, J. *Bears in the Night.*
Berne, P. *Where Is It?*
Carlson, L. *Here Come the Littles.*
Cartwright, S. *Find the Kitten.*
Children's Television Workshop. *In and Out, Up and Down.*
Hill, E. *Where is Spot?*
Hoban, T. *Over, Under and through and Other Spatial Concepts.*
Lund, D. *I Wonder What's Under.*
Oxenbury, H. *We're Going on a Bear Hunt.*
Seuss, G. *Hop on Pop.*
Slier, D. *Where's the Baby?*

Present Progressive Tense
Butler, J. *Whose Baby Am I?*
Grossman, V. & Long, S. *Ten Little Rabbits.*
Marsoli, L. *Who Hid the Honey?*
Peck & Pat. *Hiding in the Jungle.*
Sanschagrin, J. *Caillou's Potty Time.*
Walsh, M. *Do Monkeys Tweet?*

Adjectives and Adverbs
Barton, B. *Airplanes: Big and Small.*
Burningham, J. *Opposites.*
Carle, Eric. *The Very Hungry Caterpillar.*
Carle, Eric. *The Grouchy Ladybug.*
Charlip, Remy. *Fortunately.*
Freudberg, J. *The Count Counts a Party.*
Fujikawa, G. *Oh What a Busy Day.*
Heller, Ruth. *Kites Sail High: A Book about Verbs.*
Heller, Ruth. *Many Luscious Lollipops: A Book about Adjectives.*
Heller, Ruth. *Up, Up and Away: A Book about Adverbs.*
Henkes, K. *Sheila Rae's Peppermint Stick*
Lesieg, Theo. *Wacky Wednesday.*
Rius, M. *The Five Senses: Touch.*
Yorke, J. *My First Look at Touch.*

Sizes
Dunlap, G. *Big or Little?*
Hoban, T. *Is It Larger? Is It Smaller?*
Hoban, T. *Look How Big.*
Hoff, J. *Large and Small Animals.*
Huntington, D. *What Size Is This?*
Makin, C. *Sizes, Sizes, Sizes.*
Scott, D. *Do You Know Sizes?*
Yorke, J. *My First Look at Sizes.*

Shapes
Burningham, J. *Shapes, Shapes, Shapes.*
Eager, T. *Shapes and Sizes.*
Harper, T. *Round, Square, Triangle.*

Hersey, B. *Share with Us.*
Hoban, T. *Circles, Triangles, and Squares.*
Hoban, T. *So Many Circles, So Many Squares.*
Hoban, T. *Shapes, Shapes, Shapes.*
Oxenbury, H. *Shapes.*
Pragoff, F. *What Shape Is This?*
Ricklen, N. *Baby's Shapes.*
Scott, D. *Do You Know Shapes?*
York, J. *My First Look at Shapes.*

Family and Friends

Cousins, L. *Maisy's Best Friends.*
Hines, A. *Daddy Makes the Best Spaghetti.*
Hutchins, P. *My Best Friend.*
Hutchins, P. *The Doorbell Rang.*
McBratney, S. *Guess How Much I Love You.*
Penn, A. *The Kissing Hand.*
Wild, M. *Our Granny.*

Pragmatics

Bianco, M. *The Velveteen Rabbit.*
Chapman, C. *Pass the Fritters, Critters.*
Stanley, D. *The Conversation Club.*
Ziefert, H. *Mike and Tony: Best Friends.*

Daily Routines

Bauer, M. *Toes, Ears and Nose.*
Dickson, A. *I Can Dress Myself.*
Dijs, C. *Little Helpers.*
Dunn, P. *Busy, Busy Toddlers.*
Hoban, T. *I Read Signs.*
Jonas, A. *Now We Can Go.*
Katz, K. *Counting Kisses: A Kiss and Read Book.*
Katz, K. *Where is Baby's Belly Button.*
Kunhardt, D. *Pat the Bunny.*
Kunhardt, E. *Pat the Cat.*
Kunhardt, E. *Pat the Puppy.*
McGuire, L. *I Know How to Dress.*
Oxenbury, H. *Clap Hands.*
Oxenbury, H. *Playing.*
Rockwell, A. *In Our House.*
Simon, L. *Things I Like to Eat.*
Slier, D. *Hello Baby.*
Slier, D. *Little Babies.*

Synonyms

Barrett, Judi. *A Snake Is Totally Tall.*
Hanson, Joan. *More Synonyms.*
Hanson, Joan. *Synonyms.*

Antonyms (Opposites)

Allen, Pamela. *Who Sank the Boat?*
Banchek, Linda. *Snake In, Snake Out.*
Charlip, Remy. *Fortunately.*
Crews, Donald. *School Bus.*

Cuyler, Margery. *That's Good! That's Bad!*
Hoban, Tana. *Exactly the Opposite.*
Hoban, T. Push, *Pull, Empty, Full: A Book of Opposites*

"Wh-" Questions
Calmenson, S. *What Am I? Very First Riddles.*
Davis, K. *Who Hops? Who Hoots?*
Freschet, B. *Where's Henrietta's Hen?*
Gomi, T. *Where's the Fish?*
Handford, M. *Where's Waldo?*
Handford, M. *Find Waldo Now.*
Handford, M. *The Great Waldo Search.*
Hutchins, P. *What Game Shall We Play?*
Hutchins, P. *Which Witch is Which?*
Kraus, R. *Which Mouse are You?*
Kraus, R. *Where Are You Going Little Mouse?*
Martin, B. *Brown Bear, Brown Bear, What Do You See?*
Miller, M. *Whose Hat?*
Waber, B. *An Anteater Named Arthur.*
Watanabe, S. *What a Good Lunch!*
Weinburg, L. *The Forgetful Bears.*
Weinburg, L. *The Forgetful Bears Meet Mr. Memory.*
Weiss, N. *Where Does the Brown Bear Go?*
Zacharias, T. & Zacharias, W. *But Where Is the Green Parrot?*
Yabuchi, M. *Whose Footprints?*

"Why" Questions
Adams, Pam. *This Is the House That Jack Built.*
Bang, Molly. *The Grey Lady and the Strawberry Snatcher.*
Cendrars, Blaise. *Shadow.*
Cole, Joanna & Calmenson, Stephanie. *Six Sick Sheep: One Hundred One Tongue Twisters.*
De Paola, Tomie. *Hey Diddle Diddle and Other Mother Goose Rhymes.*
Emberley, Barbara. *Drummer Hoff.*
Fox, Mem. *Hattie and the Fox.*
Hoguet, Susan Ramsey. *I Unpacked My Grandmother's Trunk.*
Hutchins, Pat. *Don't Forget the Bacon.*
Lawrence, Jacob. *Harriet and the Promised Land.*
Patterson, Francine. *Koko's Kitten.*
Patterson, Francine. *Koko's Story.*

The Five Senses
Fox, Mem. *Night Noises.*
Hill, E. *Spot's Big Touch and Feel Book.*
Martin, Bill. Jr. *Polar Bear, Polar Bear, What Do You Hear?*
Martin, Bill, Jr. *Brown Bear, Brown Bear, What Do You See?*
Martin, B. & Archambault, J. *Up and Down on the Merry-Go-Round.*
Seuss, Dr. *Mr. Brown Can Moo, Can You?*
Showers, P. *The Listening Walk.*
Wells, Rosemary. *Noisy Nora.*

Index

sounds made with, 145, 146

Lisp, 118

Listening, 19, 33-34, 48, 49-51, 78. *See also* Sounds;
    Turn-taking

Literacy skills. *See* Reading

Localization, 23, 48

Love and Learning, 283-84

Loyola College, 6, 68, 143, 237, 264

MacDonald, James, 184, 263

Maloclusion, 22

Maps, 291

Massage, 34, 52, 250

Matching, visual, 280

Mayer-Johnson, 196, 262

Mean length of utterance. *See* MLU

Means-end, 59-60

Medlen, Joan, 38

Melodic intonation therapy, 133, 259

Memory
    auditory, 23
    types of, 23
    visual, 24

Mental age, 97, 230, 268

Mental retardation, 21, 185. *See also* Cognitive skills

Metronome, 259

Meyers, Laura, 203

Microscope otoscope, 17

Middle ear
    fluid, 12, 13-17, 25, 34, 118, 165
    location of, 12

Midfacial hypoplasia, 22

Milestones, communication, 10

Miller, Jon, 97

Mirrors, 62, 120, 125, 128, 138, 180

MLU
    evaluating, 226
    in Down syndrome, 26, 97, 107
    increasing, 84-90, 252
    related to linguistic stages, 105

Mobile, 34

Modeling. *See* Imitation

Modifications, classroom, 273

MORE whistles, 126

Morphemes, 26, 103, 105, 260

Morphology, 103-104, 260

Morphosyntax, 26, 103

Motherese, 35

Motor programming problems, 121. *See also* Childhood
    verbal apraxia

Mouth. *See also* Oral motor skills; Tongue
    and sensory skills, 124
    breathing through, 20, 22, 117
    exploring objects with, 19, 34, 51, 52
    movements, 22
    open, 22

size, 20

Muscle tone, 20, 22, 36, 45, 61, 62, 116, 119

Musical instruments, 126, 133, 152, 278. *See also* Songs

Music therapists, xii

Myofunctional problems, 118

Myringotomy tubes, 15-17

Name, teaching child, 33

Nasality. *See* Resonance

Nasopharynx, 12

National Down Syndrome Congress, 5, 328

National Down Syndrome Society, 5, 328

National Lekotek Center, 58

Negatives, 106, 109

NICHCY, 215

Nonverbal children, 223. *See also* Autism; Childhood Verbal
    Apraxia; Speech

Nonverbal communication, 42, 136-37, 172.
    See also Pragmatics

Nonverbal cues, 1. *See also* Pragmatics

Noise, tolerating, 31, 175

Norms
    for articulation, 148-49, 229-30
    in determining eligibility, 268
    meaning of, 219

Nose, 22

Notebook, communication, 70-71

NUK toothbrush, 34, 52, 62, 249, 251

Object permanence, 54-57

Observation, parent-child, 220-21

Occupational therapist, xii, 19, 32, 34, 37, 51, 207

Oelwein, Patricia Logan, 282, 283

Open bite, 22, 116

Ophthalmologist, 19, 44

Oral massage. *See* Massage

Oral-Motor Exercises for Speech Clarity, 38

Oral motor skills. *See also* Dysarthria
    bases for, 3
    delays in, 86
    in infants and toddlers, 62
    speech-language therapy for, 251, 254
    using straws and horns to develop,
        37, 38, 251

Orofacial mycology, 118

Otitis media, 12, 14, 23, 47. *See also* Middle ear

Otoacoustic emission testing, 11, 13

Otolaryngologist, 11, 15, 17, 118, 129

Otoscope, 13

Out of Sync Child, 31

Overextension, 96

Pacing boards, 84-85, 88, 109, 128, 133, 167, 181

Palate, 20, 22, 116, 131, 228

Parents. *See also* Home activities knowledge about
    child's communication abilities, 214, 215, 218, 222
    responsiveness of, 40
    role in IEP planning, 271-72